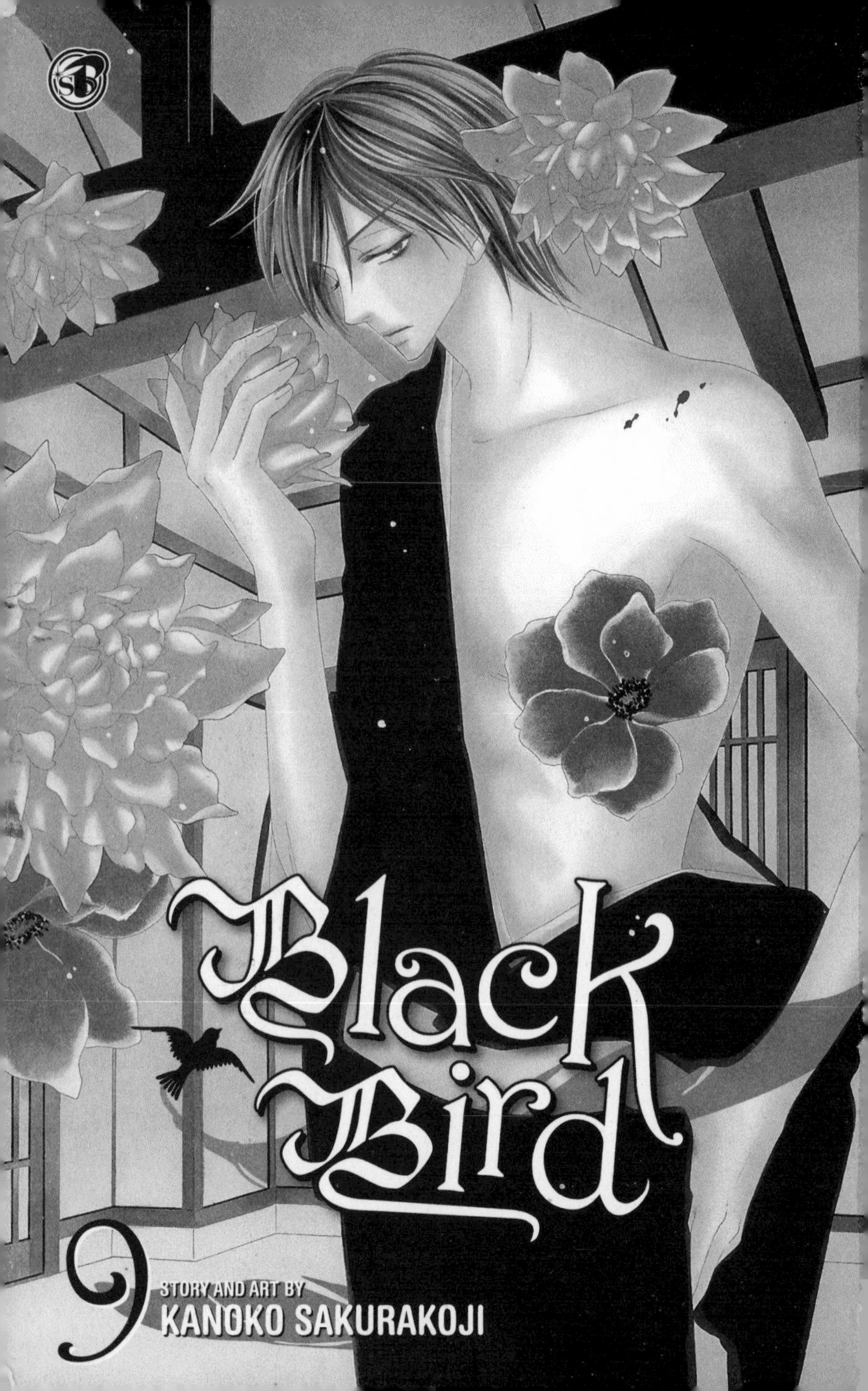
Black Bird
9
STORY AND ART BY
KANOKO SAKURAKOJI

Black Bird

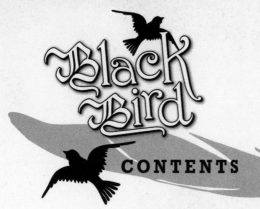

CONTENTS

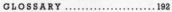

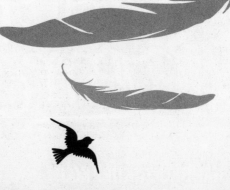

CHARACTERS

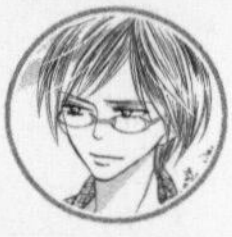

TADANOBU KUZUNOHA
Kyo's close friend since childhood. Current leader of the Kitsune clan.

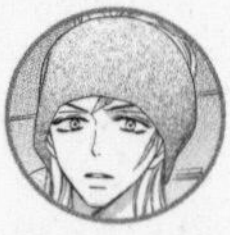

RAIKOH WATANABE
Like Misao, he can see demons and spirits. However, he refuses to believe that humans and demons can live in harmony and uses his abilities to destroy them.

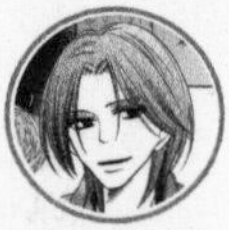

SHO USUI
Kyo's older brother and an ex-member of the Eight Daitengu. He is also known as Sojo. His whereabouts are unknown after a failed grab for the clan leadership.

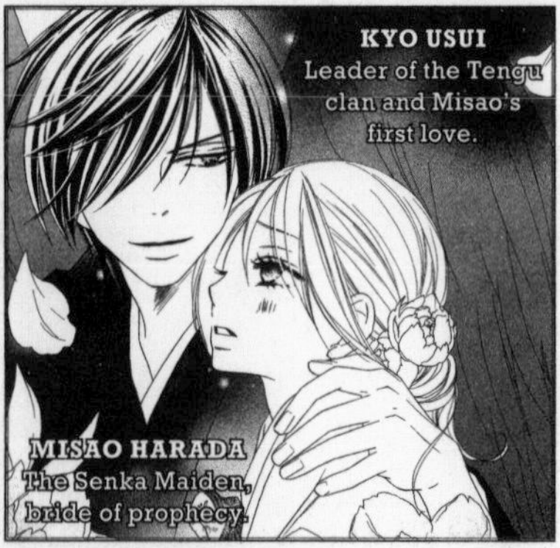
KYO USUI
Leader of the Tengu clan and Misao's first love.
MISAO HARADA
The Senka Maiden, bride of prophecy.

THE EIGHT DAITENGU
Kyo's bodyguards. Their names designate their official posts.

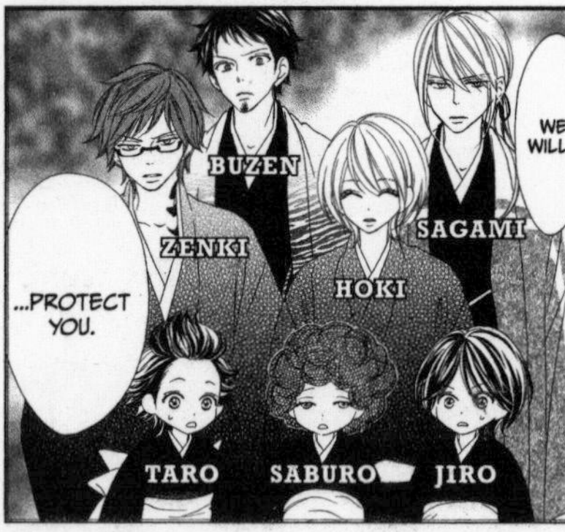
WE WILL...
...PROTECT YOU.
SAGAMI
BUZEN
HOKI
ZENKI
JIRO
SABURO
TARO

STORY THUS FAR
Misao can see spirits and demons, and her childhood sweetheart Kyo has been protecting her since she was little.

"Someday, I'll come for you, I promise." Kyo reappears the day before Misao's 16th birthday to tell her, "Your 16th birthday marks 'open season' on you." She is the Senka Maiden, and if a demon drinks her blood, he is granted a long life. If he eats her flesh, he gains eternal youth. And if he makes her his bride, his clan will prosper...And Kyo is a *tengu*, a crow demon, with his sights firmly set on her.

One day Misao's father brings home a young man named Raikoh, who bears the scars from a demon attack he suffered as a child. As a result, Raikoh holds a deep hatred for demons. When he recognizes that Kyo is a demon, he warns Misao that if she doesn't end their relationship, he will exorcise Kyo. Due to his love for Misao, Kyo hesitates to use his power against a human. He falls for Raikoh's ruse, which leaves him hovering near death.

Kyo knows that the only way he can recover is to bed Misao, but he hesitates because it's unknown what will happen to a human who lies with a demon.

Kyo and Misao are committed to being together, and after much consideration, they finally consummate their love. But what will the future bring?

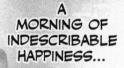

CHERRY PETALS FALLING ON MY SKIN.

A MORNING OF INDESCRIBABLE HAPPINESS...

I'LL REMEMBER IT ALL MY LIFE.

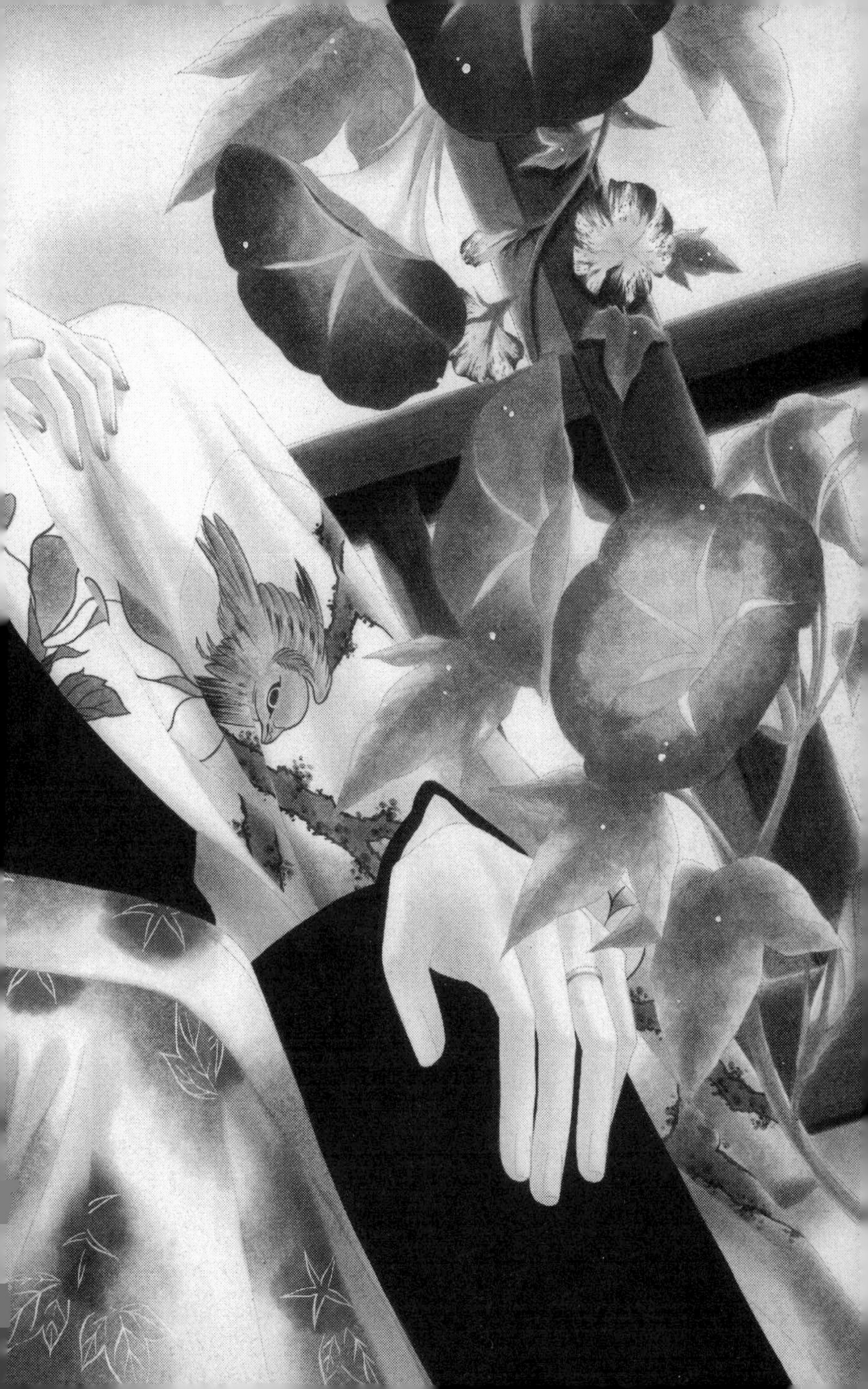

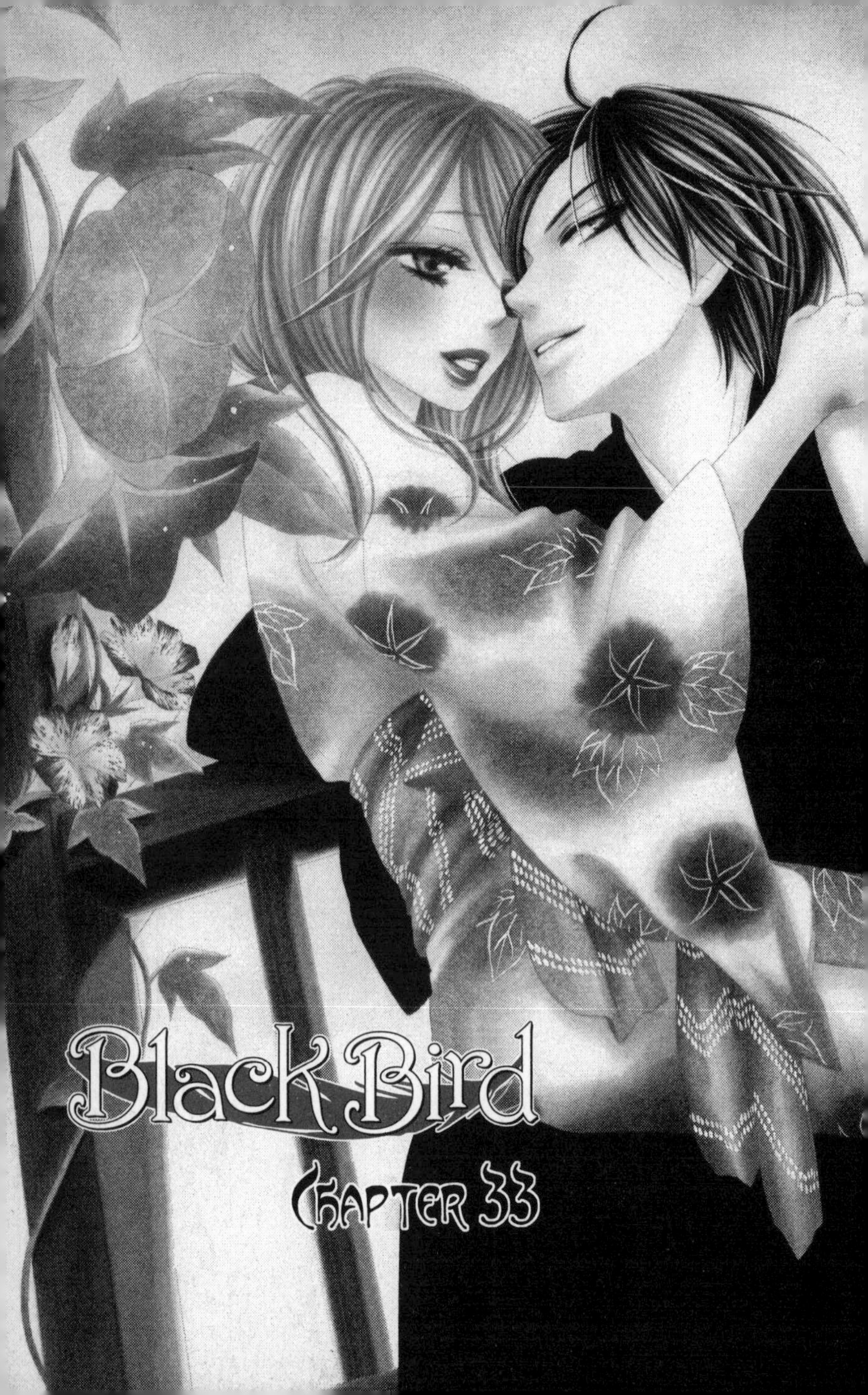
Black Bird
Chapter 33

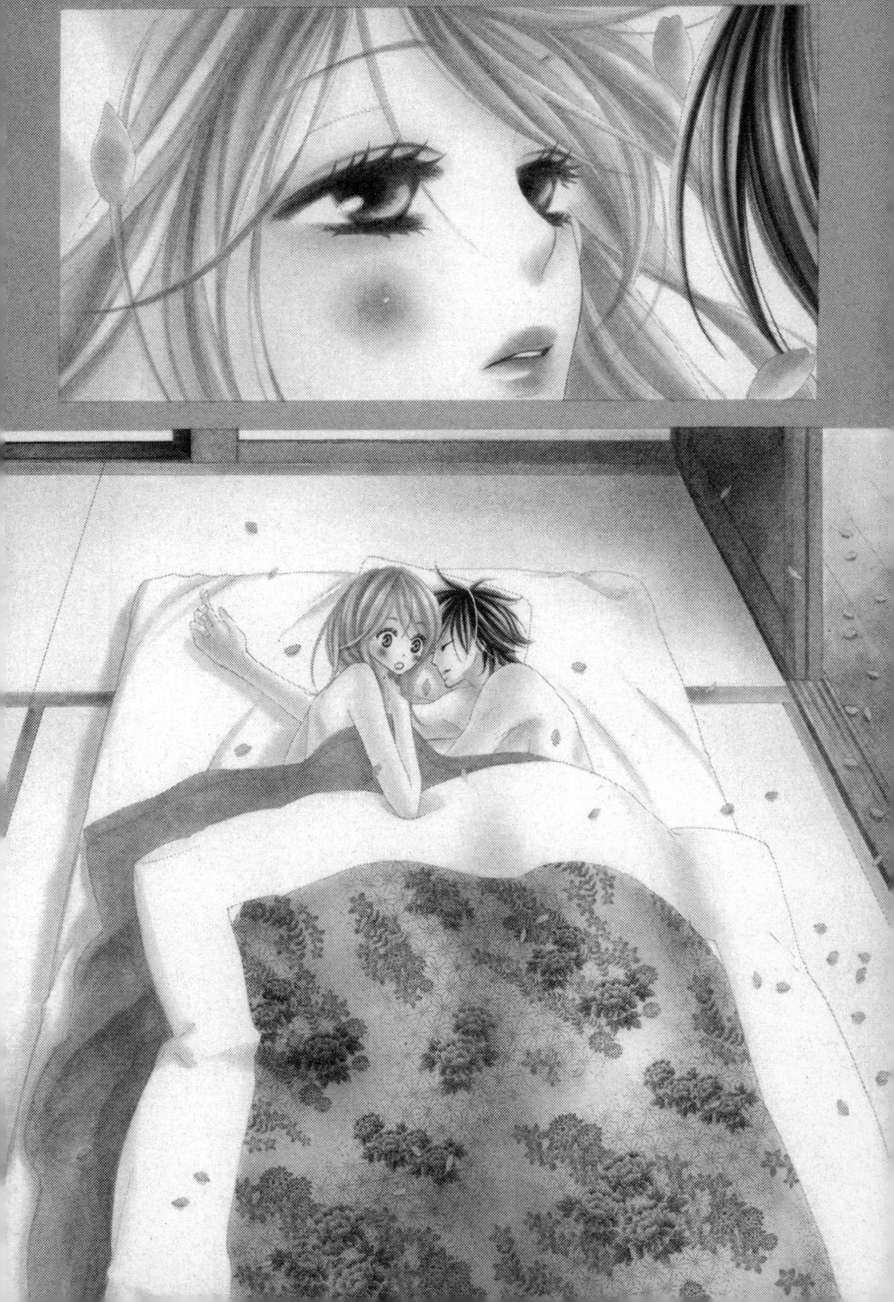

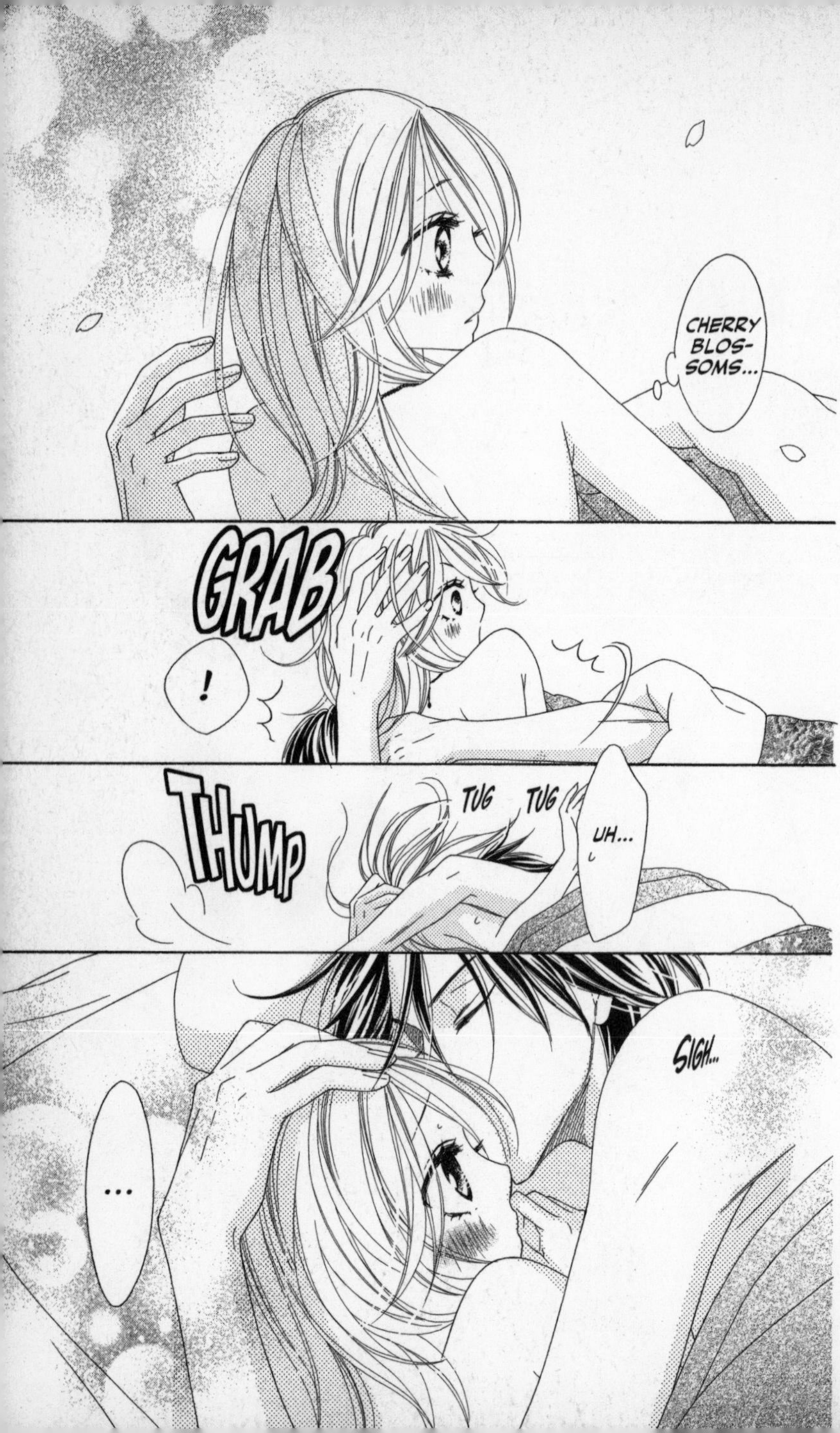
CHERRY BLOS-SOMS...
GRAB
!
TUG TUG
UH...
THUMP
SIGH...
...

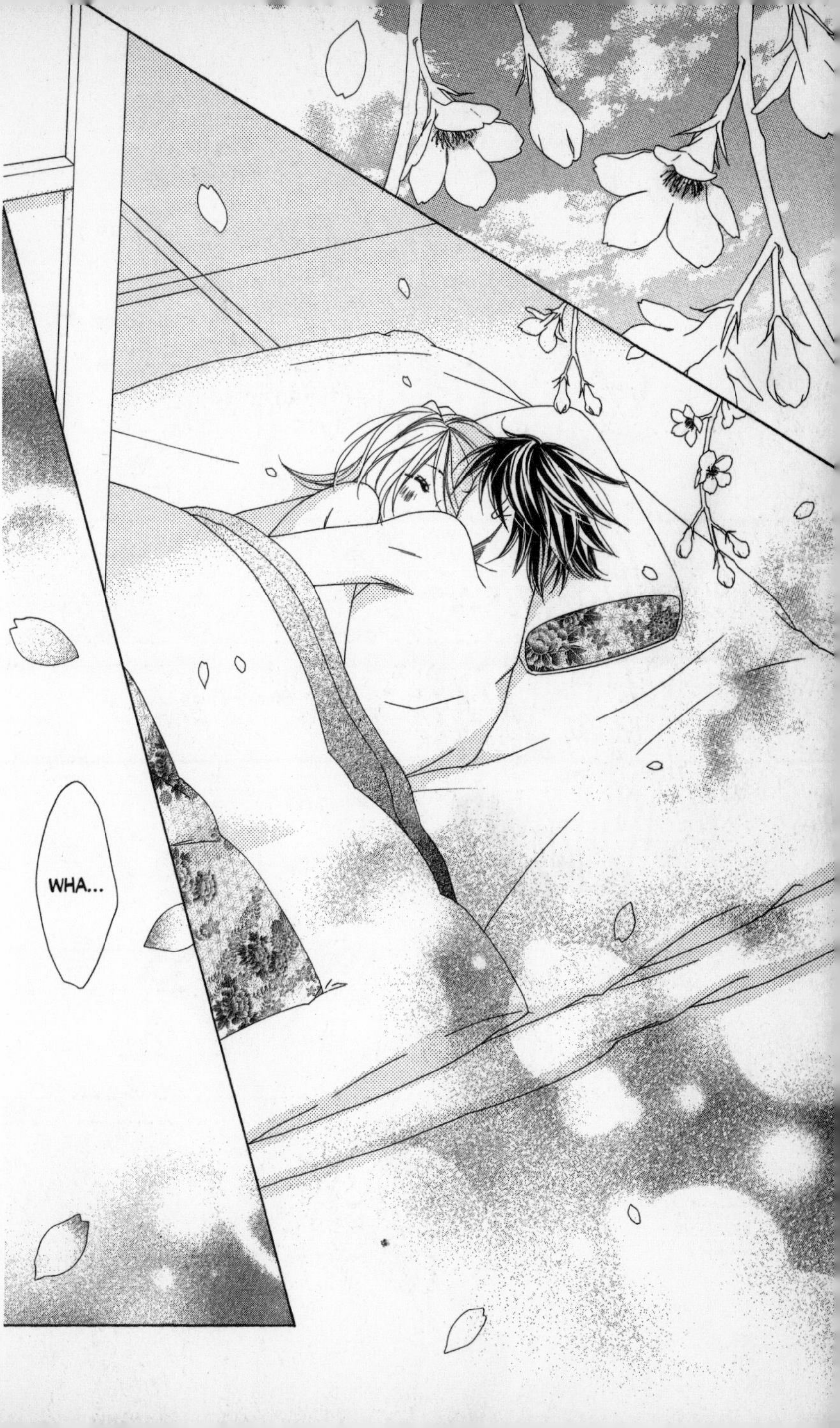
WHA...

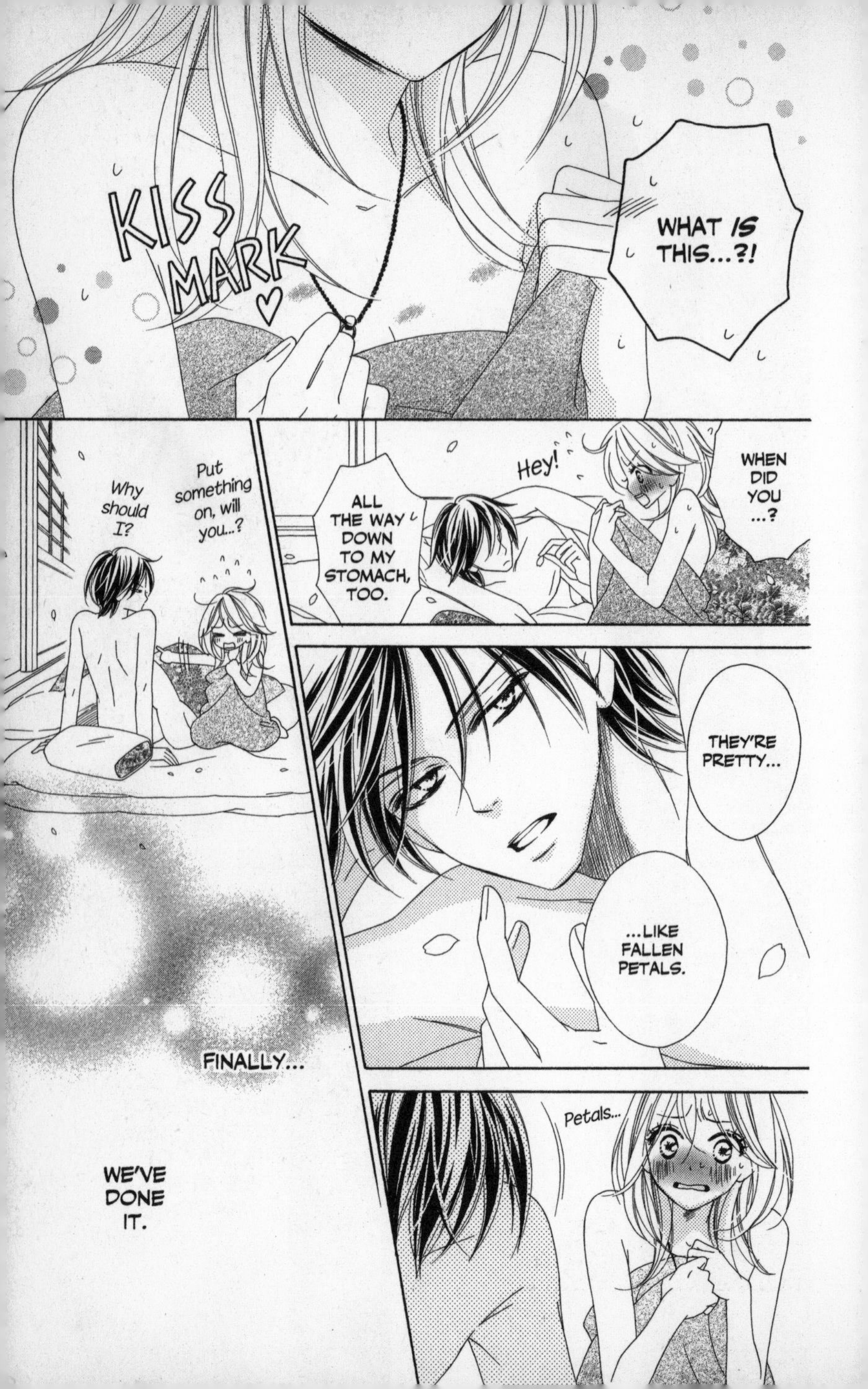
WHAT *IS* THIS...?!
KISS MARK ♥
WHEN DID YOU ...?
Hey!
ALL THE WAY DOWN TO MY STOMACH, TOO.
THEY'RE PRETTY...
...LIKE FALLEN PETALS.
Petals...
Put something on, will you...?
Why should I?
FINALLY...
WE'VE DONE IT.

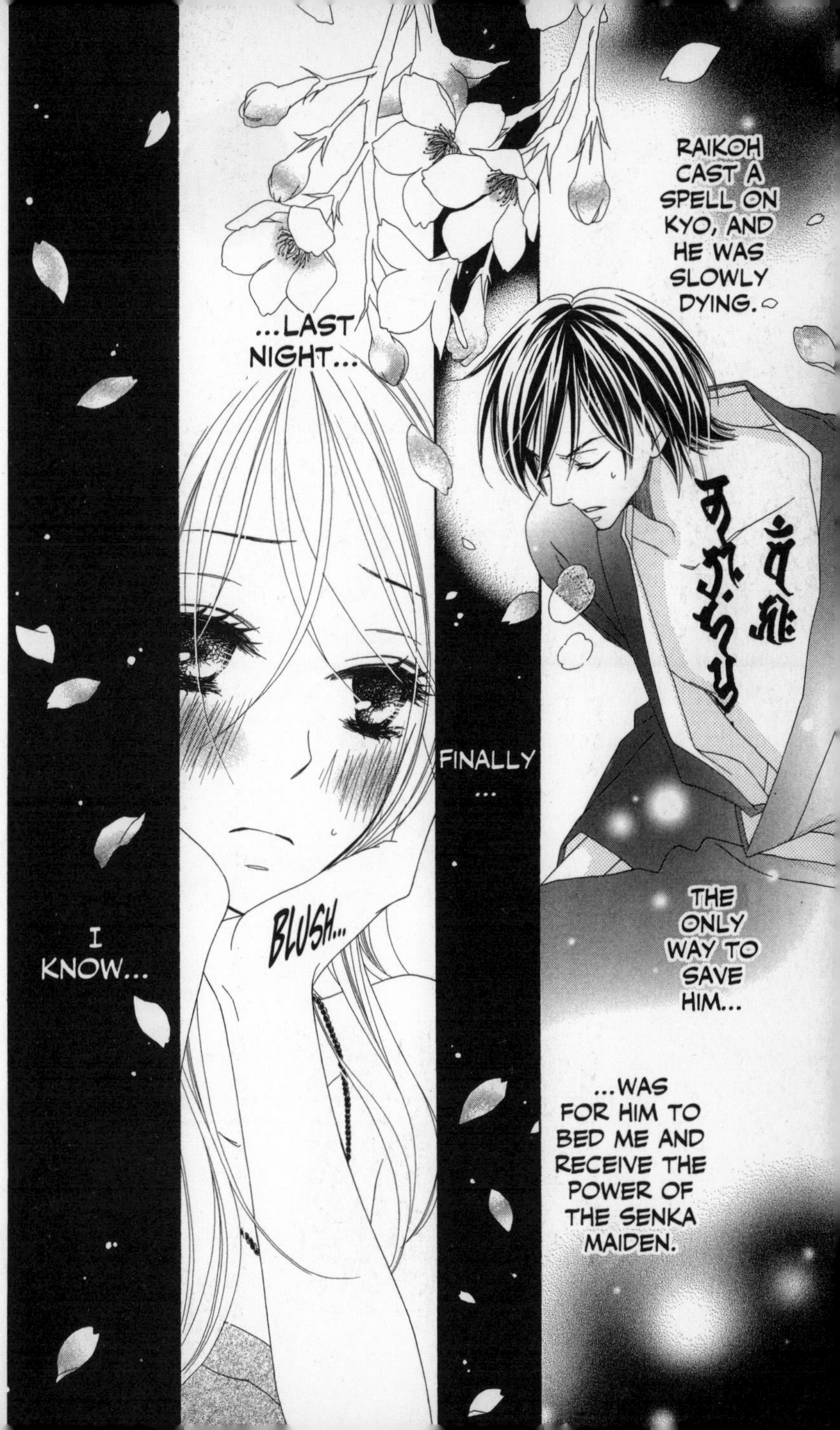
RAIKOH CAST A SPELL ON KYO, AND HE WAS SLOWLY DYING.
THE ONLY WAY TO SAVE HIM...
...WAS FOR HIM TO BED ME AND RECEIVE THE POWER OF THE SENKA MAIDEN.
FINALLY ...
...LAST NIGHT...
BLUSH...
I KNOW...

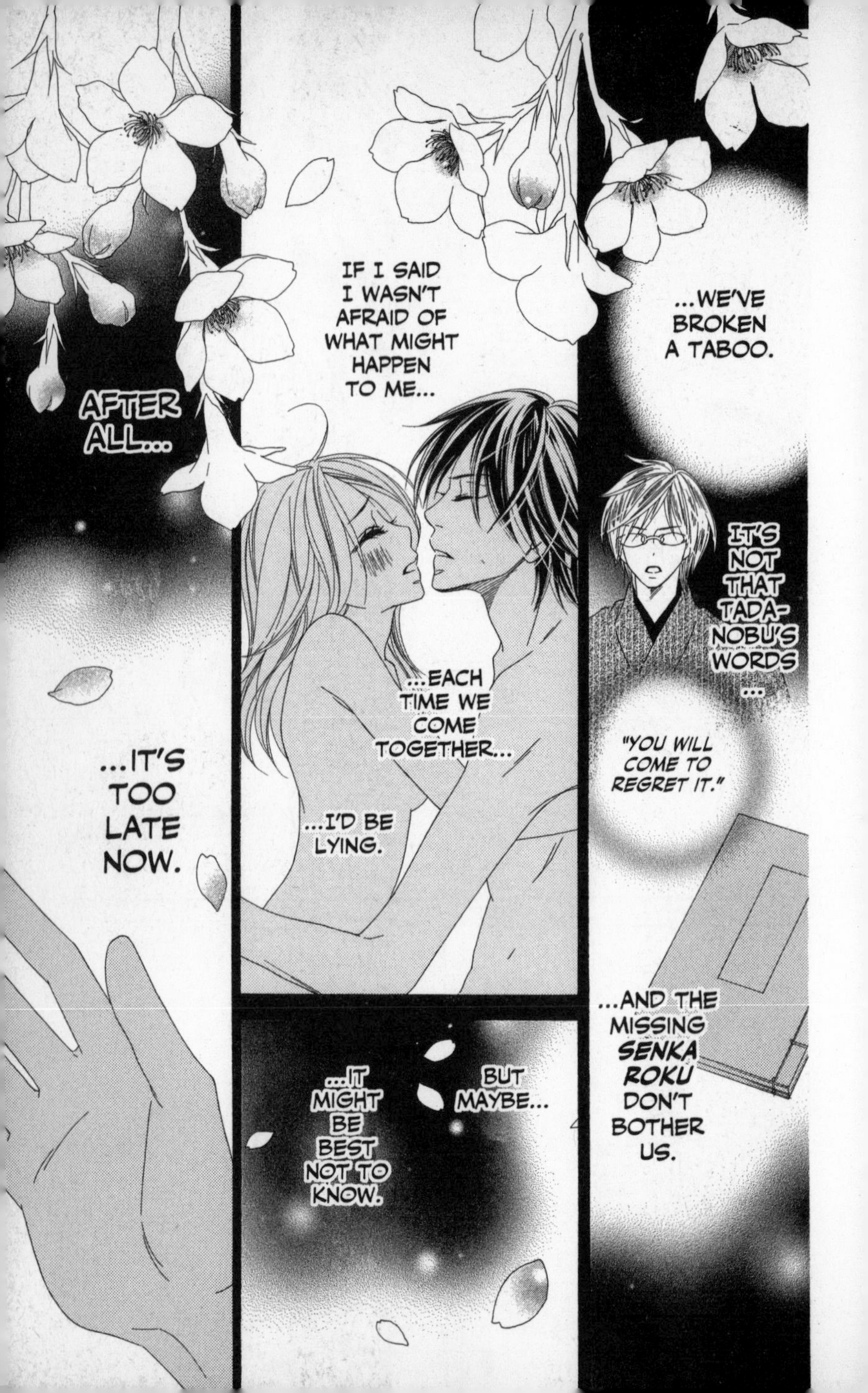
...WE'VE BROKEN A TABOO.
IT'S NOT THAT TADA-NOBU'S WORDS...
"YOU WILL COME TO REGRET IT."
...AND THE MISSING *SENKA ROKU* DON'T BOTHER US.
IF I SAID I WASN'T AFRAID OF WHAT MIGHT HAPPEN TO ME...
...EACH TIME WE COME TOGETHER...
...I'D BE LYING.
BUT MAYBE...
...IT MIGHT BE BEST NOT TO KNOW.
AFTER ALL...
...IT'S TOO LATE NOW.

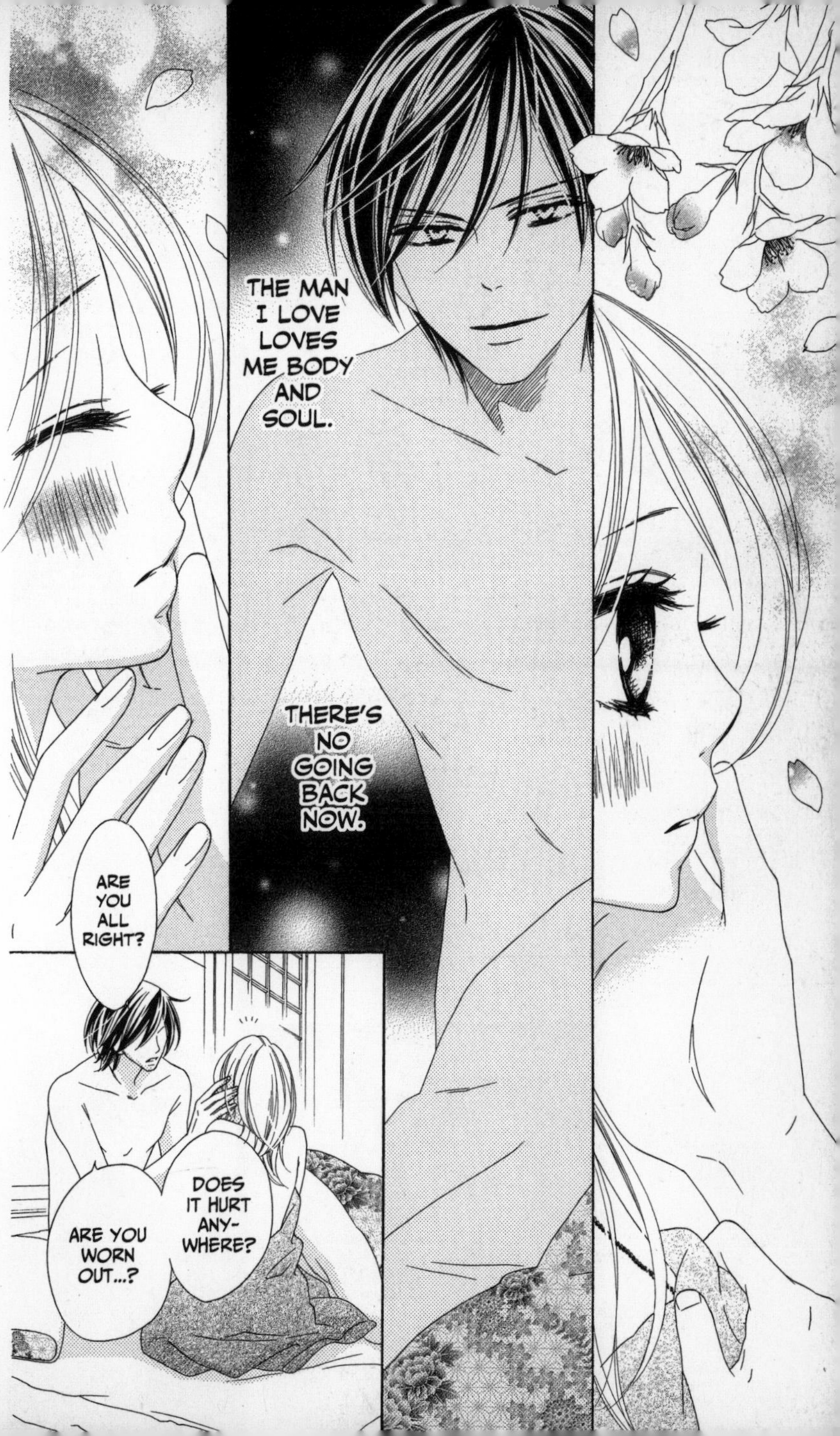
THE MAN I LOVE LOVES ME BODY AND SOUL.
THERE'S NO GOING BACK NOW.
ARE YOU ALL RIGHT?
DOES IT HURT ANY-WHERE?
ARE YOU WORN OUT...?

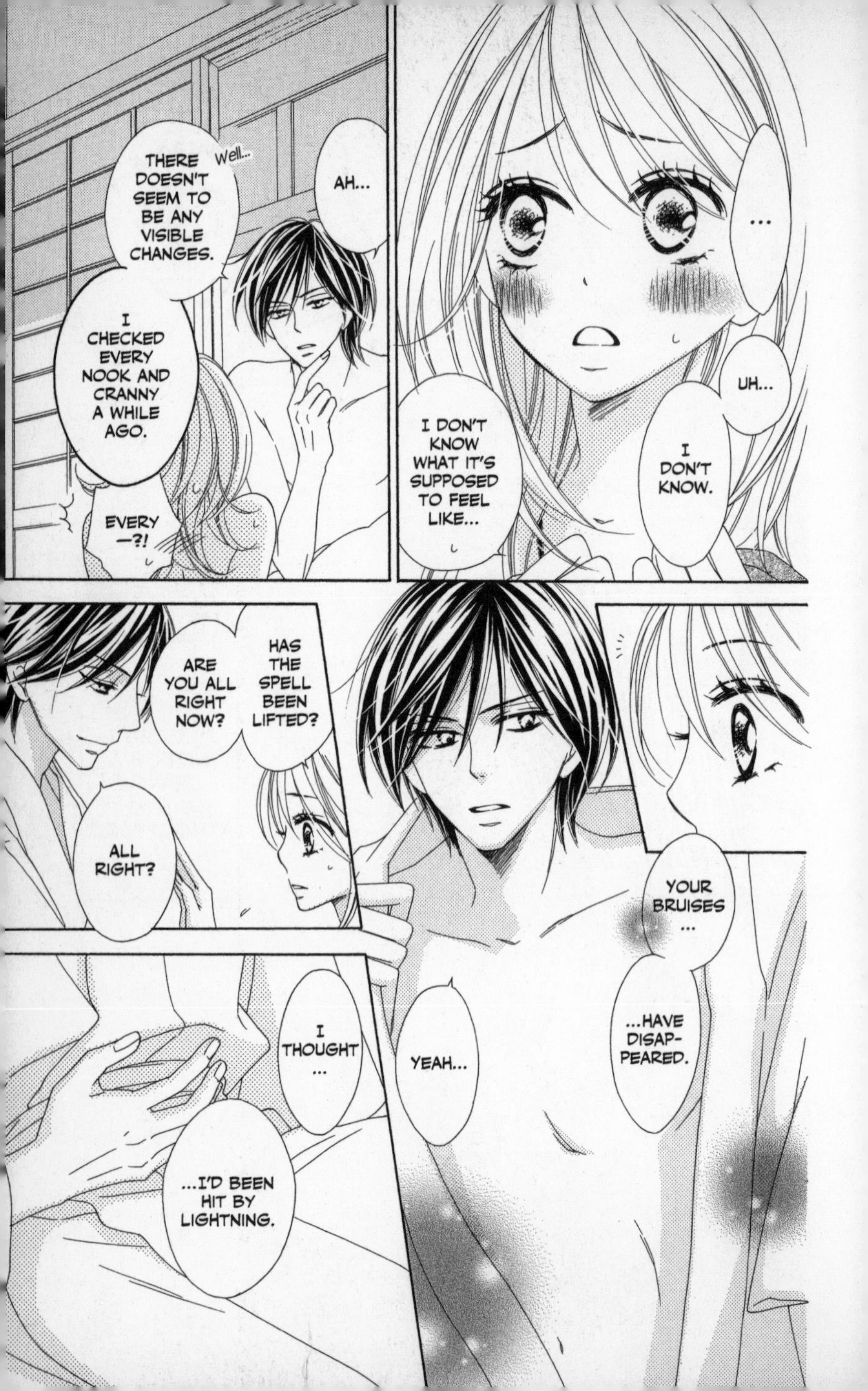
...
UH...
I DON'T KNOW.
I DON'T KNOW WHAT IT'S SUPPOSED TO FEEL LIKE...
AH...
Well...
THERE DOESN'T SEEM TO BE ANY VISIBLE CHANGES.
I CHECKED EVERY NOOK AND CRANNY A WHILE AGO.
EVERY—?!
YOUR BRUISES ...
...HAVE DISAP-PEARED.
YEAH...
HAS THE SPELL BEEN LIFTED?
ARE YOU ALL RIGHT NOW?
ALL RIGHT?
I THOUGHT ...
...I'D BEEN HIT BY LIGHTNING.

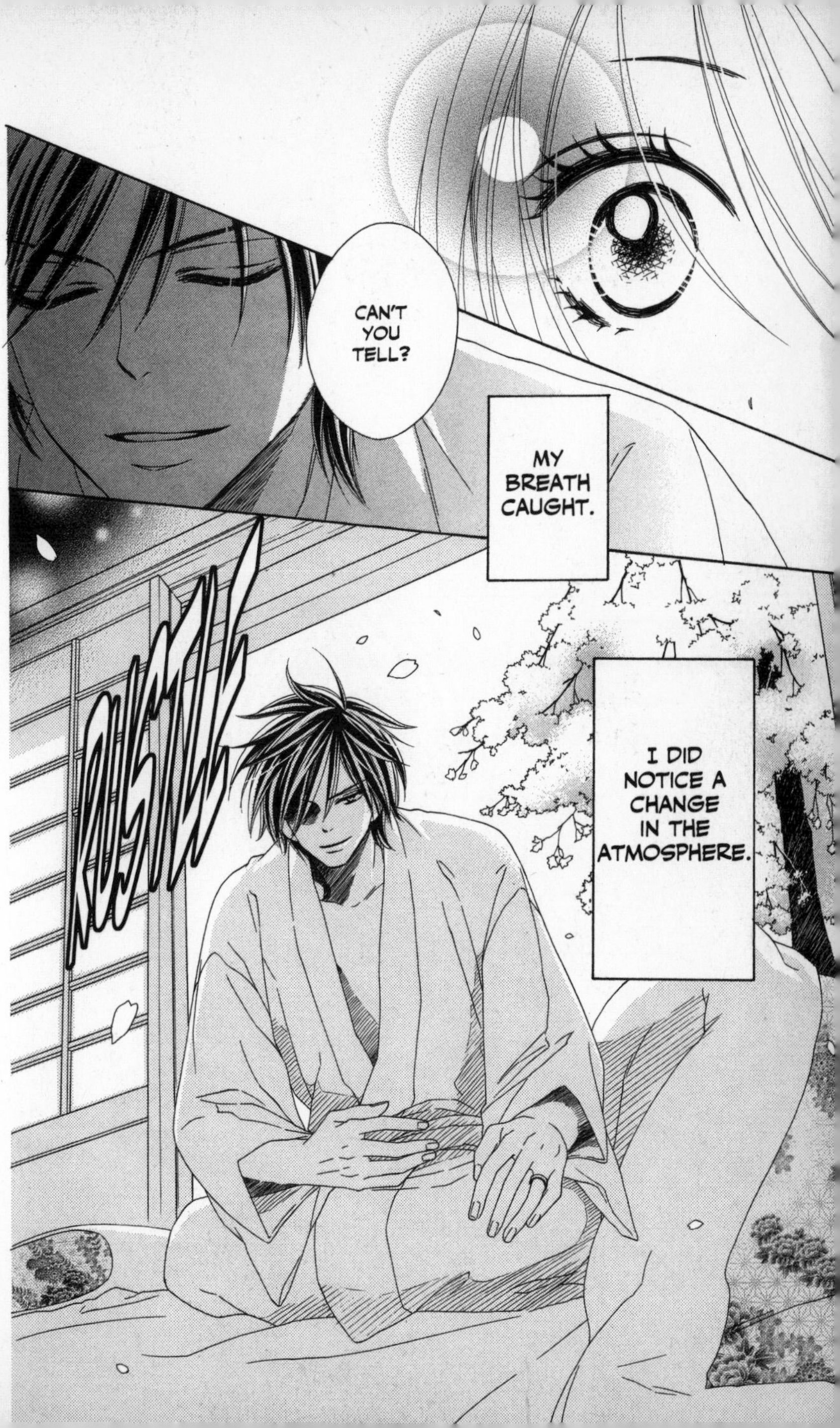
CAN'T YOU TELL?
MY BREATH CAUGHT.
I DID NOTICE A CHANGE IN THE ATMOSPHERE.
RUSTLE

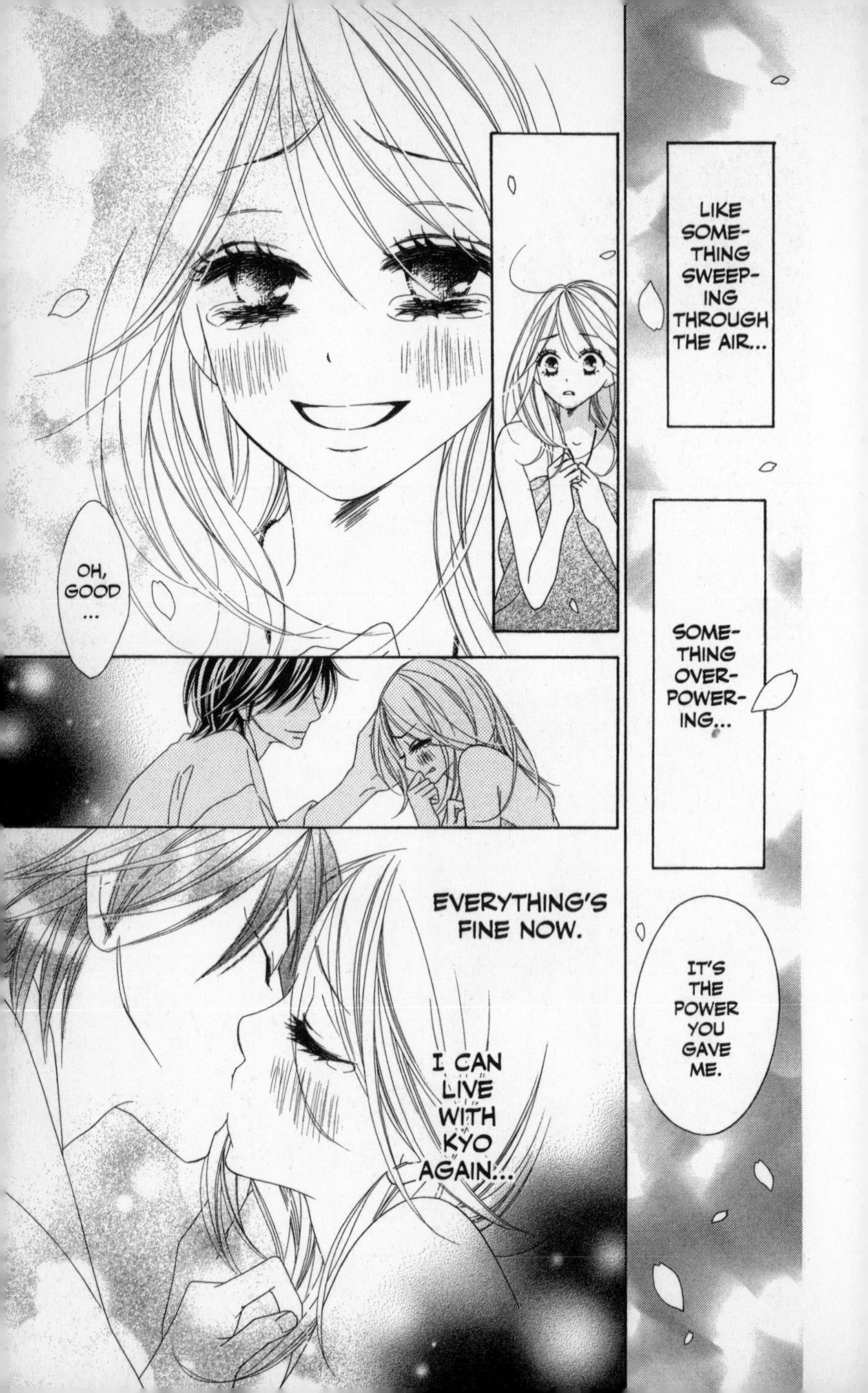
LIKE SOMETHING SWEEPING THROUGH THE AIR...
SOMETHING OVERPOWERING...
IT'S THE POWER YOU GAVE ME.
OH, GOOD...
EVERYTHING'S FINE NOW.
I CAN LIVE WITH KYO AGAIN...

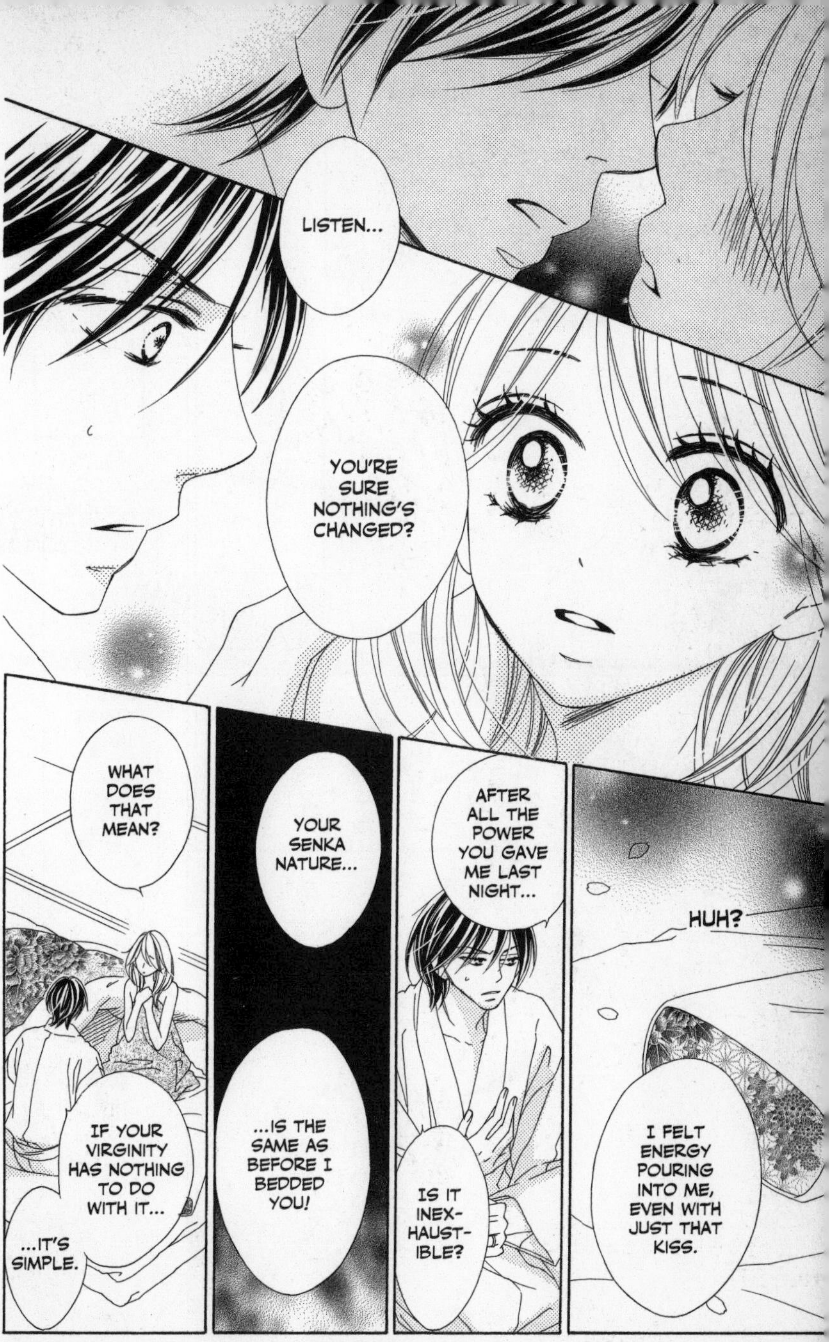
LISTEN...
YOU'RE SURE NOTHING'S CHANGED?
HUH?
I FELT ENERGY POURING INTO ME, EVEN WITH JUST THAT KISS.
AFTER ALL THE POWER YOU GAVE ME LAST NIGHT...
IS IT INEX-HAUST-IBLE?
YOUR SENKA NATURE...
...IS THE SAME AS BEFORE I BEDDED YOU!
WHAT DOES THAT MEAN?
IF YOUR VIRGINITY HAS NOTHING TO DO WITH IT...
...IT'S SIMPLE.

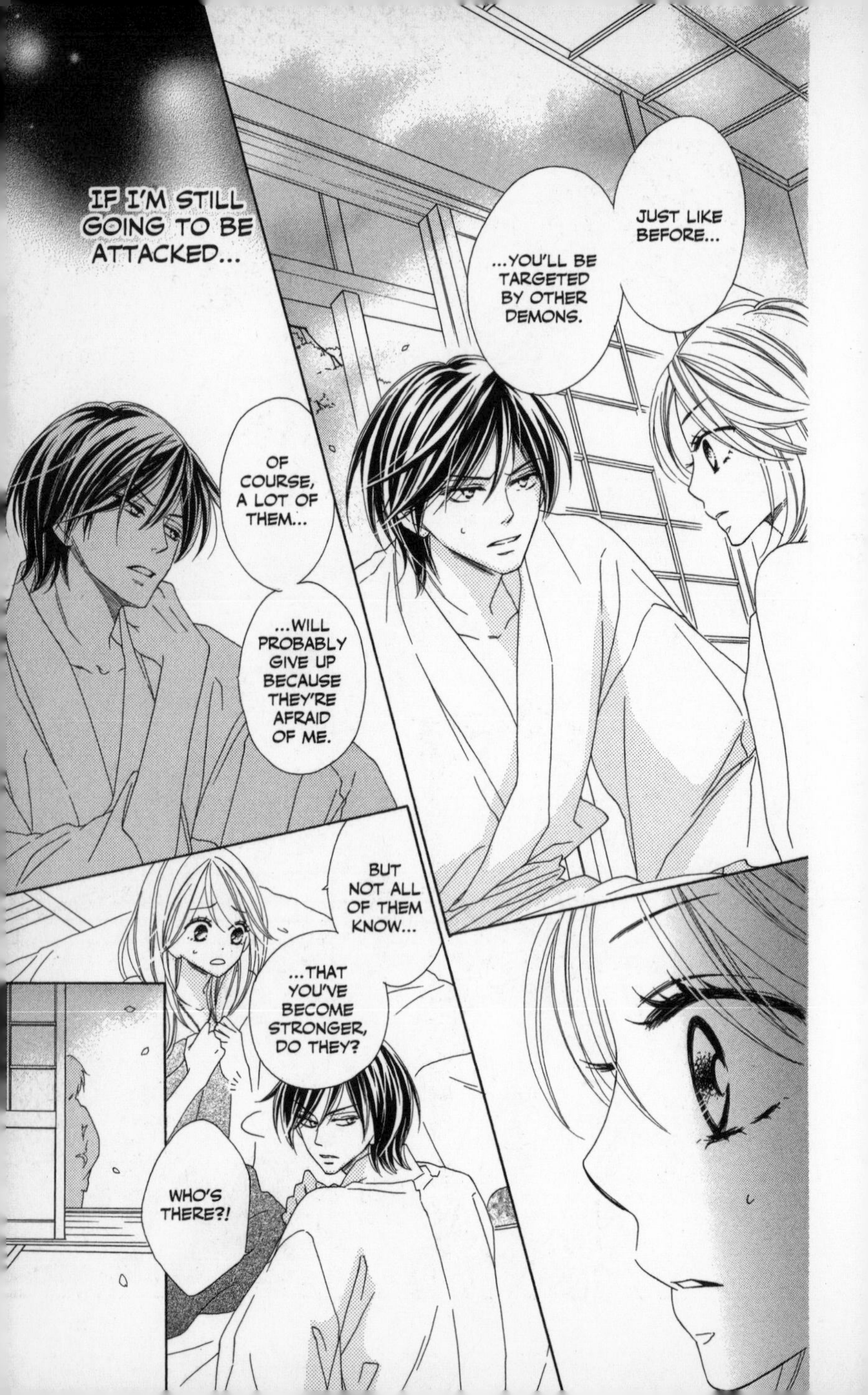
JUST LIKE BEFORE...
...YOU'LL BE TARGETED BY OTHER DEMONS.
IF I'M STILL GOING TO BE ATTACKED...
OF COURSE, A LOT OF THEM...
...WILL PROBABLY GIVE UP BECAUSE THEY'RE AFRAID OF ME.
BUT NOT ALL OF THEM KNOW...
...THAT YOU'VE BECOME STRONGER, DO THEY?
WHO'S THERE?!

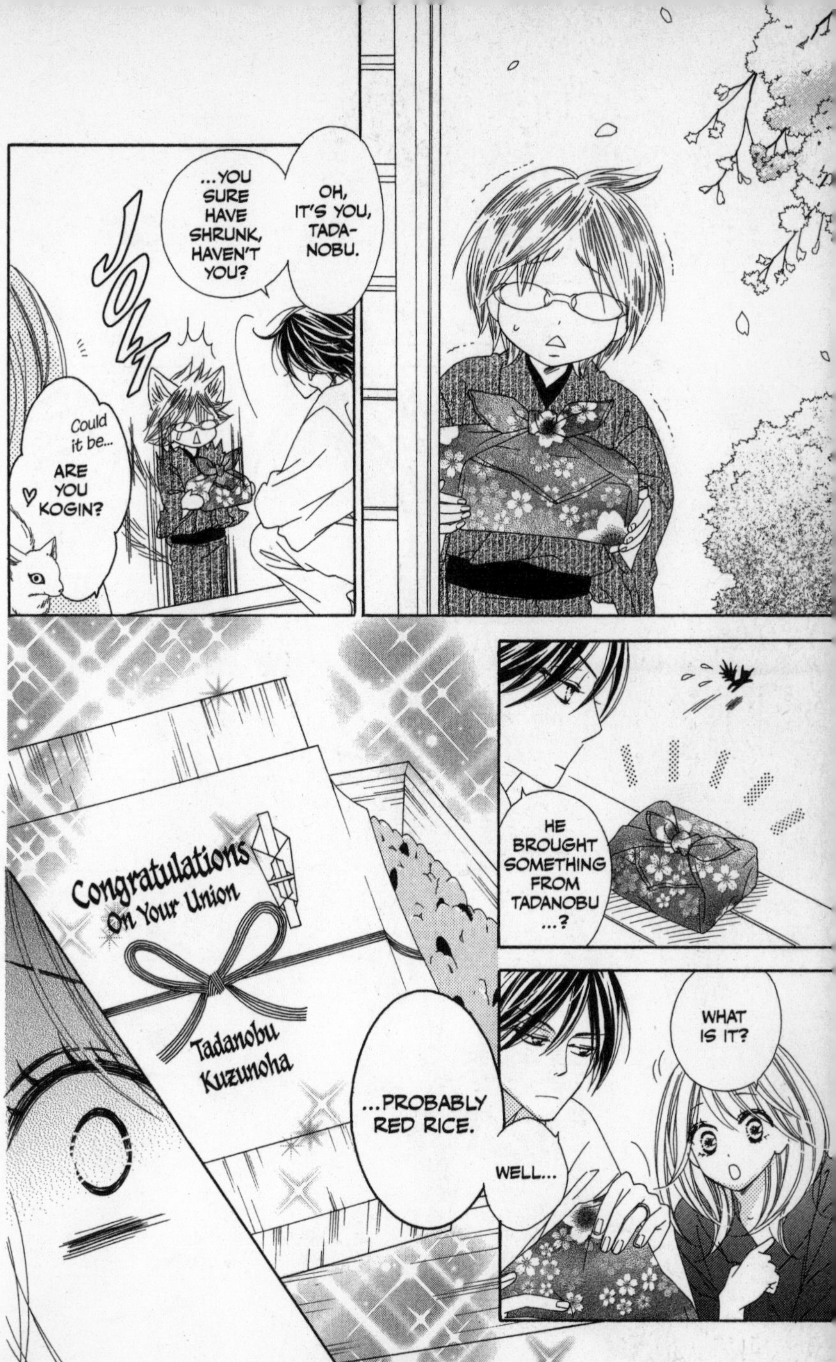
OH, IT'S YOU, TADA-NOBU.
...YOU SURE HAVE SHRUNK, HAVEN'T YOU?
JOW
Could it be... ARE YOU KOGIN?
HE BROUGHT SOMETHING FROM TADANOBU ...?
WHAT IS IT?
WELL...
...PROBABLY RED RICE.
Congratulations On Your Union
Tadanobu Kuzunoha

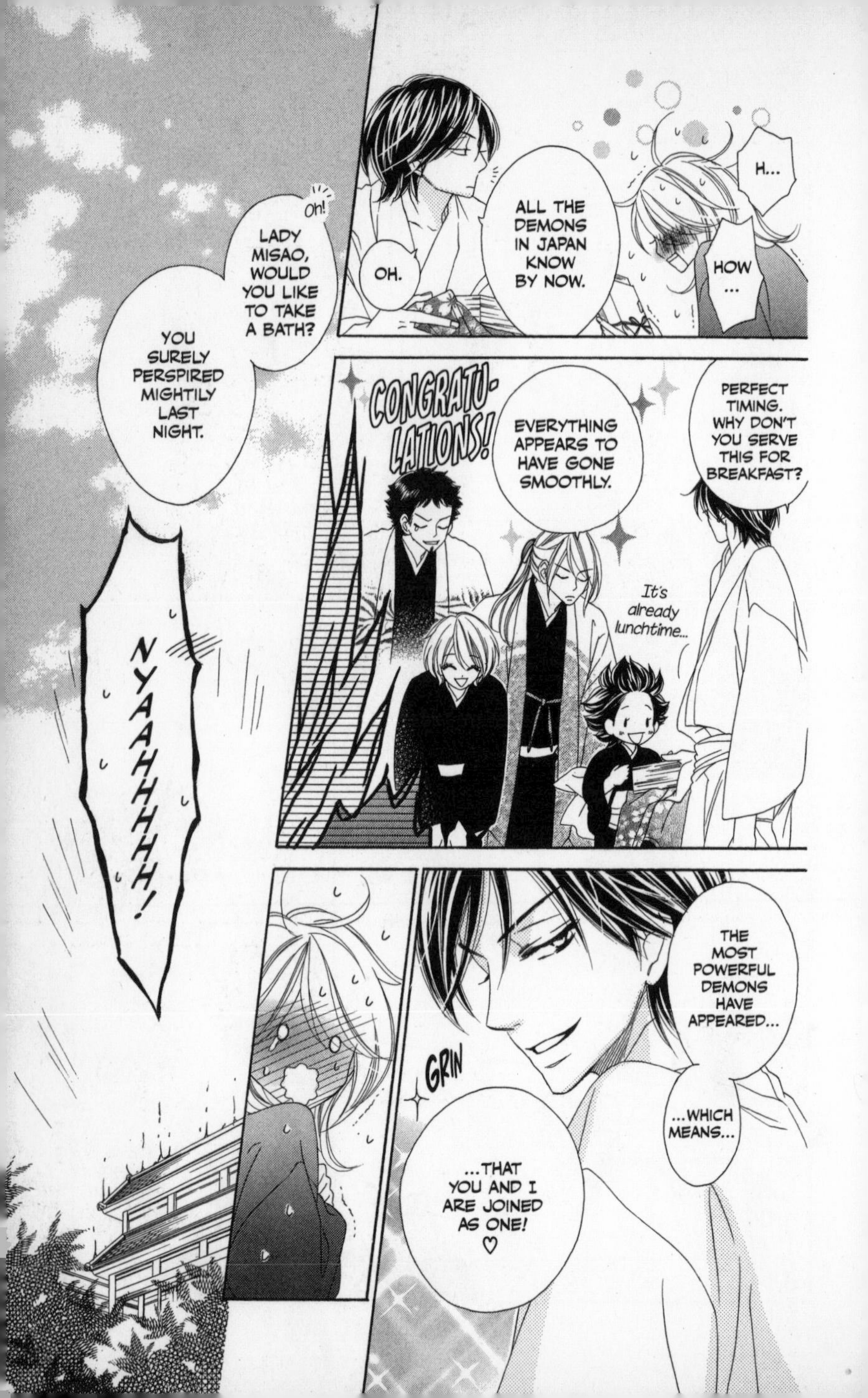
H...
HOW...
ALL THE DEMONS IN JAPAN KNOW BY NOW.
OH.
PERFECT TIMING. WHY DON'T YOU SERVE THIS FOR BREAKFAST?
EVERYTHING APPEARS TO HAVE GONE SMOOTHLY.
CONGRATULATIONS!
It's already lunchtime...
THE MOST POWERFUL DEMONS HAVE APPEARED...
...WHICH MEANS...
GRIN
...THAT YOU AND I ARE JOINED AS ONE! ♡
Oh!
LADY MISAO, WOULD YOU LIKE TO TAKE A BATH?
YOU SURELY PERSPIRED MIGHTILY LAST NIGHT.
NYAAHHHHH!

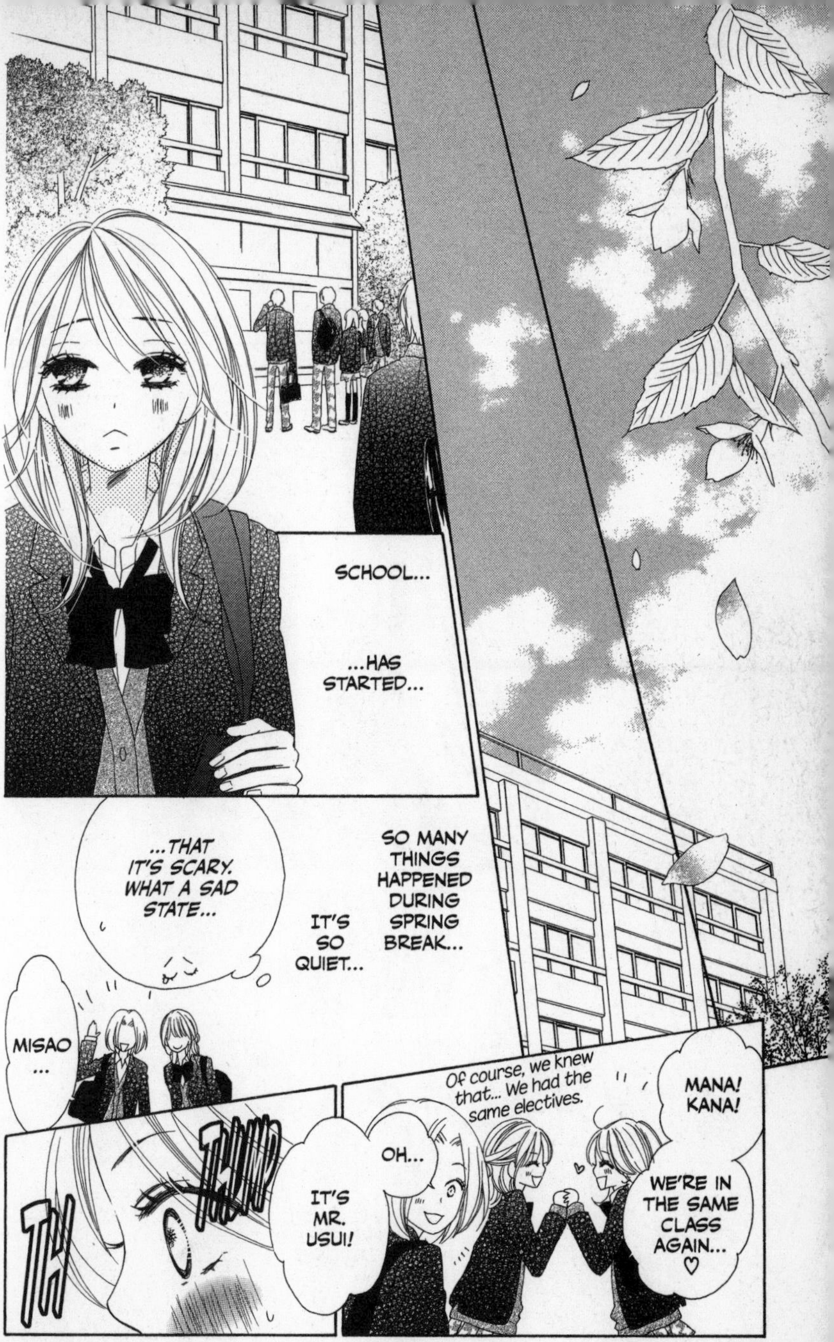
SCHOOL...
...HAS STARTED...
SO MANY THINGS HAPPENED DURING SPRING BREAK...
IT'S SO QUIET...
...THAT IT'S SCARY. WHAT A SAD STATE...
MISAO ...
MANA! KANA!
WE'RE IN THE SAME CLASS AGAIN... ♡
Of course, we knew that... We had the same electives.
OH...
IT'S MR. USUI!
THUMP
TH

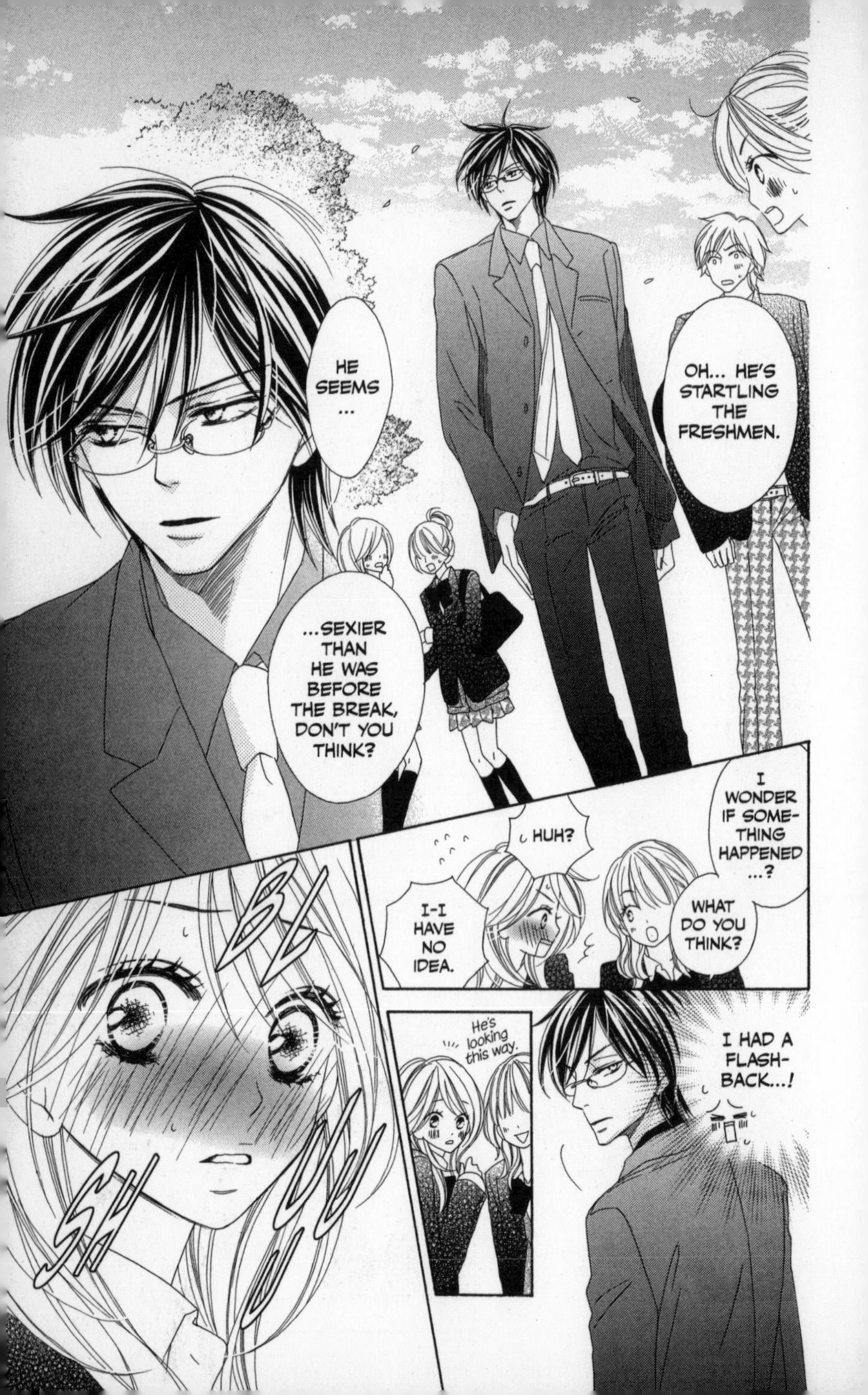
OH... HE'S STARTLING THE FRESHMEN.
HE SEEMS ...
...SEXIER THAN HE WAS BEFORE THE BREAK, DON'T YOU THINK?
I WONDER IF SOME-THING HAPPENED ...?
WHAT DO YOU THINK?
HUH?
I-I HAVE NO IDEA.
I HAD A FLASH-BACK...!
He's looking this way.

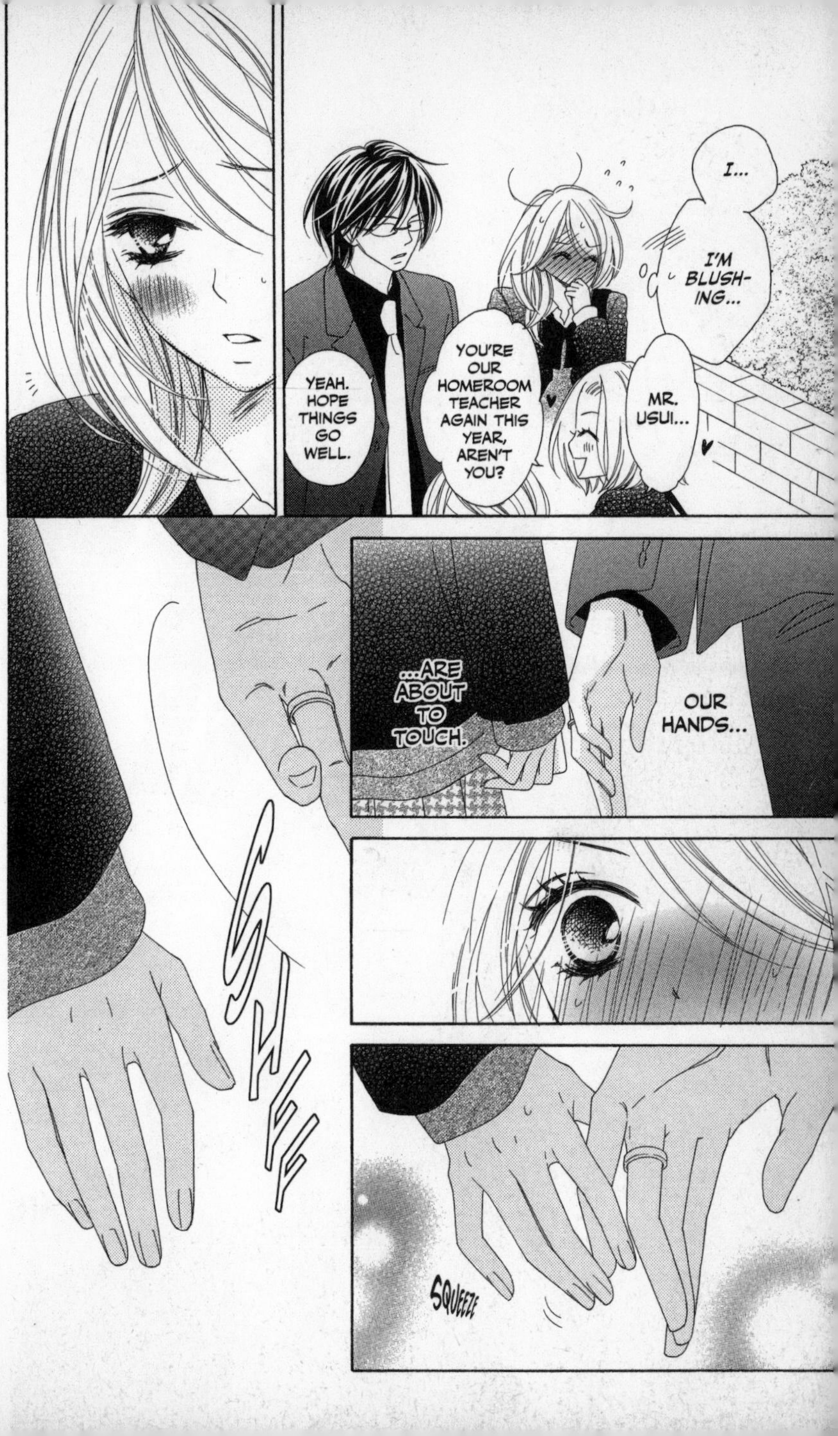
I...
I'M BLUSHING...
MR. USUI...
YOU'RE OUR HOMEROOM TEACHER AGAIN THIS YEAR, AREN'T YOU?
YEAH. HOPE THINGS GO WELL.
OUR HANDS...
...ARE ABOUT TO TOUCH.
SQUEEZE

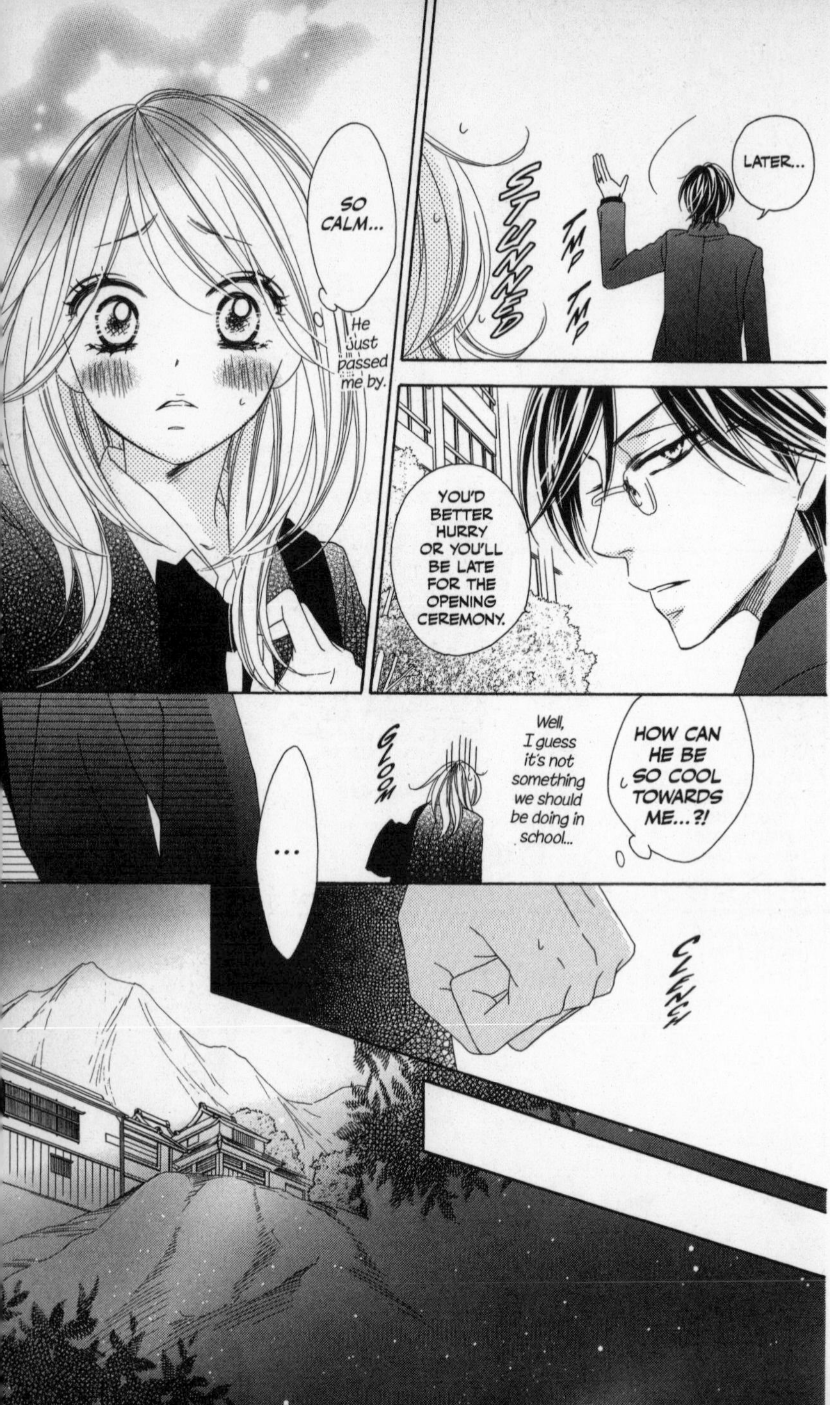
LATER...
TMP TMP
STUNNED
YOU'D BETTER HURRY OR YOU'LL BE LATE FOR THE OPENING CEREMONY.
SO CALM...
He just passed me by.
HOW CAN HE BE SO COOL TOWARDS ME...?!
Well, I guess it's not something we should be doing in school...
GLOOM
...
CLENCH

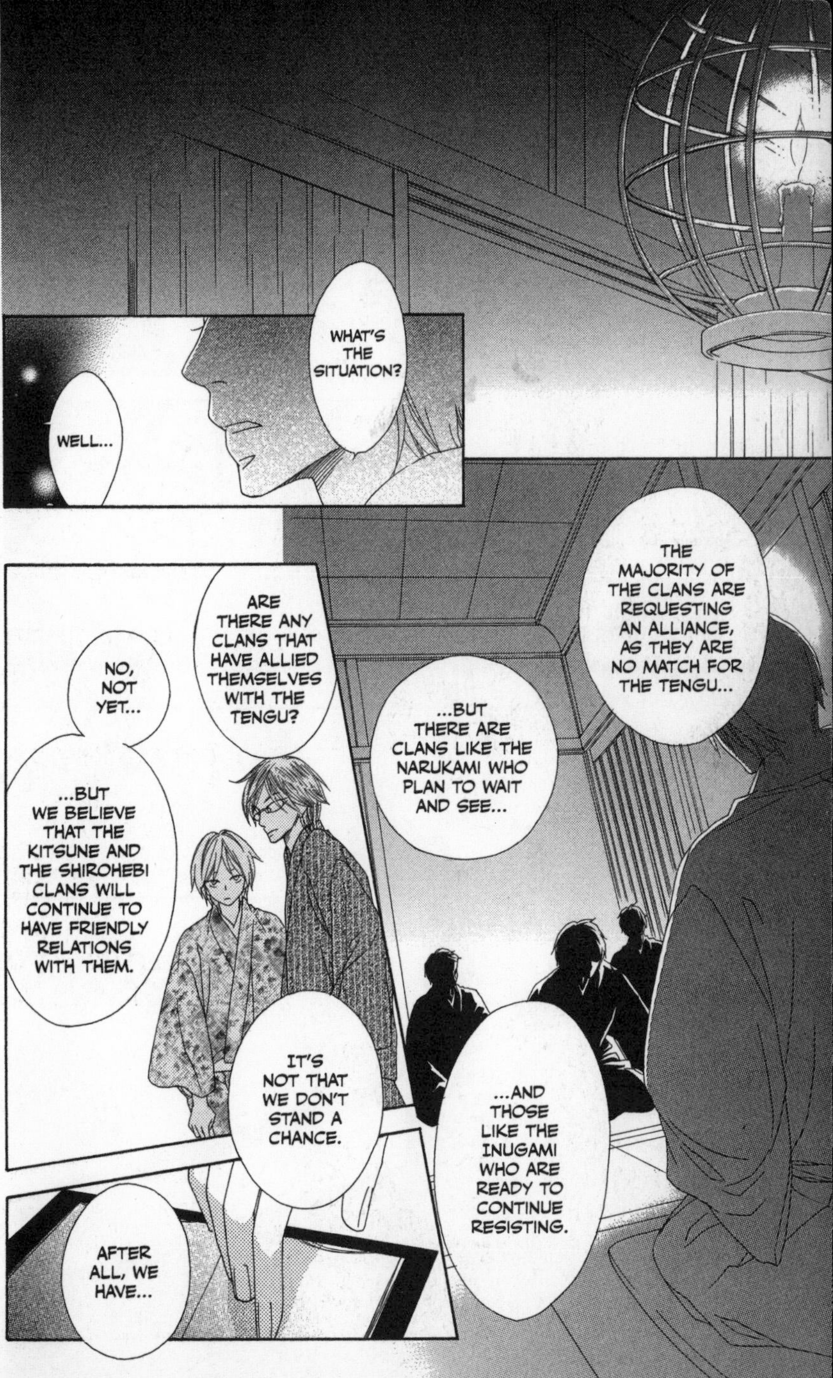
WHAT'S THE SITUATION?
WELL...
THE MAJORITY OF THE CLANS ARE REQUESTING AN ALLIANCE, AS THEY ARE NO MATCH FOR THE TENGU...
...BUT THERE ARE CLANS LIKE THE NARUKAMI WHO PLAN TO WAIT AND SEE...
...AND THOSE LIKE THE INUGAMI WHO ARE READY TO CONTINUE RESISTING.
ARE THERE ANY CLANS THAT HAVE ALLIED THEMSELVES WITH THE TENGU?
NO, NOT YET...
...BUT WE BELIEVE THAT THE KITSUNE AND THE SHIROHEBI CLANS WILL CONTINUE TO HAVE FRIENDLY RELATIONS WITH THEM.
IT'S NOT THAT WE DON'T STAND A CHANCE.
AFTER ALL, WE HAVE...

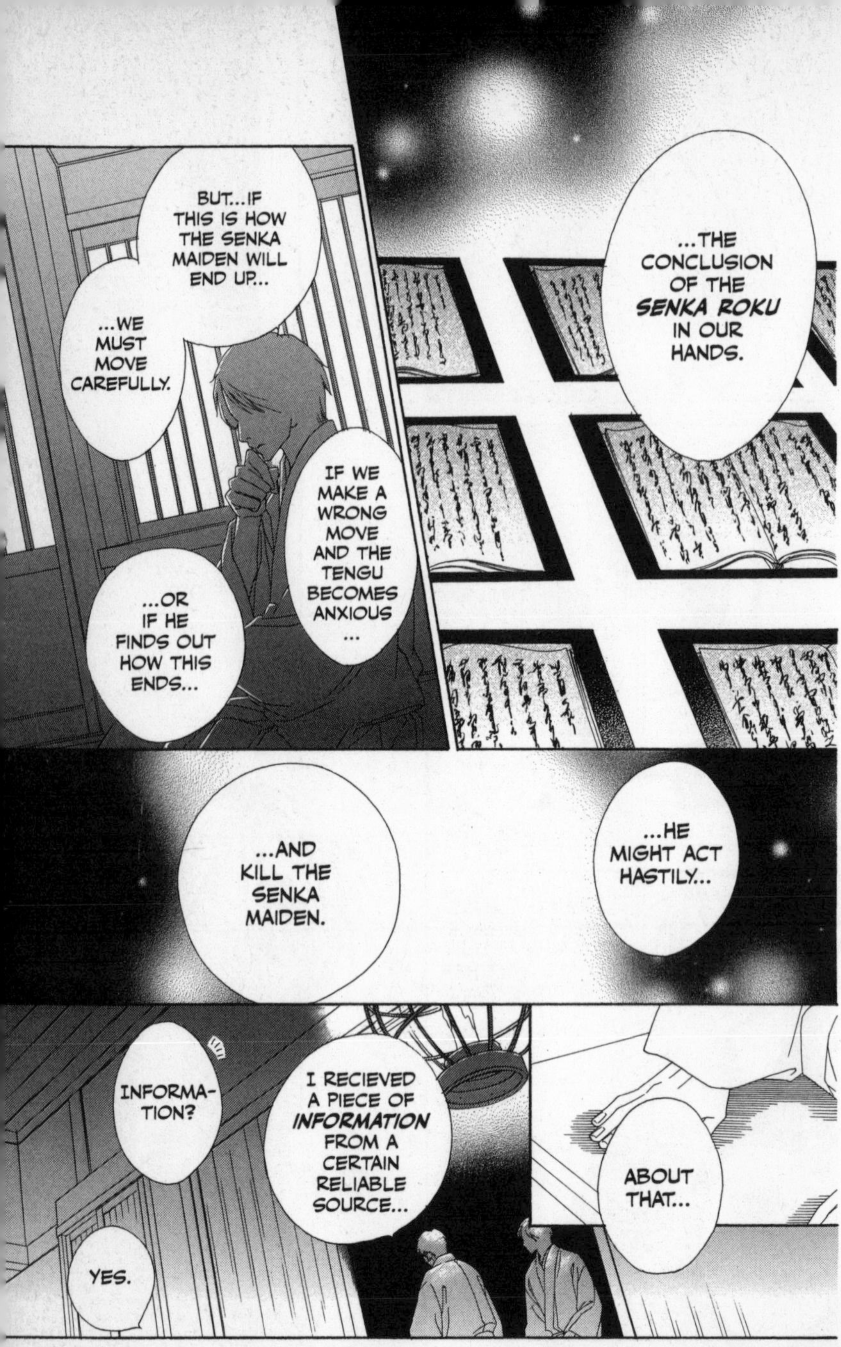
...THE CONCLUSION OF THE *SENKA ROKU* IN OUR HANDS.
BUT...IF THIS IS HOW THE SENKA MAIDEN WILL END UP...
...WE MUST MOVE CAREFULLY.
IF WE MAKE A WRONG MOVE AND THE TENGU BECOMES ANXIOUS...
...OR IF HE FINDS OUT HOW THIS ENDS...
...HE MIGHT ACT HASTILY...
...AND KILL THE SENKA MAIDEN.
ABOUT THAT...
I RECIEVED A PIECE OF *INFORMATION* FROM A CERTAIN RELIABLE SOURCE...
INFORMATION?
YES.

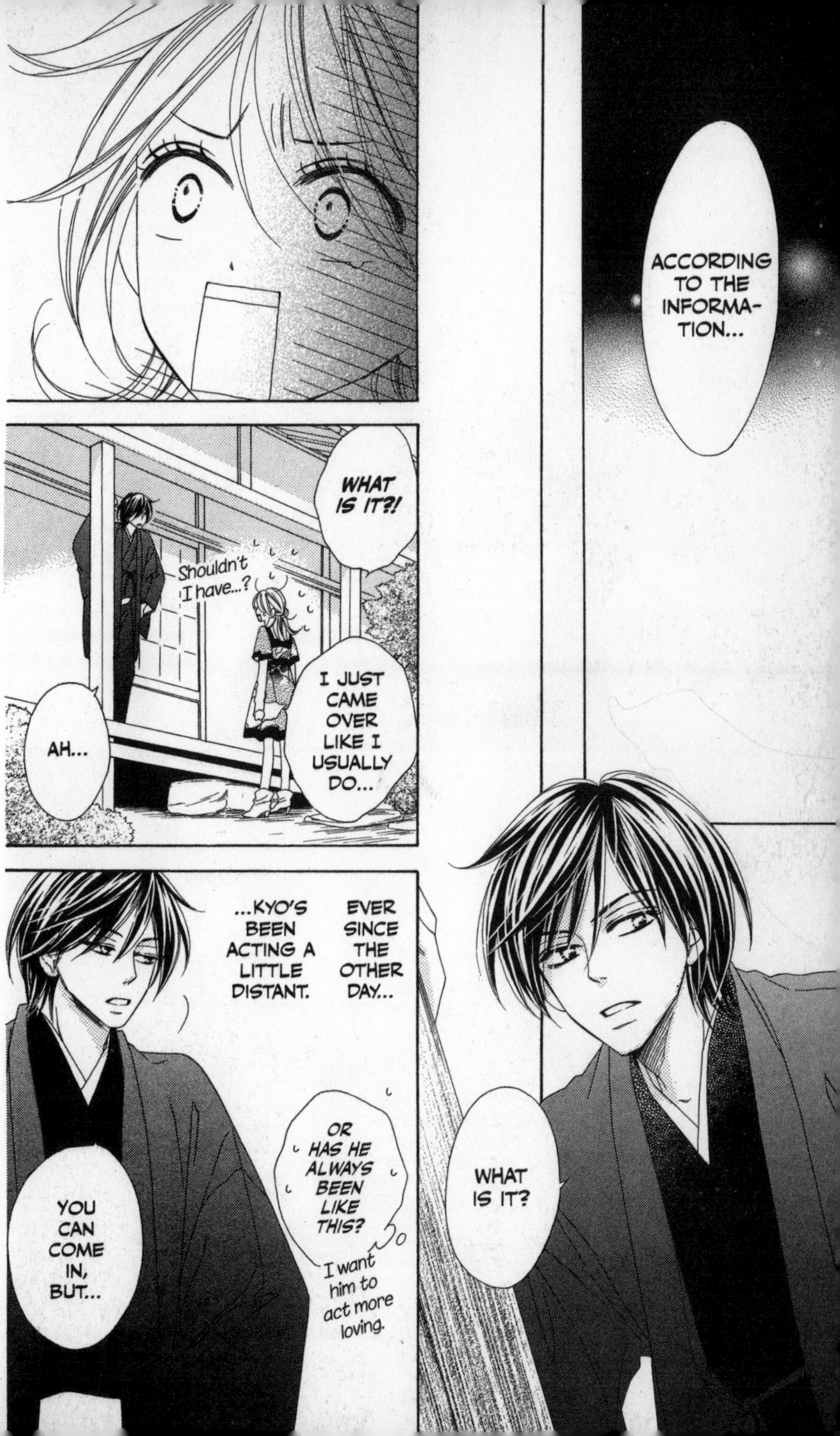
ACCORDING TO THE INFORMATION...
WHAT IS IT?!
Shouldn't I have...?
I JUST CAME OVER LIKE I USUALLY DO...
AH...
WHAT IS IT?
EVER SINCE THE OTHER DAY...
...KYO'S BEEN ACTING A LITTLE DISTANT.
OR HAS HE ALWAYS BEEN LIKE THIS?
I want him to act more loving.
YOU CAN COME IN, BUT...

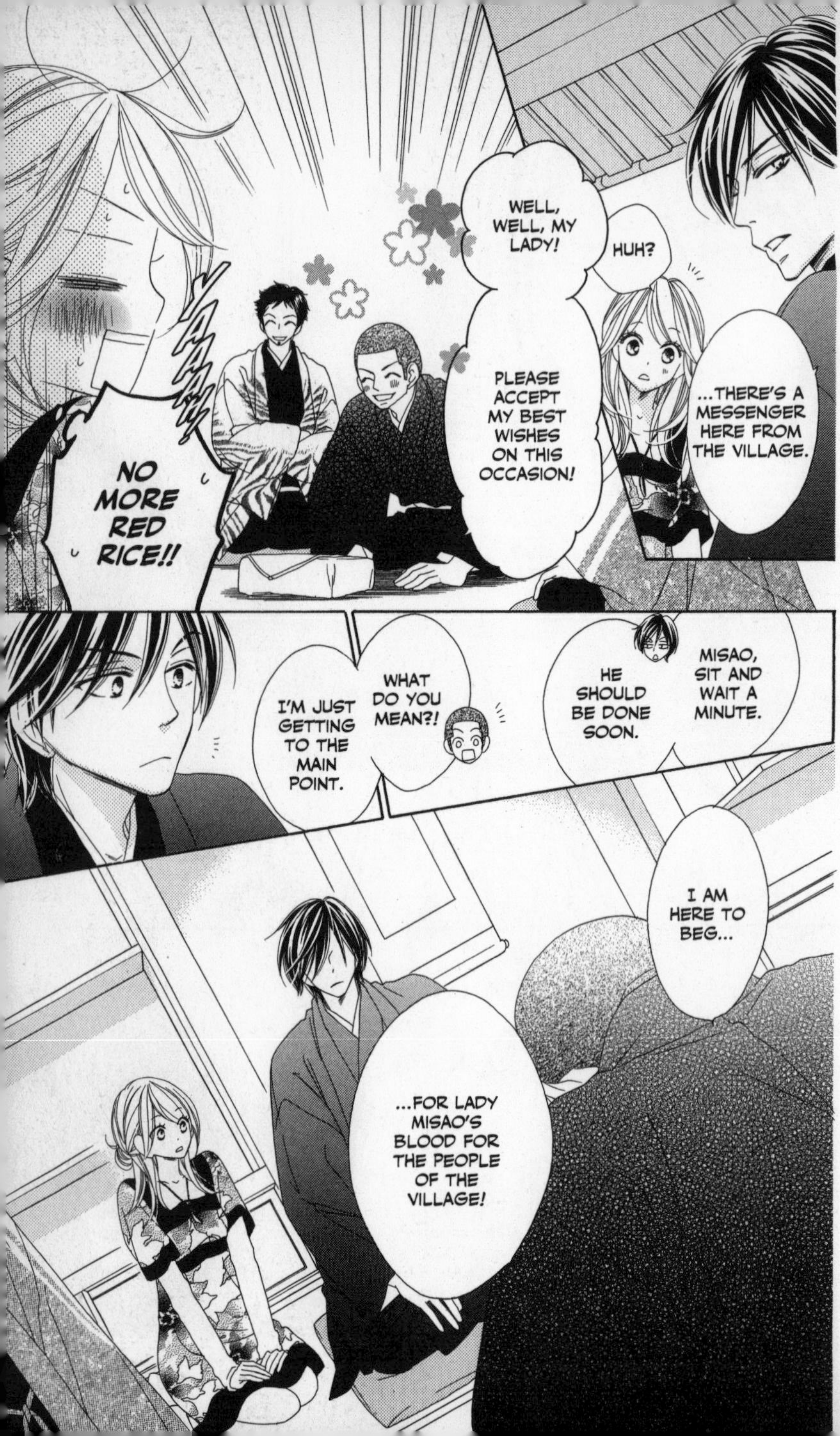
...THERE'S A MESSENGER HERE FROM THE VILLAGE.
HUH?
WELL, WELL, MY LADY!
PLEASE ACCEPT MY BEST WISHES ON THIS OCCASION!
NO MORE RED RICE!!
MISAO, SIT AND WAIT A MINUTE.
HE SHOULD BE DONE SOON.
WHAT DO YOU MEAN?!
I'M JUST GETTING TO THE MAIN POINT.
I AM HERE TO BEG...
...FOR LADY MISAO'S BLOOD FOR THE PEOPLE OF THE VILLAGE!

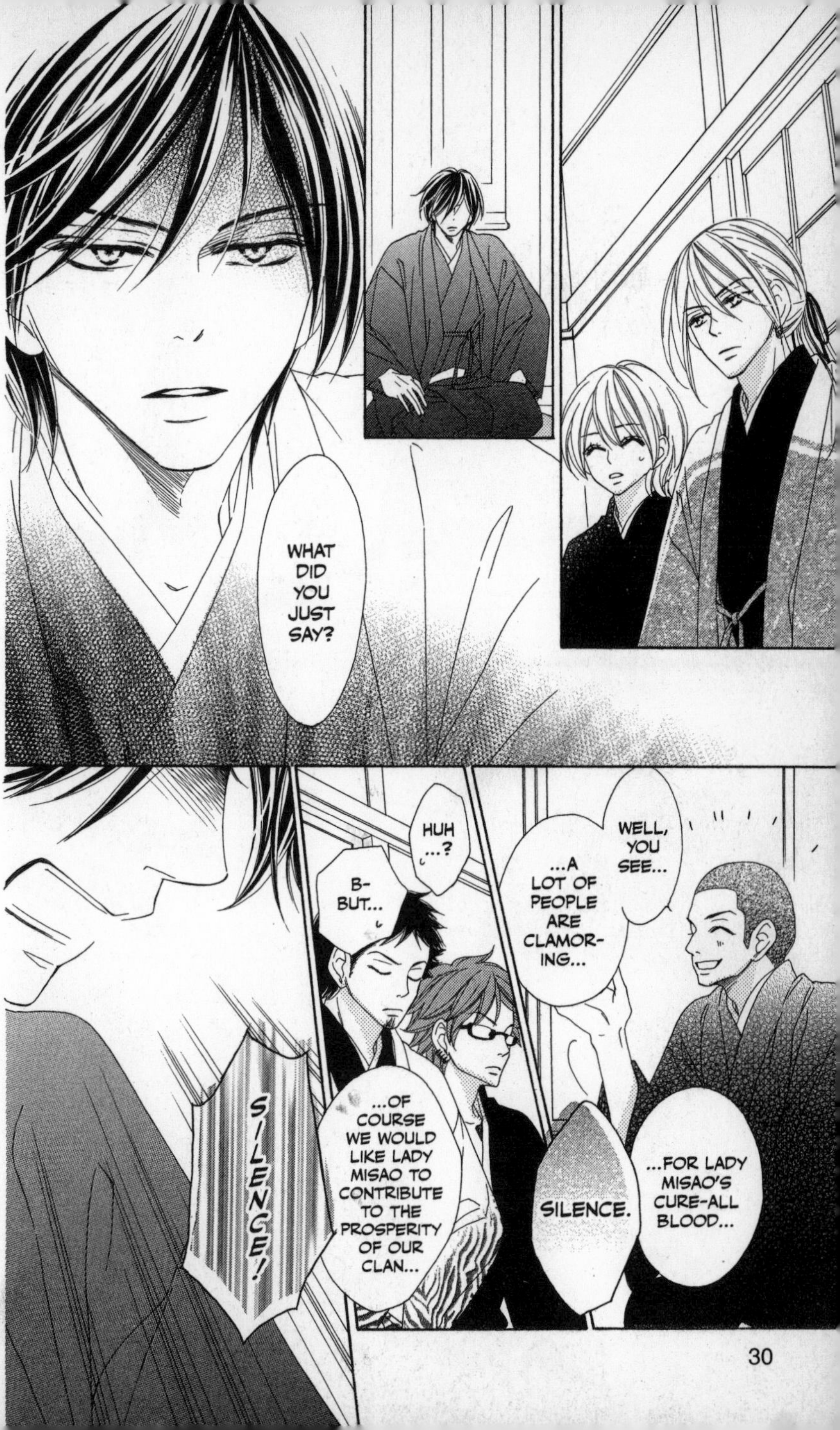
WHAT DID YOU JUST SAY?
WELL, YOU SEE...
...A LOT OF PEOPLE ARE CLAMORING...
...FOR LADY MISAO'S CURE-ALL BLOOD...
HUH ...?
B-BUT...
...OF COURSE WE WOULD LIKE LADY MISAO TO CONTRIBUTE TO THE PROSPERITY OF OUR CLAN...
SILENCE.
SILENCE!

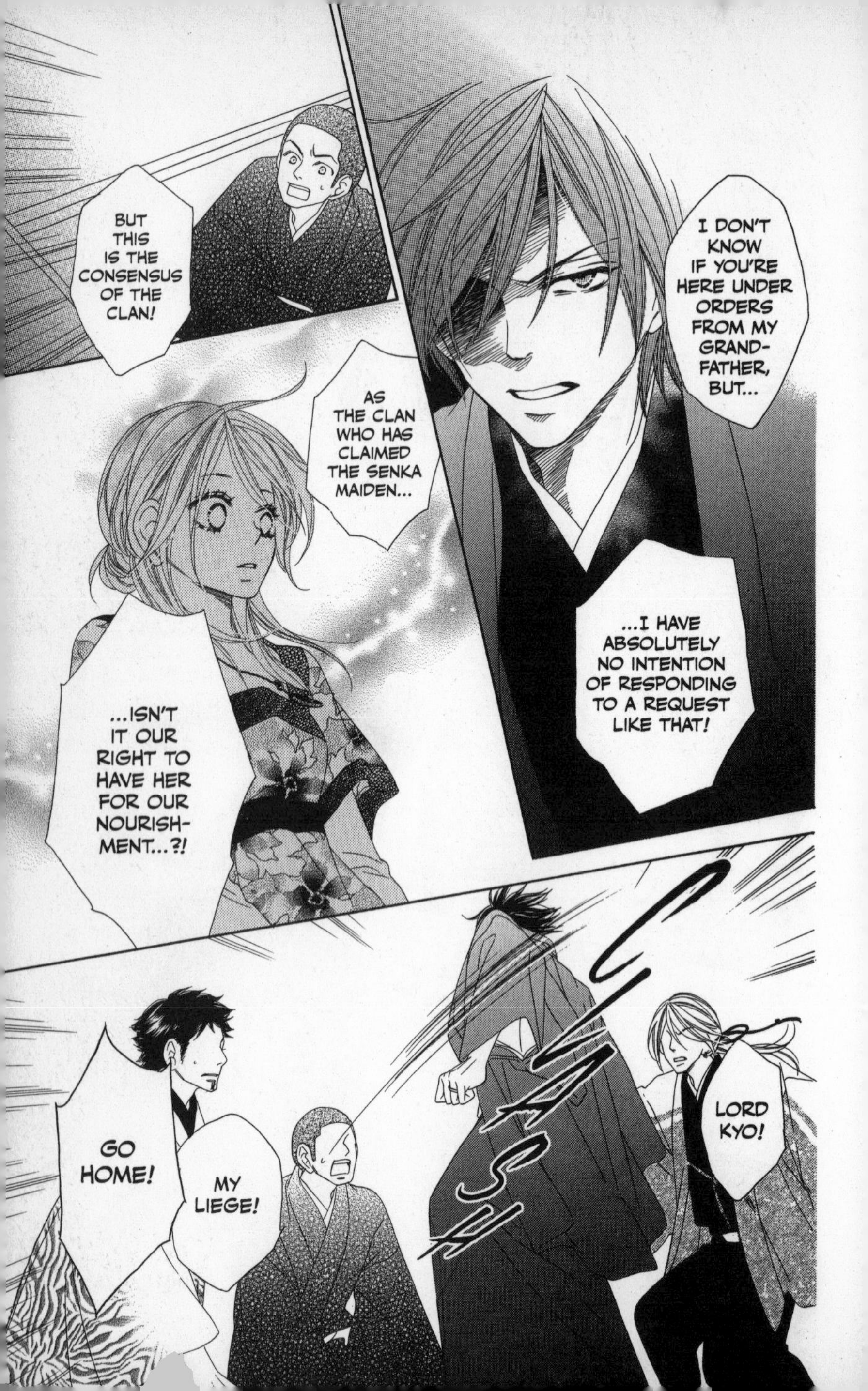
I DON'T KNOW IF YOU'RE HERE UNDER ORDERS FROM MY GRANDFATHER, BUT...
...I HAVE ABSOLUTELY NO INTENTION OF RESPONDING TO A REQUEST LIKE THAT!
BUT THIS IS THE CONSENSUS OF THE CLAN!
AS THE CLAN WHO HAS CLAIMED THE SENKA MAIDEN...
...ISN'T IT OUR RIGHT TO HAVE HER FOR OUR NOURISHMENT...?!
LORD KYO!
MY LIEGE!
GO HOME!

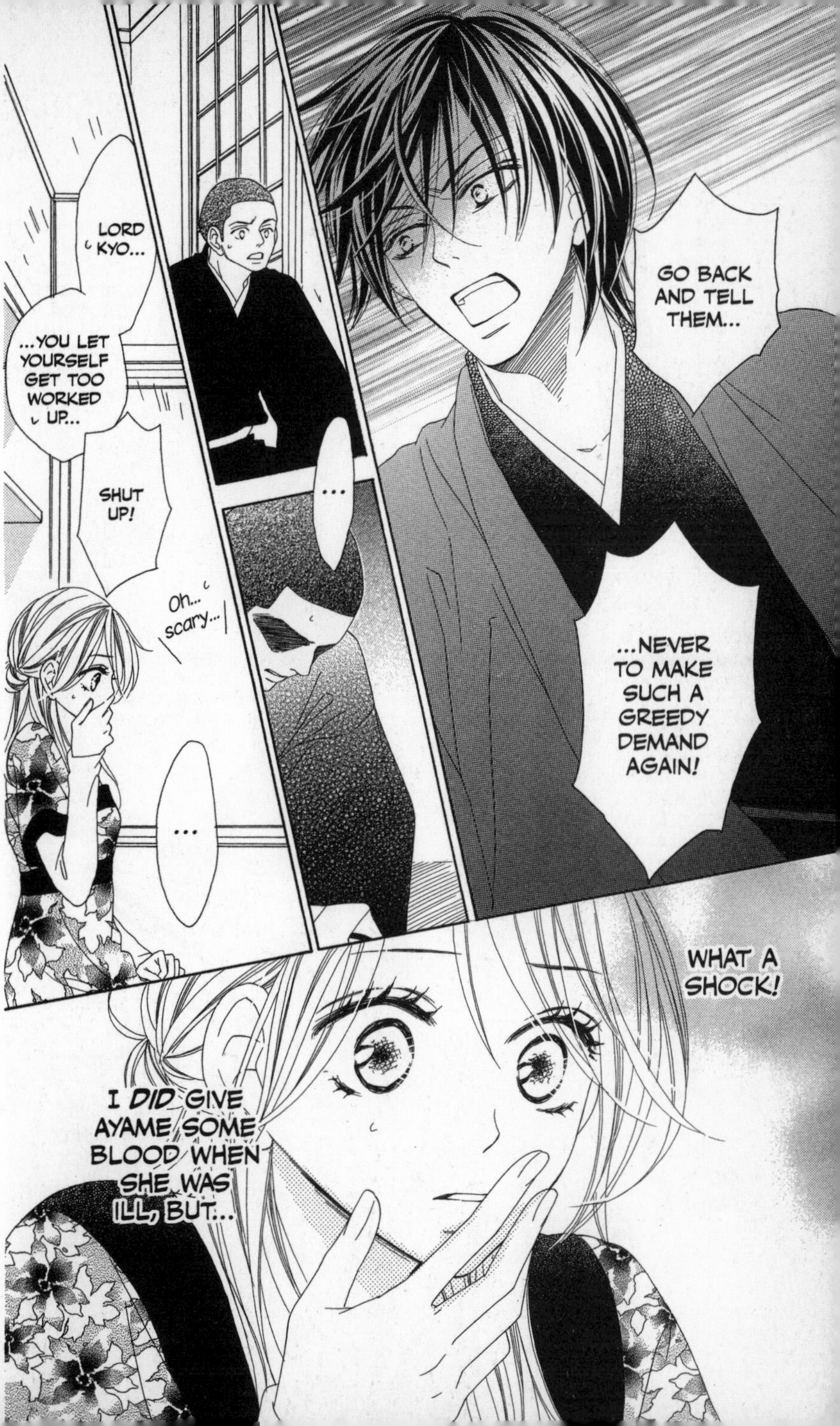
GO BACK AND TELL THEM...
...NEVER TO MAKE SUCH A GREEDY DEMAND AGAIN!
...
LORD KYO...
...YOU LET YOURSELF GET TOO WORKED UP...
SHUT UP!
Oh... scary...
...
WHAT A SHOCK!
I *DID* GIVE AYAME SOME BLOOD WHEN SHE WAS ILL, BUT...

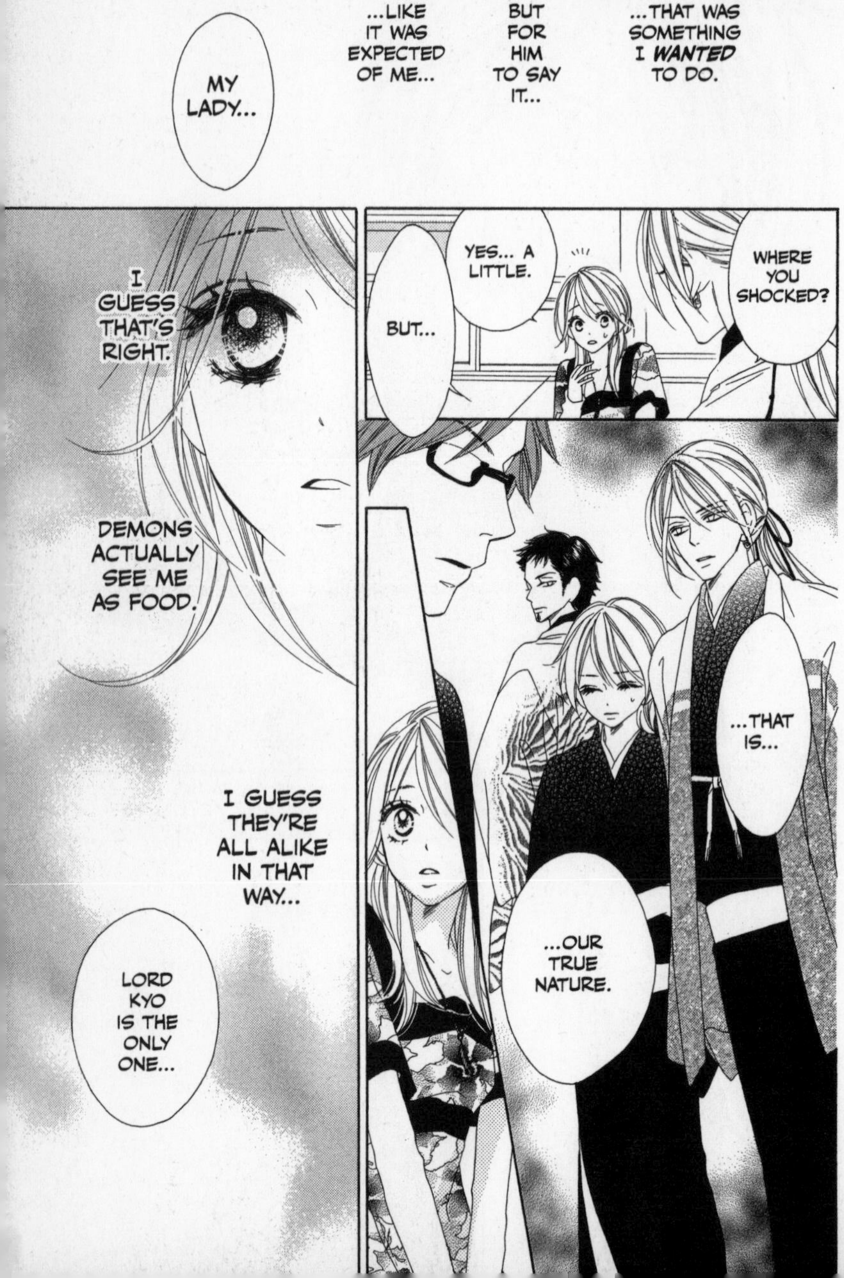
...THAT WAS SOMETHING I *WANTED* TO DO.
BUT FOR HIM TO SAY IT...
...LIKE IT WAS EXPECTED OF ME...
MY LADY...
WHERE YOU SHOCKED?
YES... A LITTLE.
BUT...
...THAT IS...
...OUR TRUE NATURE.
I GUESS THAT'S RIGHT.
DEMONS ACTUALLY SEE ME AS FOOD.
I GUESS THEY'RE ALL ALIKE IN THAT WAY...
LORD KYO IS THE ONLY ONE...

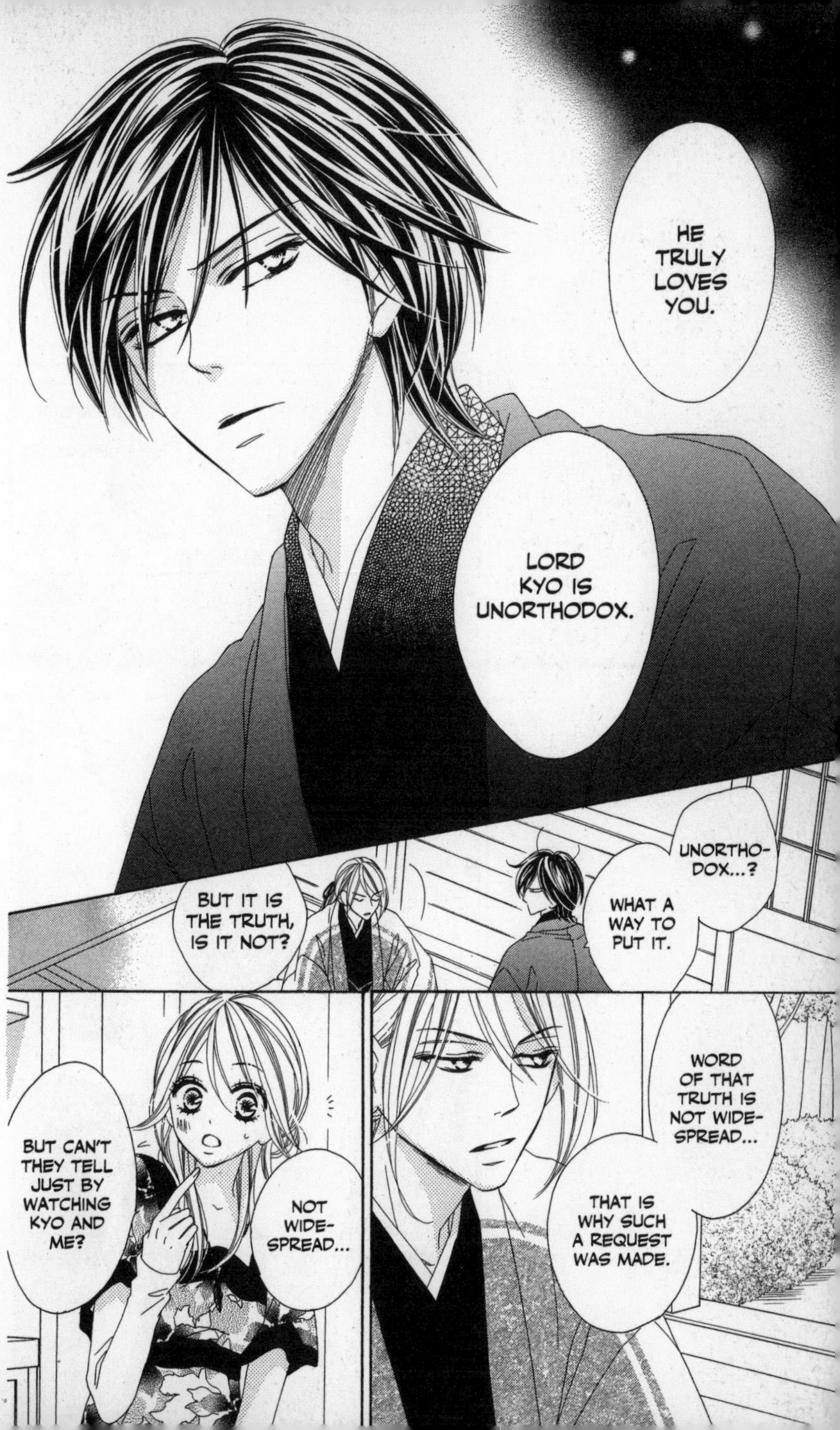
HE TRULY LOVES YOU.
LORD KYO IS UNORTHODOX.
UNORTHO-DOX...?
WHAT A WAY TO PUT IT.
BUT IT IS THE TRUTH, IS IT NOT?
WORD OF THAT TRUTH IS NOT WIDE-SPREAD...
THAT IS WHY SUCH A REQUEST WAS MADE.
NOT WIDE-SPREAD...
BUT CAN'T THEY TELL JUST BY WATCHING KYO AND ME?

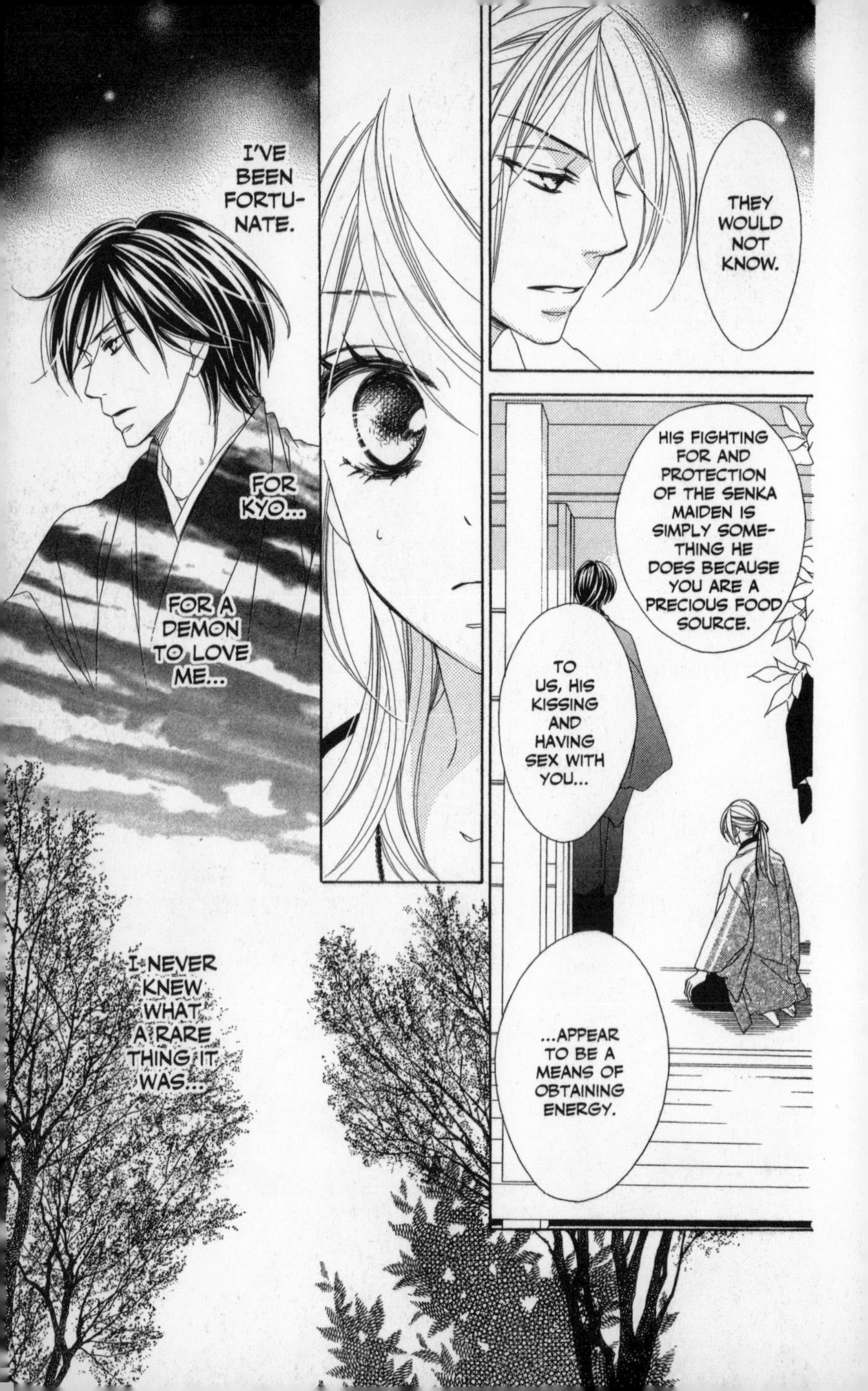
THEY WOULD NOT KNOW.
HIS FIGHTING FOR AND PROTECTION OF THE SENKA MAIDEN IS SIMPLY SOME-THING HE DOES BECAUSE YOU ARE A PRECIOUS FOOD SOURCE.
TO US, HIS KISSING AND HAVING SEX WITH YOU...
...APPEAR TO BE A MEANS OF OBTAINING ENERGY.
I'VE BEEN FORTU-NATE.
FOR KYO...
FOR A DEMON TO LOVE ME...
I NEVER KNEW WHAT A RARE THING IT WAS...

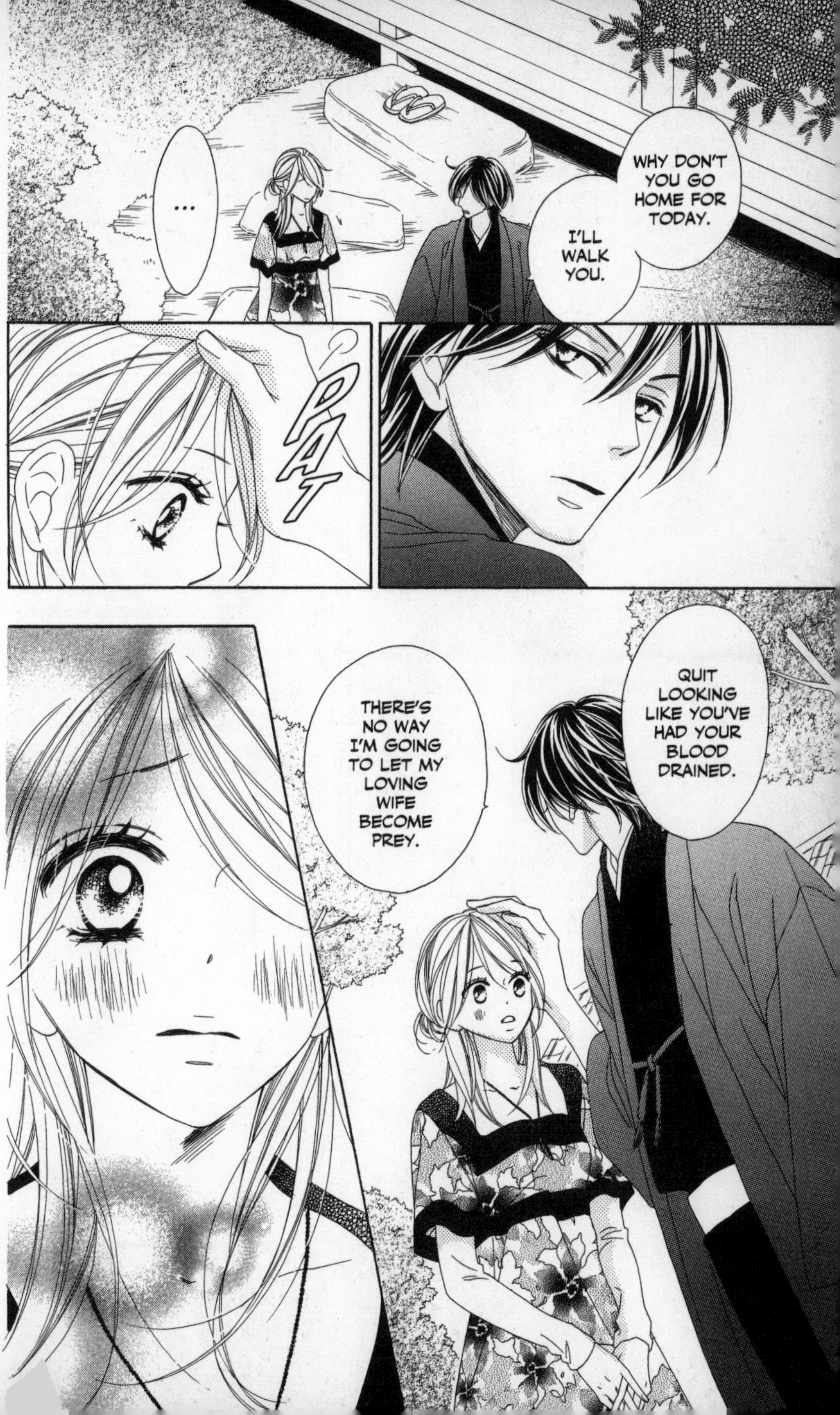
WHY DON'T YOU GO HOME FOR TODAY.
I'LL WALK YOU.
...
PAT
QUIT LOOKING LIKE YOU'VE HAD YOUR BLOOD DRAINED.
THERE'S NO WAY I'M GOING TO LET MY LOVING WIFE BECOME PREY.

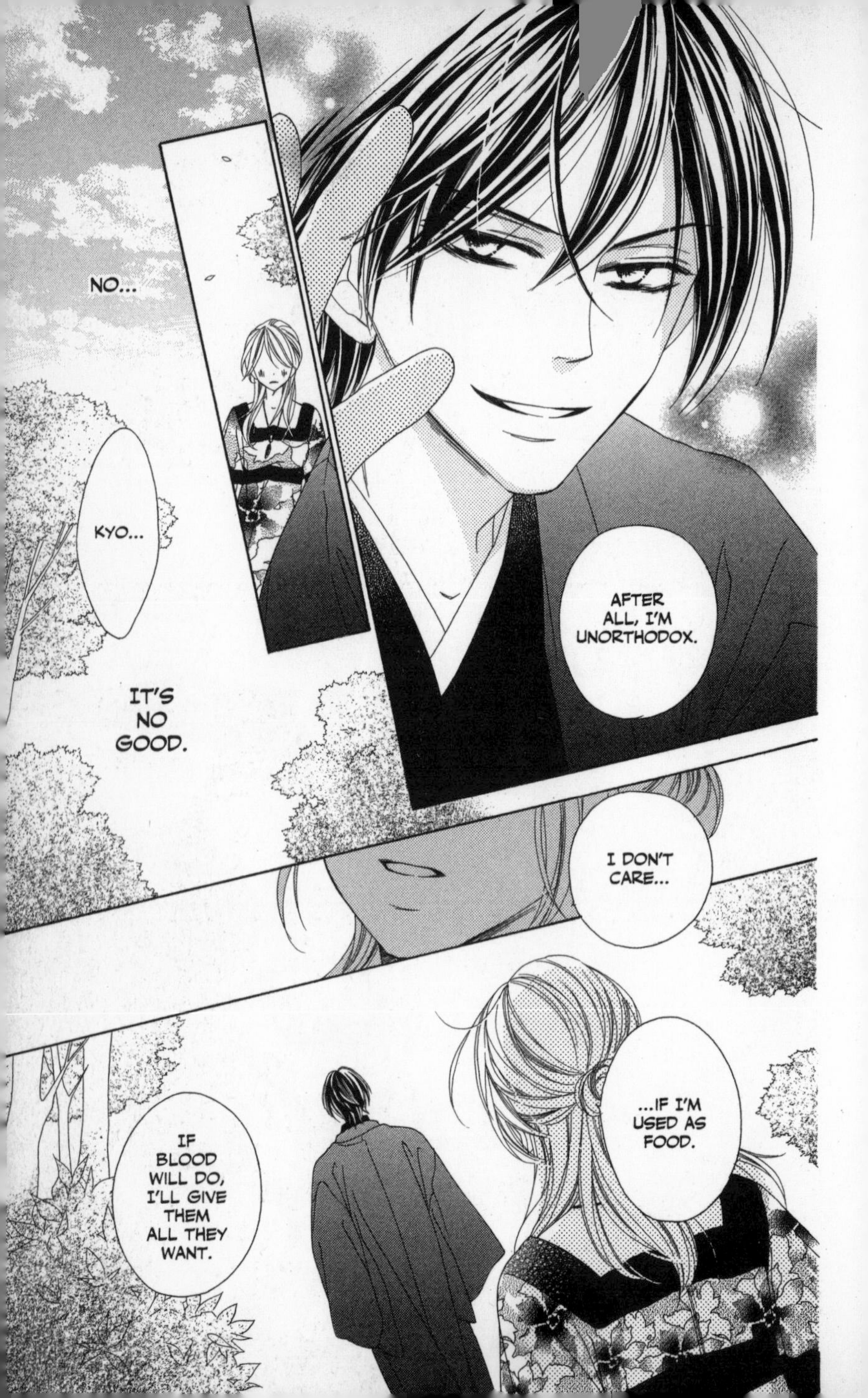
AFTER ALL, I'M UNORTHODOX.
NO...
KYO...
IT'S NO GOOD.
I DON'T CARE...
...IF I'M USED AS FOOD.
IF BLOOD WILL DO, I'LL GIVE THEM ALL THEY WANT.

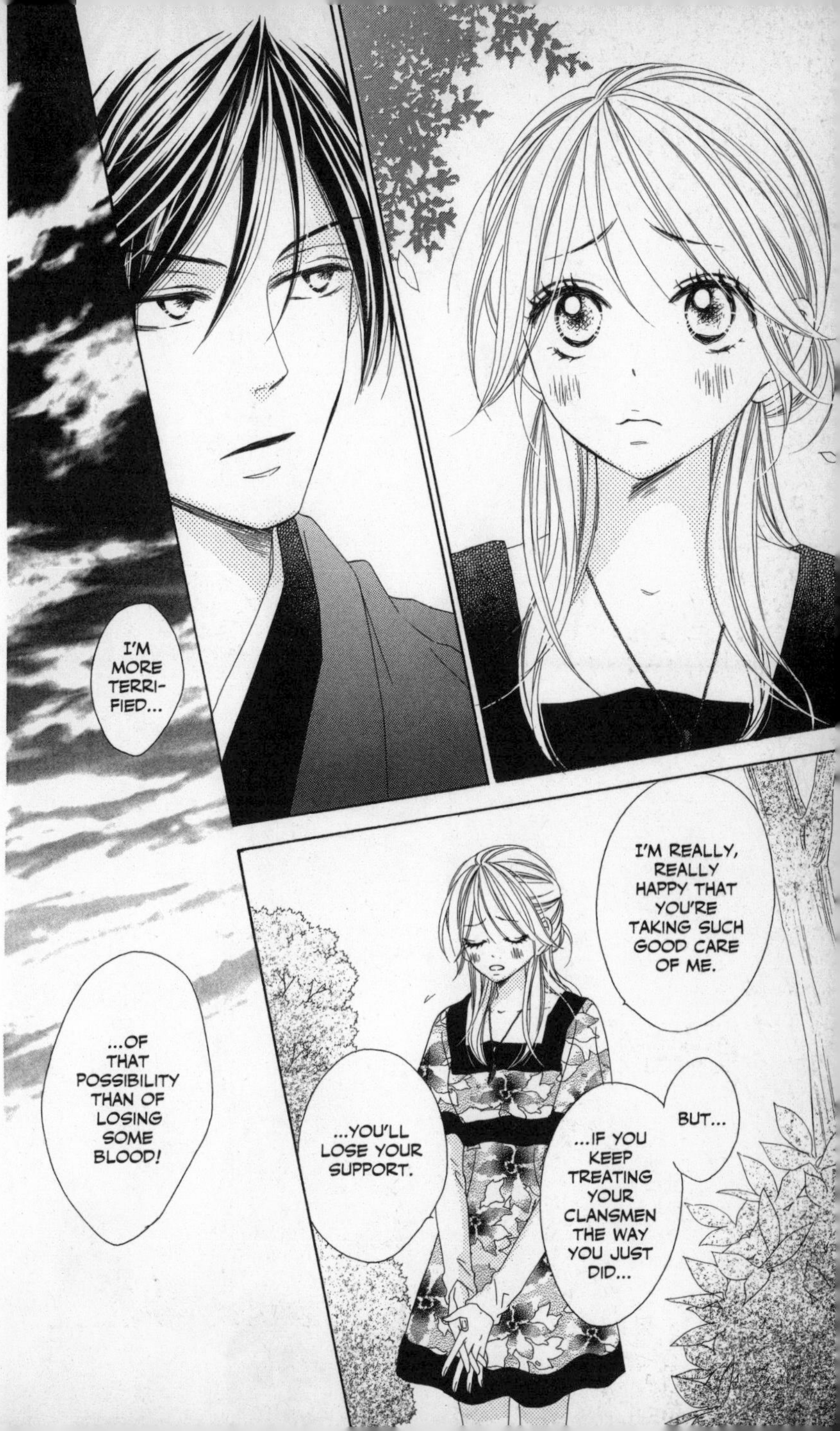
I'M REALLY, REALLY HAPPY THAT YOU'RE TAKING SUCH GOOD CARE OF ME.
BUT...
...IF YOU KEEP TREATING YOUR CLANSMEN THE WAY YOU JUST DID...
...YOU'LL LOSE YOUR SUPPORT.
I'M MORE TERRI-FIED...
...OF THAT POSSIBILITY THAN OF LOSING SOME BLOOD!

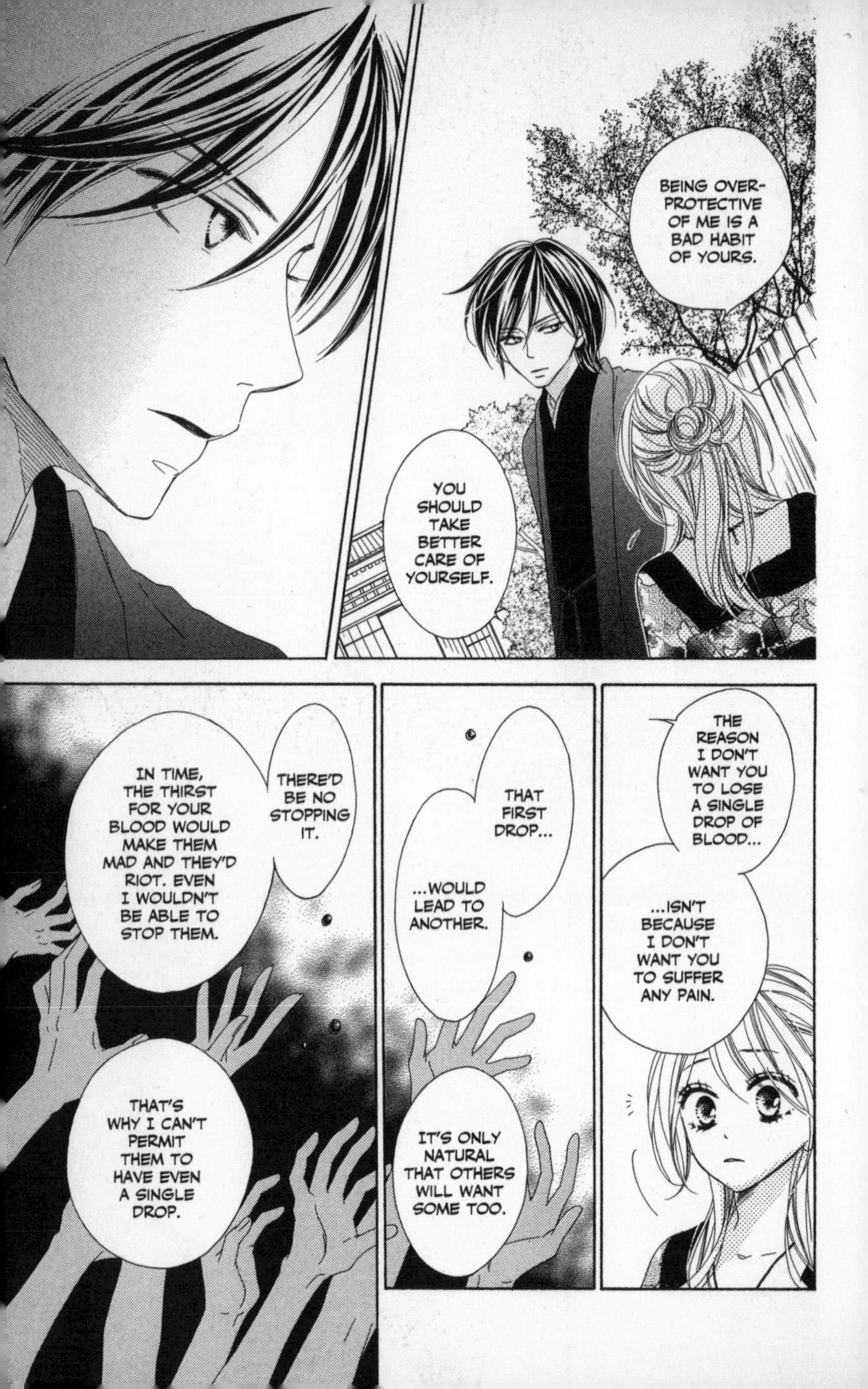
BEING OVER-PROTECTIVE OF ME IS A BAD HABIT OF YOURS.
YOU SHOULD TAKE BETTER CARE OF YOURSELF.
THE REASON I DON'T WANT YOU TO LOSE A SINGLE DROP OF BLOOD...
...ISN'T BECAUSE I DON'T WANT YOU TO SUFFER ANY PAIN.
THAT FIRST DROP...
...WOULD LEAD TO ANOTHER.
IT'S ONLY NATURAL THAT OTHERS WILL WANT SOME TOO.
THERE'D BE NO STOPPING IT.
IN TIME, THE THIRST FOR YOUR BLOOD WOULD MAKE THEM MAD AND THEY'D RIOT. EVEN I WOULDN'T BE ABLE TO STOP THEM.
THAT'S WHY I CAN'T PERMIT THEM TO HAVE EVEN A SINGLE DROP.

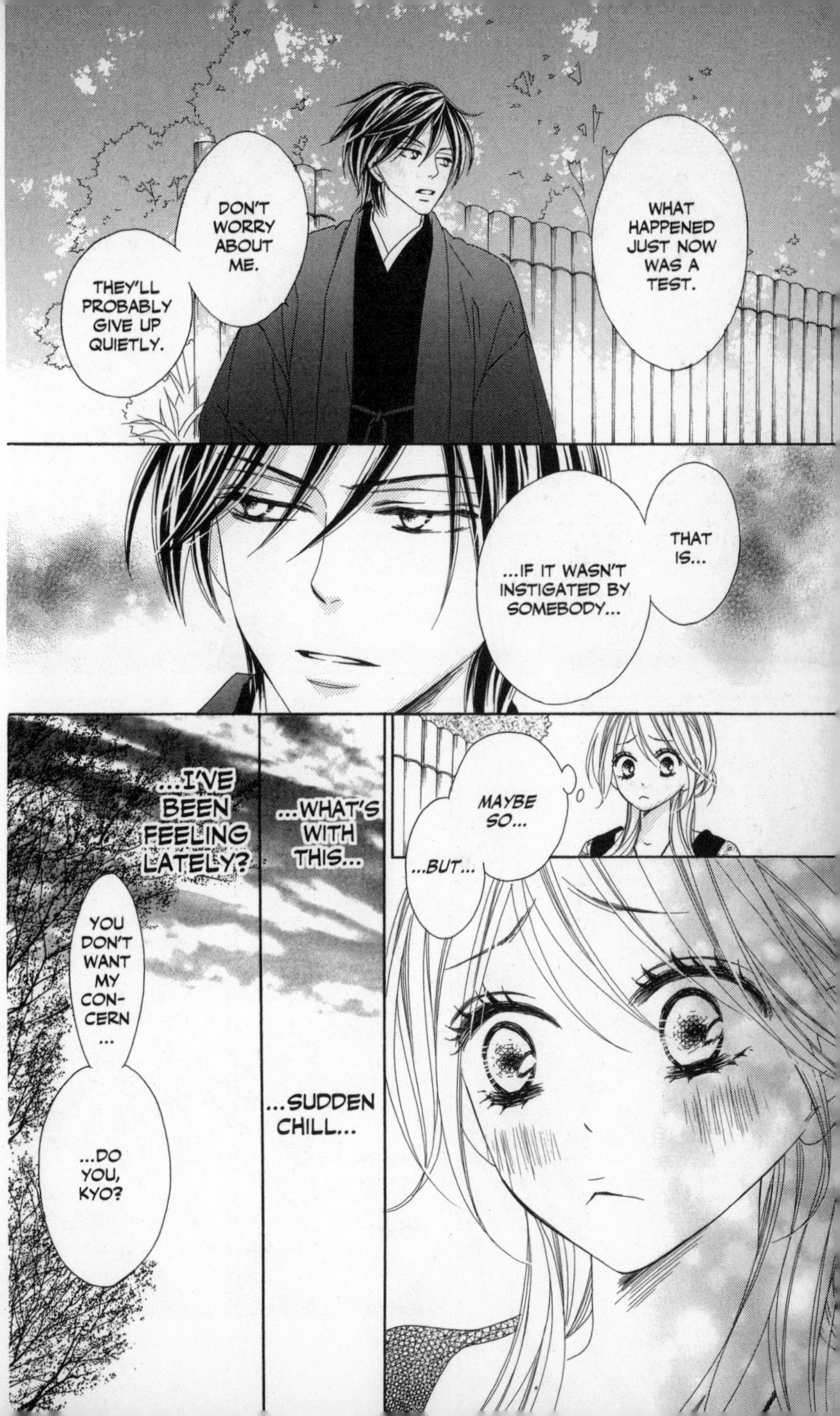
WHAT HAPPENED JUST NOW WAS A TEST.
DON'T WORRY ABOUT ME.
THEY'LL PROBABLY GIVE UP QUIETLY.
THAT IS...
...IF IT WASN'T INSTIGATED BY SOMEBODY...
MAYBE SO...
...BUT...
...WHAT'S WITH THIS...
...SUDDEN CHILL...
...I'VE BEEN FEELING LATELY?
YOU DON'T WANT MY CON-CERN...
...DO YOU, KYO?

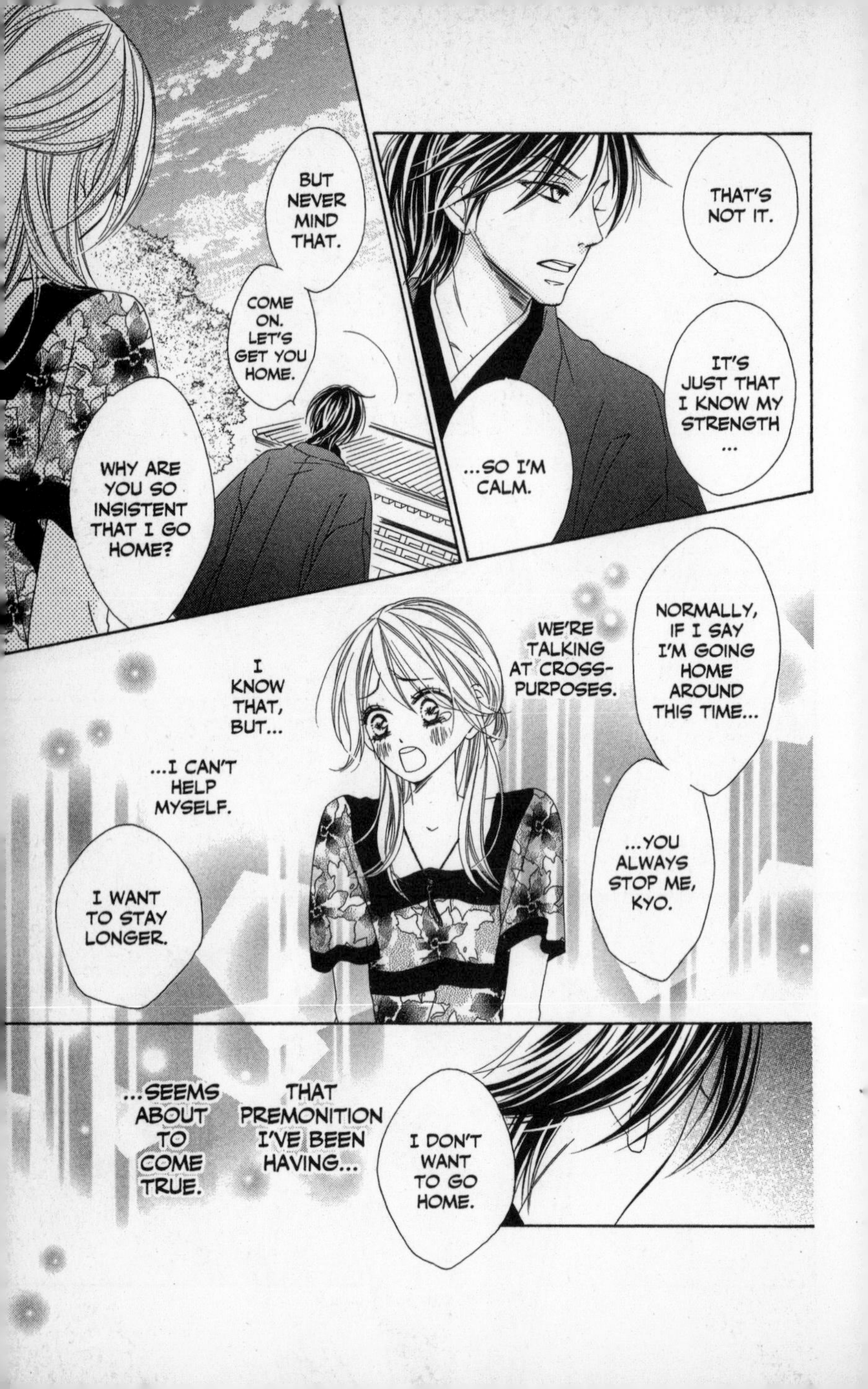
THAT'S NOT IT.
IT'S JUST THAT I KNOW MY STRENGTH...
...SO I'M CALM.
BUT NEVER MIND THAT.
COME ON. LET'S GET YOU HOME.
WHY ARE YOU SO INSISTENT THAT I GO HOME?
NORMALLY, IF I SAY I'M GOING HOME AROUND THIS TIME...
...YOU ALWAYS STOP ME, KYO.
WE'RE TALKING AT CROSS-PURPOSES.
I KNOW THAT, BUT...
...I CAN'T HELP MYSELF.
I WANT TO STAY LONGER.
I DON'T WANT TO GO HOME.
THAT PREMONITION I'VE BEEN HAVING...
...SEEMS ABOUT TO COME TRUE.

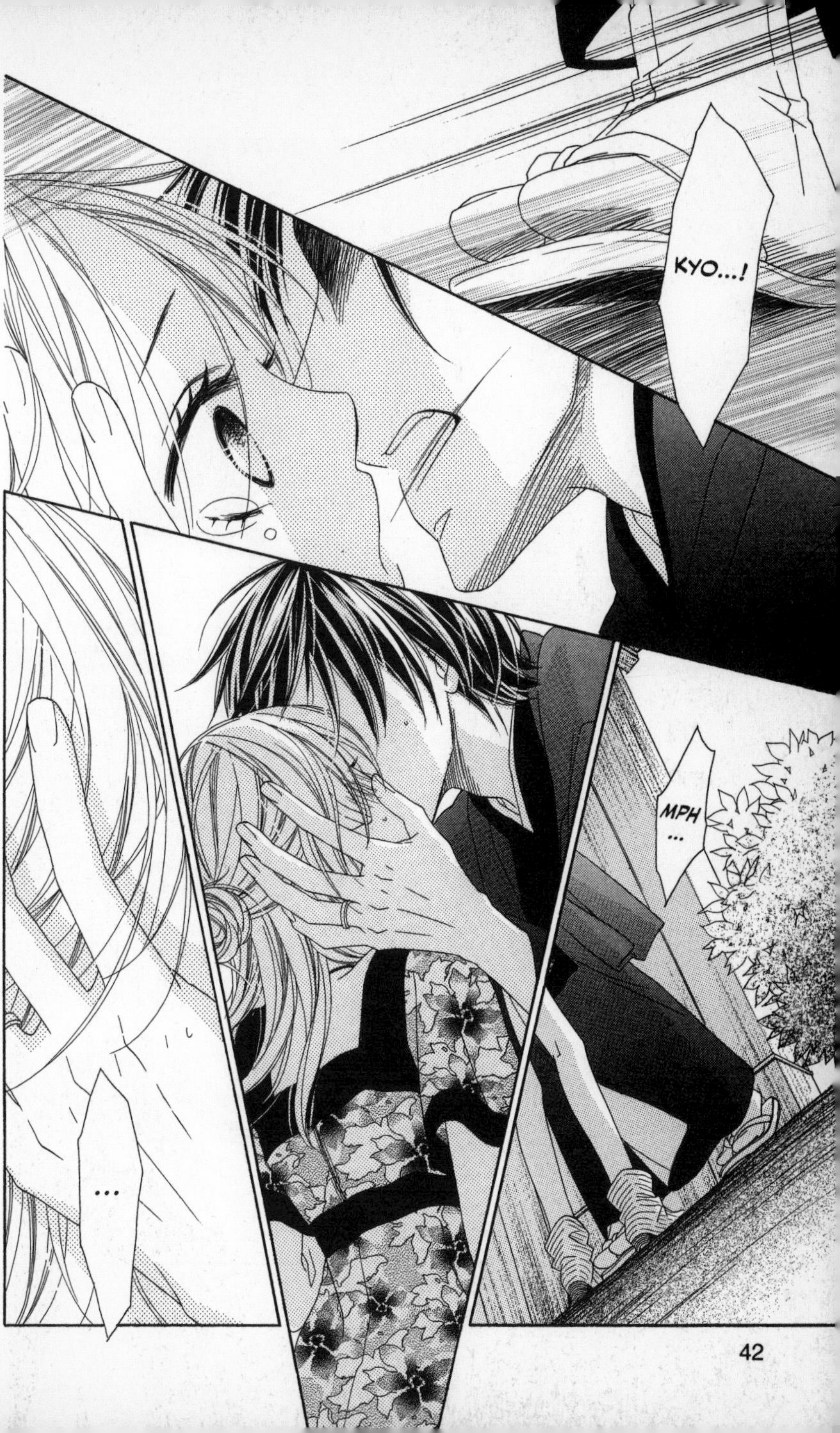
KYO...!
MPH ...
...

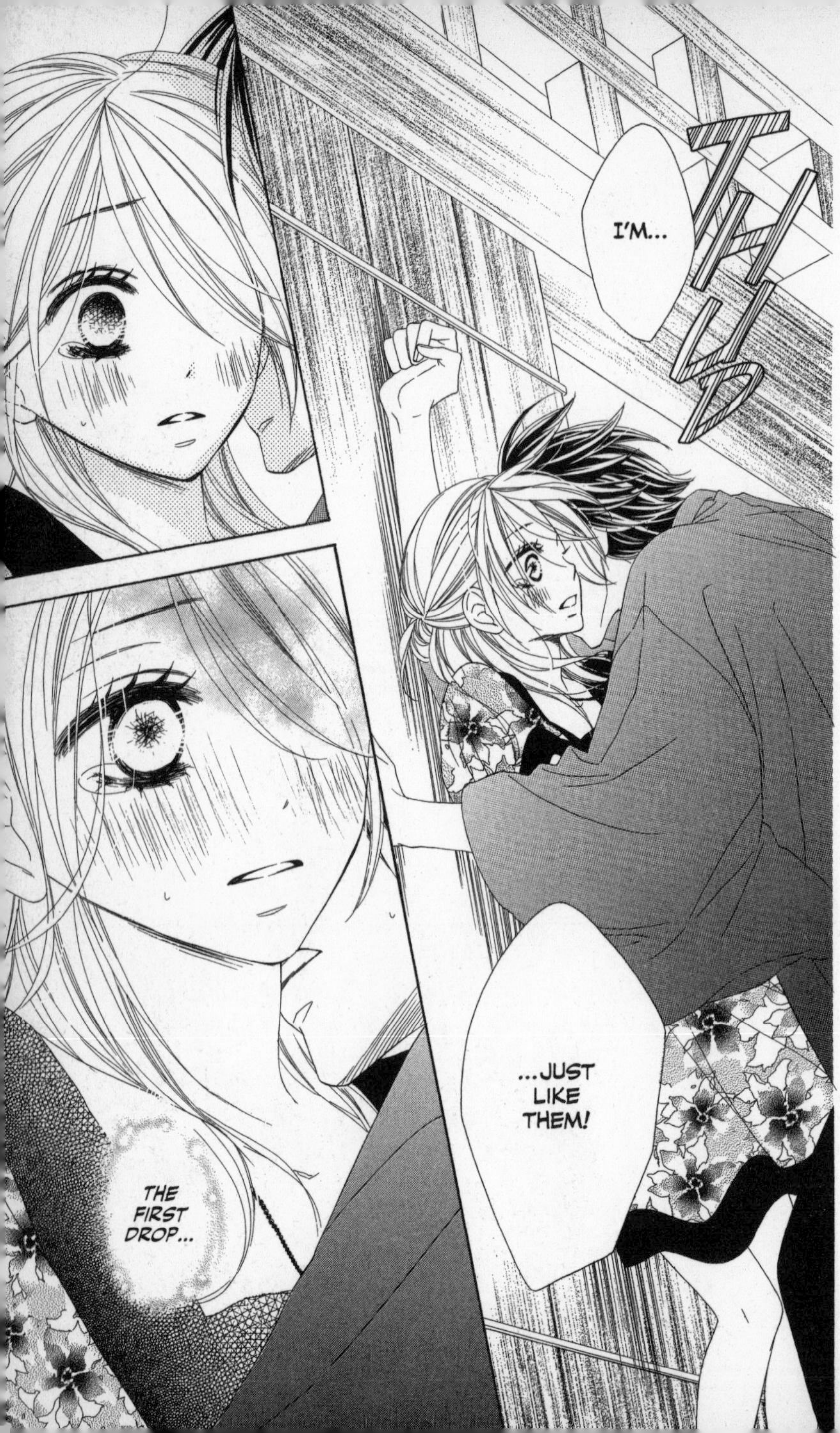
THUD
I'M...
...JUST LIKE THEM!
THE FIRST DROP...

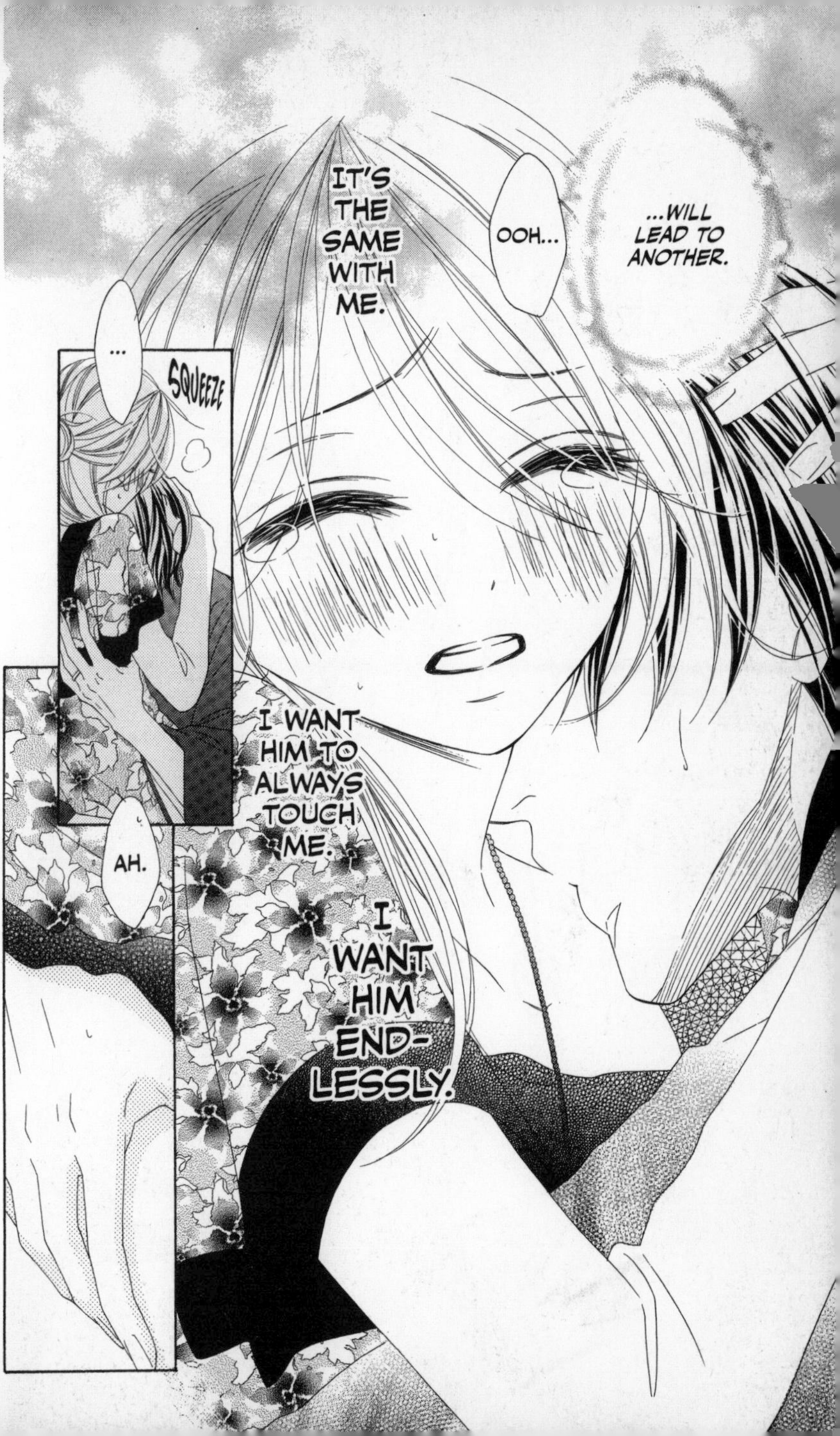
...WILL LEAD TO ANOTHER.
OOH...
IT'S THE SAME WITH ME.
...
SQUEEZE
I WANT HIM TO ALWAYS TOUCH ME.
I WANT HIM END-LESSLY.
AH.

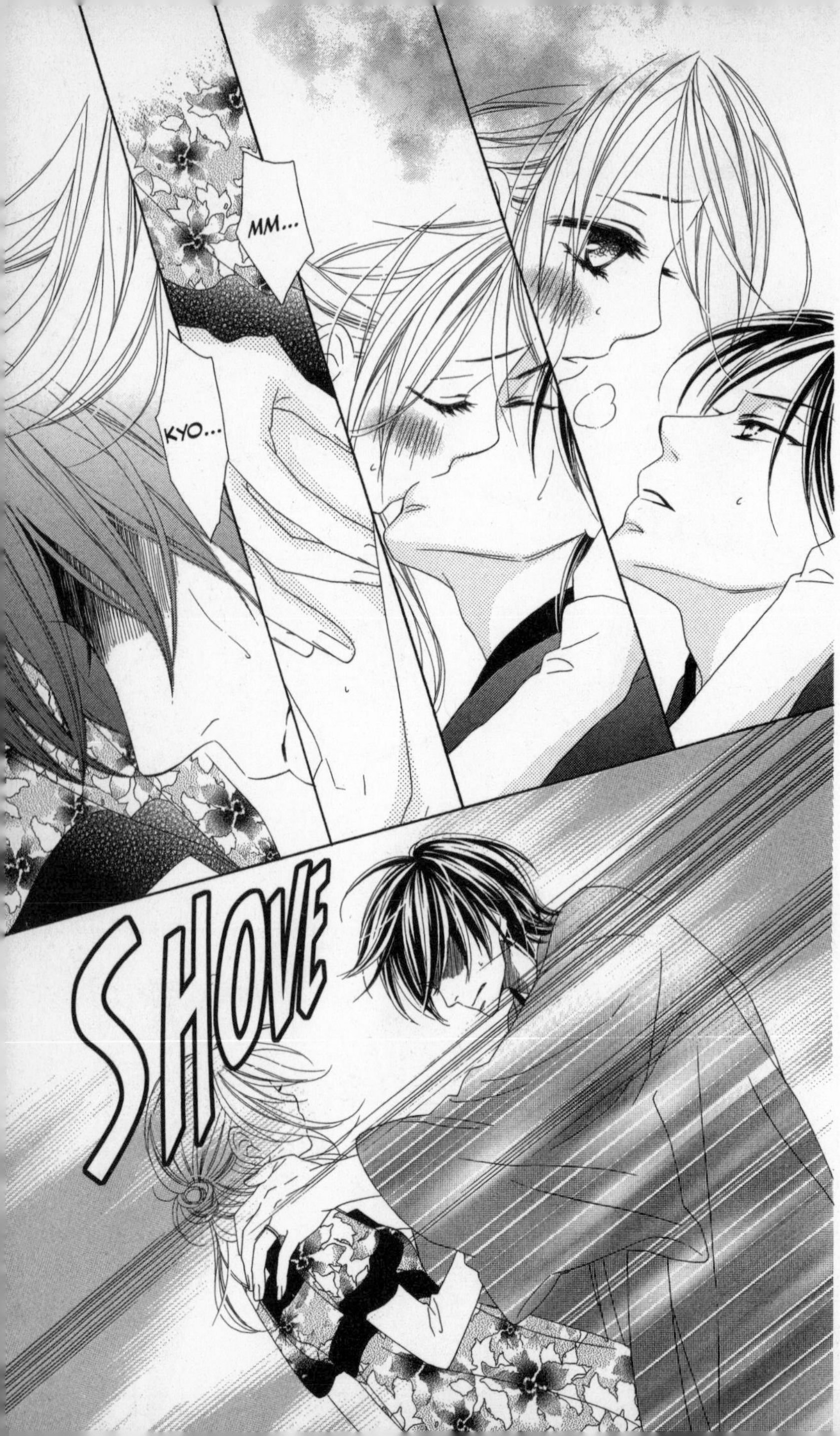
MM...
KYO...
SHOVE

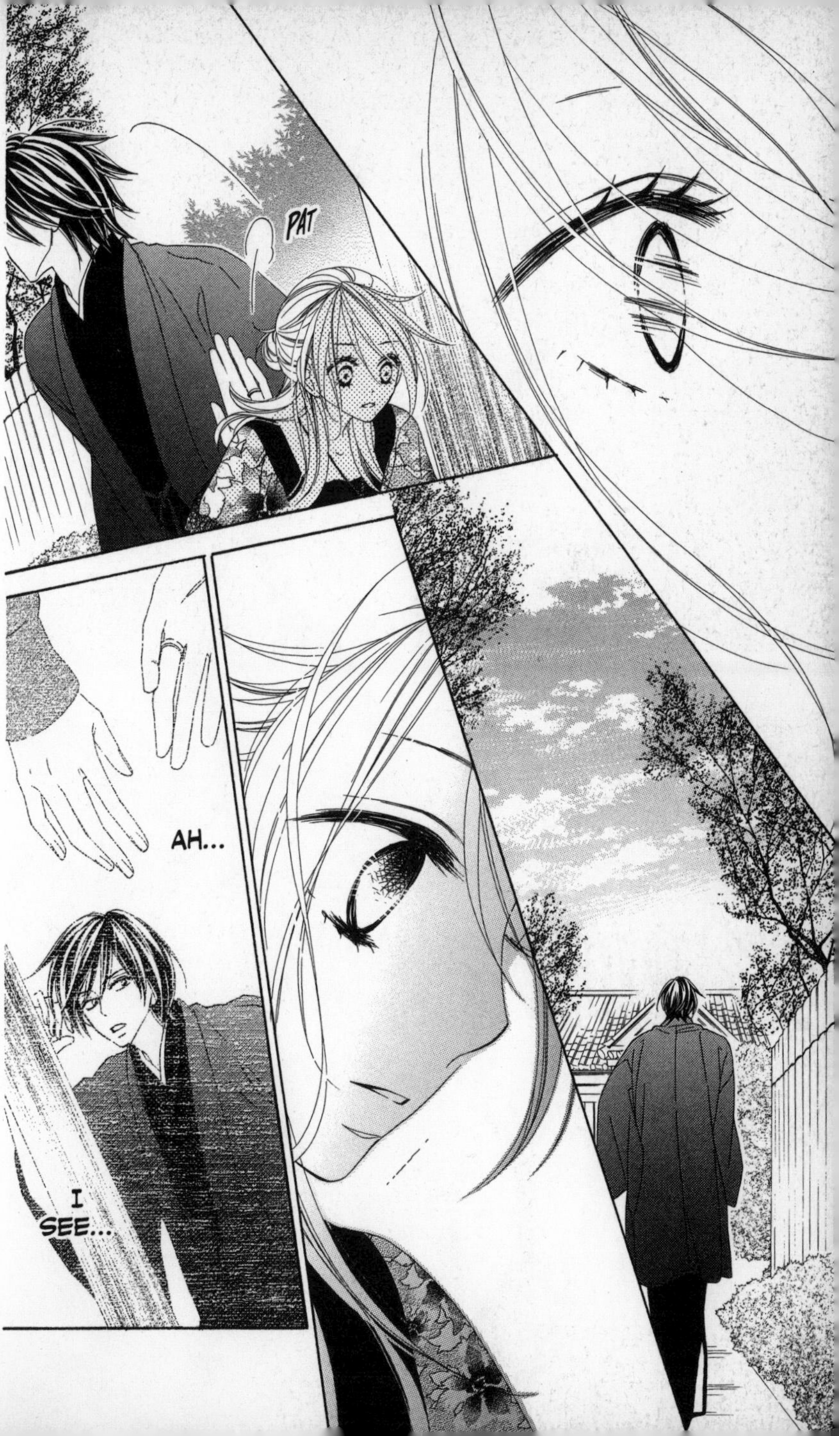
PAT
AH...
I SEE...

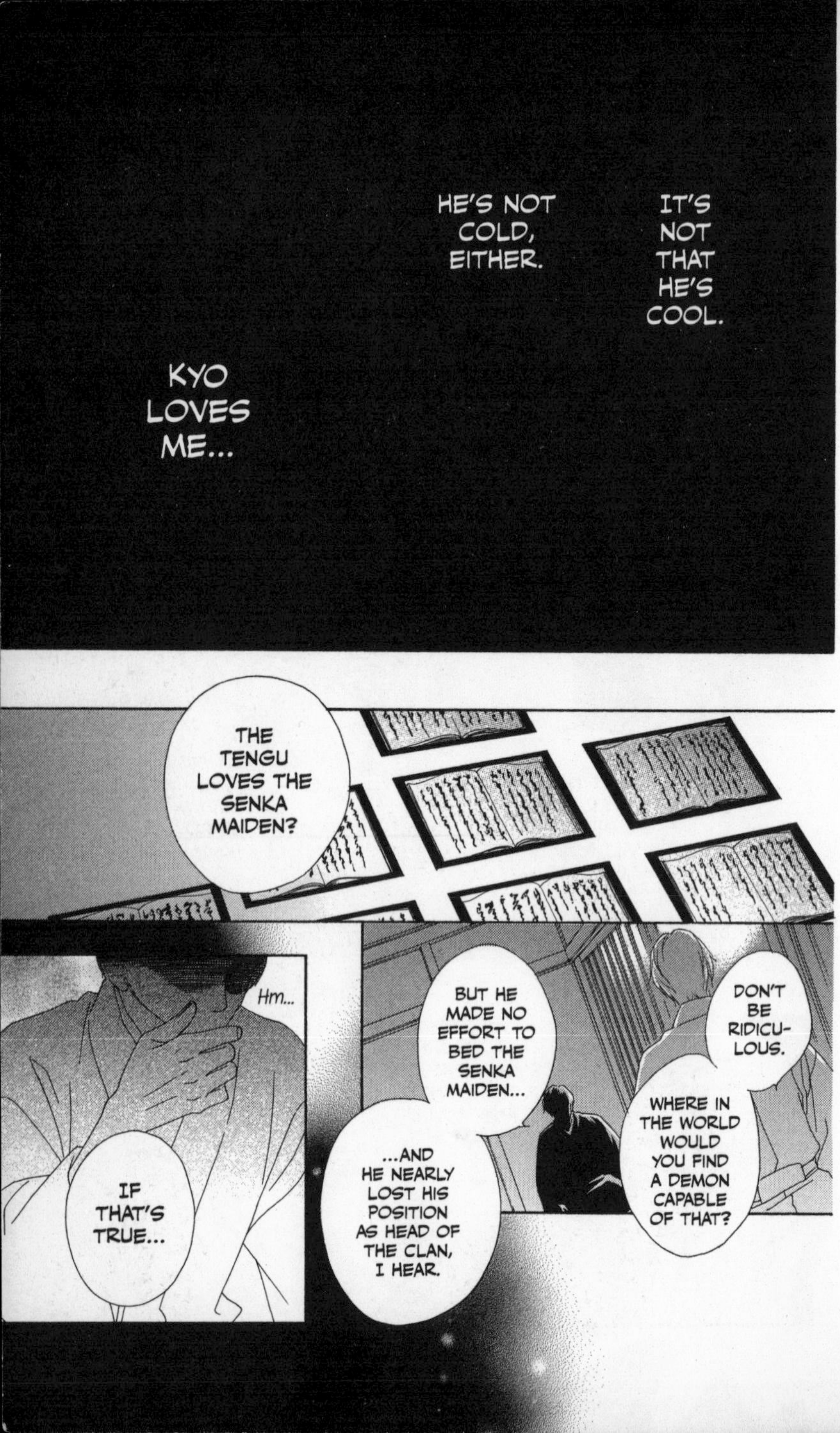
IT'S NOT THAT HE'S COOL.
HE'S NOT COLD, EITHER.
KYO LOVES ME...
THE TENGU LOVES THE SENKA MAIDEN?
DON'T BE RIDICULOUS.
WHERE IN THE WORLD WOULD YOU FIND A DEMON CAPABLE OF THAT?
BUT HE MADE NO EFFORT TO BED THE SENKA MAIDEN...
...AND HE NEARLY LOST HIS POSITION AS HEAD OF THE CLAN, I HEAR.
Hm...
IF THAT'S TRUE...

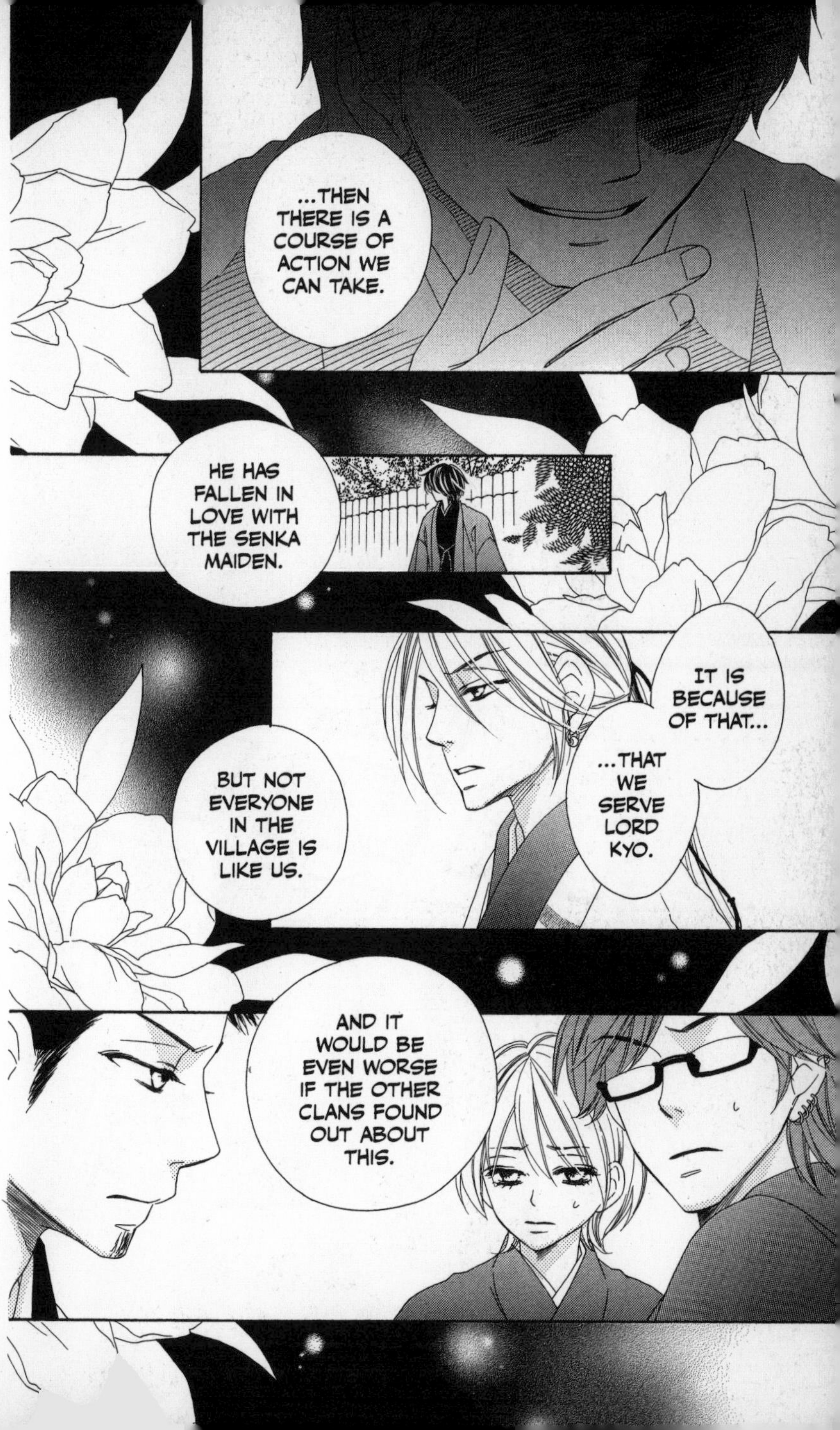
...THEN THERE IS A COURSE OF ACTION WE CAN TAKE.
HE HAS FALLEN IN LOVE WITH THE SENKA MAIDEN.
IT IS BECAUSE OF THAT...
...THAT WE SERVE LORD KYO.
BUT NOT EVERYONE IN THE VILLAGE IS LIKE US.
AND IT WOULD BE EVEN WORSE IF THE OTHER CLANS FOUND OUT ABOUT THIS.

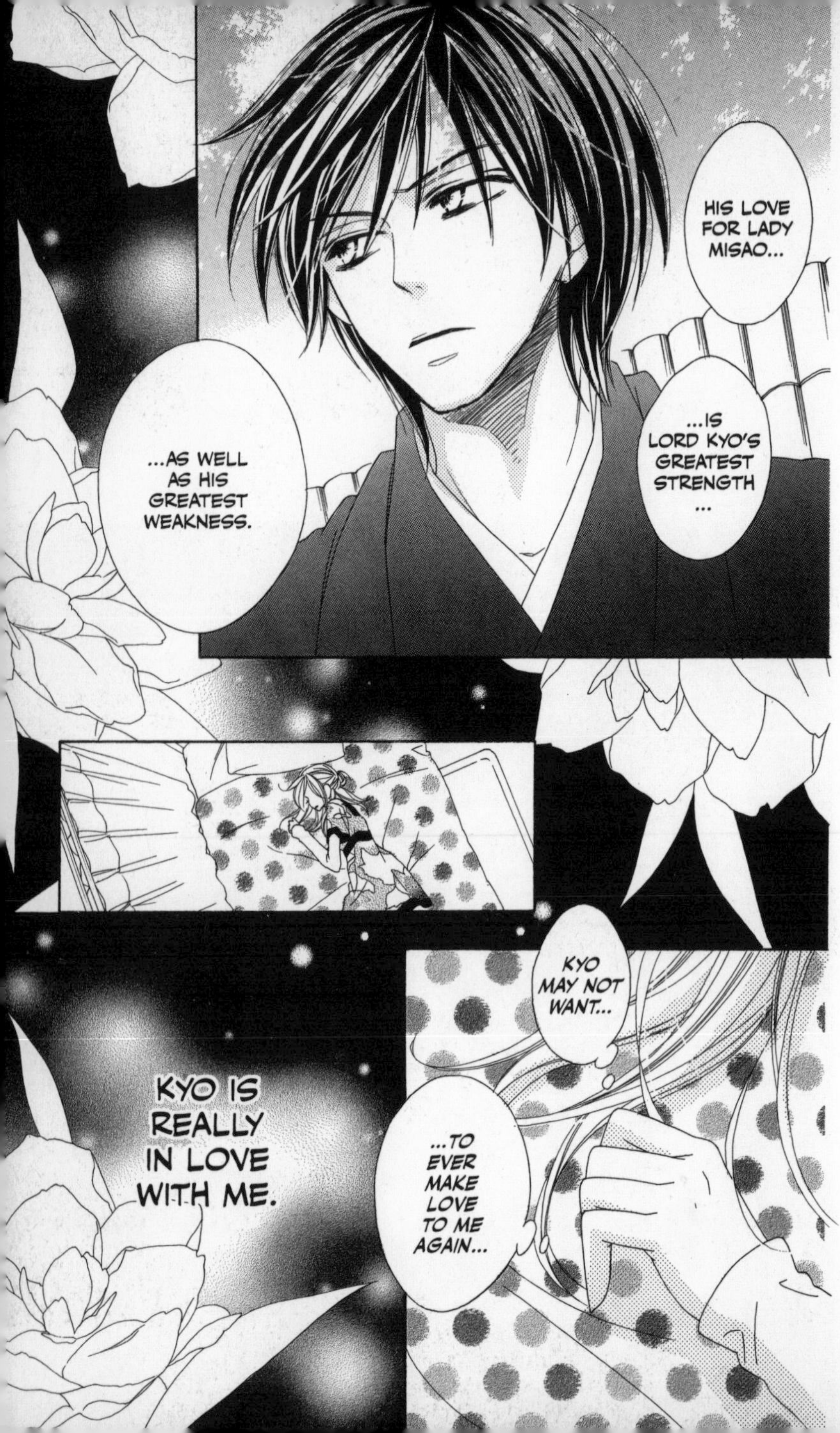
HIS LOVE FOR LADY MISAO...
...IS LORD KYO'S GREATEST STRENGTH ...
...AS WELL AS HIS GREATEST WEAKNESS.
KYO MAY NOT WANT...
...TO EVER MAKE LOVE TO ME AGAIN...
KYO IS REALLY IN LOVE WITH ME.

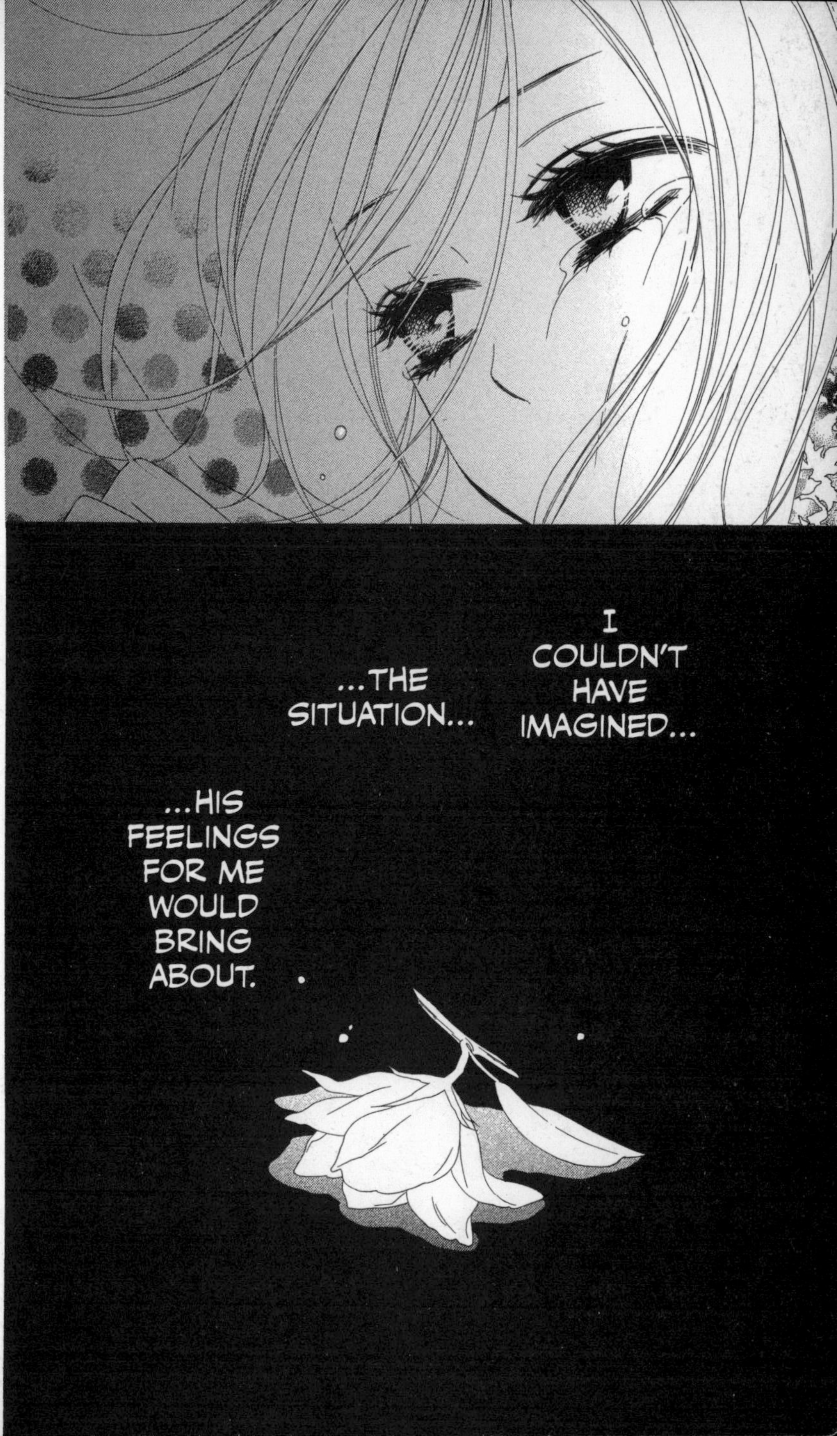
I COULDN'T HAVE IMAGINED...
...THE SITUATION...
...HIS FEELINGS FOR ME WOULD BRING ABOUT.

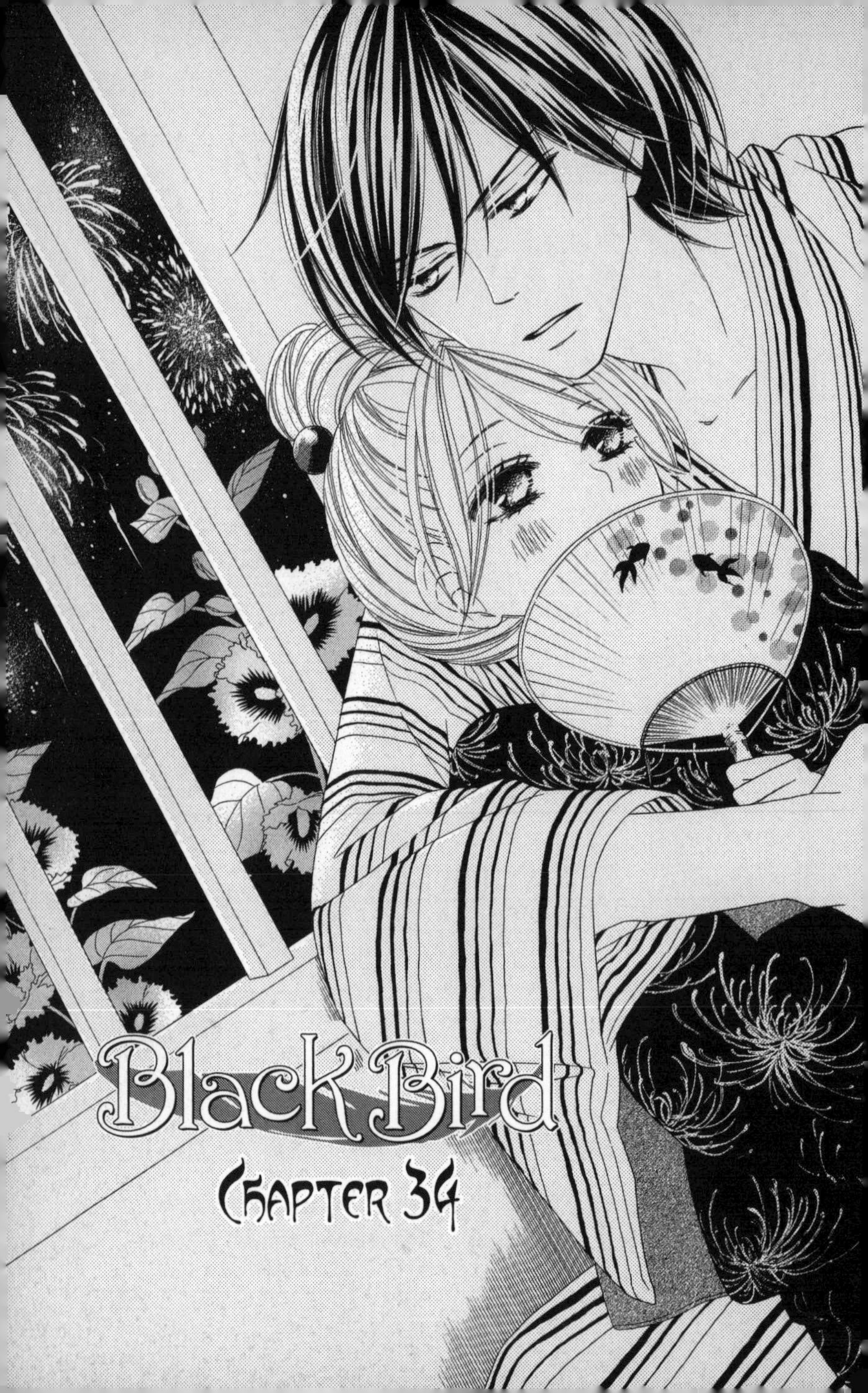
Black Bird
Chapter 34

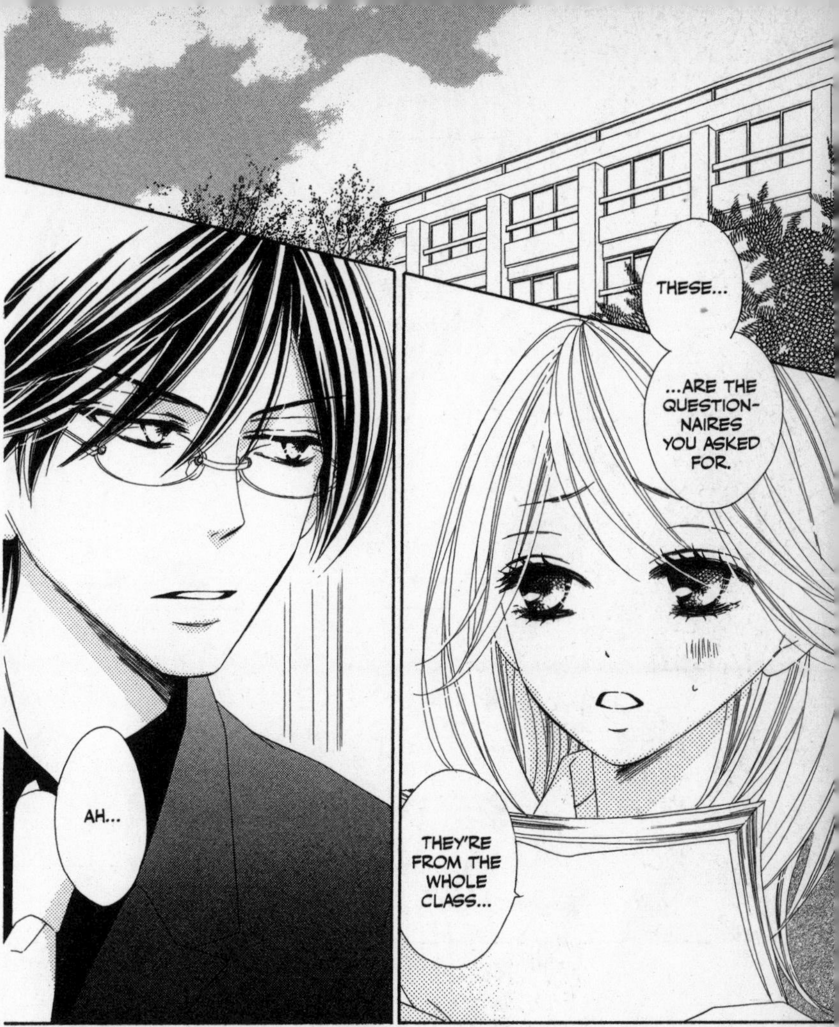
THESE...
...ARE THE QUESTION-NAIRES YOU ASKED FOR.
THEY'RE FROM THE WHOLE CLASS...
AH...

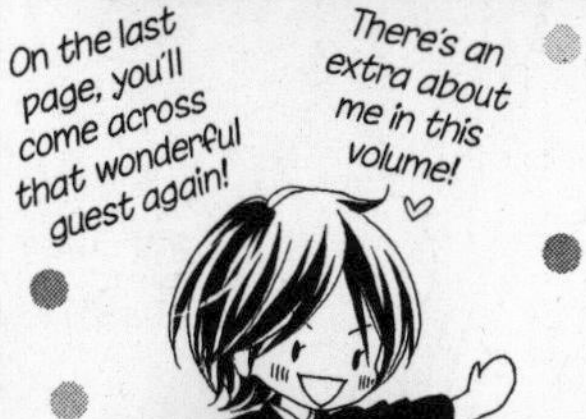
There's an extra about me in this volume!
On the last page, you'll come across that wonderful guest again!

Hello, this is Sakurakoji. ♡

Thank you very much for picking up Volume 9 of *Black Bird!*

I'm excited because I feel, more than ever, as though I've stepped into an unknown world...

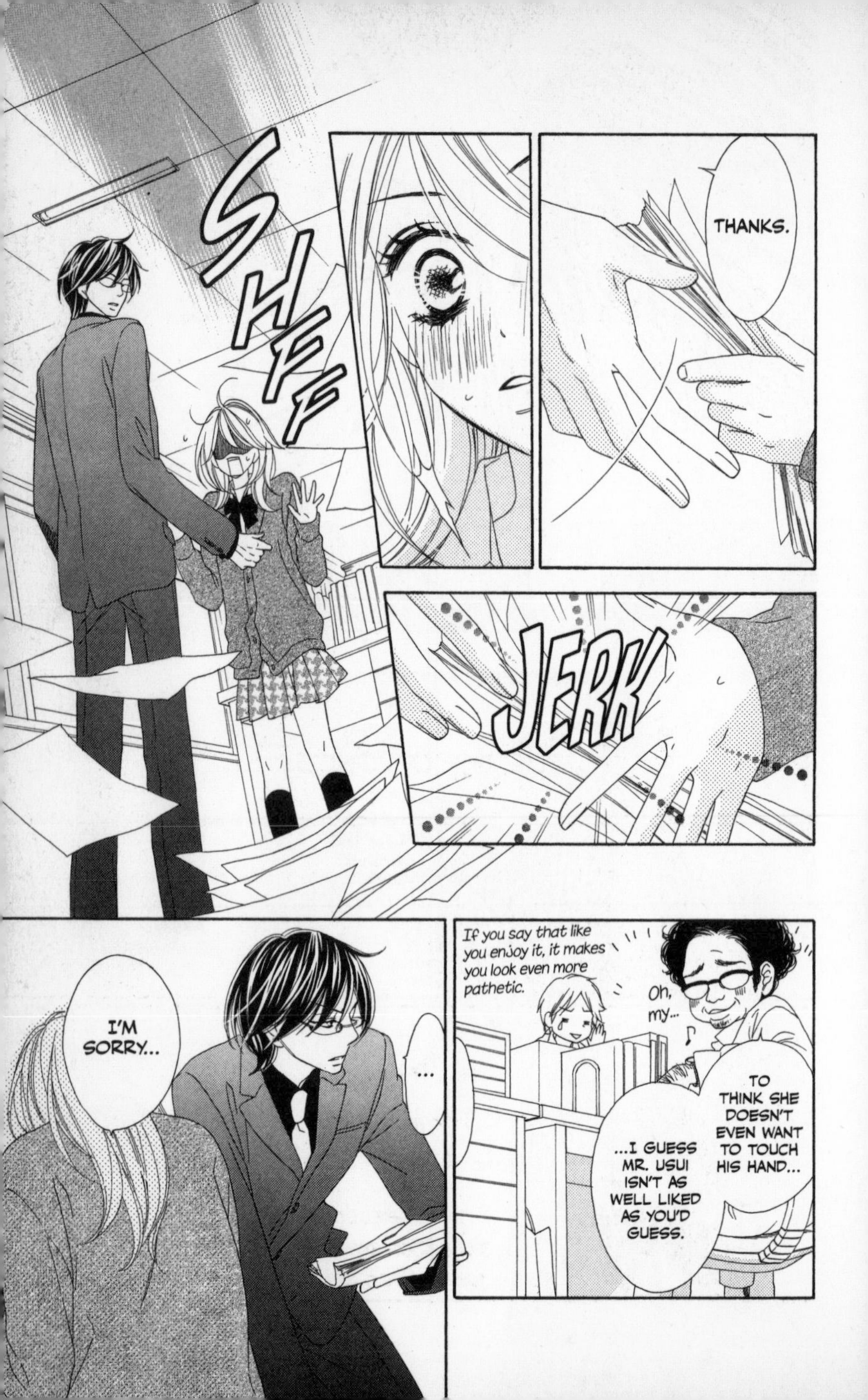
THANKS.
JERK
SHFFF
TO THINK SHE DOESN'T EVEN WANT TO TOUCH HIS HAND...
...I GUESS MR. USUI ISN'T AS WELL LIKED AS YOU'D GUESS.
If you say that like you enjoy it, it makes you look even more pathetic.
Oh, my... ♪
I'M SORRY...
...

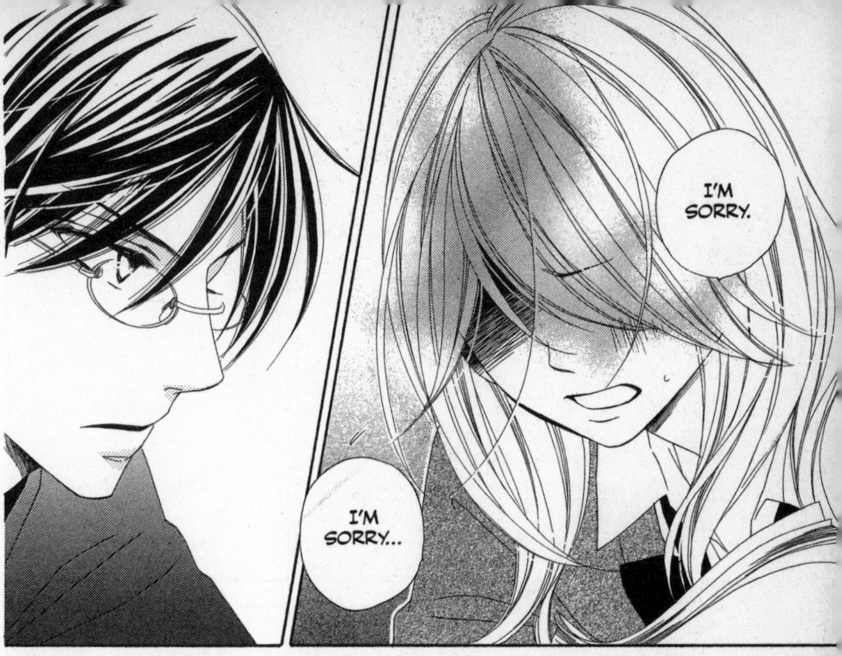
I'M SORRY.
I'M SORRY...

...DOESN'T EVEN WANT TO TOUCH HIS HAND?

IT'S THE OPPOSITE.

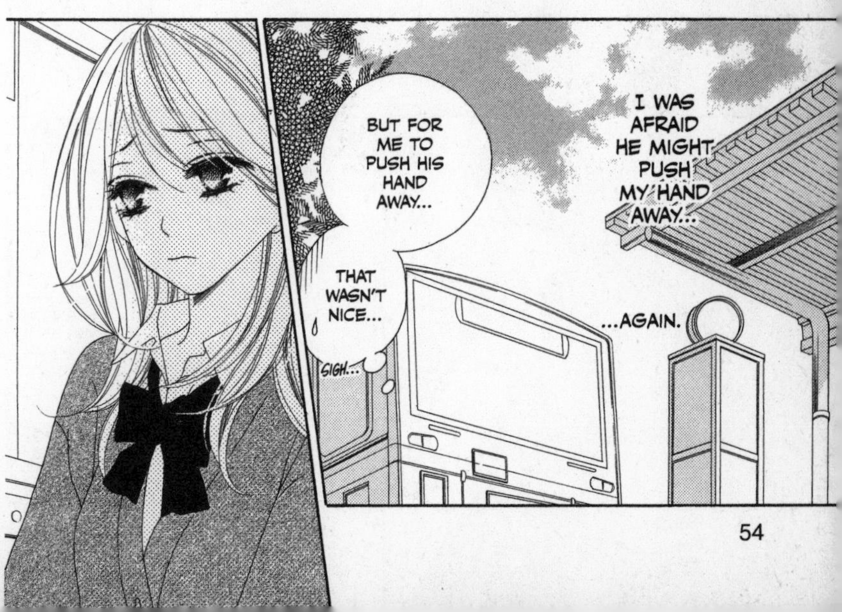
I WAS AFRAID HE MIGHT PUSH MY HAND AWAY...
...AGAIN.
BUT FOR ME TO PUSH HIS HAND AWAY...
THAT WASN'T NICE...
SIGH...

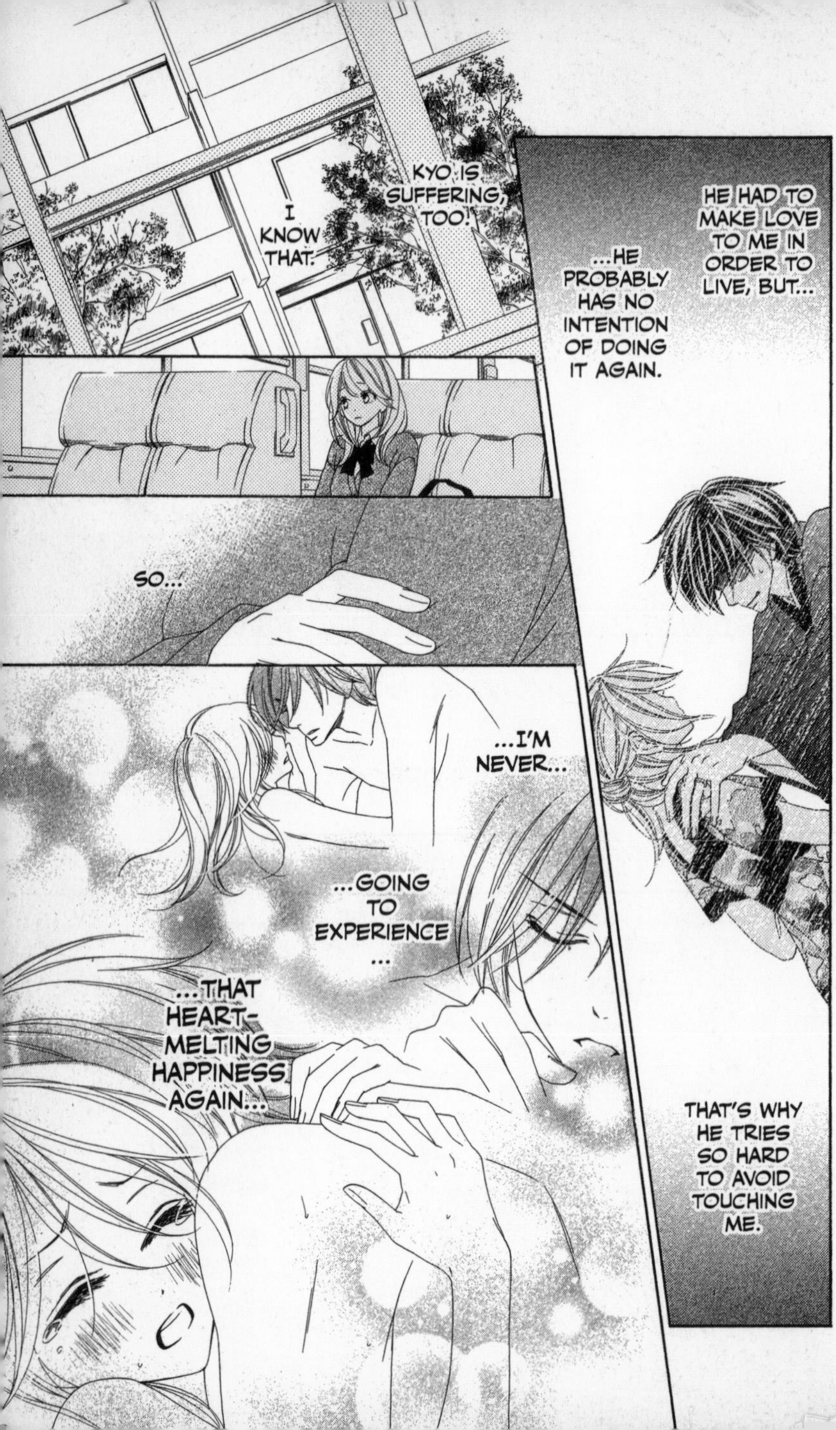
KYO IS SUFFERING, TOO!
I KNOW THAT.
HE HAD TO MAKE LOVE TO ME IN ORDER TO LIVE, BUT...
...HE PROBABLY HAS NO INTENTION OF DOING IT AGAIN.
THAT'S WHY HE TRIES SO HARD TO AVOID TOUCHING ME.
SO...
...I'M NEVER...
...GOING TO EXPERIENCE...
...THAT HEART-MELTING HAPPINESS AGAIN...

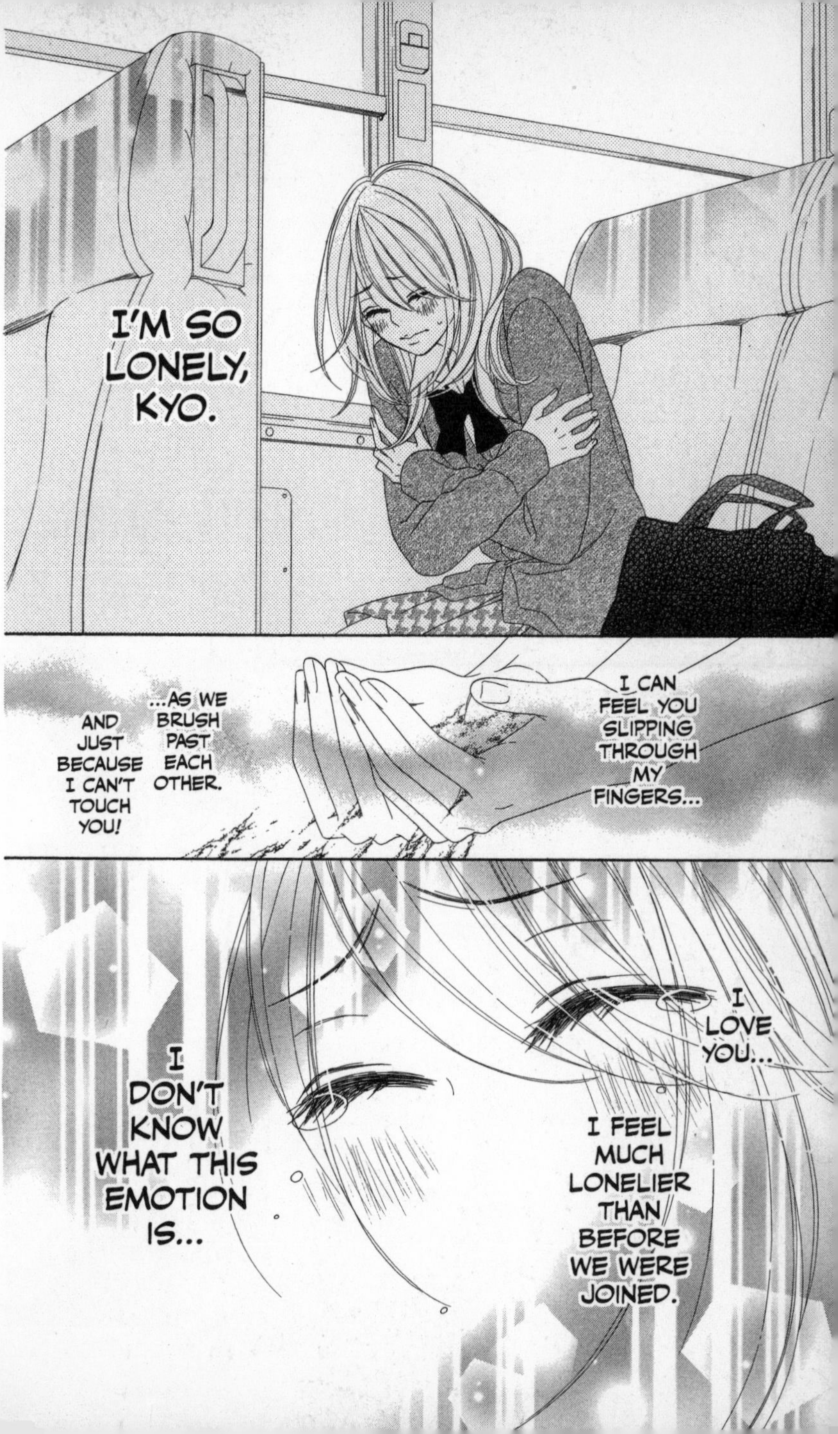
I'M SO LONELY, KYO.
I CAN FEEL YOU SLIPPING THROUGH MY FINGERS...
...AS WE BRUSH PAST EACH OTHER.
AND JUST BECAUSE I CAN'T TOUCH YOU!
I LOVE YOU...
I FEEL MUCH LONELIER THAN BEFORE WE WERE JOINED.
I DON'T KNOW WHAT THIS EMOTION IS...

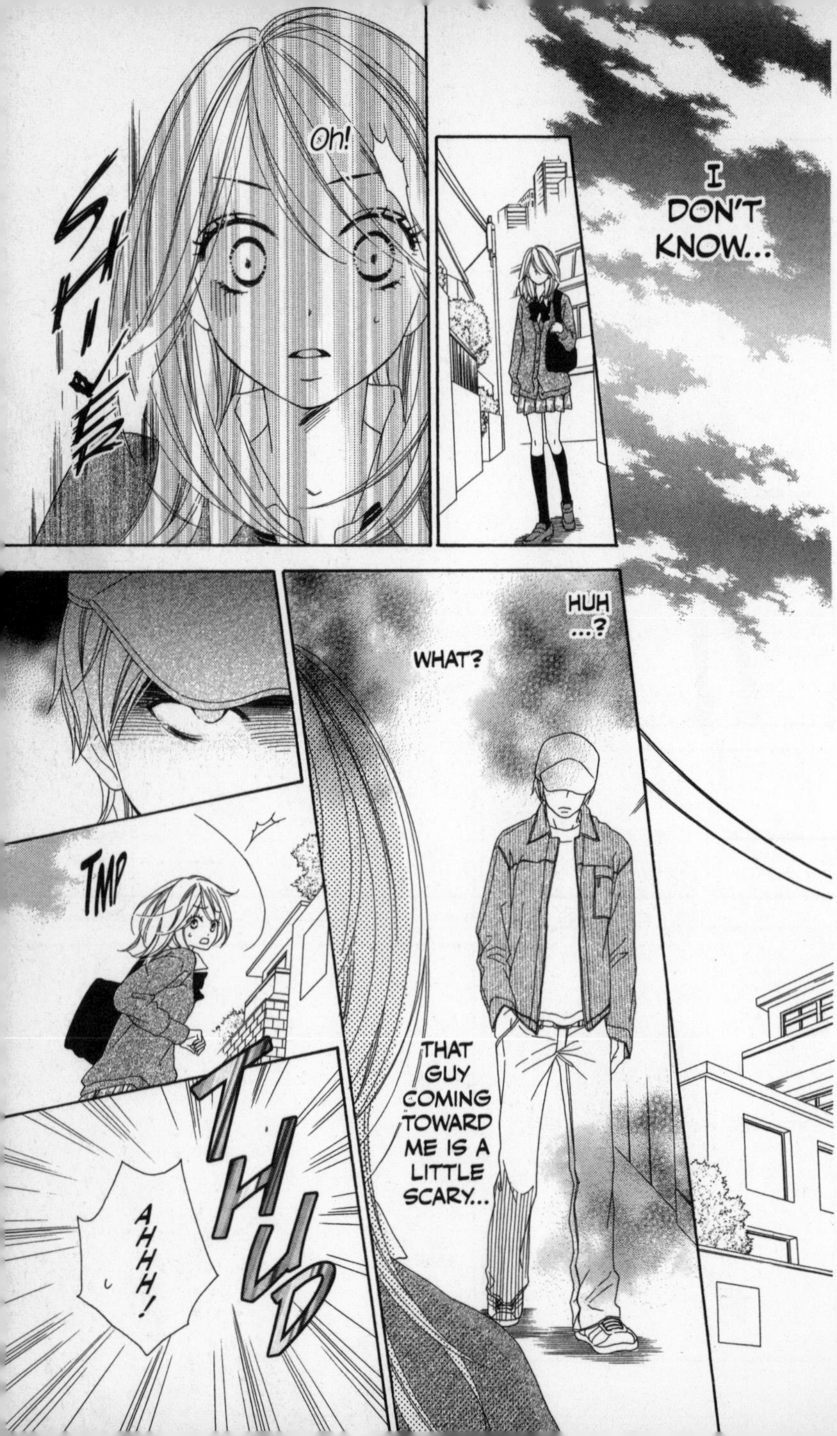
I DON'T KNOW...
Oh!
HUH ...?
WHAT?
THAT GUY COMING TOWARD ME IS A LITTLE SCARY...
TMP
THUD
AHHH!

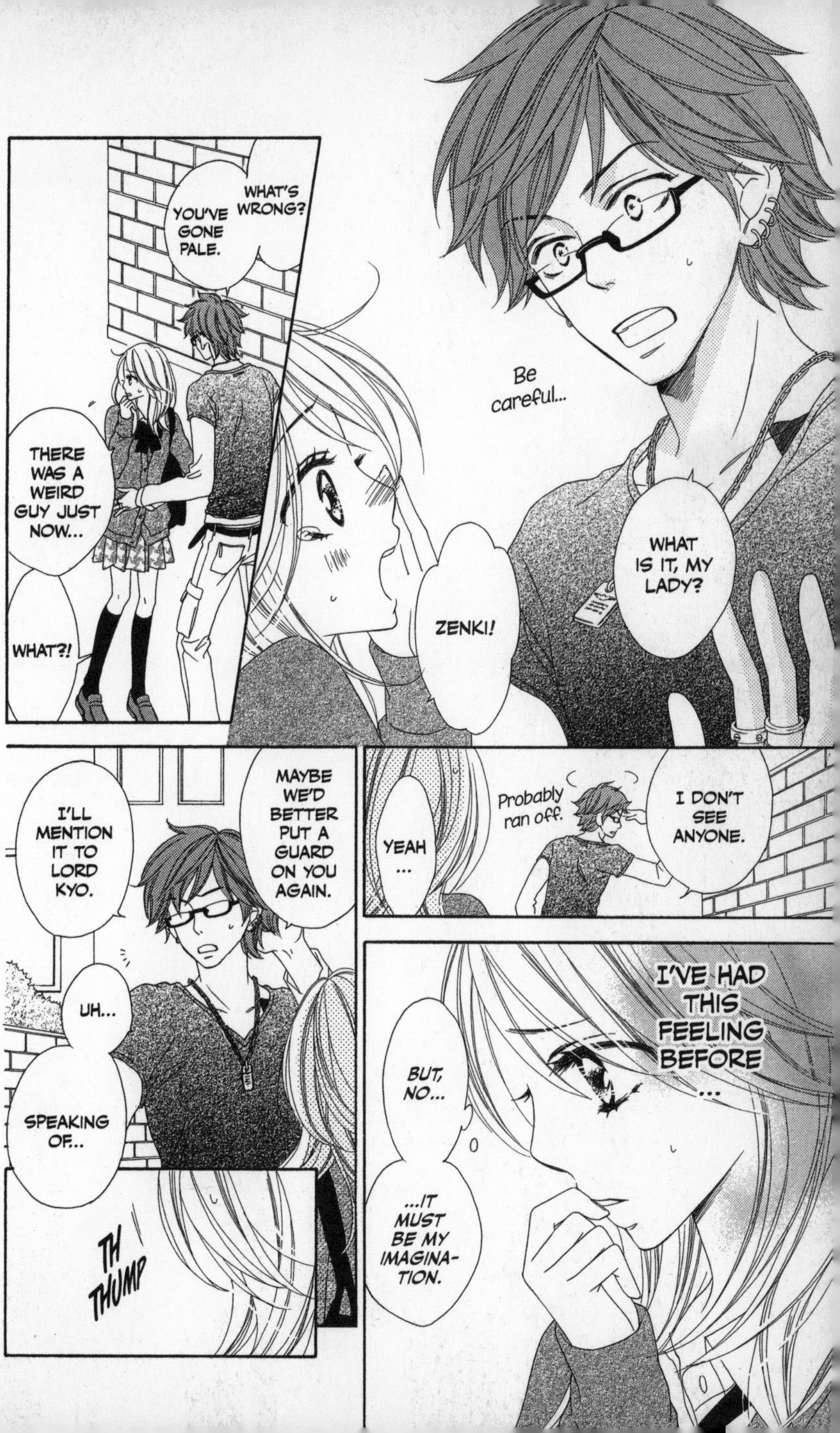
Be careful...
ZENKI!
WHAT IS IT, MY LADY?
WHAT'S WRONG?
YOU'VE GONE PALE.
THERE WAS A WEIRD GUY JUST NOW...
WHAT?!
I DON'T SEE ANYONE.
Probably ran off.
YEAH...
I'VE HAD THIS FEELING BEFORE...
BUT, NO...
...IT MUST BE MY IMAGINATION.
MAYBE WE'D BETTER PUT A GUARD ON YOU AGAIN.
I'LL MENTION IT TO LORD KYO.
UH...
SPEAKING OF...
TH THUMP

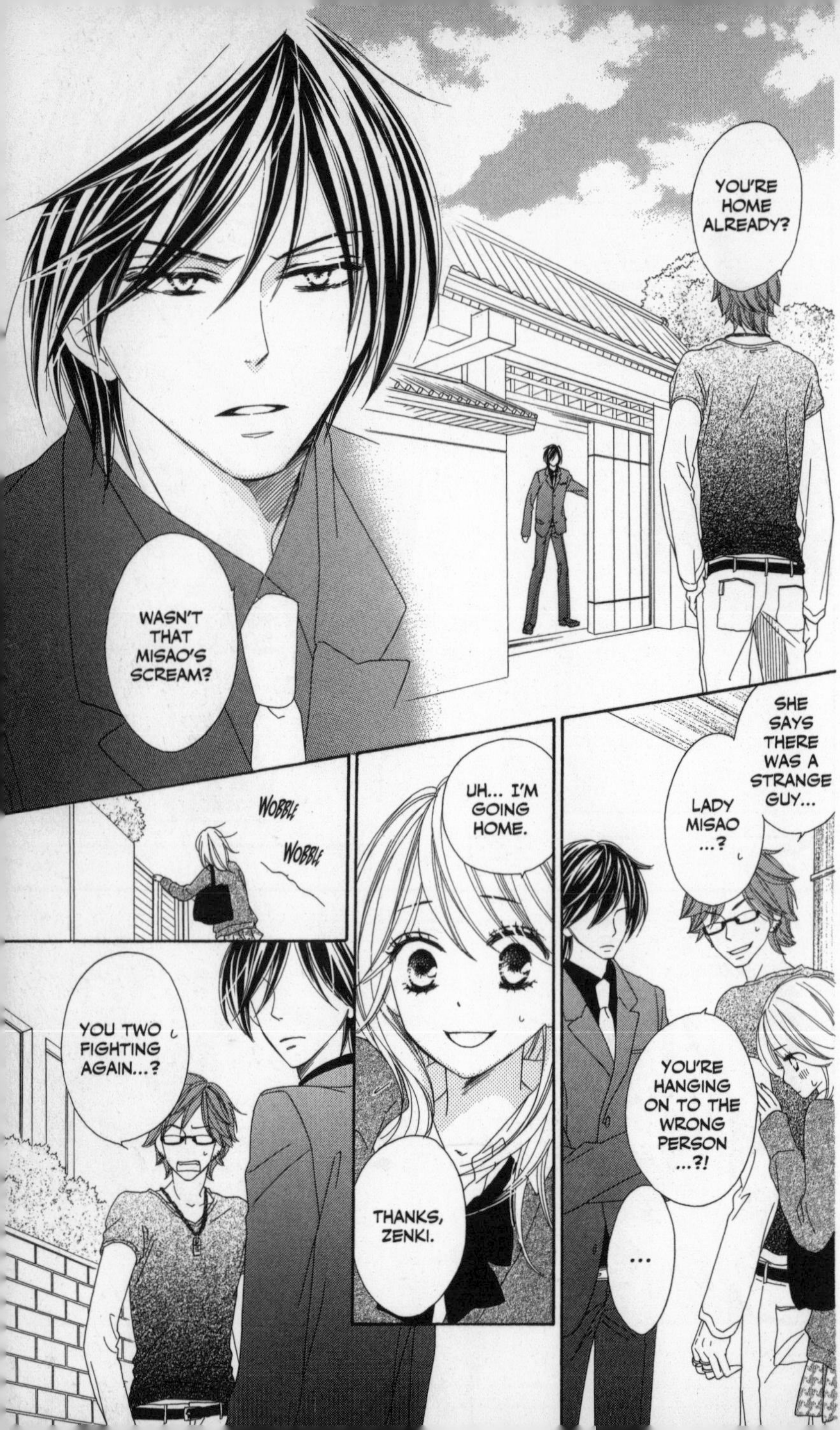
YOU'RE HOME ALREADY?
WASN'T THAT MISAO'S SCREAM?
SHE SAYS THERE WAS A STRANGE GUY...
LADY MISAO ...?
YOU'RE HANGING ON TO THE WRONG PERSON ...?!
...
UH... I'M GOING HOME.
THANKS, ZENKI.
WOBBLE
WOBBLE
YOU TWO FIGHTING AGAIN...?

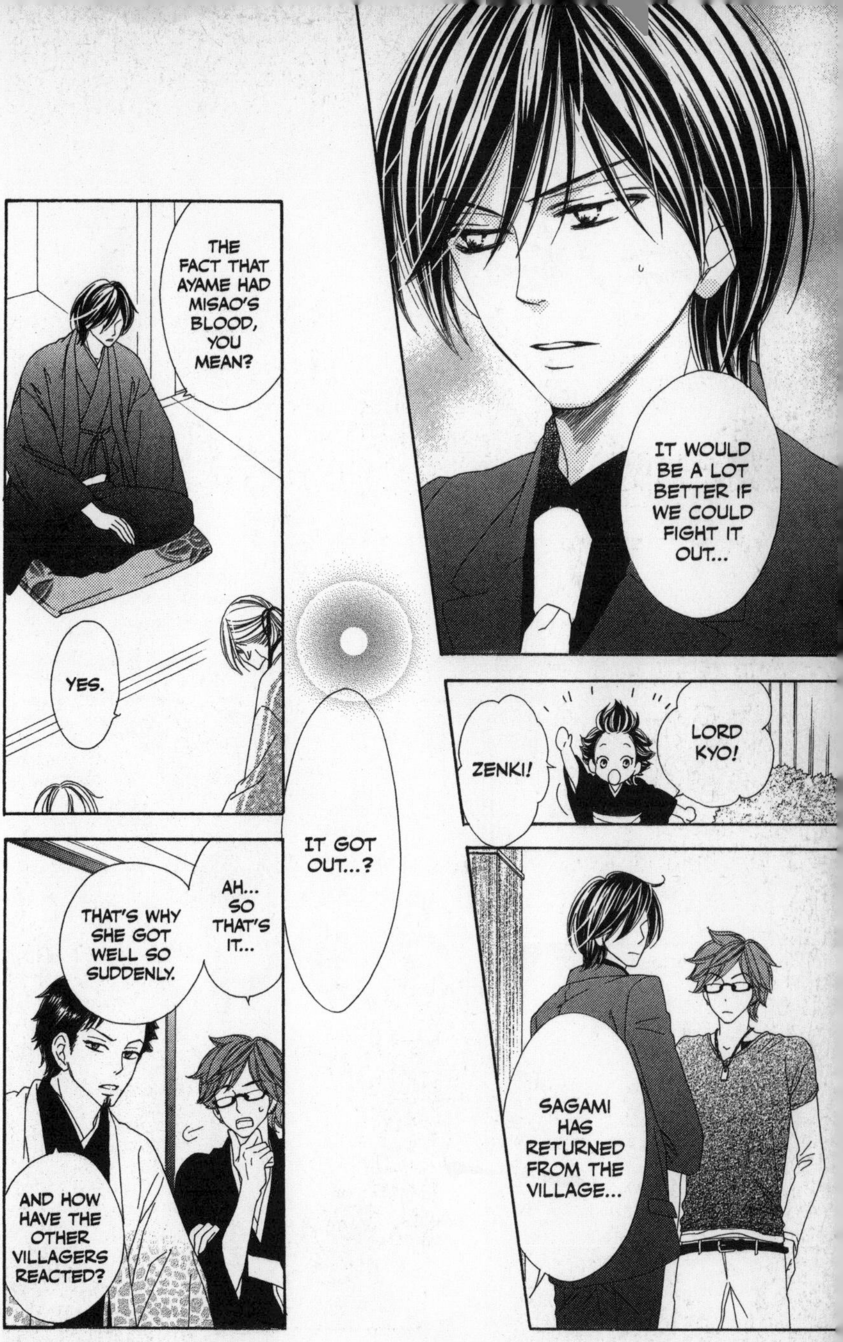

IT WOULD BE A LOT BETTER IF WE COULD FIGHT IT OUT...
THE FACT THAT AYAME HAD MISAO'S BLOOD, YOU MEAN?
YES.
IT GOT OUT...?
LORD KYO!
ZENKI!
SAGAMI HAS RETURNED FROM THE VILLAGE...
AH... SO THAT'S IT...
THAT'S WHY SHE GOT WELL SO SUDDENLY.
AND HOW HAVE THE OTHER VILLAGERS REACTED?

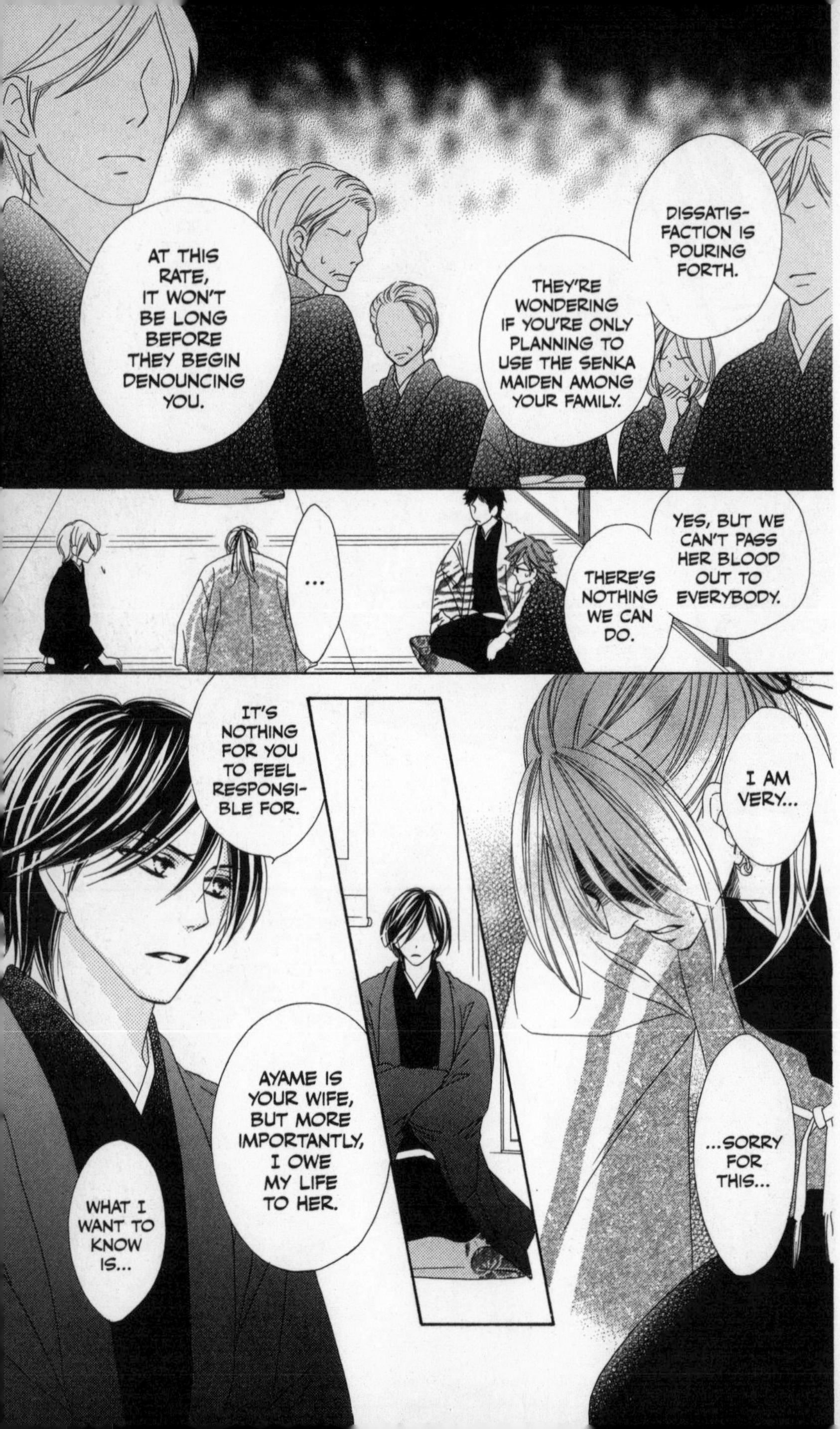
DISSATIS-FACTION IS POURING FORTH.
THEY'RE WONDERING IF YOU'RE ONLY PLANNING TO USE THE SENKA MAIDEN AMONG YOUR FAMILY.
AT THIS RATE, IT WON'T BE LONG BEFORE THEY BEGIN DENOUNCING YOU.
YES, BUT WE CAN'T PASS HER BLOOD OUT TO EVERYBODY.
THERE'S NOTHING WE CAN DO.
...
I AM VERY...
...SORRY FOR THIS...
IT'S NOTHING FOR YOU TO FEEL RESPONSI-BLE FOR.
AYAME IS YOUR WIFE, BUT MORE IMPORTANTLY, I OWE MY LIFE TO HER.
WHAT I WANT TO KNOW IS...

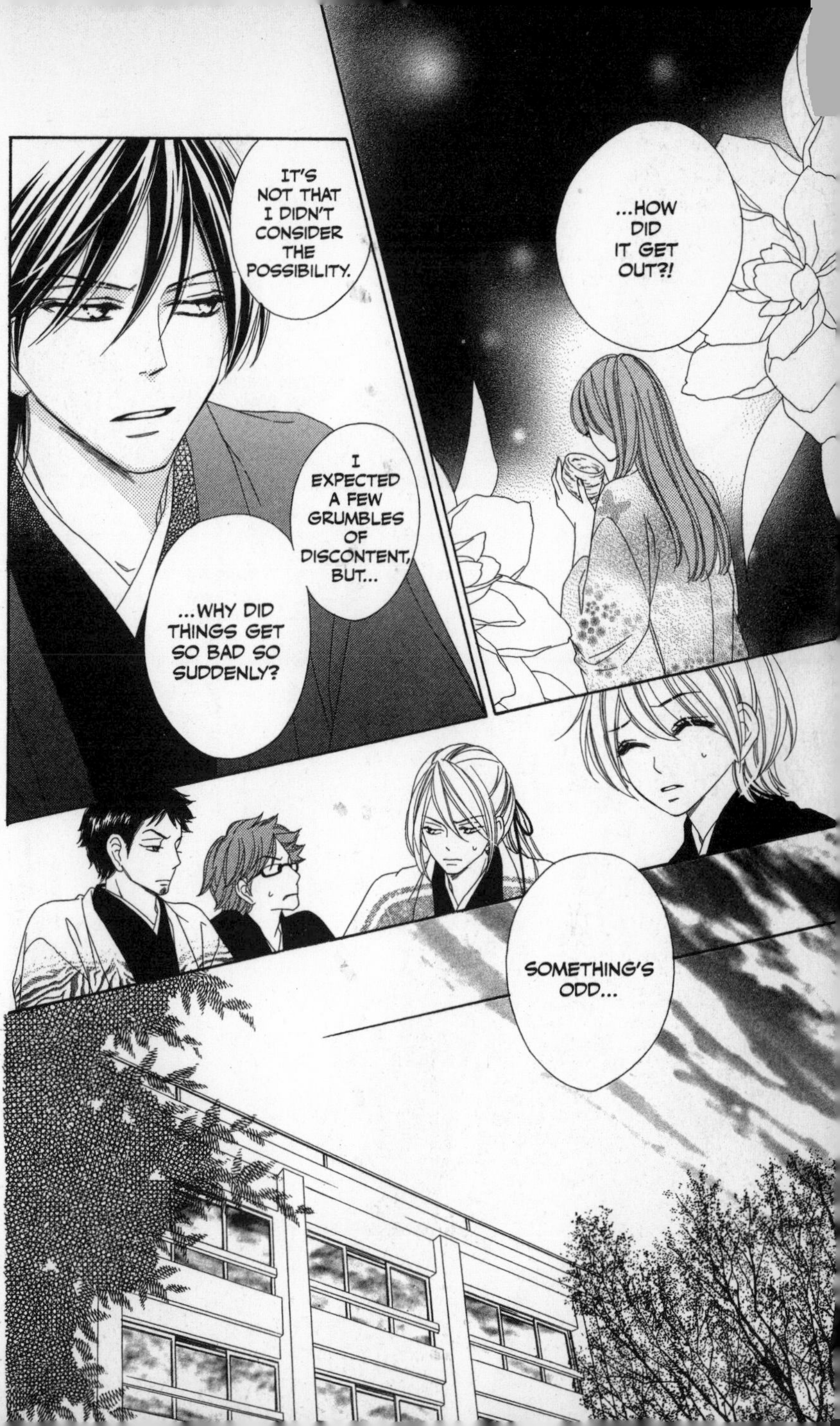
...HOW DID IT GET OUT?!
IT'S NOT THAT I DIDN'T CONSIDER THE POSSIBILITY.
I EXPECTED A FEW GRUMBLES OF DISCONTENT, BUT...
...WHY DID THINGS GET SO BAD SO SUDDENLY?
SOMETHING'S ODD...

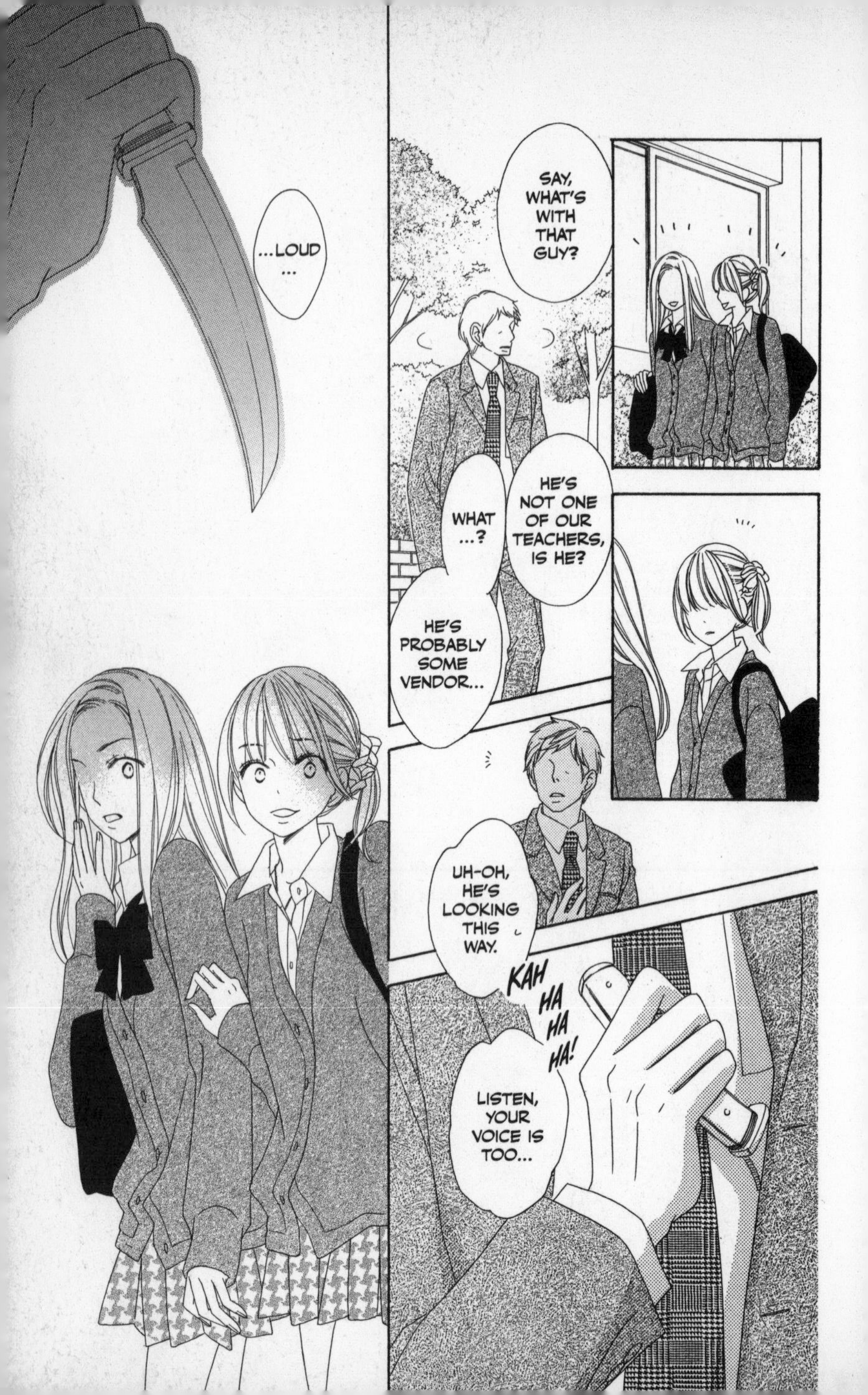
SAY, WHAT'S WITH THAT GUY?
HE'S NOT ONE OF OUR TEACHERS, IS HE?
WHAT ...?
HE'S PROBABLY SOME VENDOR...
UH-OH, HE'S LOOKING THIS WAY.
KAH HA HA HA!
LISTEN, YOUR VOICE IS TOO...
...LOUD ...

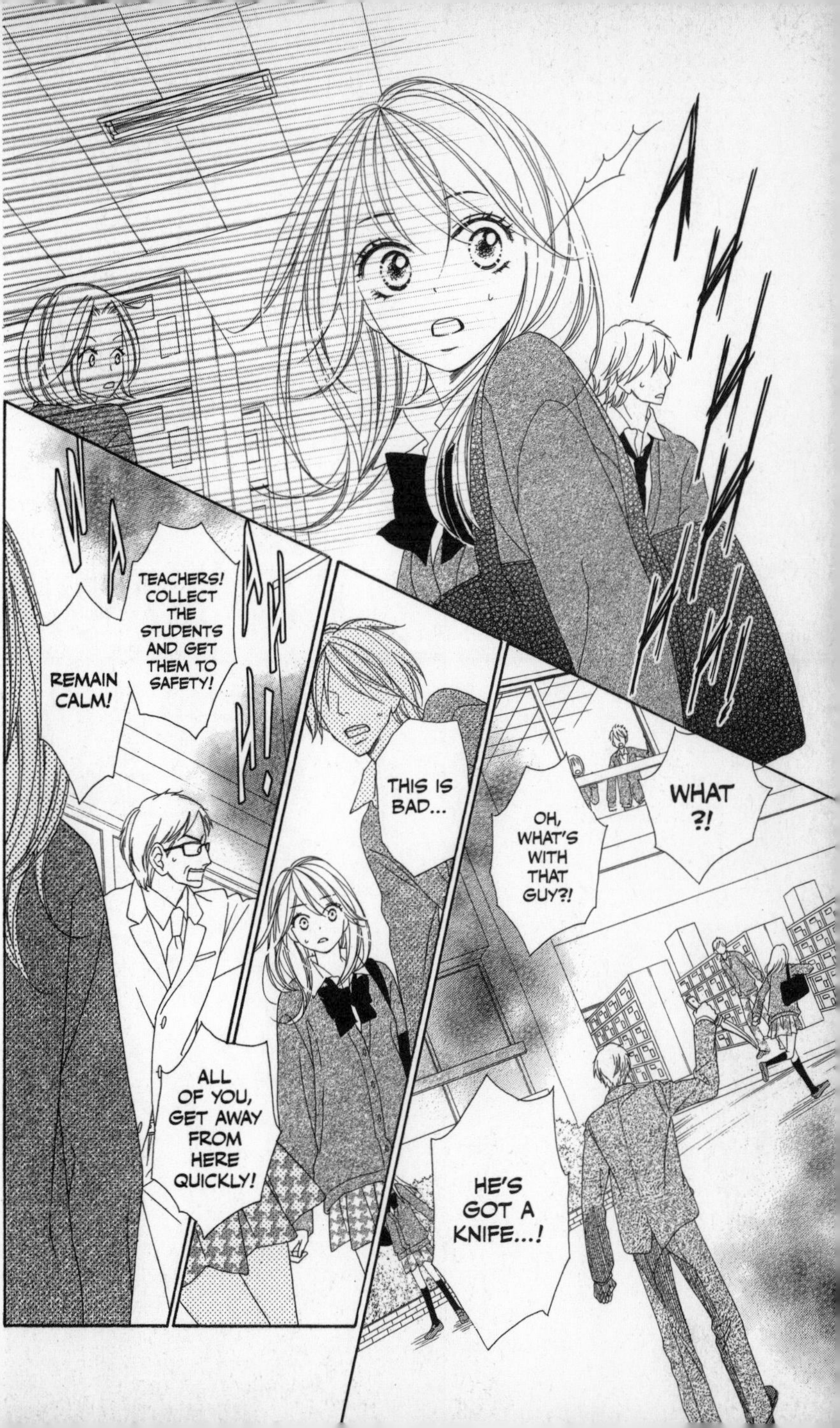
WHAT ?!
OH, WHAT'S WITH THAT GUY?!
HE'S GOT A KNIFE...!
THIS IS BAD...
TEACHERS! COLLECT THE STUDENTS AND GET THEM TO SAFETY!
REMAIN CALM!
ALL OF YOU, GET AWAY FROM HERE QUICKLY!

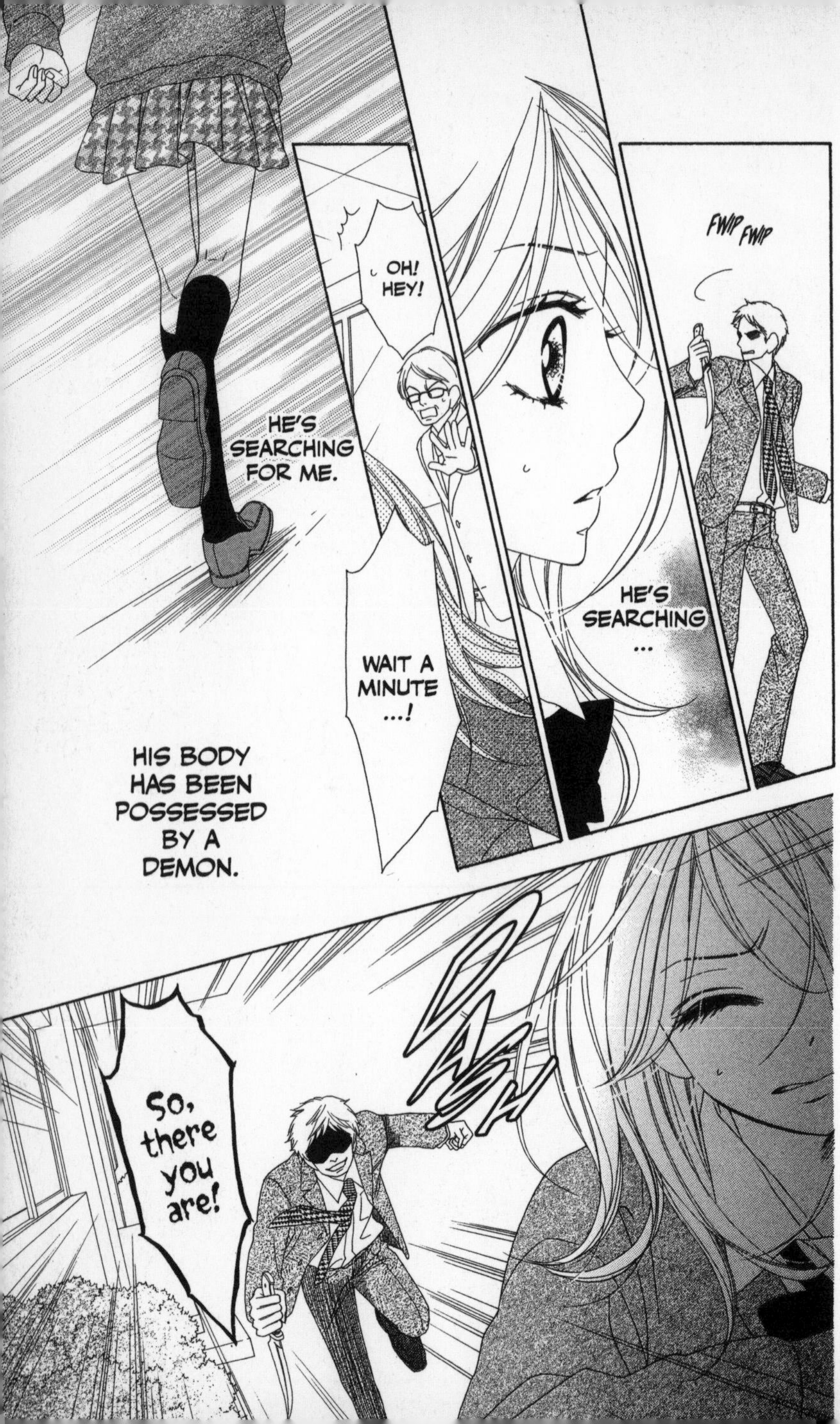
FWIP FWIP
HE'S SEARCHING ...
OH! HEY!
WAIT A MINUTE ...!
HE'S SEARCHING FOR ME.
HIS BODY HAS BEEN POSSESSED BY A DEMON.
So, there you are!

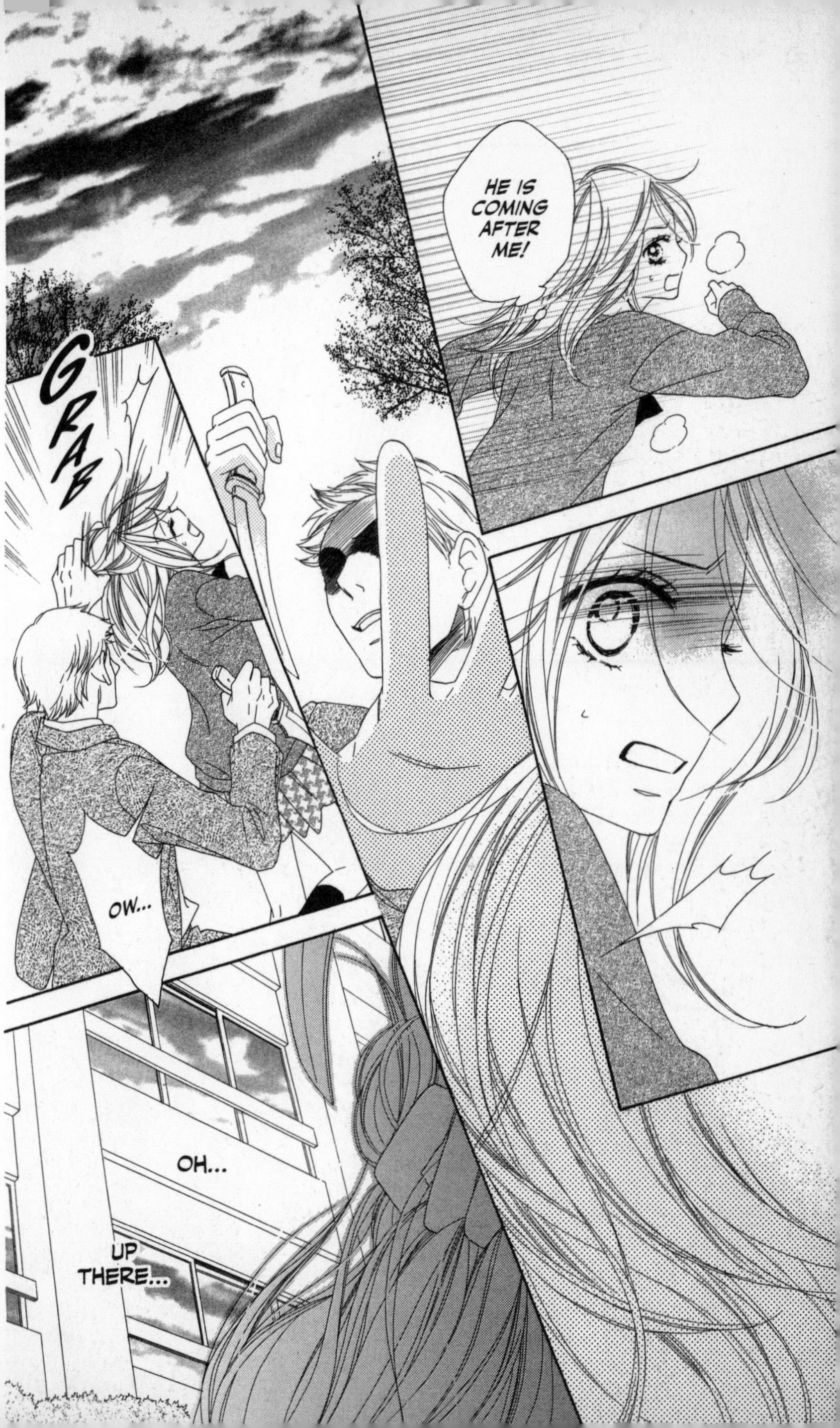
HE IS COMING AFTER ME!
GRAB
OW...
OH...
UP THERE...

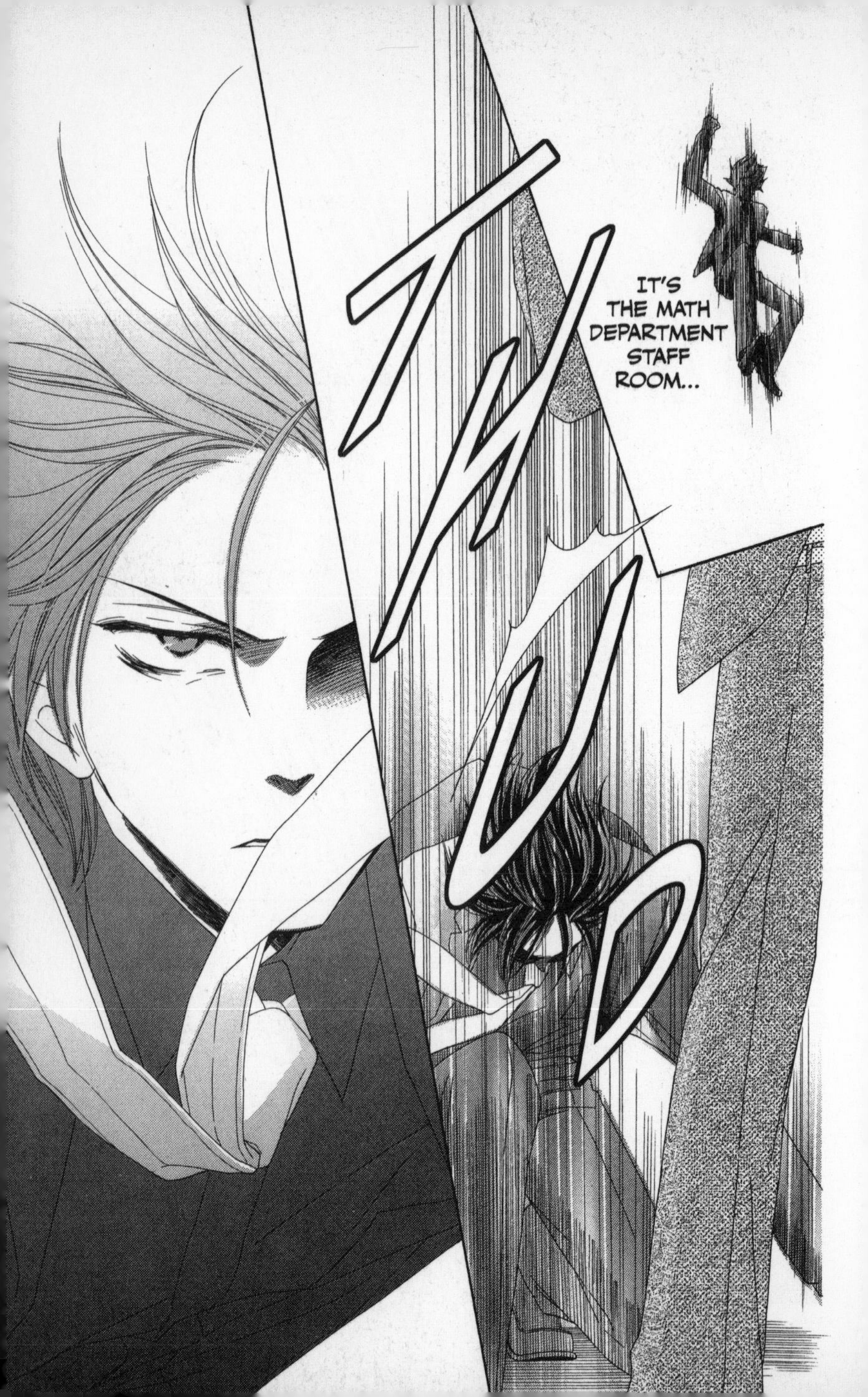
IT'S THE MATH DEPARTMENT STAFF ROOM...
THUD

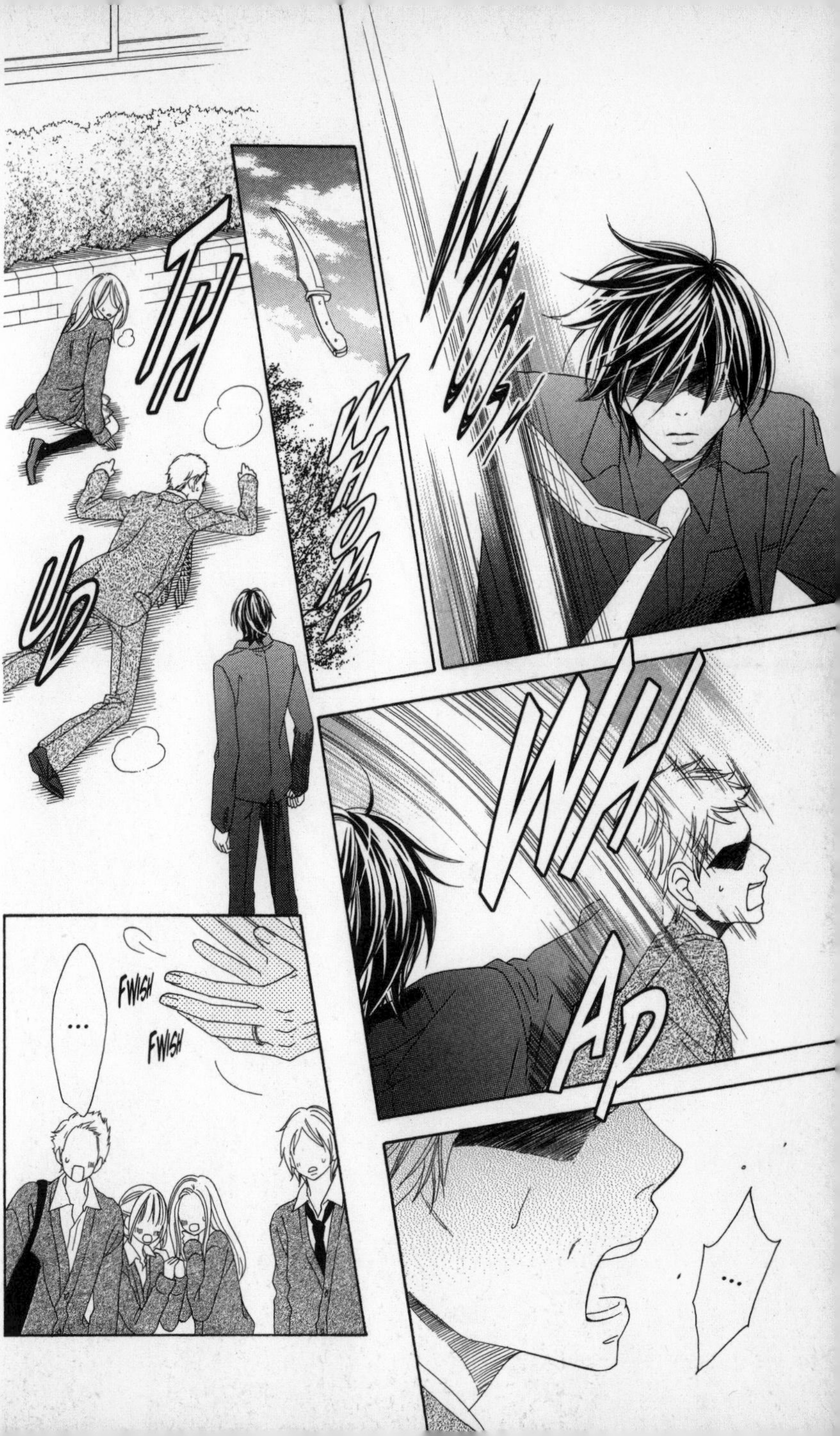

WHOOSH
WHAP
...
WHOOMP
THUD
FWISH
FWISH
...

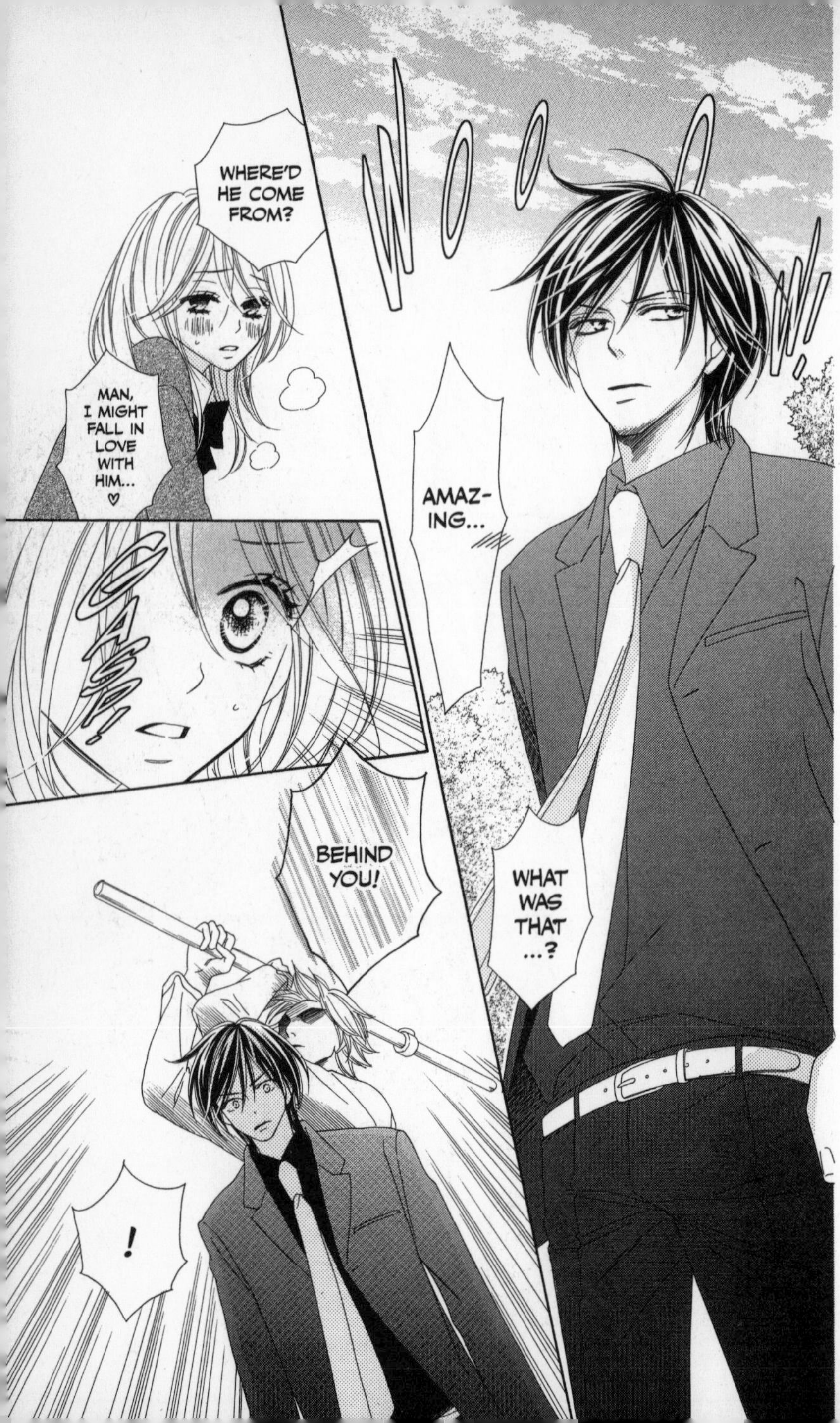
WOOOW!!
AMAZ-ING...
WHAT WAS THAT ...?
WHERE'D HE COME FROM?
MAN, I MIGHT FALL IN LOVE WITH HIM... ♡
GASP!
BEHIND YOU!
!

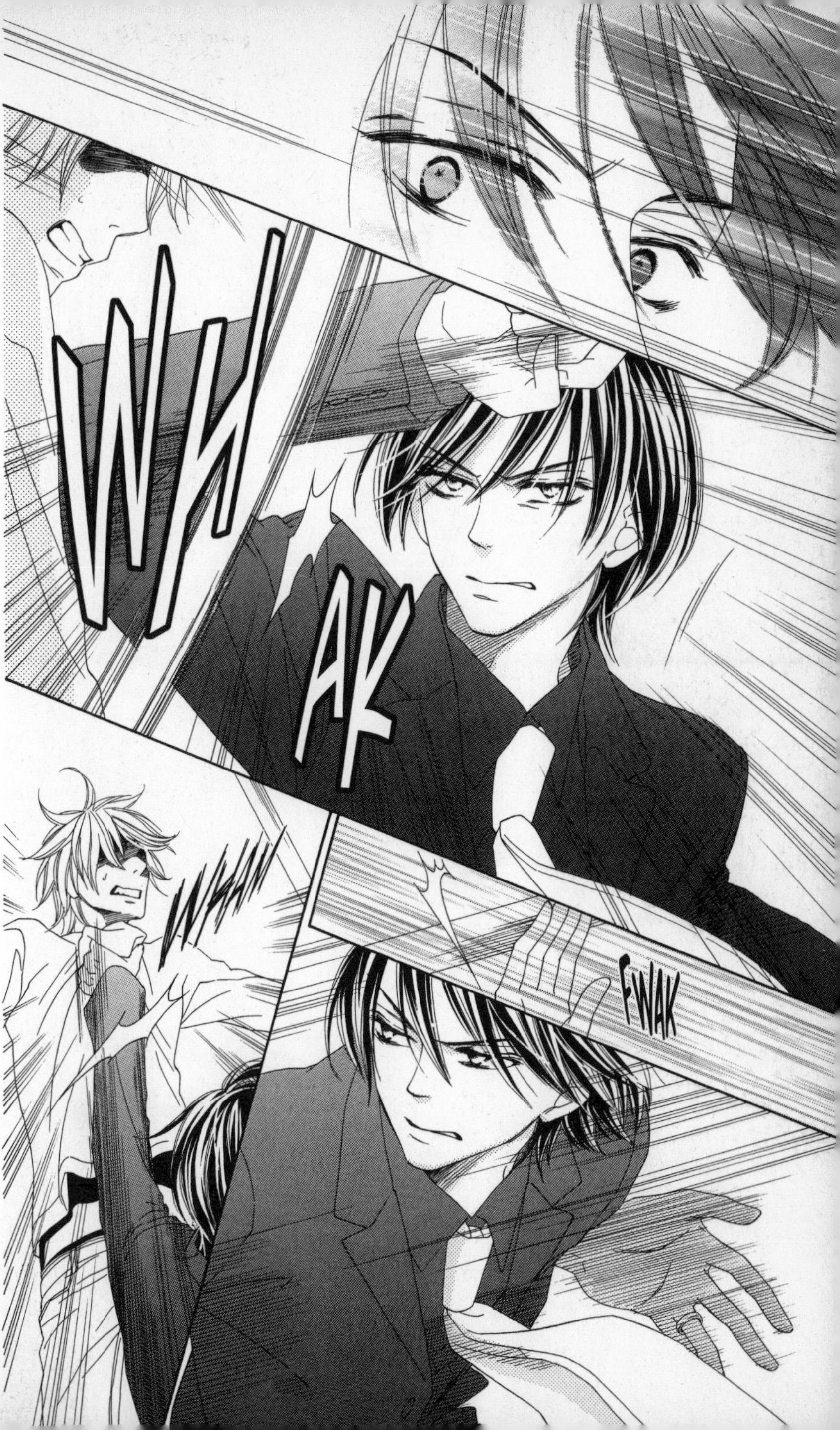
WH
AK
FWAK

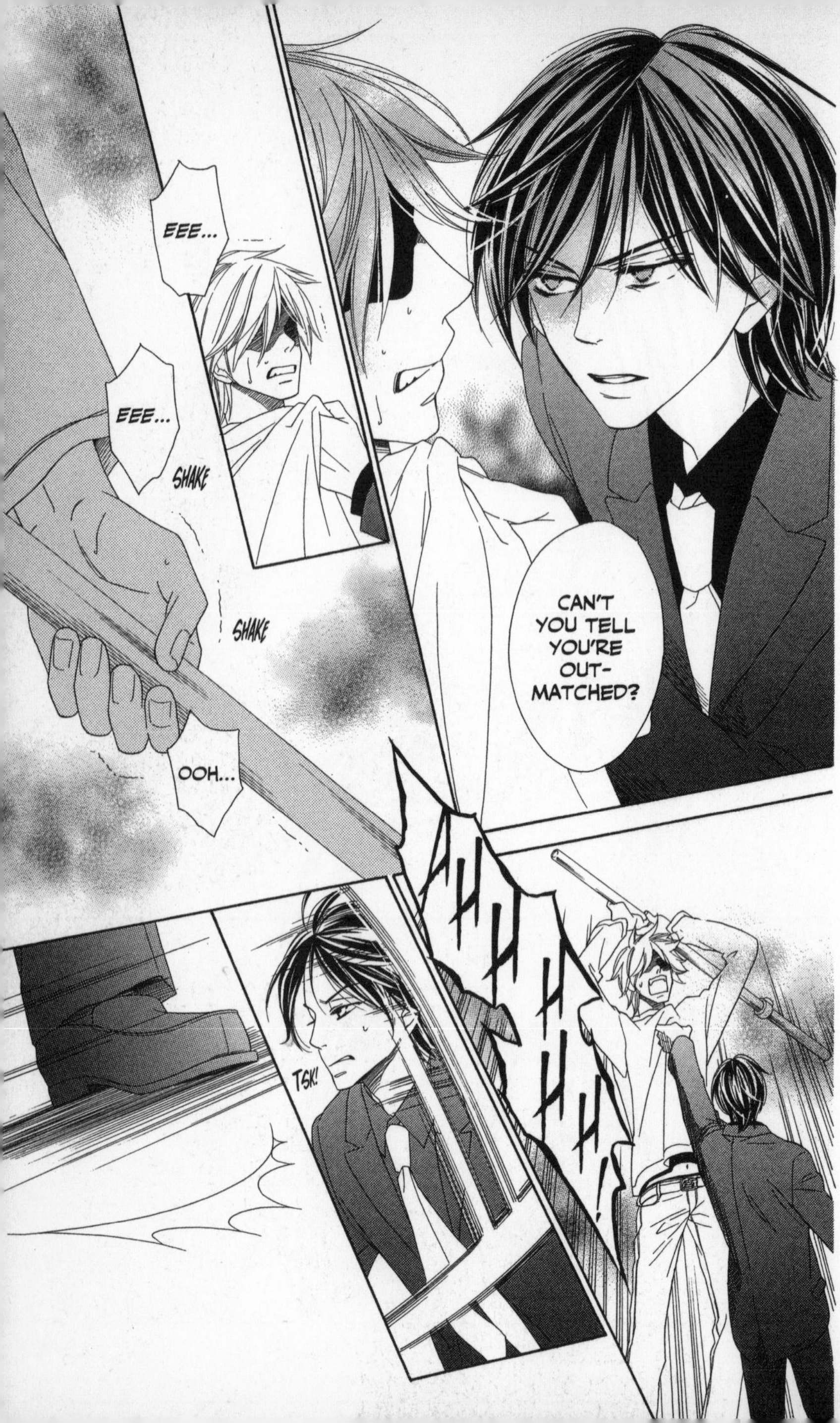
CAN'T YOU TELL YOU'RE OUT-MATCHED?
EEE...
EEE...
SHAKE
SHAKE
OOH...
AHHHHHHH!
TSK!

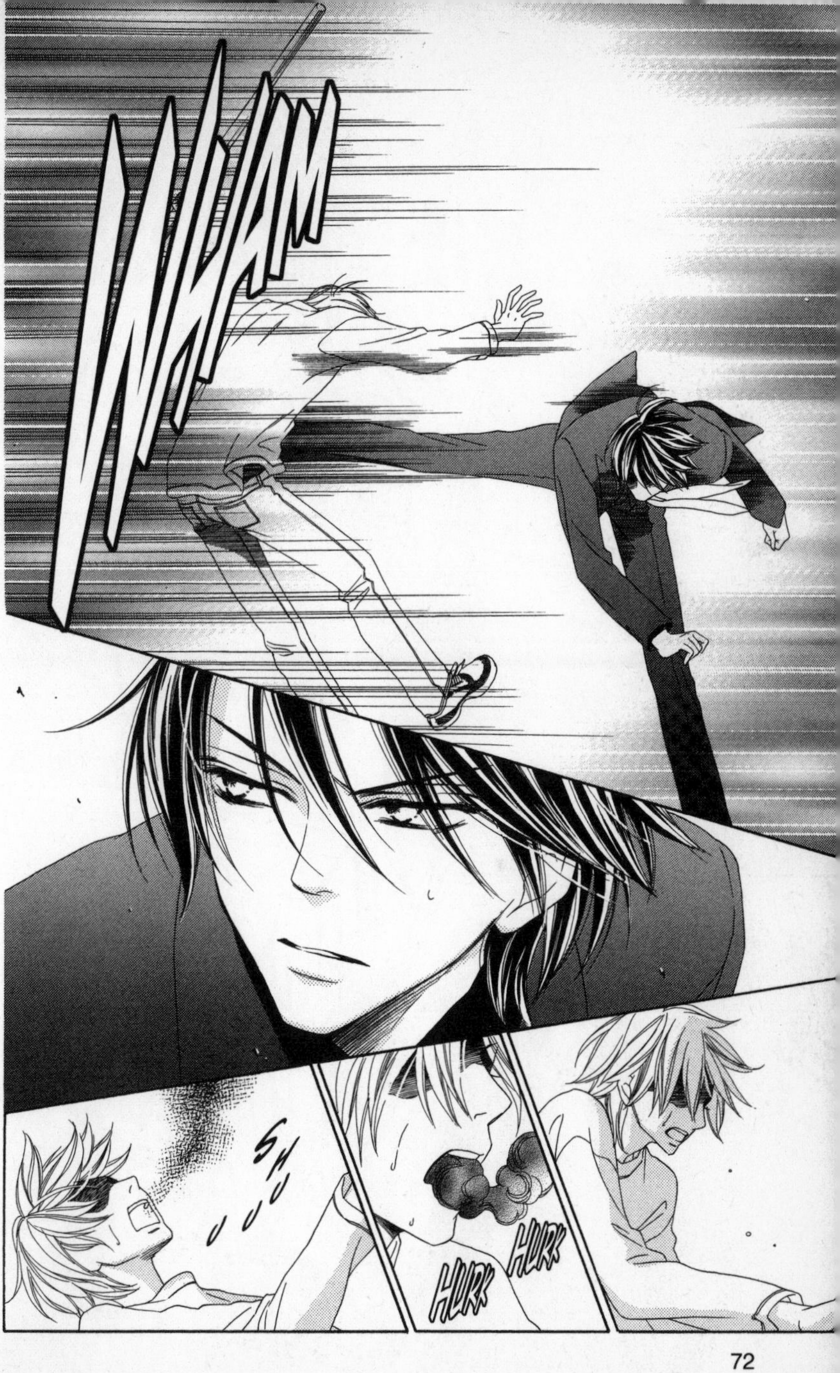
WHAM
SHUUU
HURK
HURK

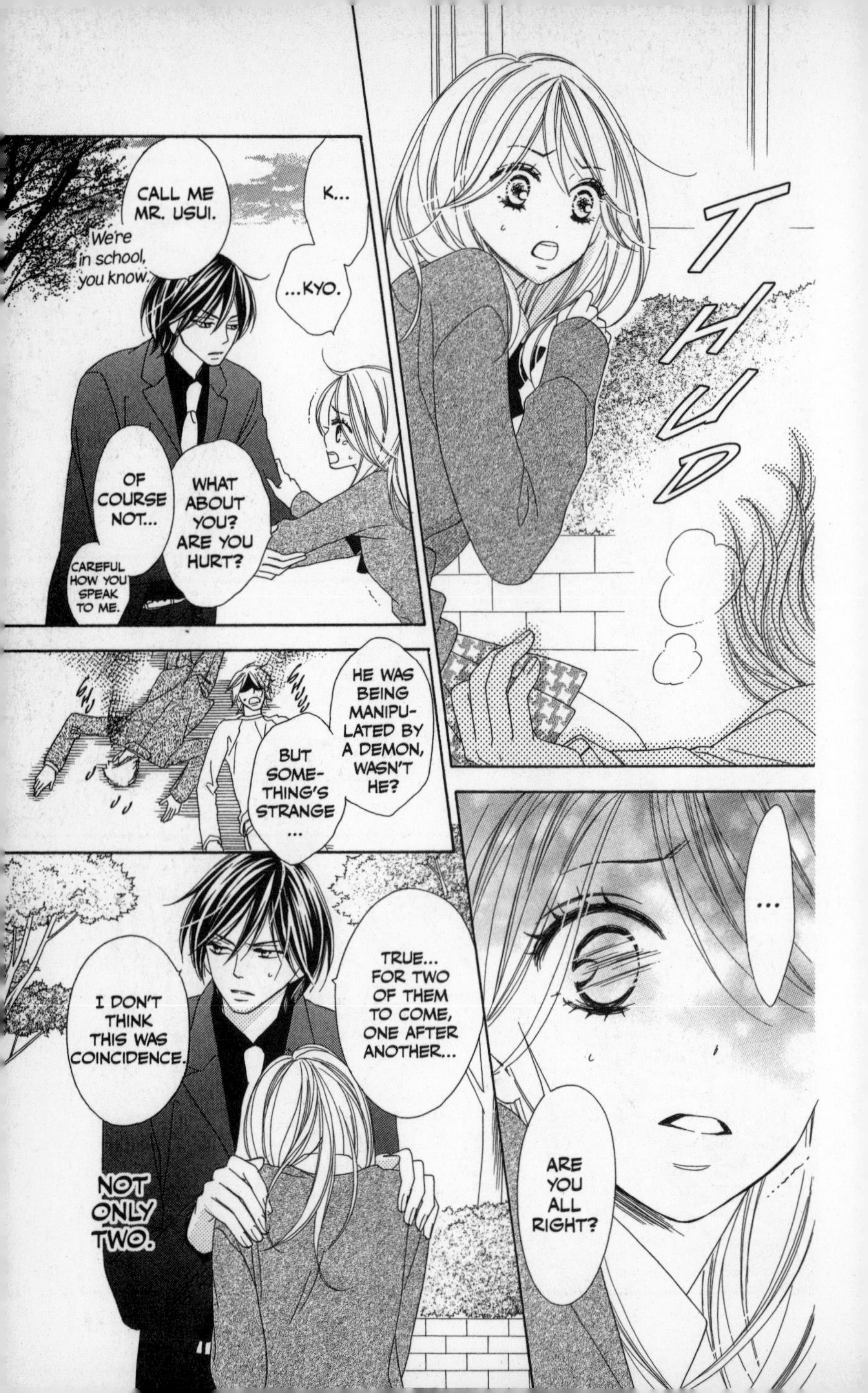
THUD
K...
...KYO.
CALL ME MR. USUI.
We're in school, you know.
WHAT ABOUT YOU? ARE YOU HURT?
OF COURSE NOT...
CAREFUL HOW YOU SPEAK TO ME.
HE WAS BEING MANIPULATED BY A DEMON, WASN'T HE?
BUT SOMETHING'S STRANGE...
...
ARE YOU ALL RIGHT?
TRUE... FOR TWO OF THEM TO COME, ONE AFTER ANOTHER...
I DON'T THINK THIS WAS COINCIDENCE.
NOT ONLY TWO.

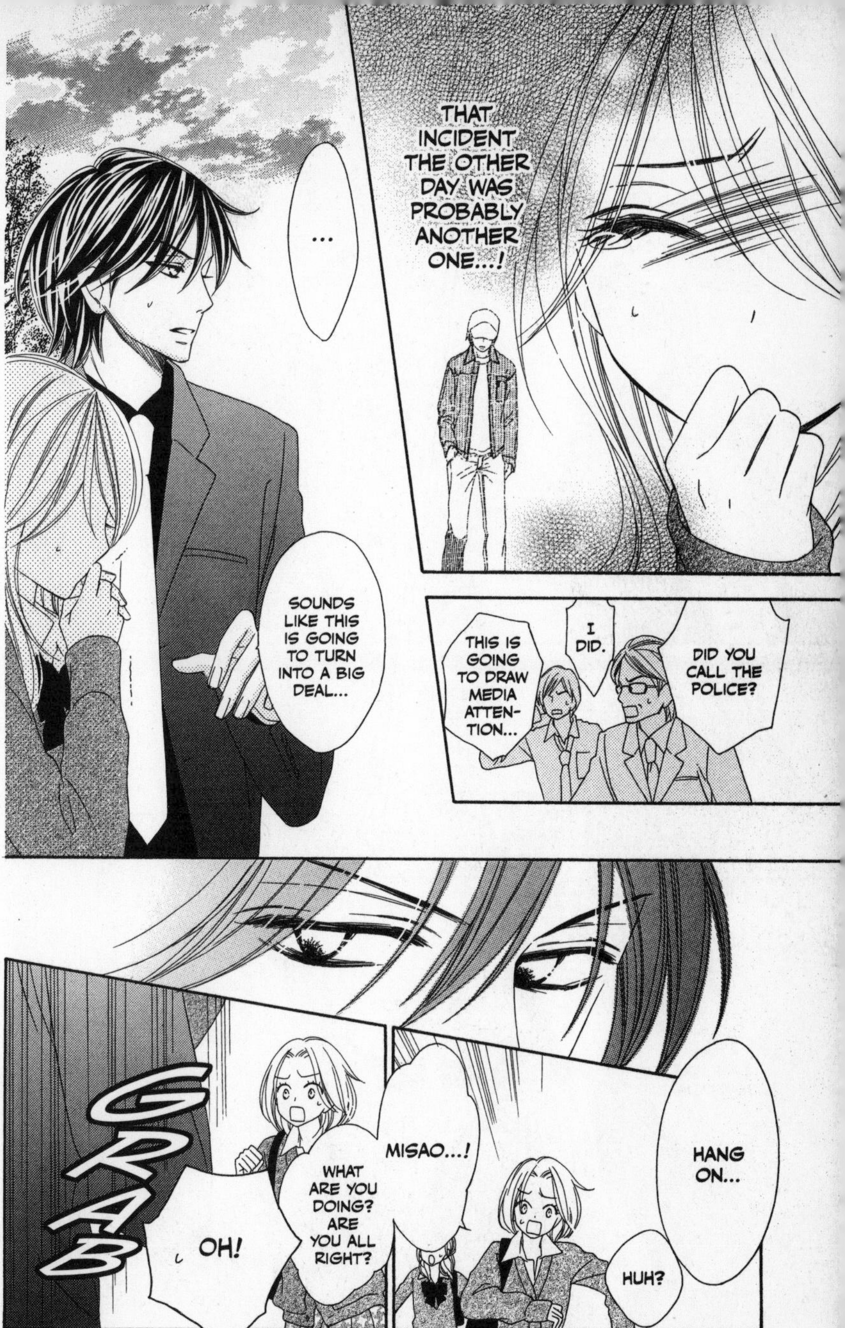
THAT INCIDENT THE OTHER DAY WAS PROBABLY ANOTHER ONE...!
DID YOU CALL THE POLICE?
I DID.
THIS IS GOING TO DRAW MEDIA ATTEN-TION...
...
SOUNDS LIKE THIS IS GOING TO TURN INTO A BIG DEAL...
HANG ON...
HUH?
MISAO...!
WHAT ARE YOU DOING? ARE YOU ALL RIGHT?
OH!
GRAB

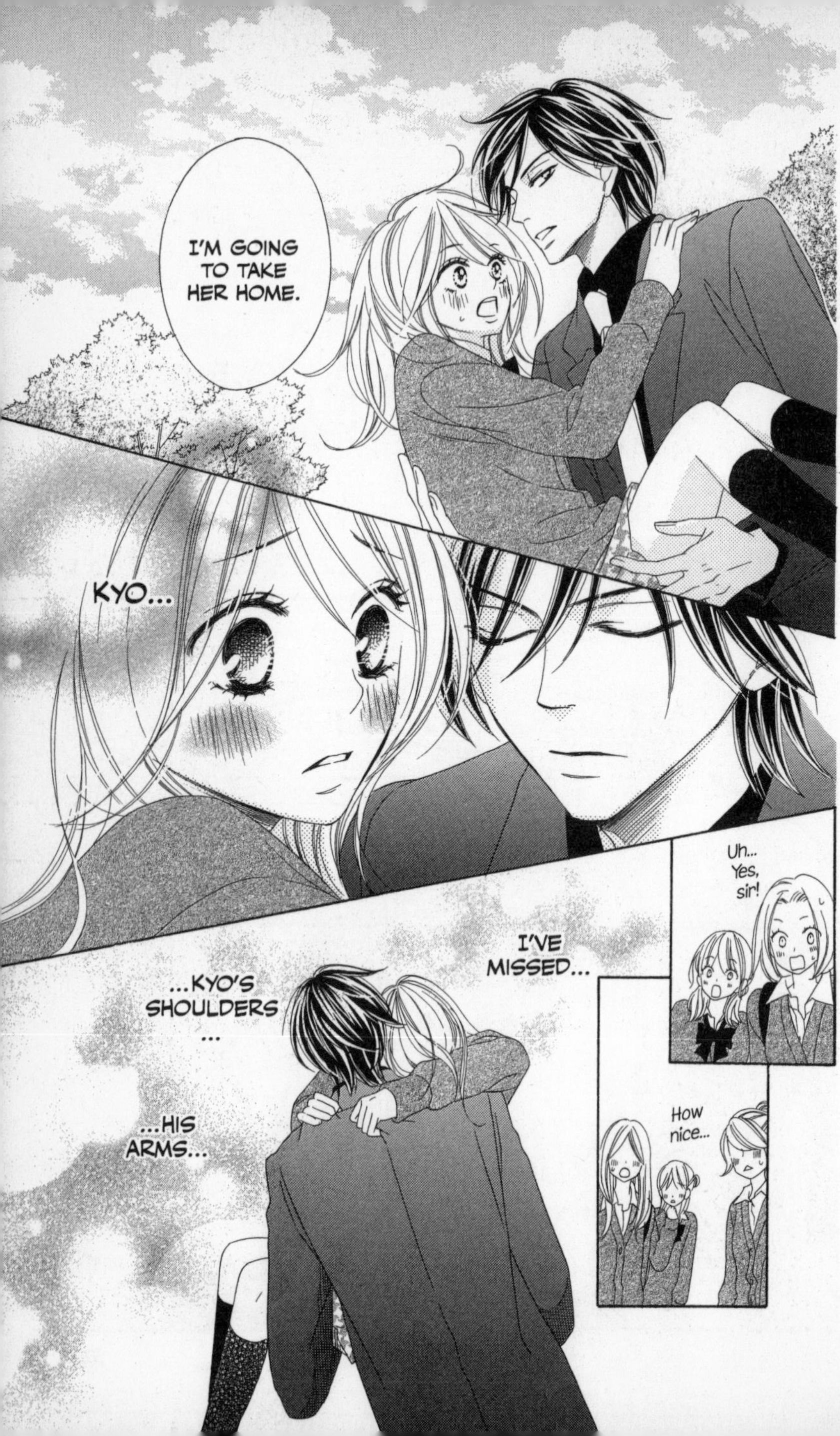
I'M GOING TO TAKE HER HOME.
KYO...
Uh... Yes, sir!
How nice...
I'VE MISSED...
...KYO'S SHOULDERS ...
...HIS ARMS...

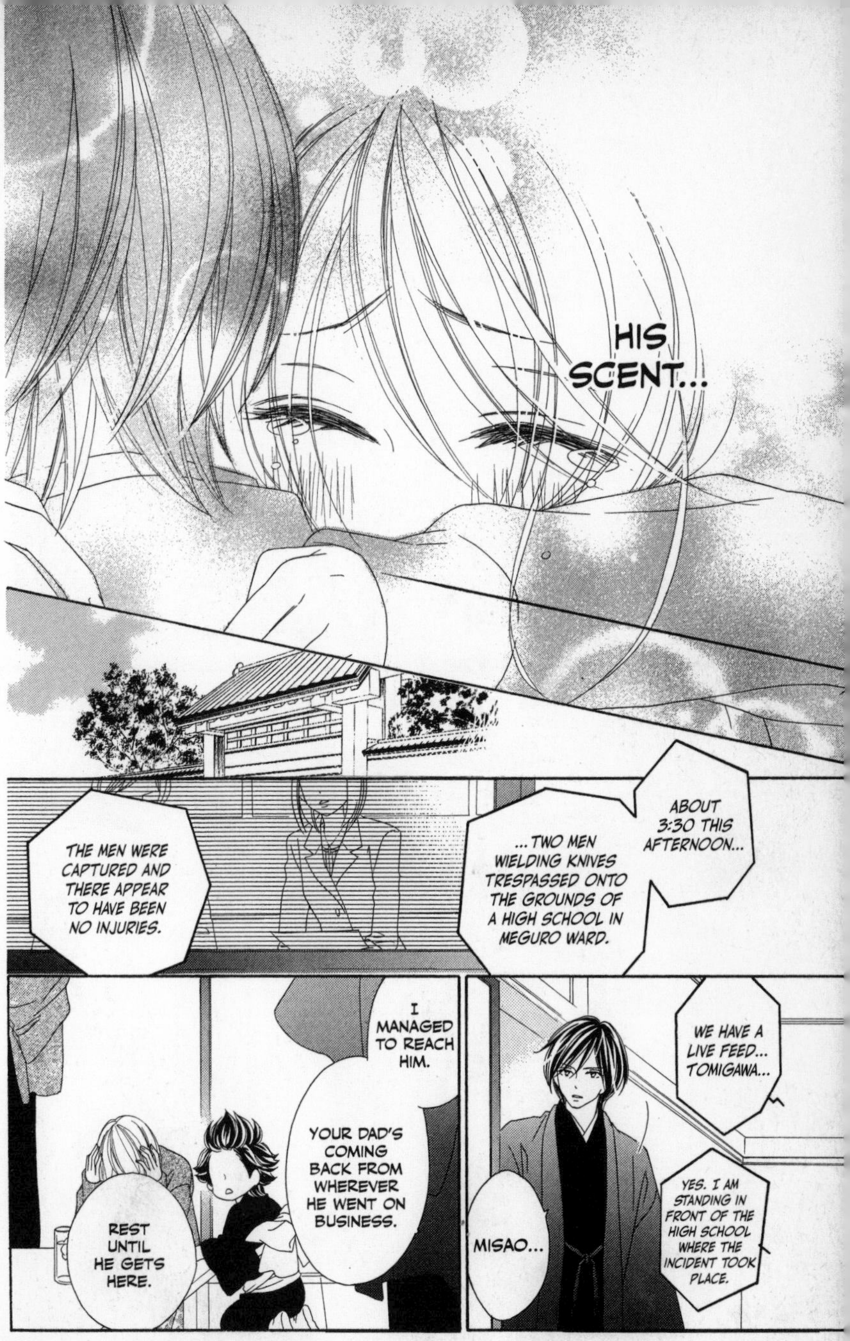
HIS SCENT...
ABOUT 3:30 THIS AFTERNOON...
...TWO MEN WIELDING KNIVES TRESPASSED ONTO THE GROUNDS OF A HIGH SCHOOL IN MEGURO WARD.
THE MEN WERE CAPTURED AND THERE APPEAR TO HAVE BEEN NO INJURIES.
WE HAVE A LIVE FEED... TOMIGAWA...
YES. I AM STANDING IN FRONT OF THE HIGH SCHOOL WHERE THE INCIDENT TOOK PLACE.
MISAO...
I MANAGED TO REACH HIM.
YOUR DAD'S COMING BACK FROM WHEREVER HE WENT ON BUSINESS.
REST UNTIL HE GETS HERE.

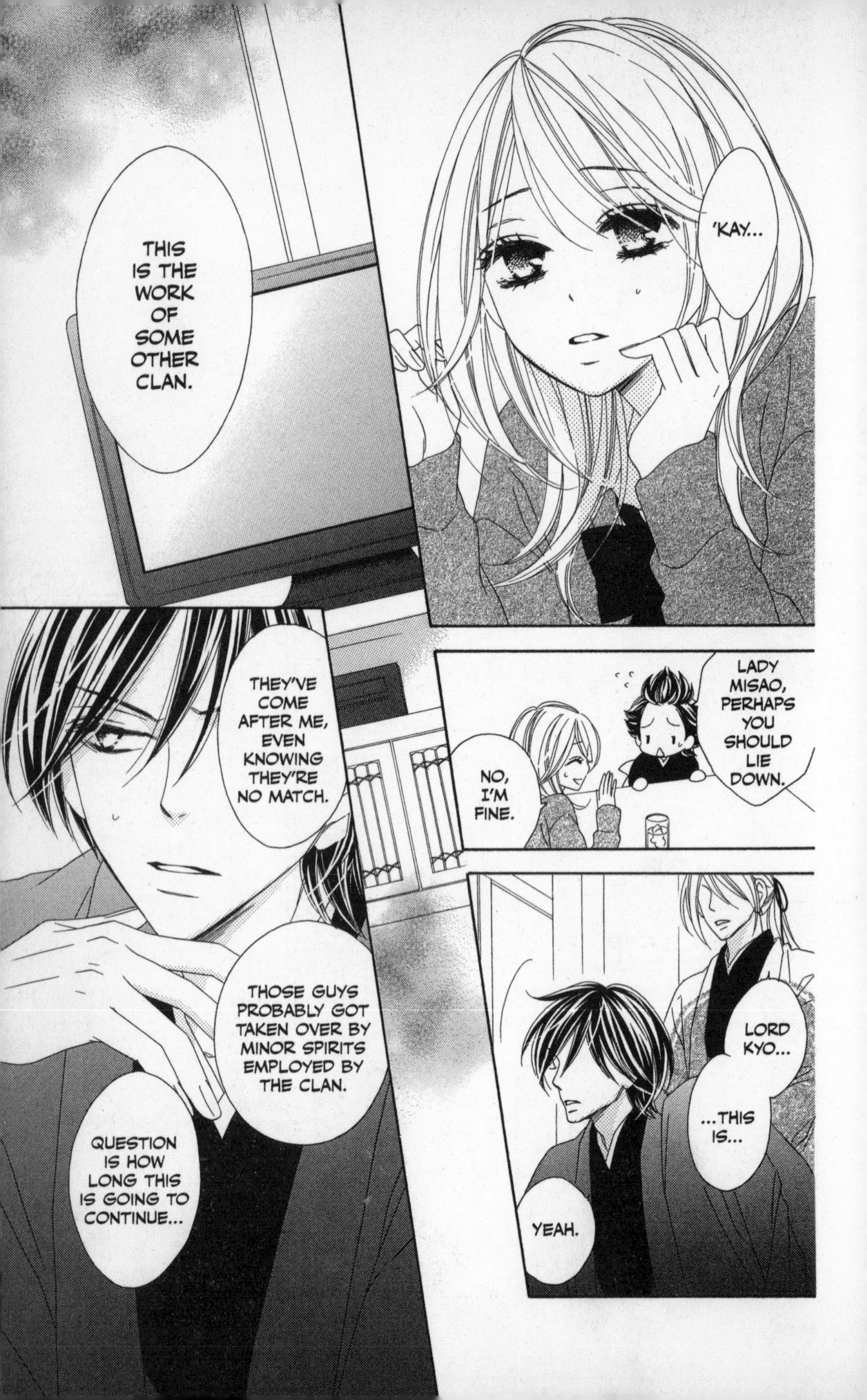
'KAY...
THIS IS THE WORK OF SOME OTHER CLAN.
LADY MISAO, PERHAPS YOU SHOULD LIE DOWN.
NO, I'M FINE.
LORD KYO...
...THIS IS...
YEAH.
THEY'VE COME AFTER ME, EVEN KNOWING THEY'RE NO MATCH.
THOSE GUYS PROBABLY GOT TAKEN OVER BY MINOR SPIRITS EMPLOYED BY THE CLAN.
QUESTION IS HOW LONG THIS IS GOING TO CONTINUE...

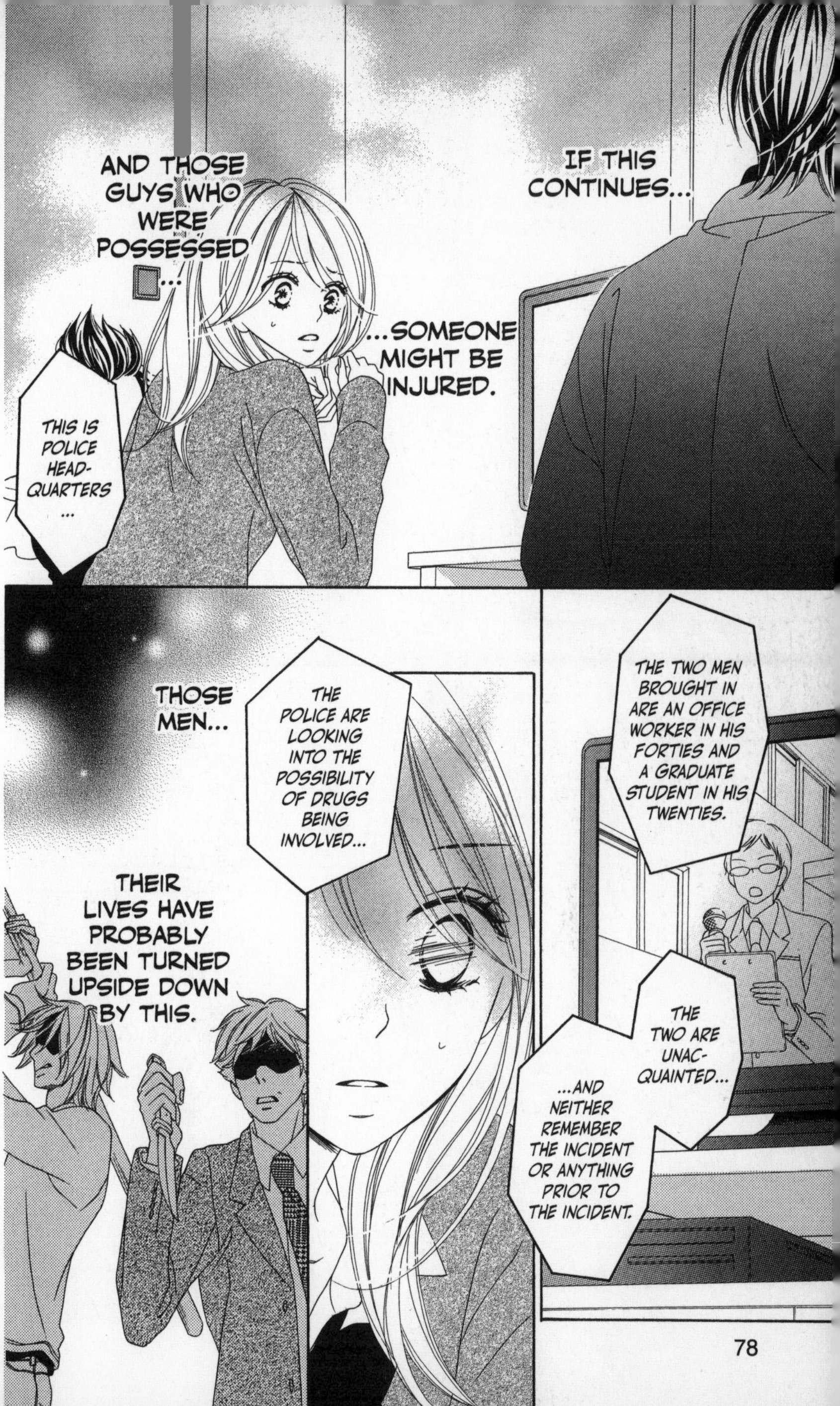
IF THIS CONTINUES...
AND THOSE GUYS WHO WERE POSSESSED...
...SOMEONE MIGHT BE INJURED.
THIS IS POLICE HEAD-QUARTERS...
THE TWO MEN BROUGHT IN ARE AN OFFICE WORKER IN HIS FORTIES AND A GRADUATE STUDENT IN HIS TWENTIES.
THE TWO ARE UNAC-QUAINTED...
...AND NEITHER REMEMBER THE INCIDENT OR ANYTHING PRIOR TO THE INCIDENT.
THE POLICE ARE LOOKING INTO THE POSSIBILITY OF DRUGS BEING INVOLVED...
THOSE MEN...
THEIR LIVES HAVE PROBABLY BEEN TURNED UPSIDE DOWN BY THIS.

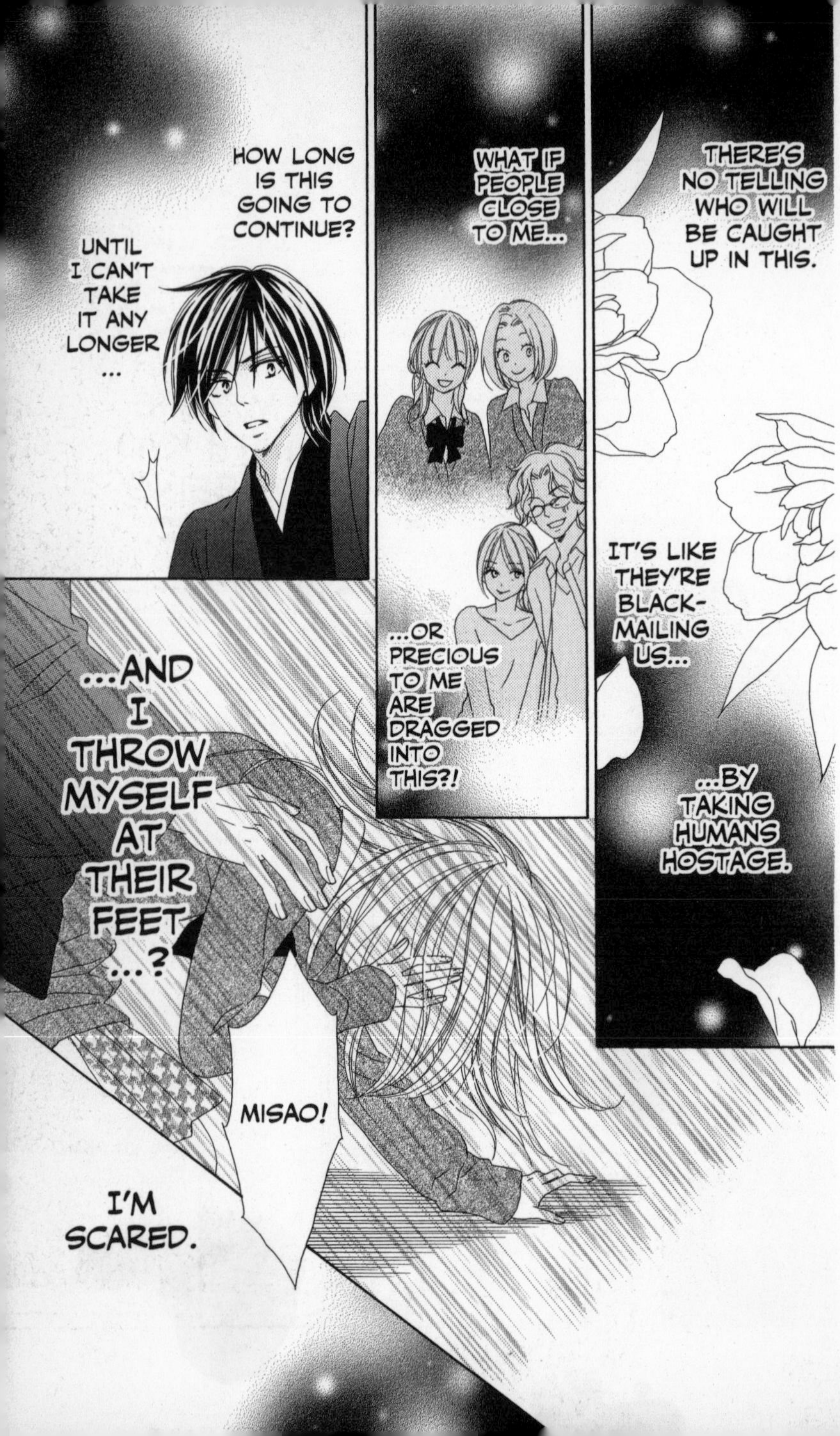
THERE'S NO TELLING WHO WILL BE CAUGHT UP IN THIS.
IT'S LIKE THEY'RE BLACK-MAILING US...
...BY TAKING HUMANS HOSTAGE.
WHAT IF PEOPLE CLOSE TO ME...
...OR PRECIOUS TO ME ARE DRAGGED INTO THIS?!
HOW LONG IS THIS GOING TO CONTINUE?
UNTIL I CAN'T TAKE IT ANY LONGER...
...AND I THROW MYSELF AT THEIR FEET...?
MISAO!
I'M SCARED.

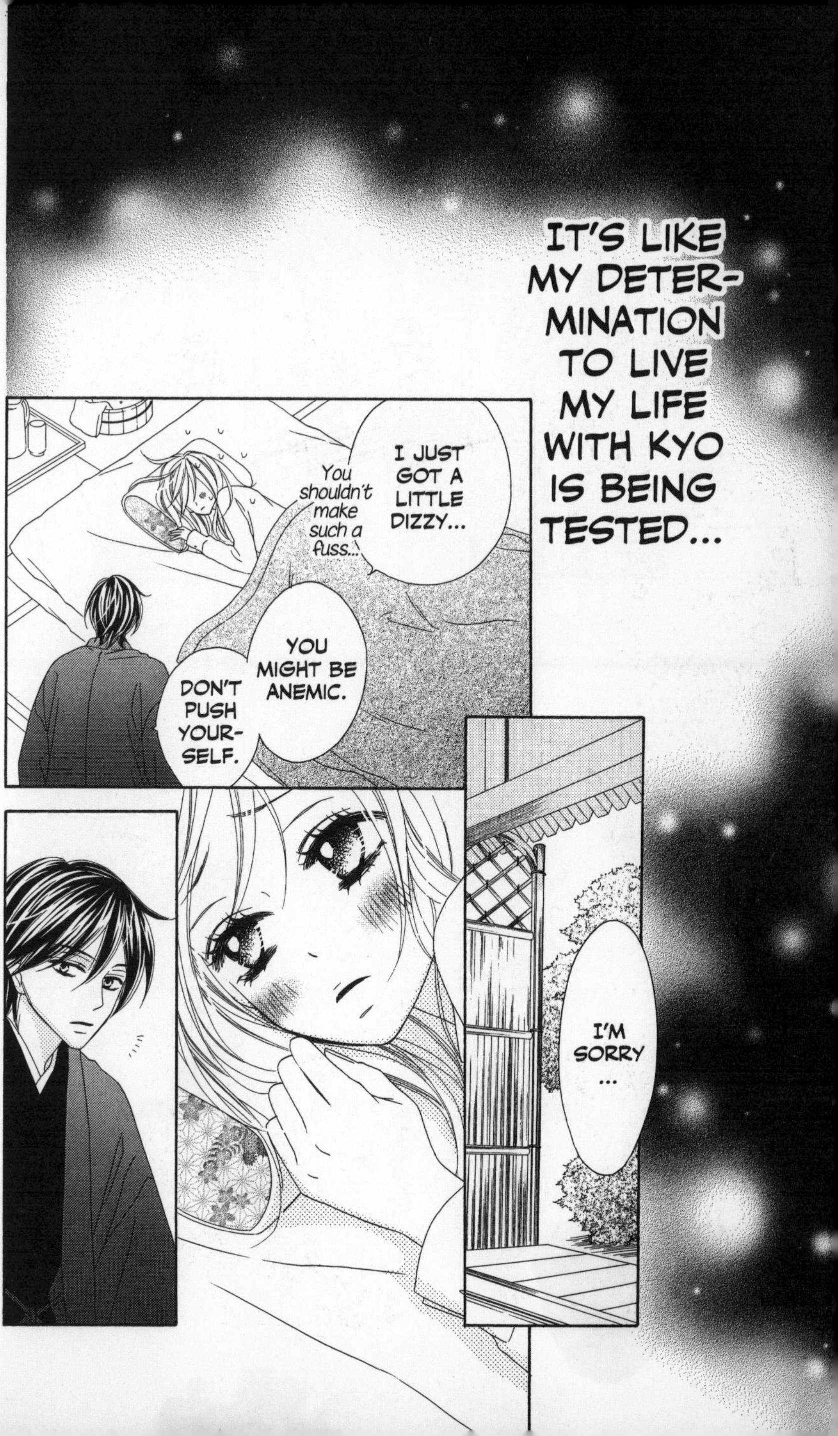
IT'S LIKE MY DETERMINATION TO LIVE MY LIFE WITH KYO IS BEING TESTED...
I JUST GOT A LITTLE DIZZY...
You shouldn't make such a fuss...
YOU MIGHT BE ANEMIC.
DON'T PUSH YOURSELF.
I'M SORRY...

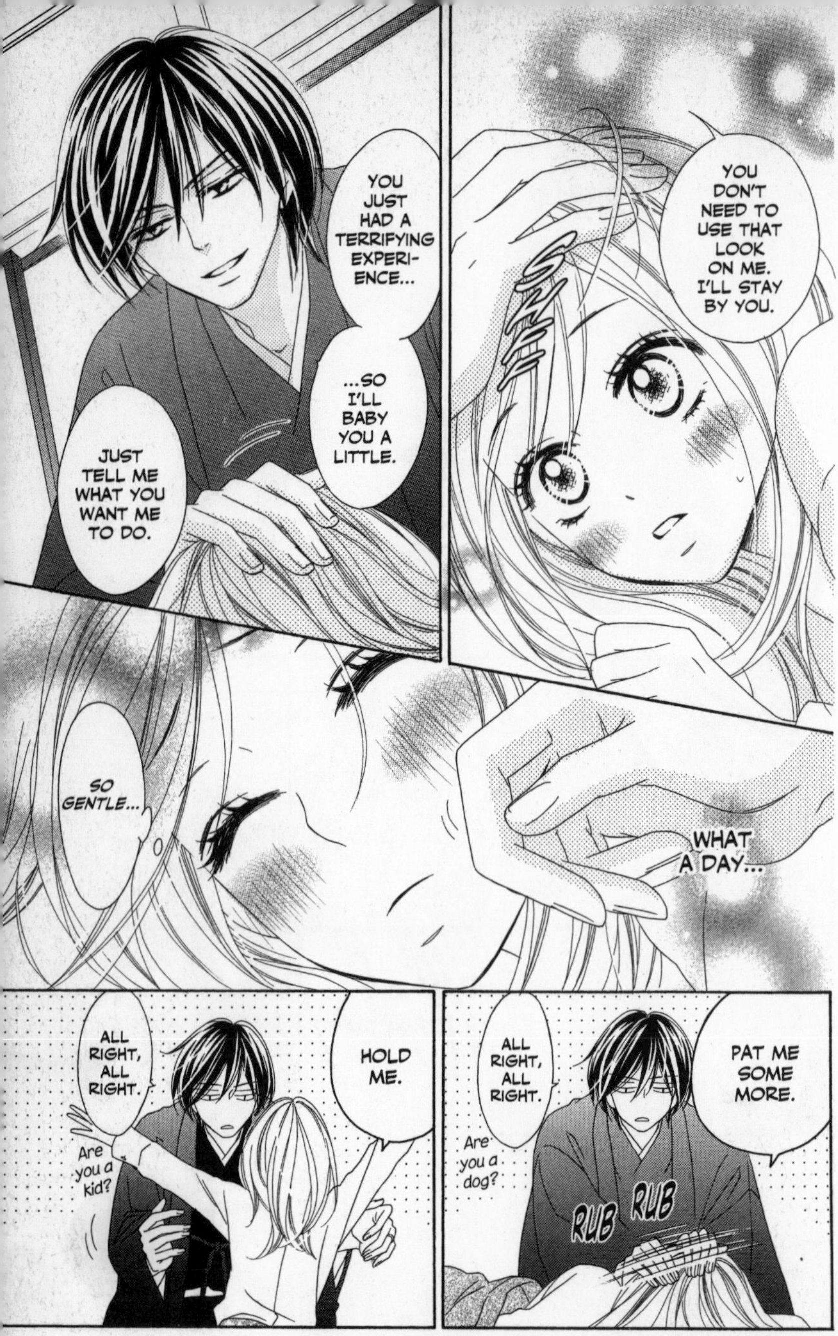
YOU DON'T NEED TO USE THAT LOOK ON ME. I'LL STAY BY YOU.
YOU JUST HAD A TERRIFYING EXPERIENCE...
...SO I'LL BABY YOU A LITTLE.
JUST TELL ME WHAT YOU WANT ME TO DO.
WHAT A DAY...
SO GENTLE...
PAT ME SOME MORE.
ALL RIGHT, ALL RIGHT.
Are you a dog?
RUB RUB
HOLD ME.
ALL RIGHT, ALL RIGHT.
Are you a kid?

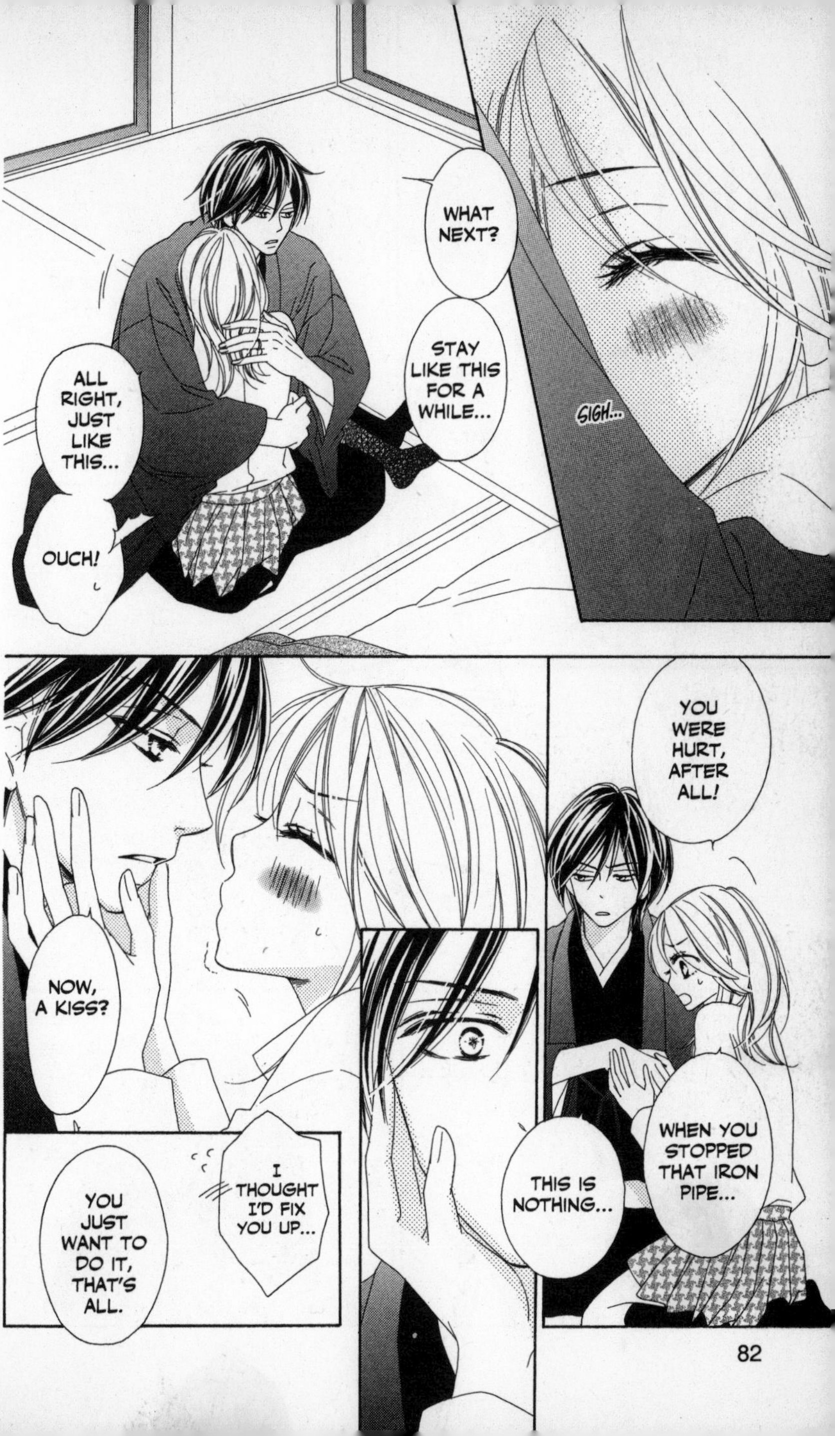
SIGH...
WHAT NEXT?
STAY LIKE THIS FOR A WHILE...
ALL RIGHT, JUST LIKE THIS...
OUCH!
YOU WERE HURT, AFTER ALL!
WHEN YOU STOPPED THAT IRON PIPE...
THIS IS NOTHING...
NOW, A KISS?
I THOUGHT I'D FIX YOU UP...
YOU JUST WANT TO DO IT, THAT'S ALL.

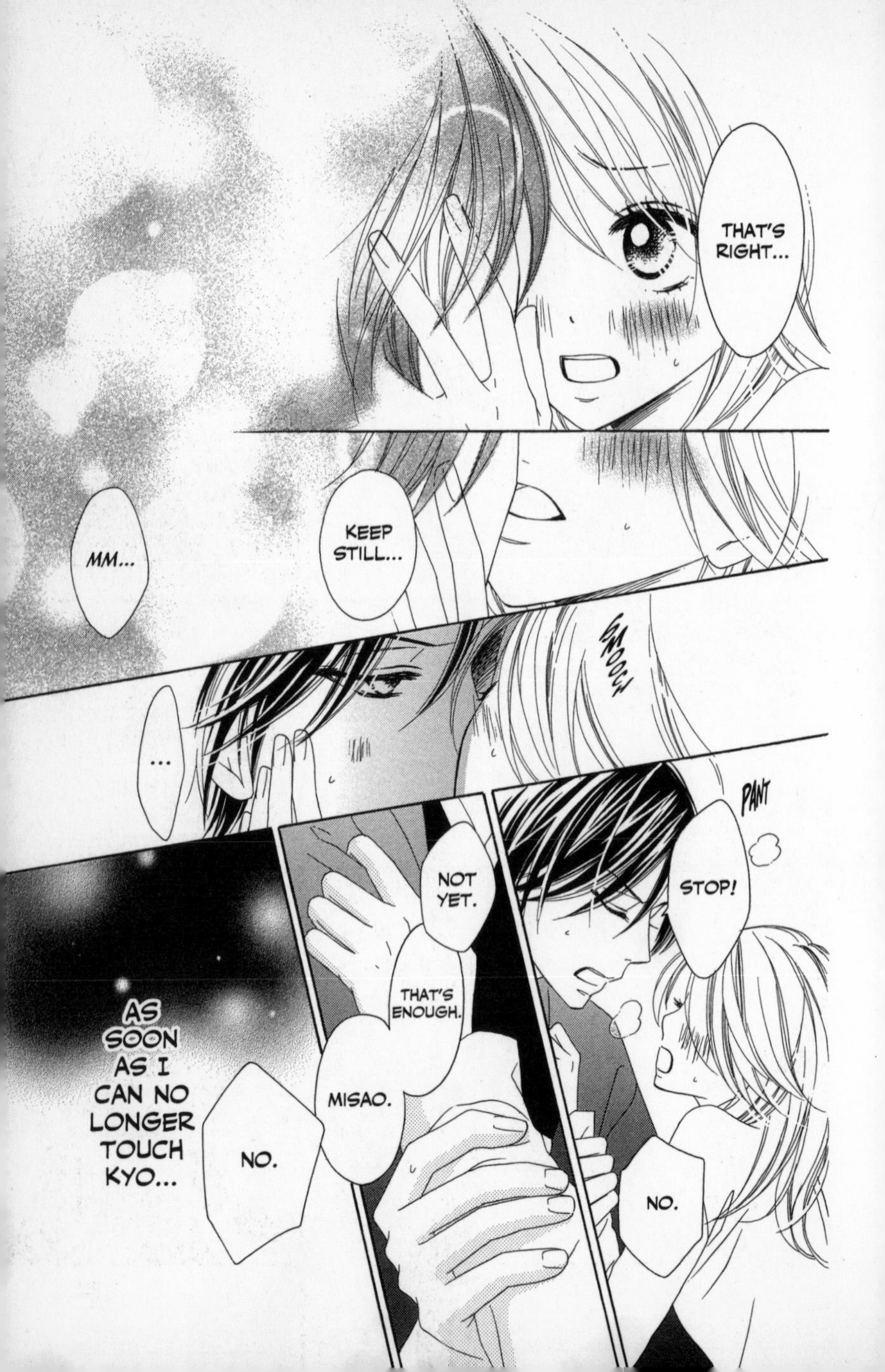
THAT'S RIGHT...
KEEP STILL...
MM...
SMOOCH
...
PANT
STOP!
NO.
NOT YET.
THAT'S ENOUGH.
MISAO.
NO.
AS SOON AS I CAN NO LONGER TOUCH KYO...

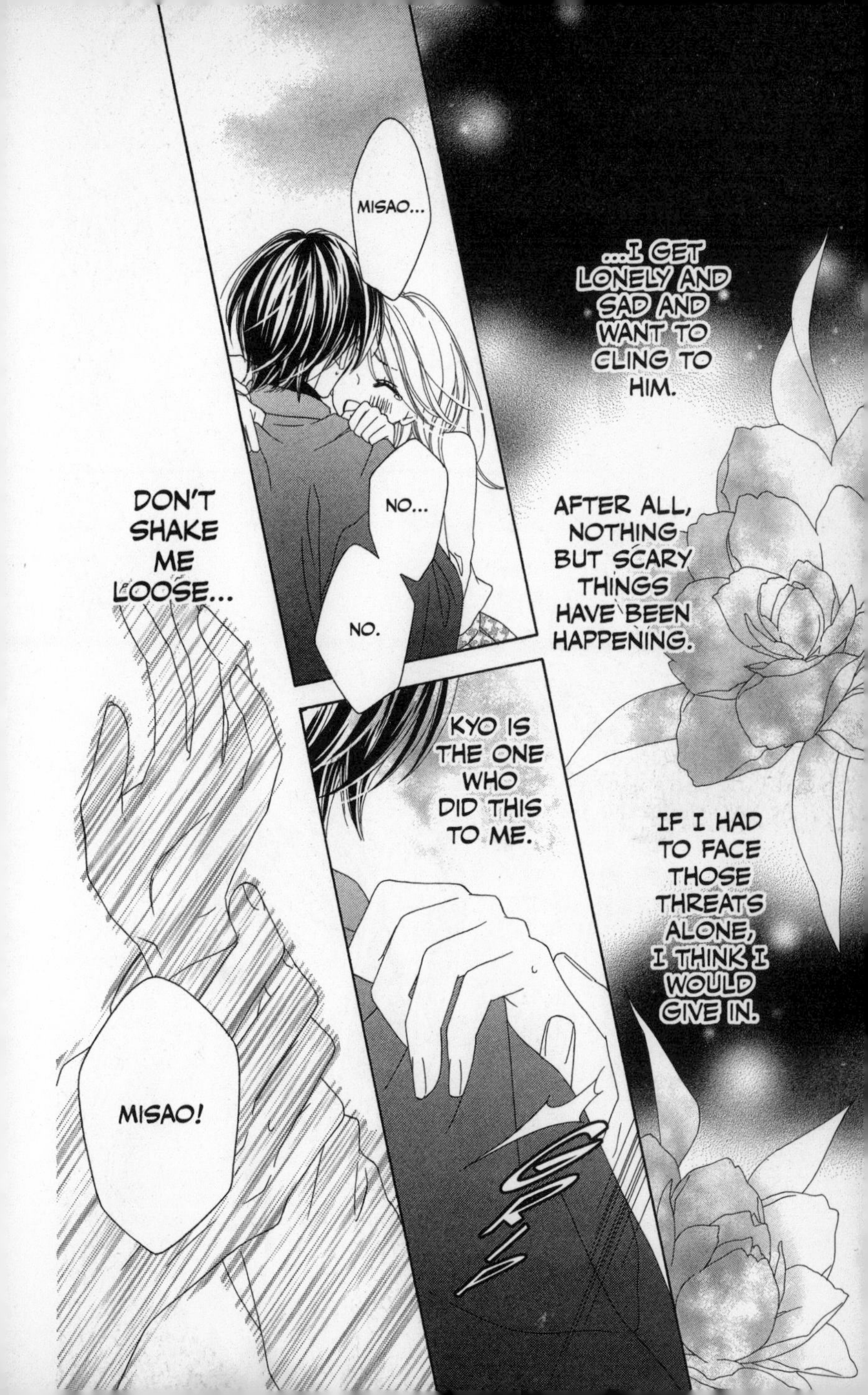
...I GET LONELY AND SAD AND WANT TO CLING TO HIM.
MISAO...
NO...
NO.
AFTER ALL, NOTHING BUT SCARY THINGS HAVE BEEN HAPPENING.
IF I HAD TO FACE THOSE THREATS ALONE, I THINK I WOULD GIVE IN.
KYO IS THE ONE WHO DID THIS TO ME.
DON'T SHAKE ME LOOSE...
MISAO!

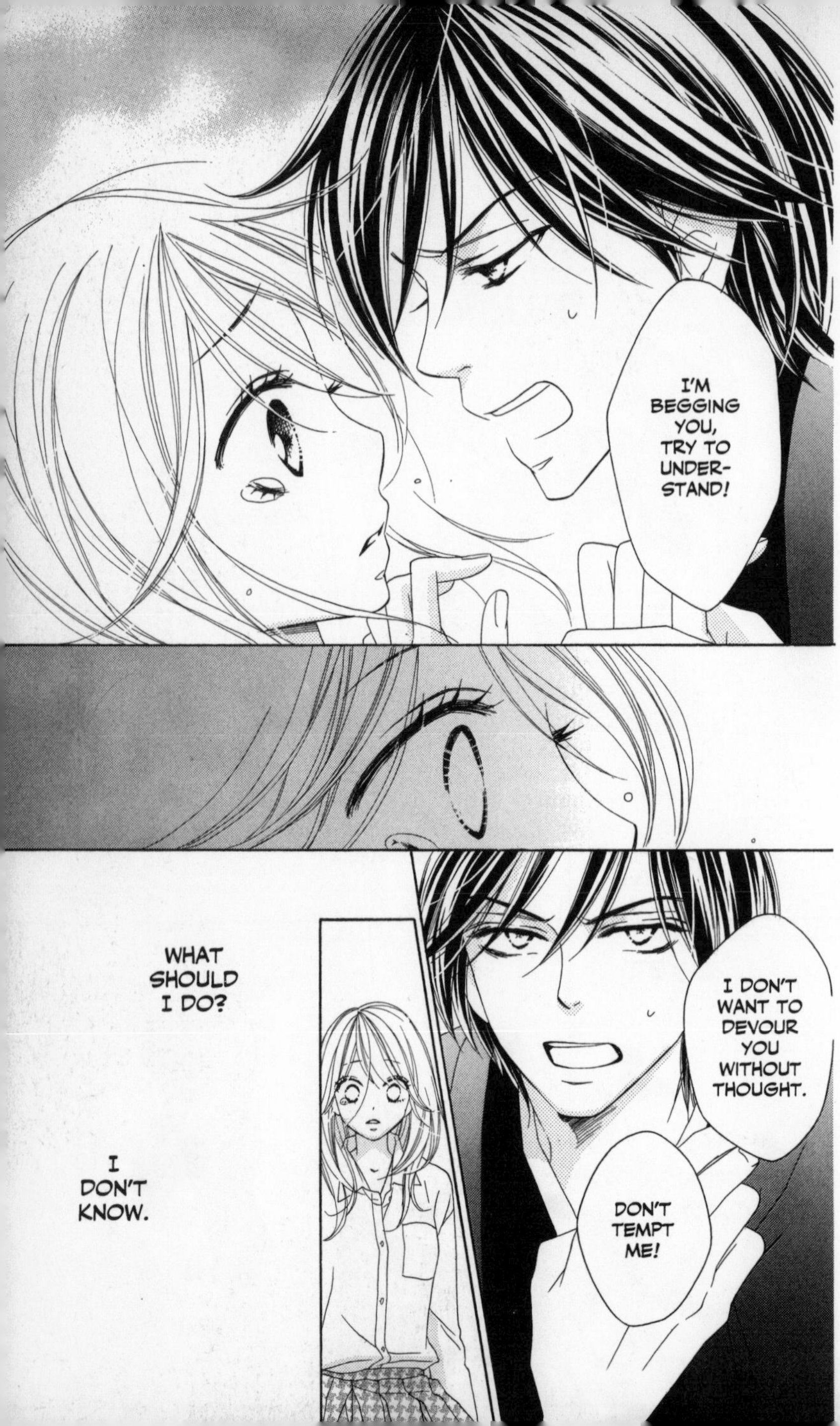
I'M BEGGING YOU, TRY TO UNDER-STAND!
I DON'T WANT TO DEVOUR YOU WITHOUT THOUGHT.
DON'T TEMPT ME!
WHAT SHOULD I DO?
I DON'T KNOW.

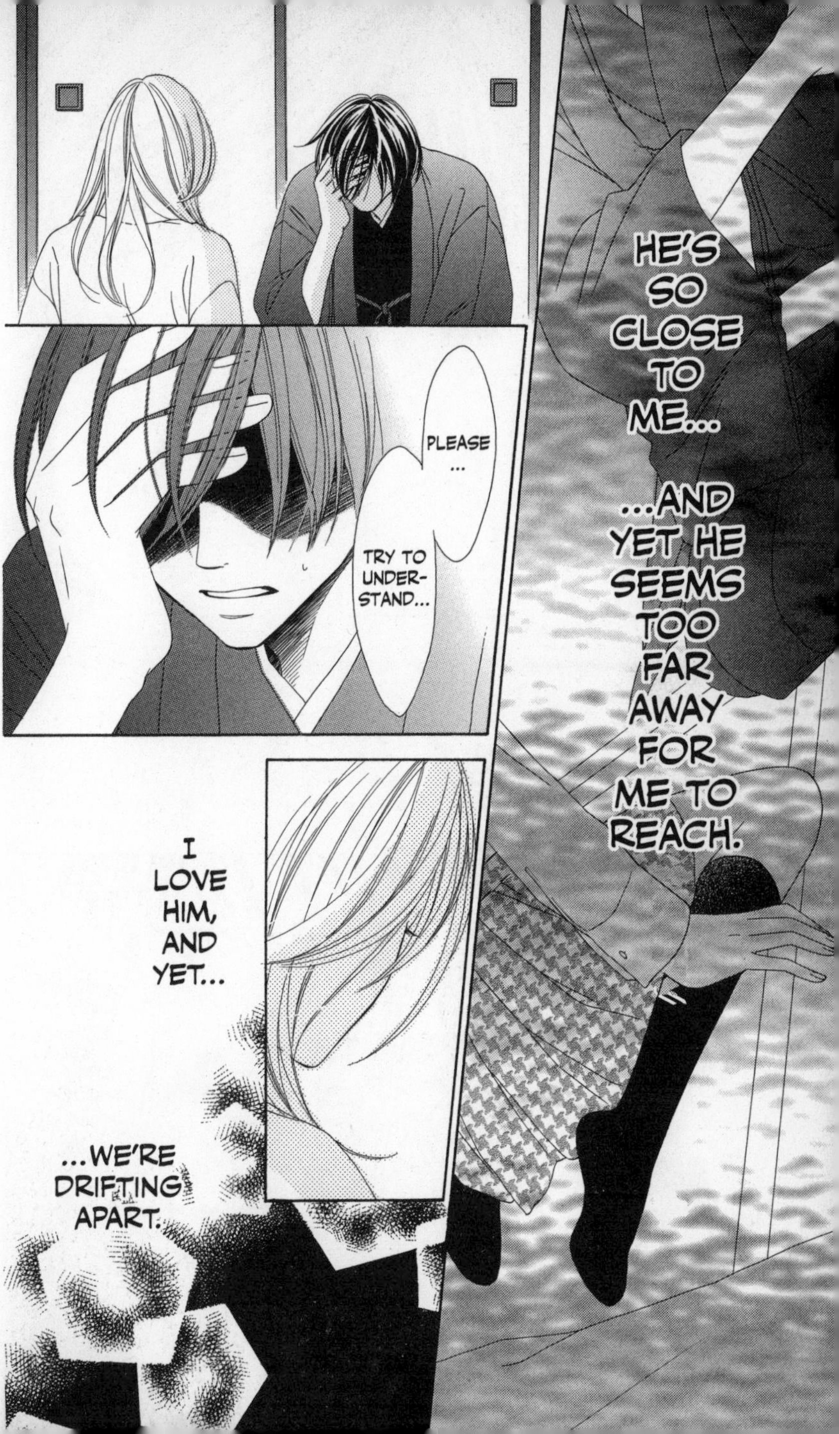
HE'S SO CLOSE TO ME...
...AND YET HE SEEMS TOO FAR AWAY FOR ME TO REACH.
PLEASE...
TRY TO UNDER-STAND...
I LOVE HIM, AND YET...
...WE'RE DRIFTING APART.

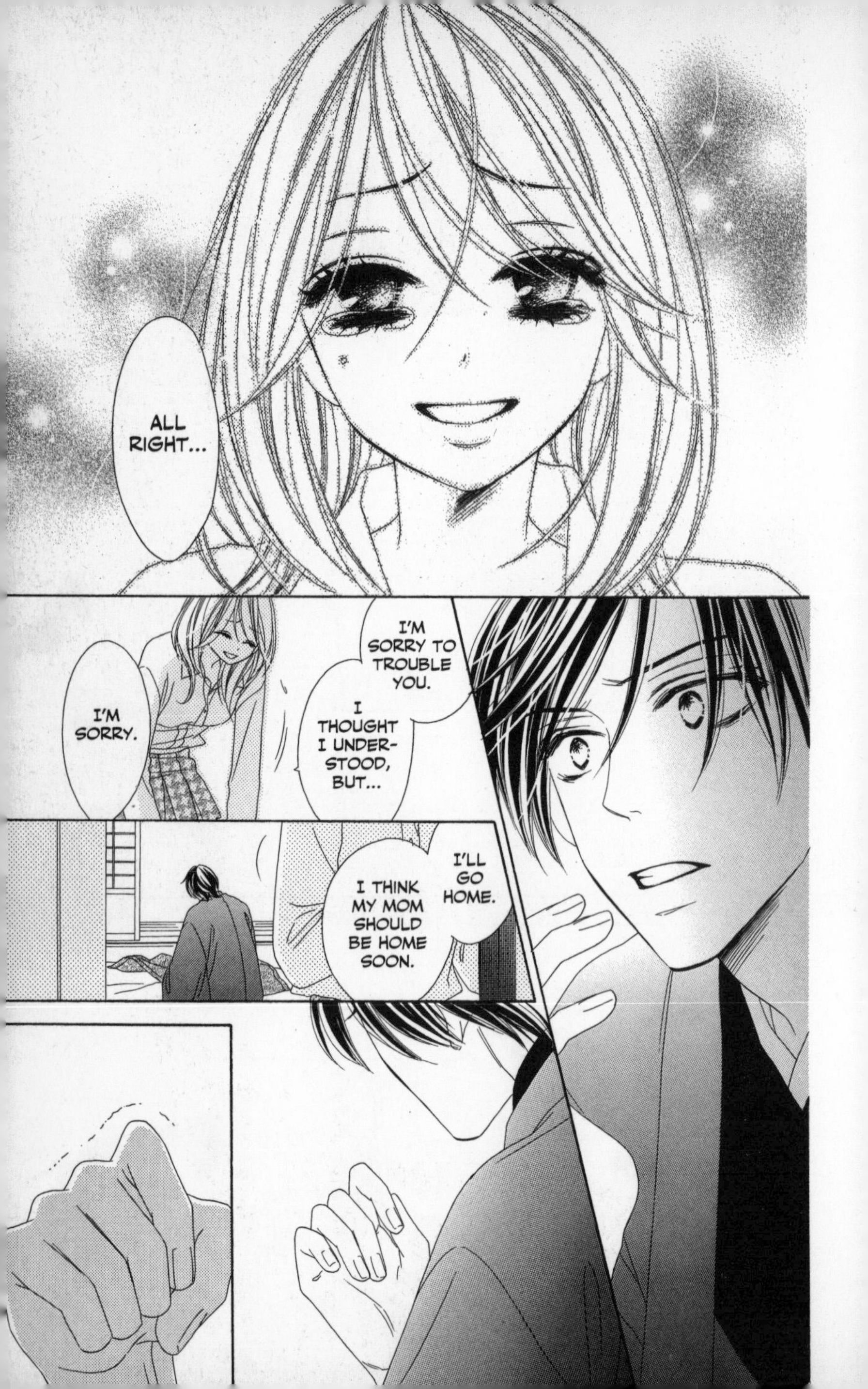
ALL RIGHT...
I'M SORRY TO TROUBLE YOU.
I THOUGHT I UNDER-STOOD, BUT...
I'M SORRY.
I'LL GO HOME.
I THINK MY MOM SHOULD BE HOME SOON.

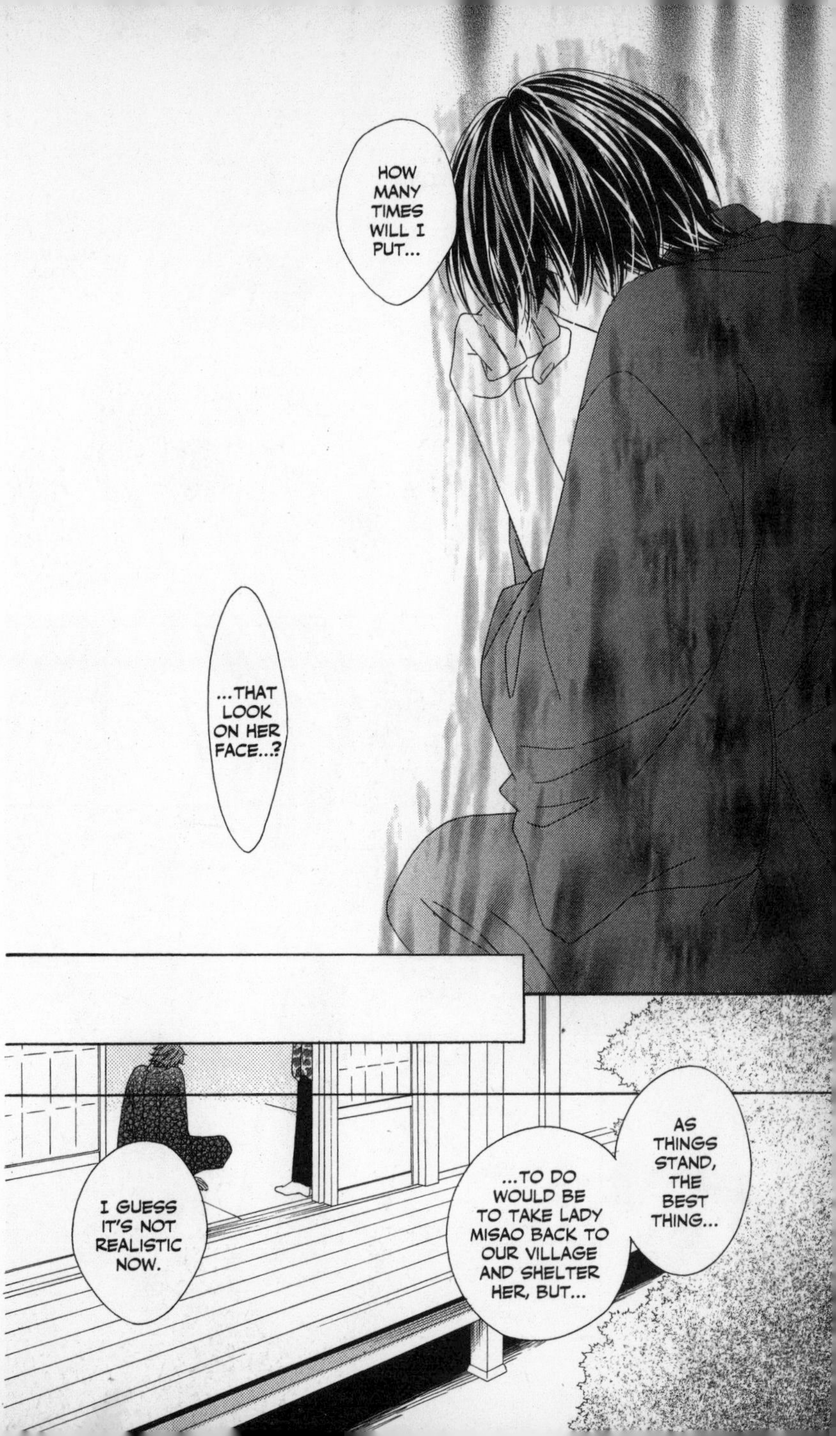
HOW MANY TIMES WILL I PUT...
...THAT LOOK ON HER FACE...?
AS THINGS STAND, THE BEST THING...
...TO DO WOULD BE TO TAKE LADY MISAO BACK TO OUR VILLAGE AND SHELTER HER, BUT...
I GUESS IT'S NOT REALISTIC NOW.

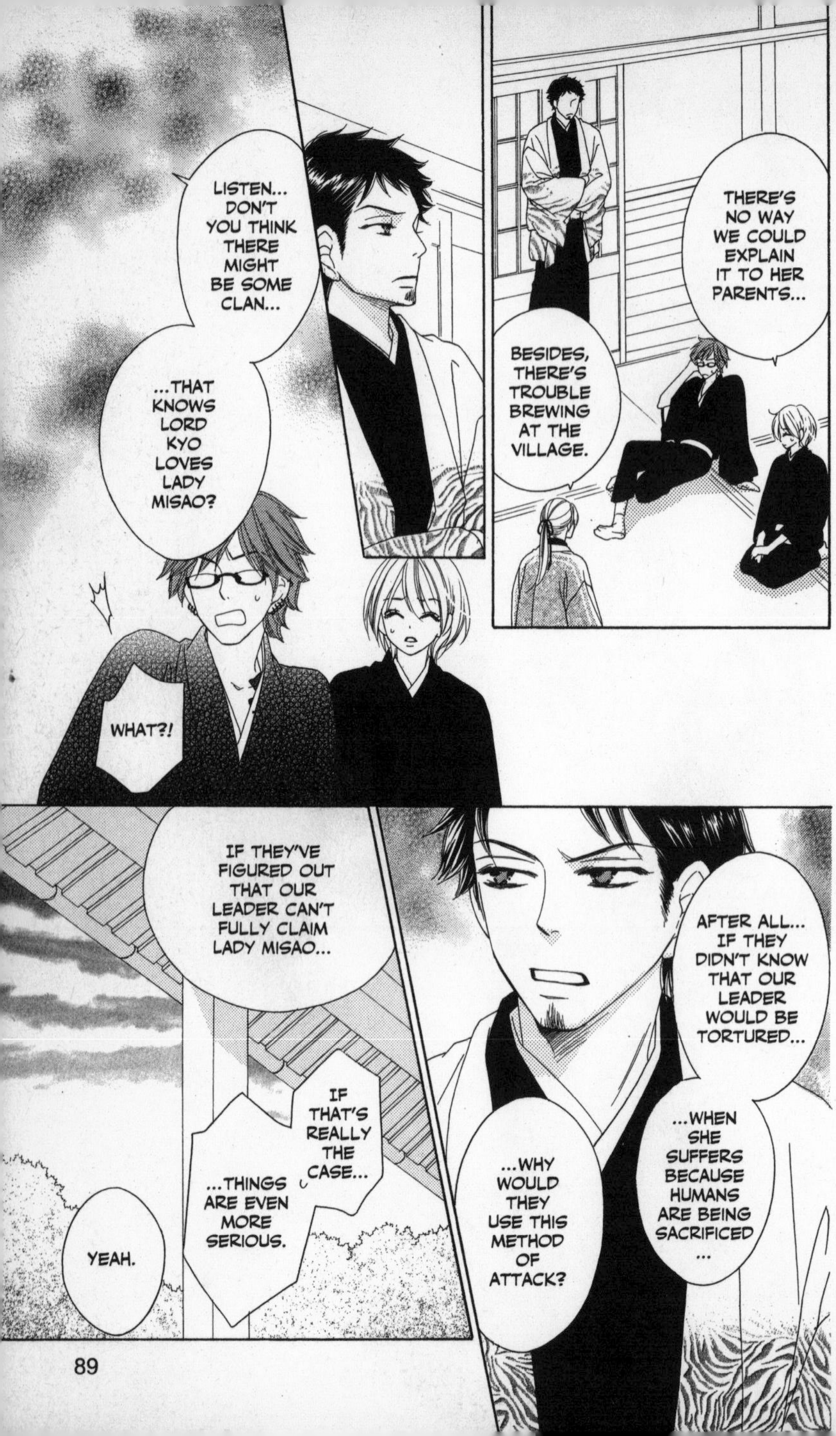
THERE'S NO WAY WE COULD EXPLAIN IT TO HER PARENTS...
BESIDES, THERE'S TROUBLE BREWING AT THE VILLAGE.
LISTEN... DON'T YOU THINK THERE MIGHT BE SOME CLAN...
...THAT KNOWS LORD KYO LOVES LADY MISAO?
WHAT?!
AFTER ALL... IF THEY DIDN'T KNOW THAT OUR LEADER WOULD BE TORTURED...
...WHEN SHE SUFFERS BECAUSE HUMANS ARE BEING SACRIFICED...
...WHY WOULD THEY USE THIS METHOD OF ATTACK?
IF THEY'VE FIGURED OUT THAT OUR LEADER CAN'T FULLY CLAIM LADY MISAO...
IF THAT'S REALLY THE CASE...
...THINGS ARE EVEN MORE SERIOUS.
YEAH.

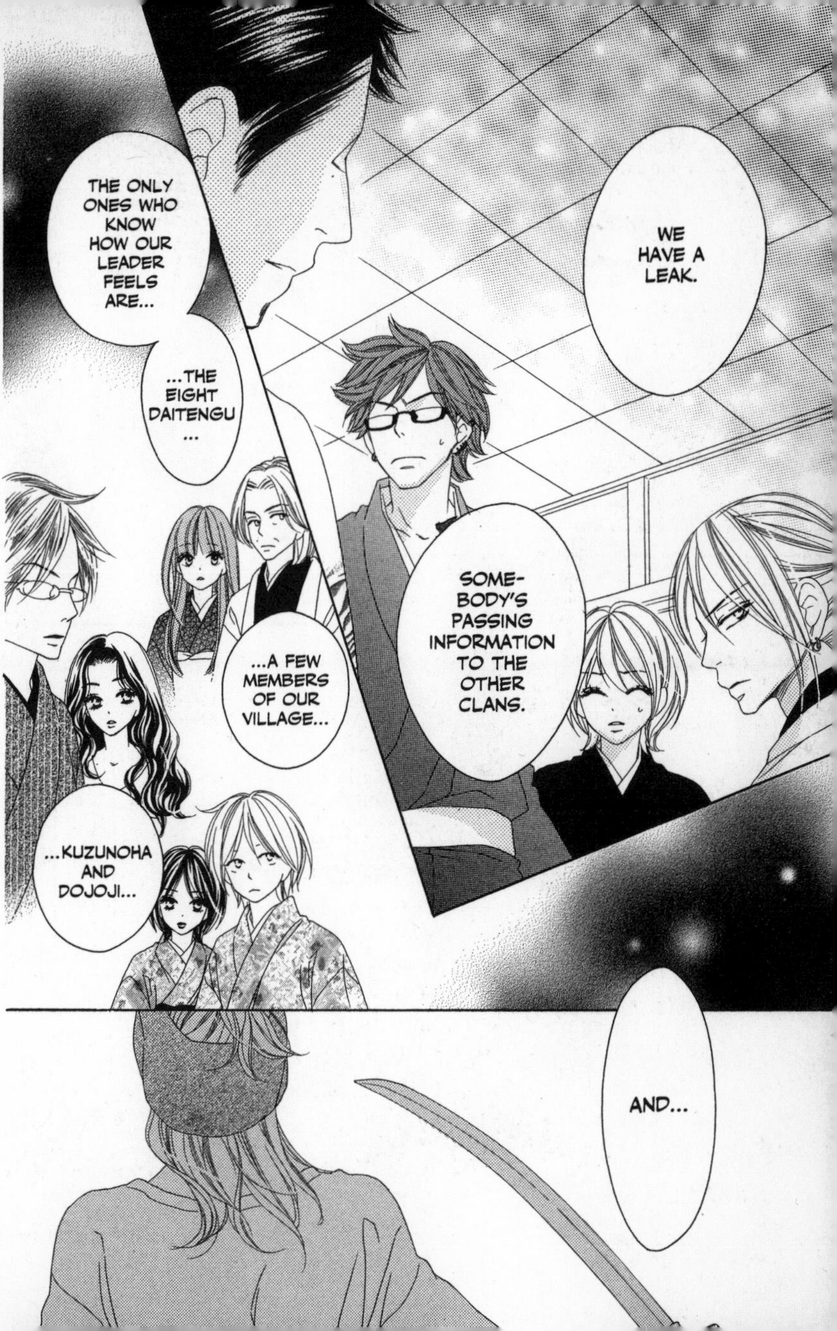
WE HAVE A LEAK.
SOME-BODY'S PASSING INFORMATION TO THE OTHER CLANS.
THE ONLY ONES WHO KNOW HOW OUR LEADER FEELS ARE...
...THE EIGHT DAITENGU...
...A FEW MEMBERS OF OUR VILLAGE...
...KUZUNOHA AND DOJOJI...
AND...

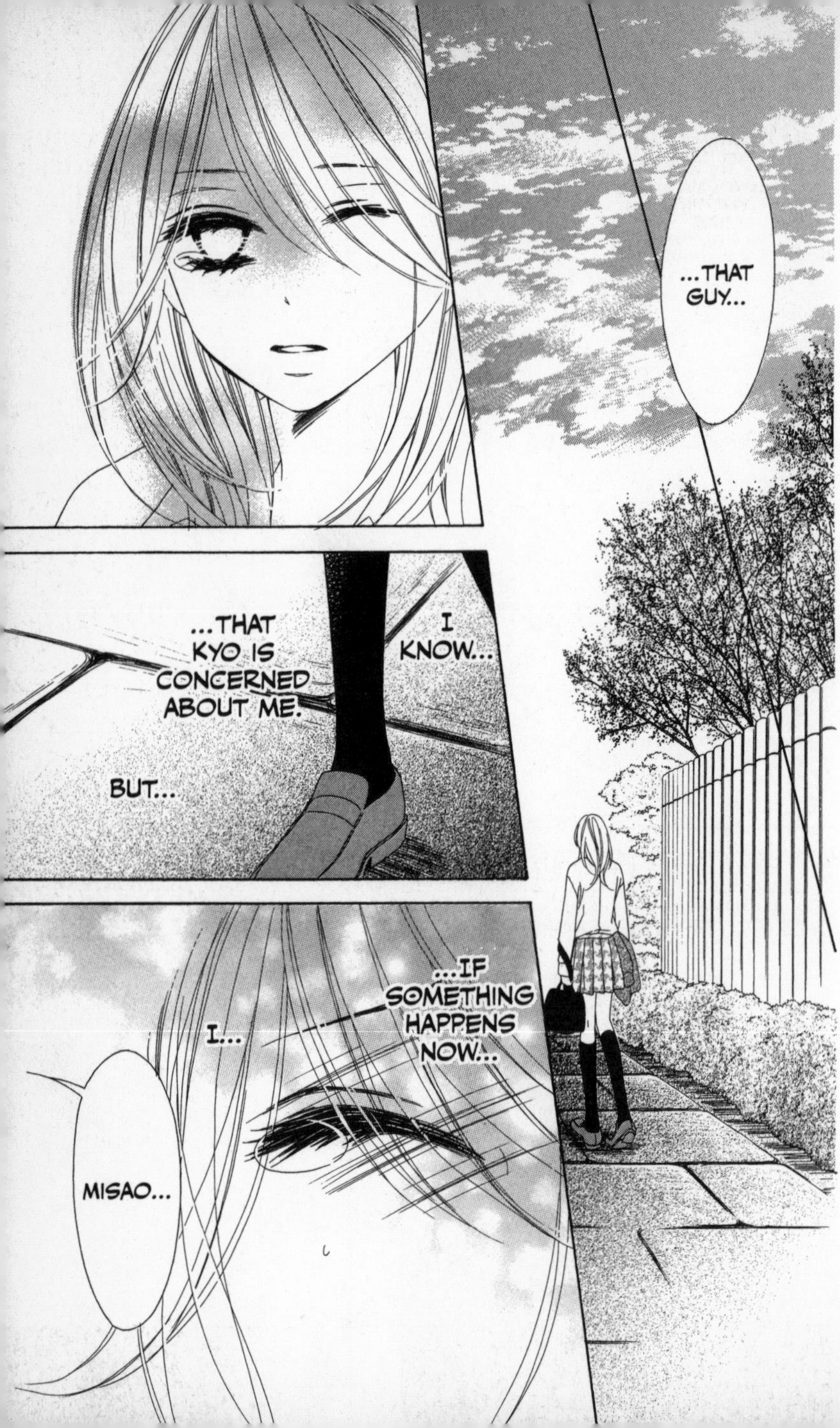
...THAT GUY...
I KNOW...
...THAT KYO IS CONCERNED ABOUT ME.
BUT...
...IF SOMETHING HAPPENS NOW...
I...
MISAO...

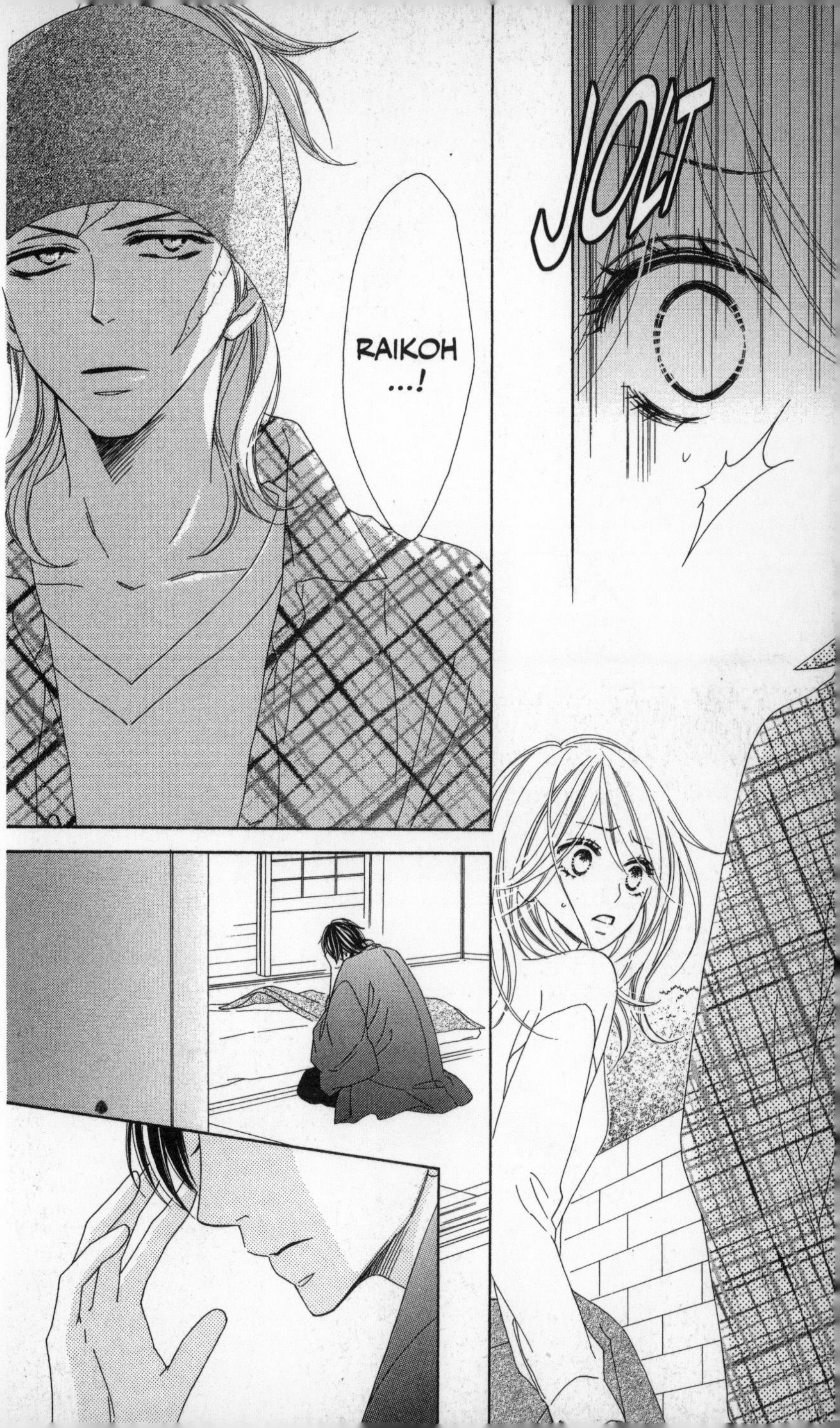
JOLT
RAIKOH ...!

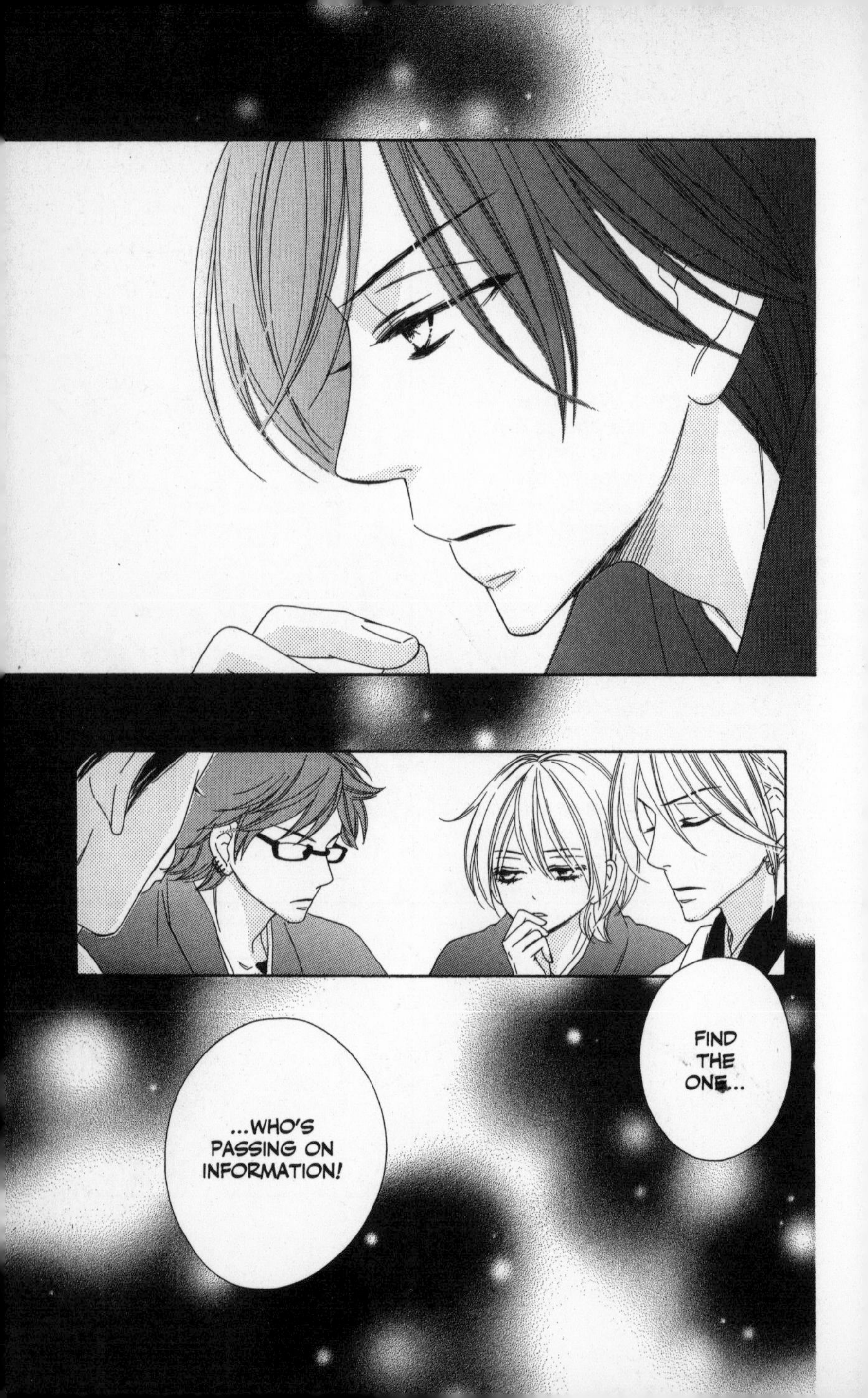
FIND THE ONE...
...WHO'S PASSING ON INFORMATION!

In Volume 7, Kyo said he didn't like "blue-backed fish," but he's not the only one. According to legend, all Tengu hate blue-backed fish, so I thought something like this → could happen.

Hinako Sugiura, researcher of lifestyles and customs of Japan's Edo period, wrote in her book *Sarusuberi* that in order to keep them from being stolen by tengu, people would feed their children blue-backed fish every day. If that were the case, Kyo would not have been able to take part in this bride-taking competition... Well, if you could please overlook that...

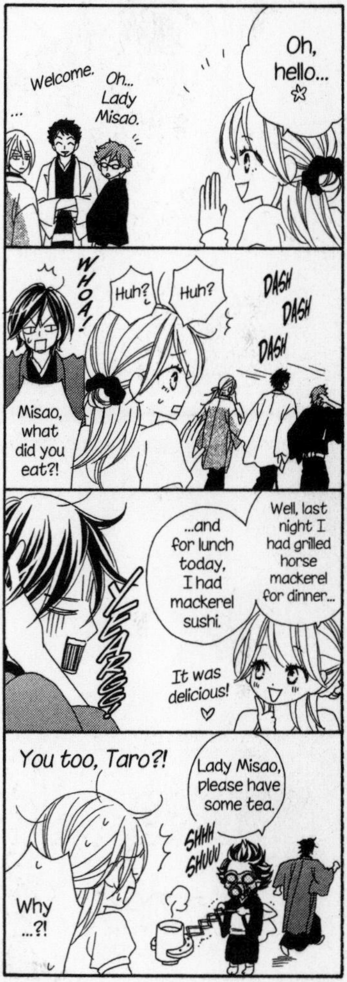
Oh, hello...
Oh... Lady Misao.
Welcome.
...
DASH
DASH
DASH
Huh?
Huh?
WHOA!
Misao, what did you eat?!
Well, last night I had grilled horse mackerel for dinner...
...and for lunch today, I had mackerel sushi.
It was delicious!
Lady Misao, please have some tea.
SHHH
SHUUU
You too, Taro?!
Why ...?!

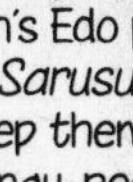

Could it be like garlic to vampires?

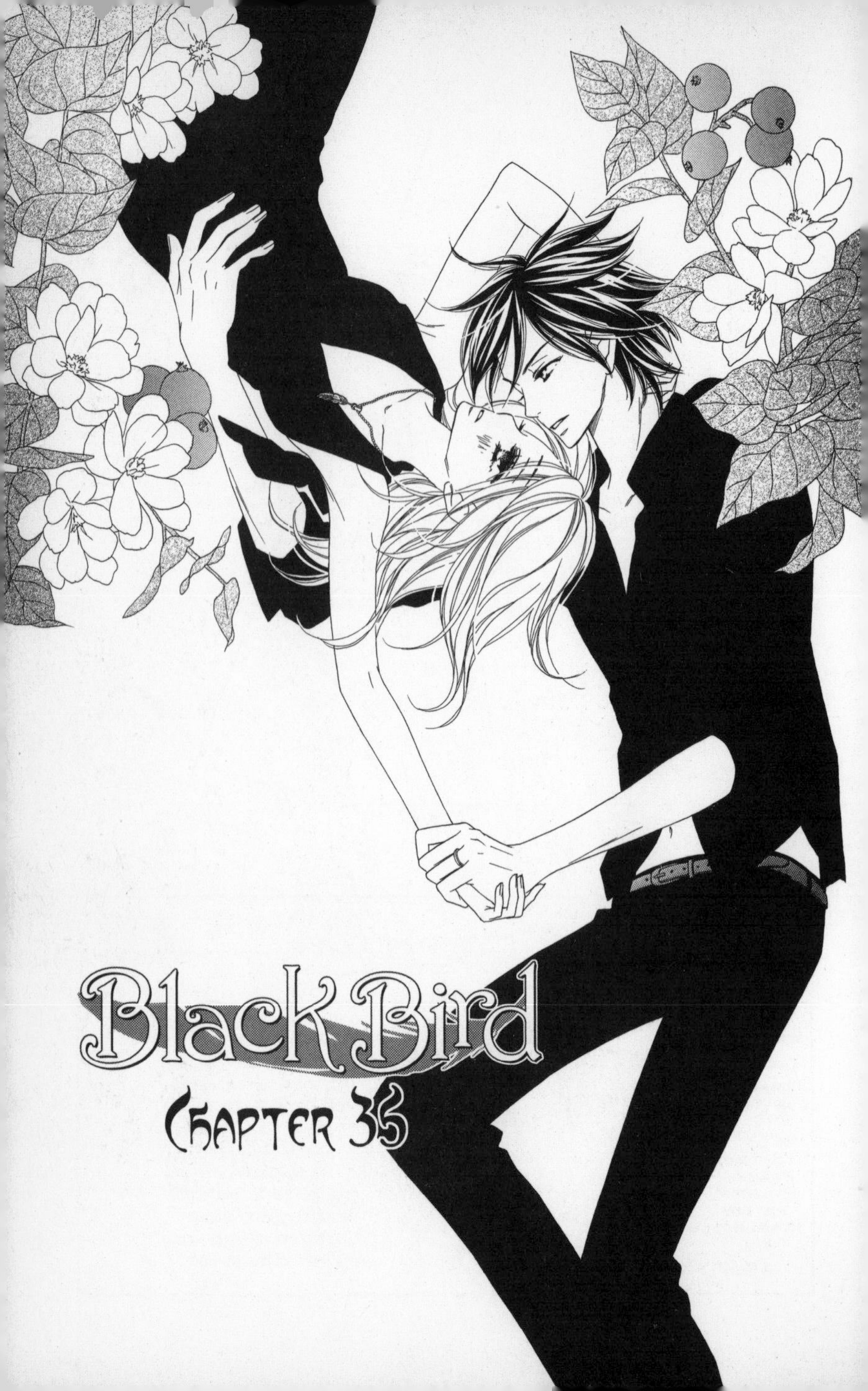
Black Bird
Chapter 36

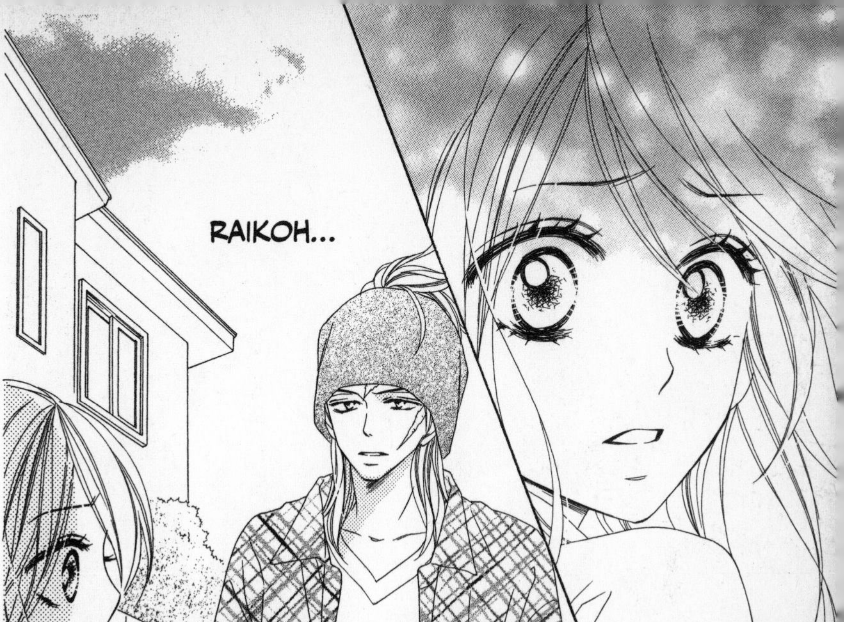
RAIKOH...
MISAO...

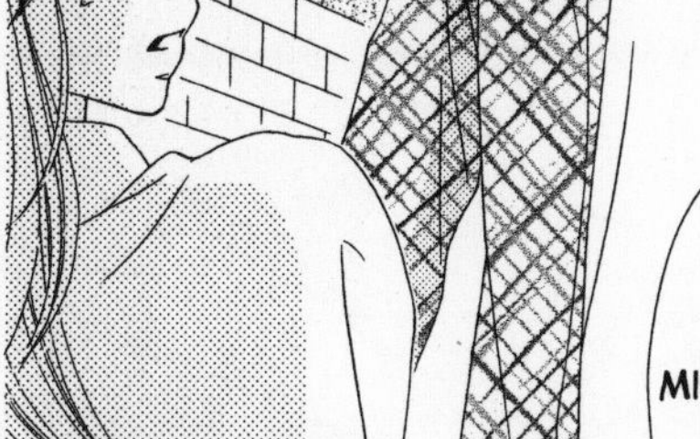
Repeating
Mind blank
Not a wink of sleep two nights before.
Thank you very much.
Thank you very much.
Smile frozen on face
I didn't even realize my under-kimono was **really** showing at my wrist.
Finger shaking

I'm sorry for being a creator like this.

When Volume 8 went on sale, I did my first book signing. Thank you very much to all who came, to those who sent me letters and emails saying that they wanted to come, and to the people from Nishizawa Bookstore's Kita Store in Fukushima who invited me to come!!

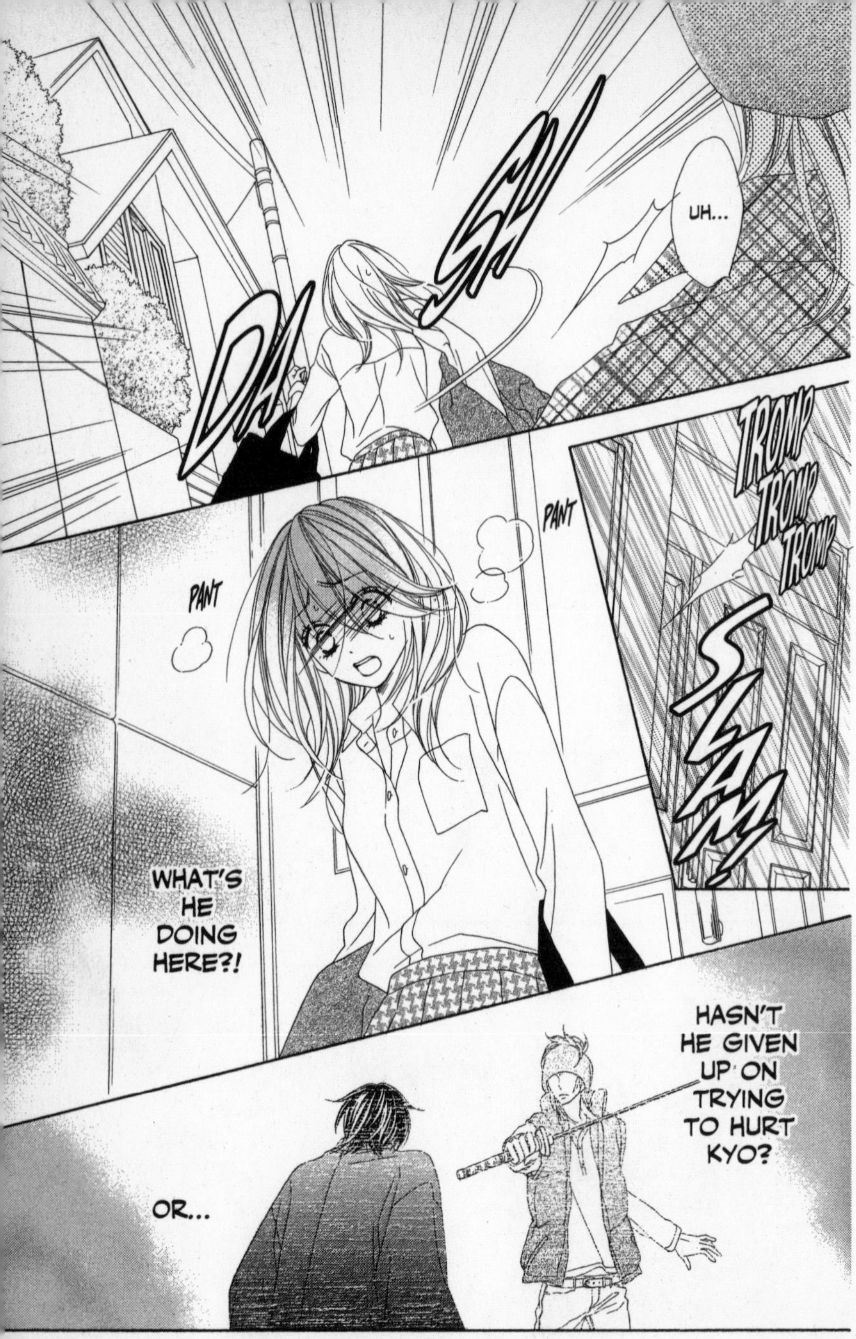
UH...
DASH
TROMP TROMP TROMP
SLAM!
PANT
PANT
WHAT'S HE DOING HERE?!
HASN'T HE GIVEN UP ON TRYING TO HURT KYO?
OR...

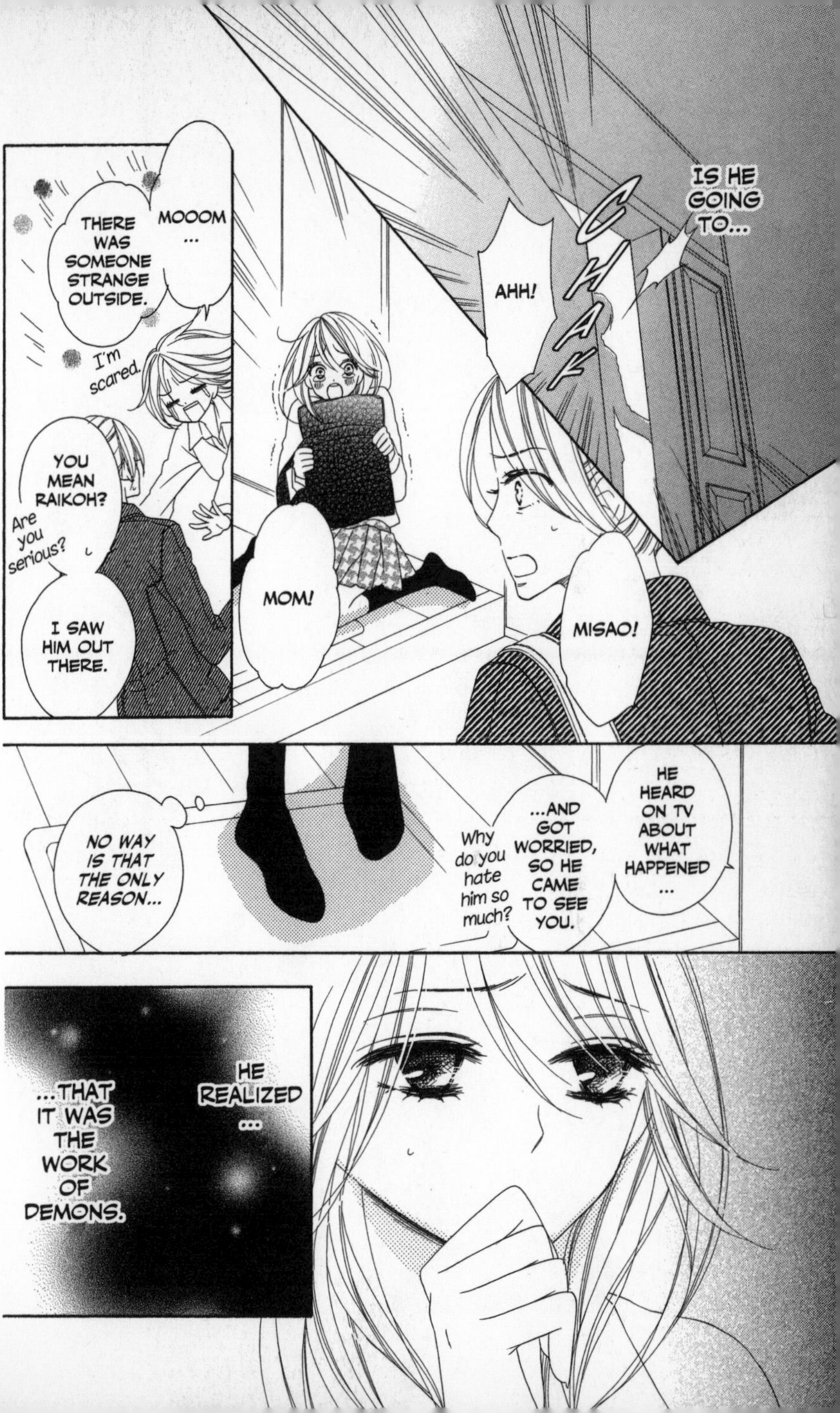
IS HE GOING TO...
CHAK
AHH!
MISAO!
MOM!
MOOOM...
THERE WAS SOMEONE STRANGE OUTSIDE.
I'm scared.
YOU MEAN RAIKOH?
Are you serious?
I SAW HIM OUT THERE.
HE HEARD ON TV ABOUT WHAT HAPPENED...
...AND GOT WORRIED, SO HE CAME TO SEE YOU.
Why do you hate him so much?
NO WAY IS THAT THE ONLY REASON...
HE REALIZED...
...THAT IT WAS THE WORK OF DEMONS.

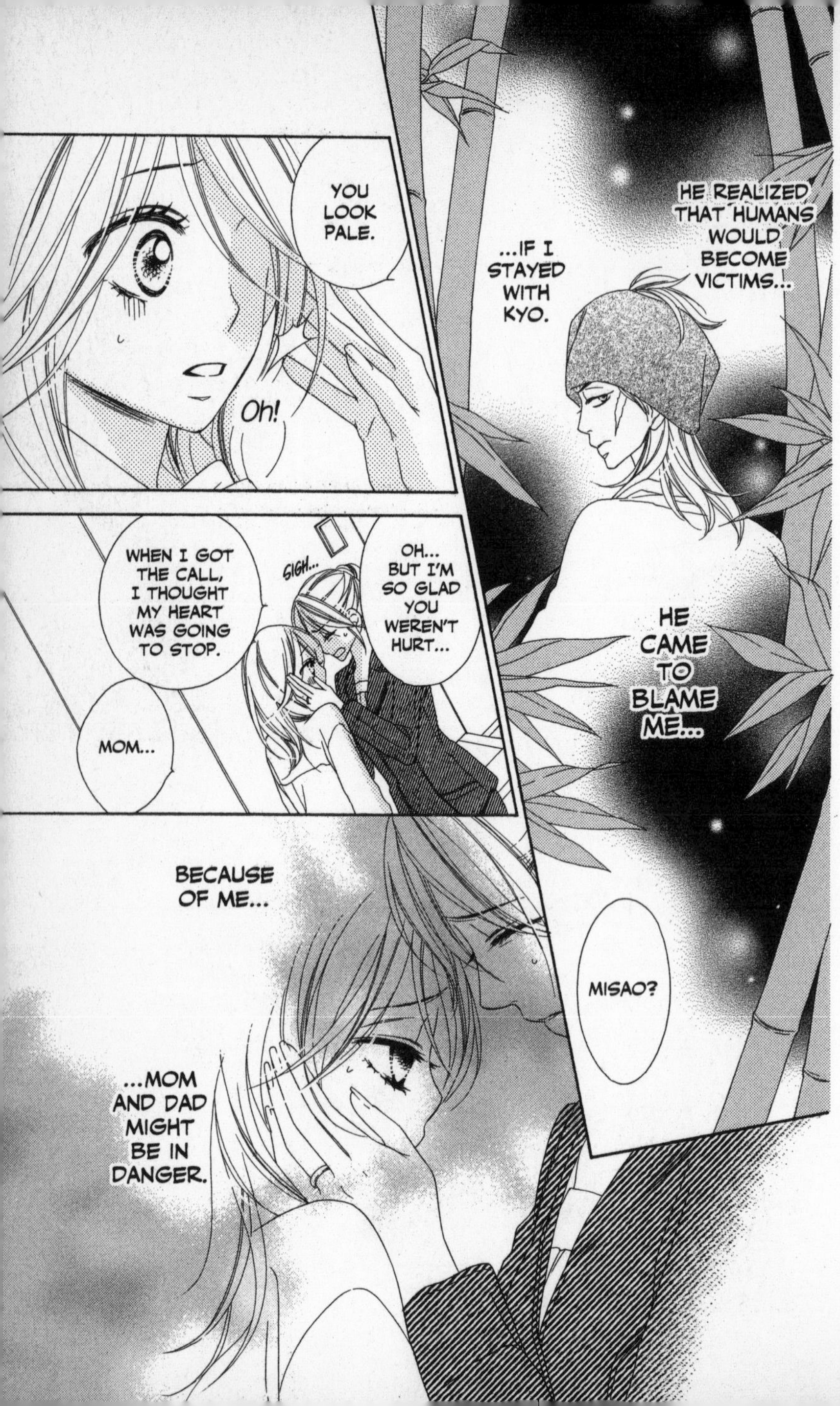
HE REALIZED THAT HUMANS WOULD BECOME VICTIMS...
...IF I STAYED WITH KYO.
HE CAME TO BLAME ME...
MISAO?
YOU LOOK PALE.
Oh!
OH... BUT I'M SO GLAD YOU WEREN'T HURT...
SIGH...
WHEN I GOT THE CALL, I THOUGHT MY HEART WAS GOING TO STOP.
MOM...
BECAUSE OF ME...
...MOM AND DAD MIGHT BE IN DANGER.

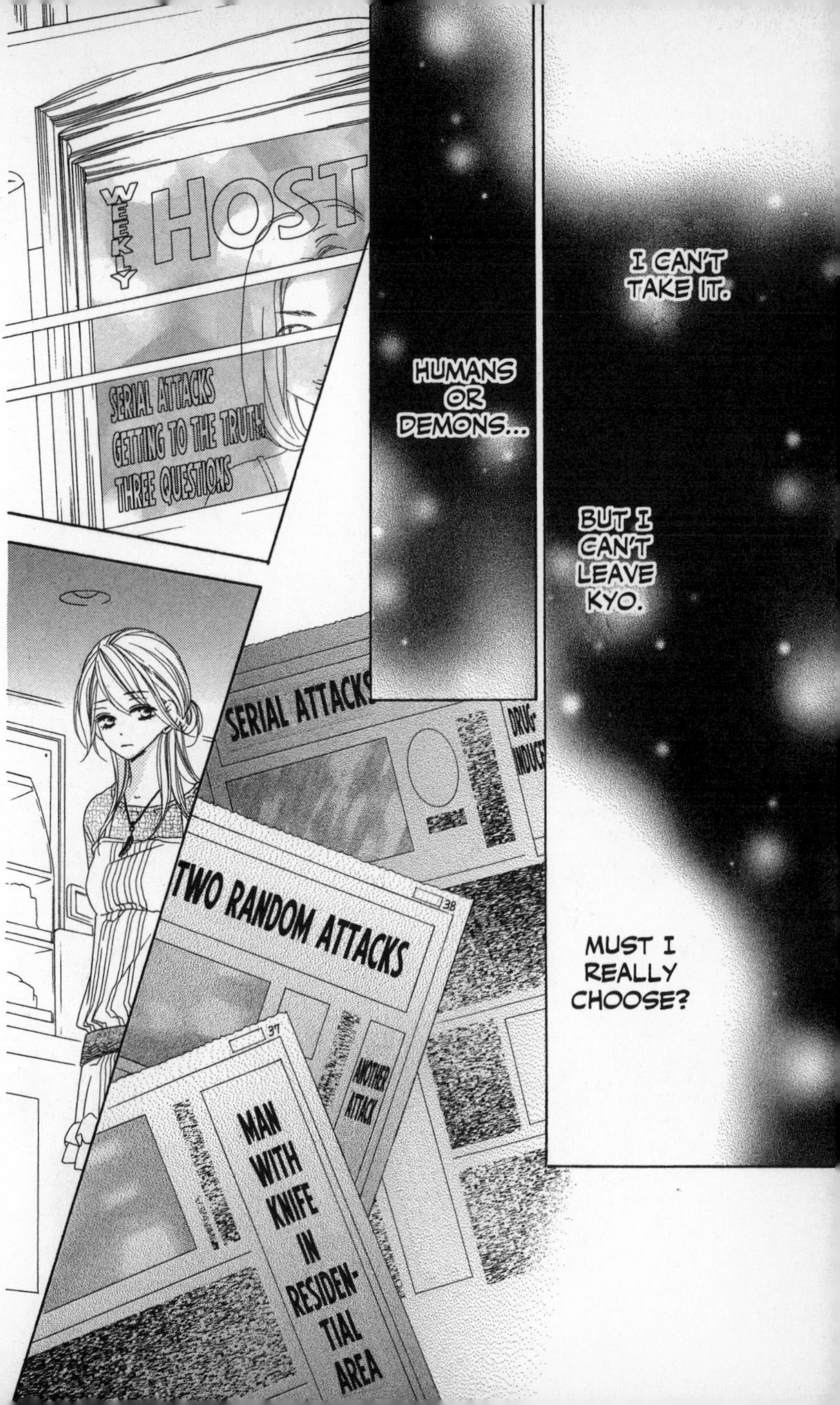
I CAN'T TAKE IT.
HUMANS OR DEMONS...
BUT I CAN'T LEAVE KYO.
MUST I REALLY CHOOSE?
WEEKLY HOST
SERIAL ATTACKS
GETTING TO THE TRUTH!
THREE QUESTIONS
SERIAL ATTACKS
TWO RANDOM ATTACKS
ANOTHER ATTACK
MAN WITH KNIFE IN RESIDENTIAL AREA

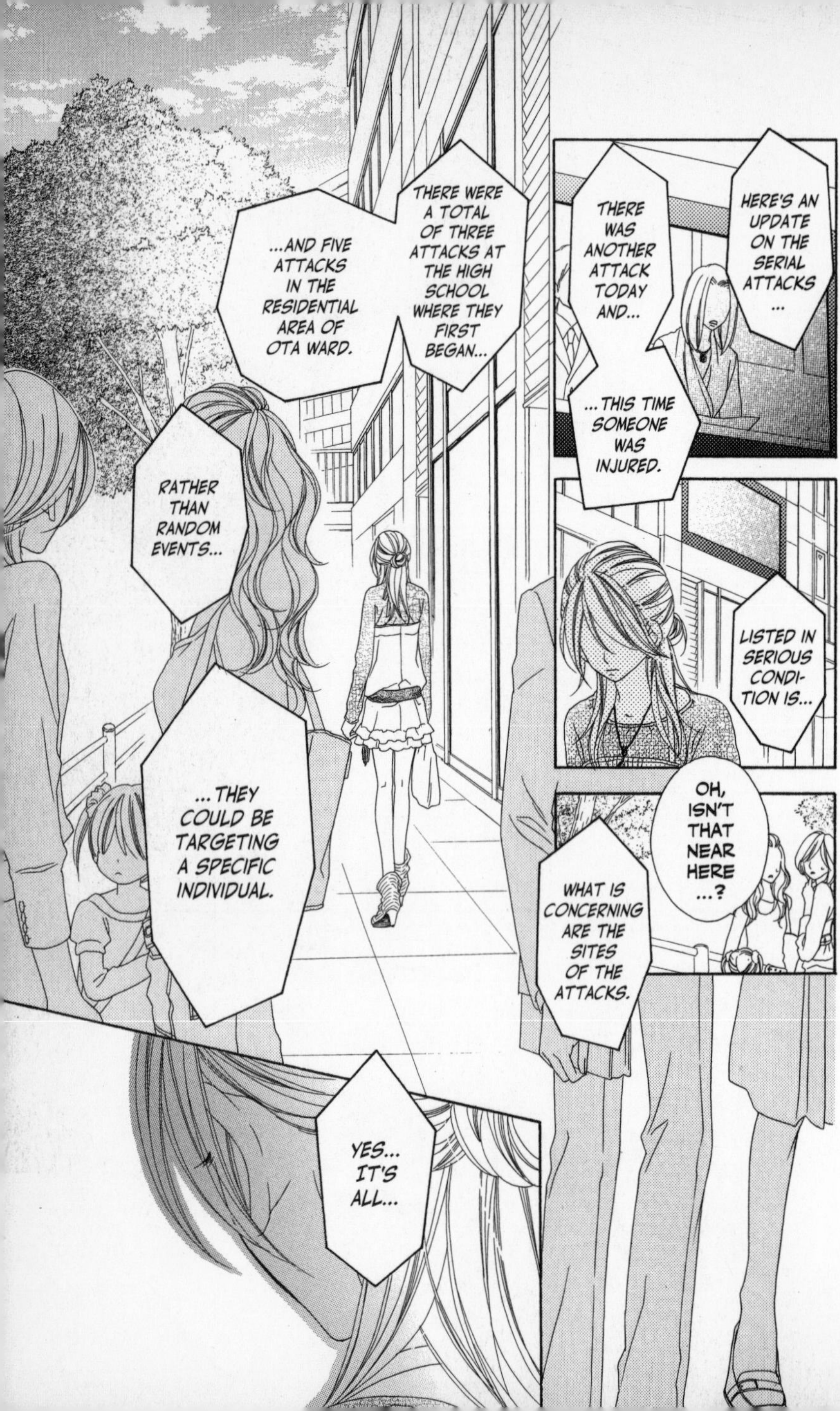
HERE'S AN UPDATE ON THE SERIAL ATTACKS ...
THERE WAS ANOTHER ATTACK TODAY AND...
...THIS TIME SOMEONE WAS INJURED.
LISTED IN SERIOUS CONDITION IS...
OH, ISN'T THAT NEAR HERE ...?
WHAT IS CONCERNING ARE THE SITES OF THE ATTACKS.
THERE WERE A TOTAL OF THREE ATTACKS AT THE HIGH SCHOOL WHERE THEY FIRST BEGAN...
...AND FIVE ATTACKS IN THE RESIDENTIAL AREA OF OTA WARD.
RATHER THAN RANDOM EVENTS...
...THEY COULD BE TARGETING A SPECIFIC INDIVIDUAL.
YES... IT'S ALL...

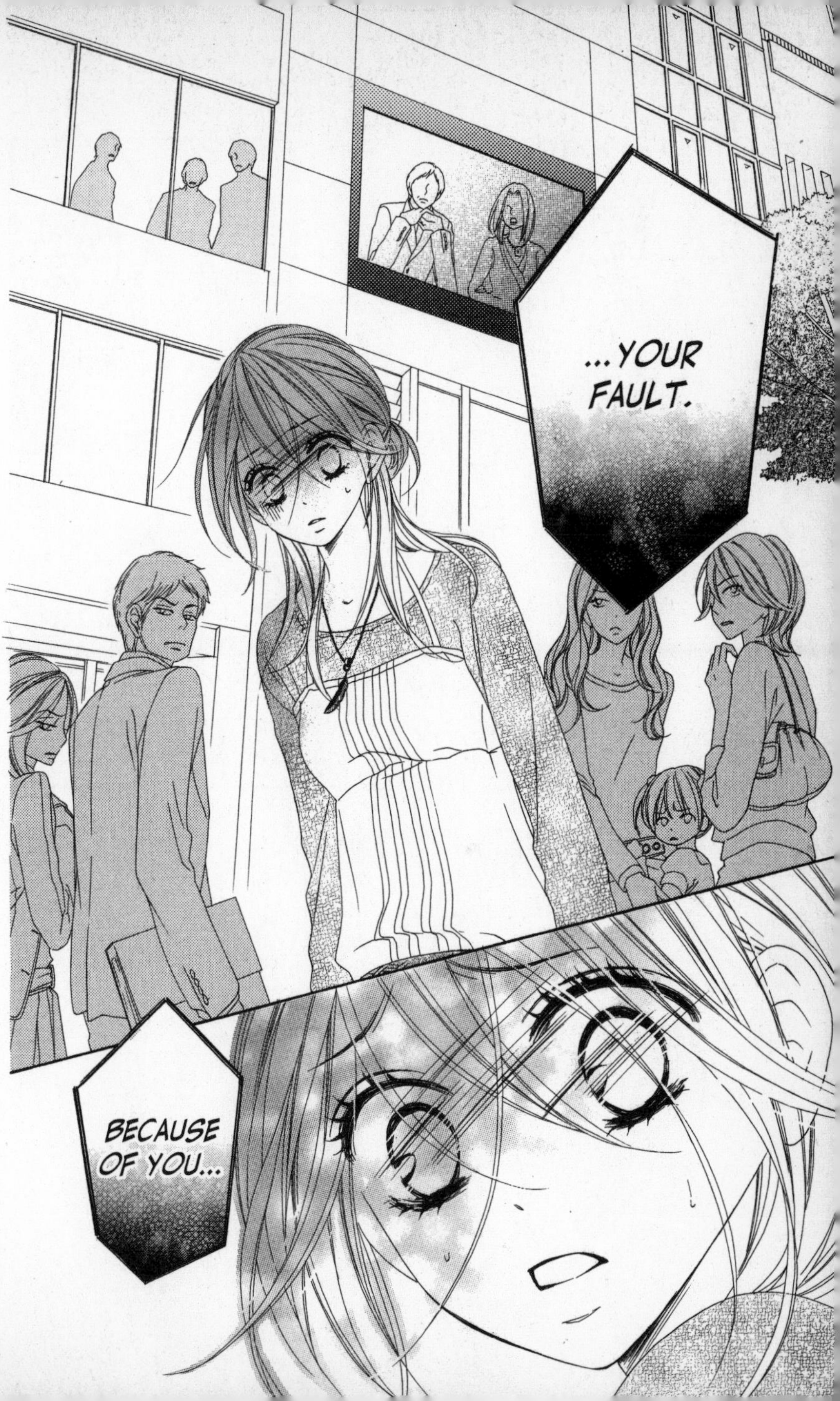
...YOUR FAULT.
BECAUSE OF YOU...

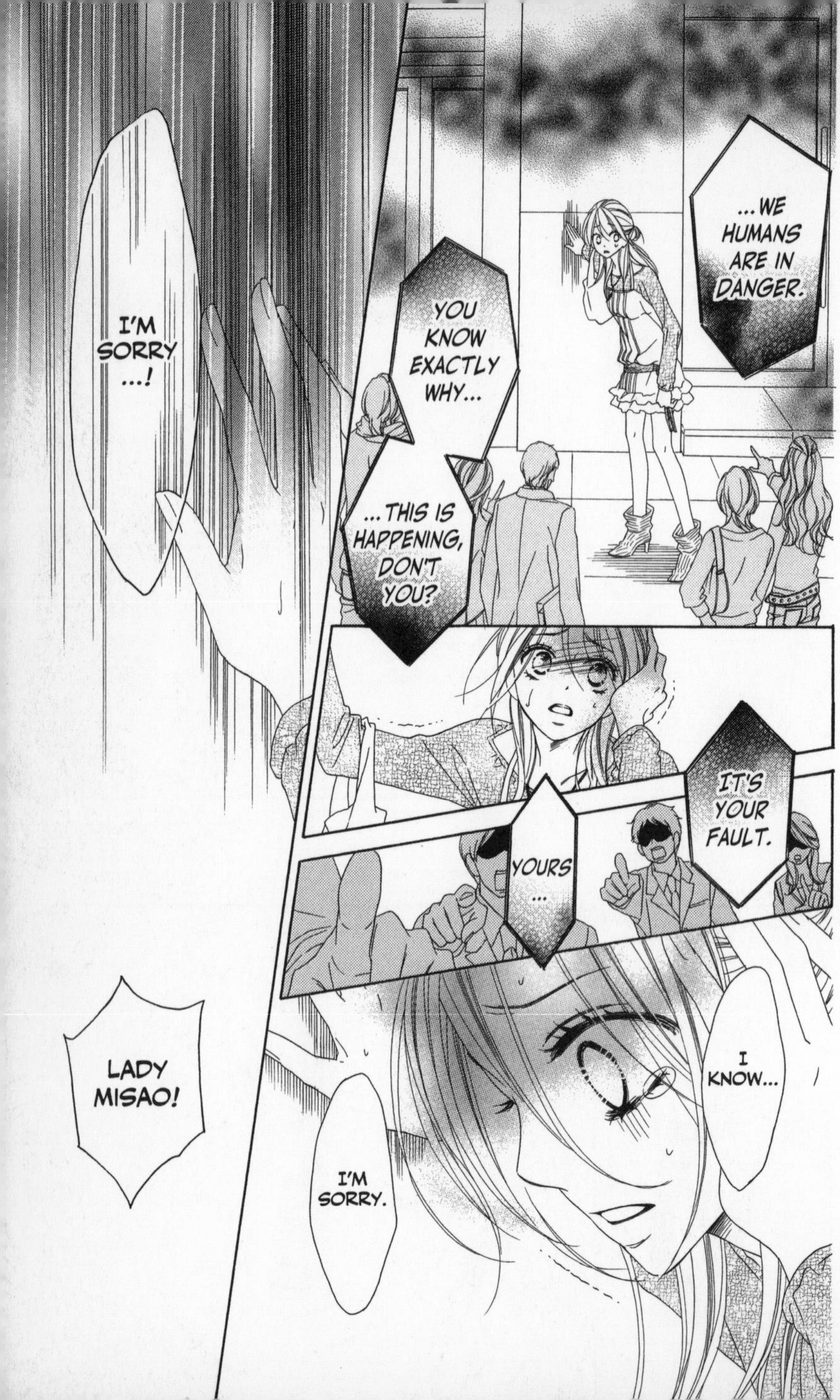
...WE HUMANS ARE IN DANGER.
YOU KNOW EXACTLY WHY...
...THIS IS HAPPENING, DON'T YOU?
IT'S YOUR FAULT.
YOURS...
I KNOW...
I'M SORRY.
I'M SORRY...!
LADY MISAO!

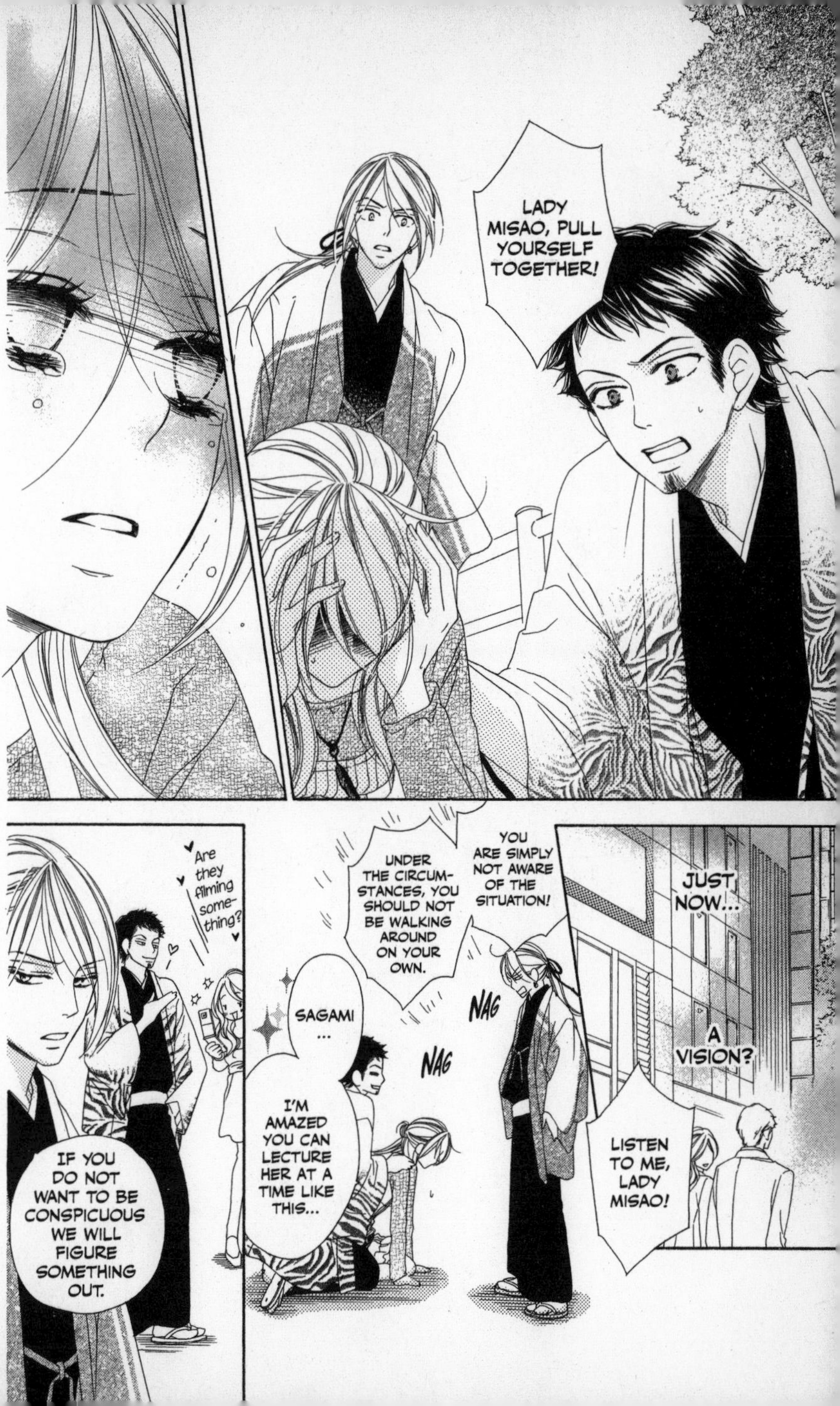

LADY MISAO, PULL YOURSELF TOGETHER!
JUST NOW...
A VISION?
LISTEN TO ME, LADY MISAO!
YOU ARE SIMPLY NOT AWARE OF THE SITUATION!
UNDER THE CIRCUMSTANCES, YOU SHOULD NOT BE WALKING AROUND ON YOUR OWN.
NAG
NAG
SAGAMI ...
I'M AMAZED YOU CAN LECTURE HER AT A TIME LIKE THIS...
Are they filming something?
IF YOU DO NOT WANT TO BE CONSPICUOUS WE WILL FIGURE SOMETHING OUT.

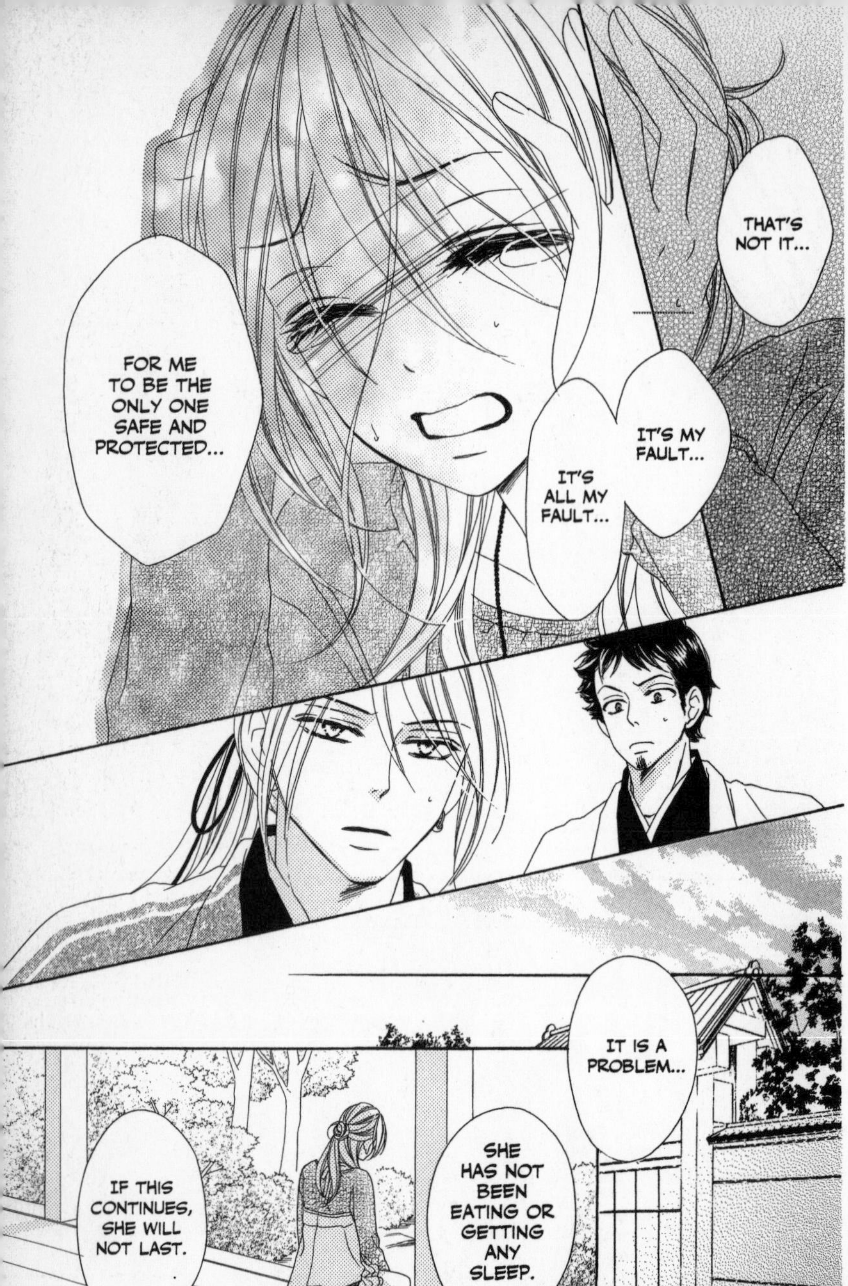
THAT'S NOT IT...
IT'S MY FAULT...
IT'S ALL MY FAULT...
FOR ME TO BE THE ONLY ONE SAFE AND PROTECTED...
IT IS A PROBLEM...
SHE HAS NOT BEEN EATING OR GETTING ANY SLEEP.
IF THIS CONTINUES, SHE WILL NOT LAST.

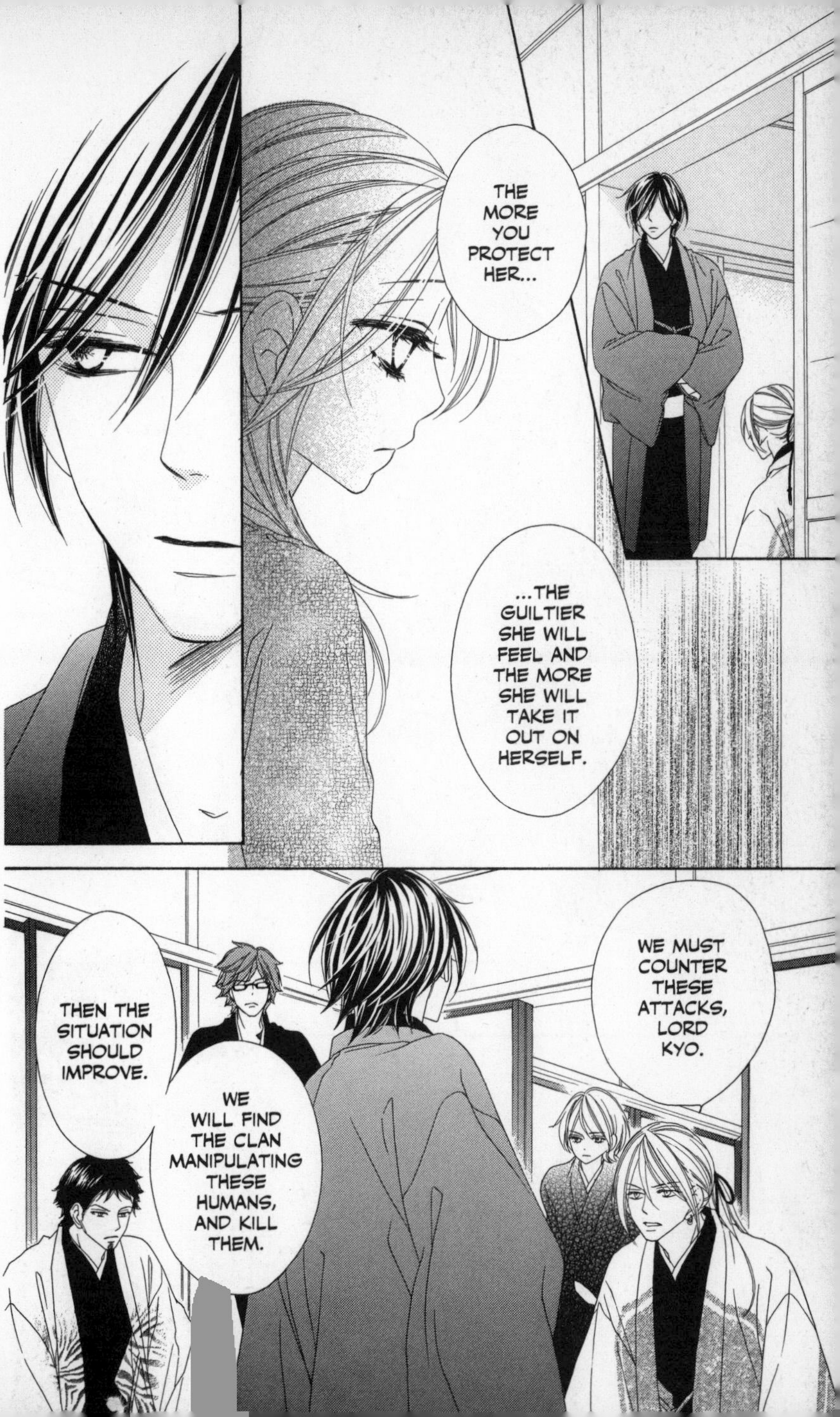
THE MORE YOU PROTECT HER...
...THE GUILTIER SHE WILL FEEL AND THE MORE SHE WILL TAKE IT OUT ON HERSELF.
WE MUST COUNTER THESE ATTACKS, LORD KYO.
THEN THE SITUATION SHOULD IMPROVE.
WE WILL FIND THE CLAN MANIPULATING THESE HUMANS, AND KILL THEM.

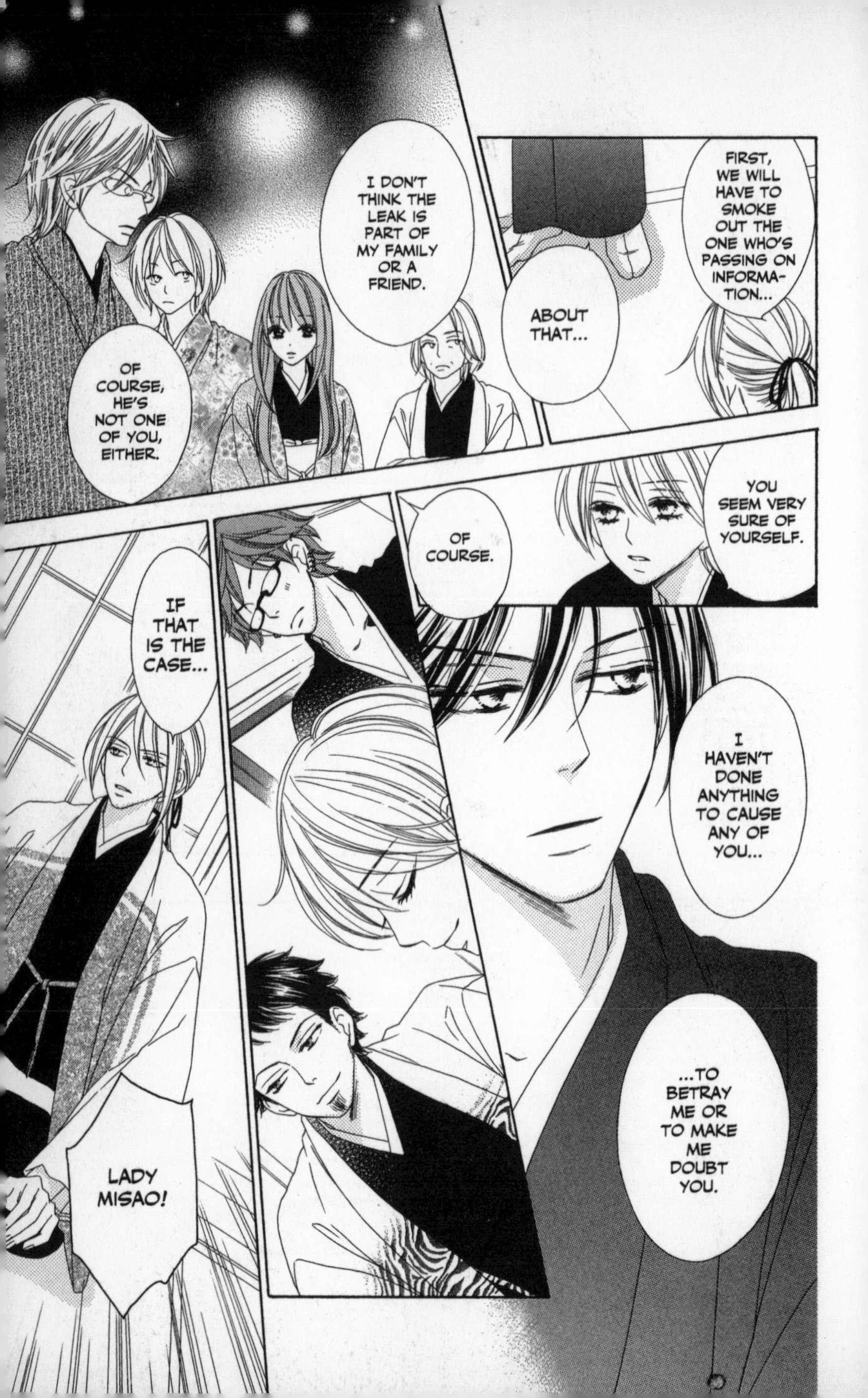
FIRST, WE WILL HAVE TO SMOKE OUT THE ONE WHO'S PASSING ON INFORMATION...
ABOUT THAT...
I DON'T THINK THE LEAK IS PART OF MY FAMILY OR A FRIEND.
OF COURSE, HE'S NOT ONE OF YOU, EITHER.
YOU SEEM VERY SURE OF YOURSELF.
OF COURSE.
I HAVEN'T DONE ANYTHING TO CAUSE ANY OF YOU...
...TO BETRAY ME OR TO MAKE ME DOUBT YOU.
IF THAT IS THE CASE...
LADY MISAO!

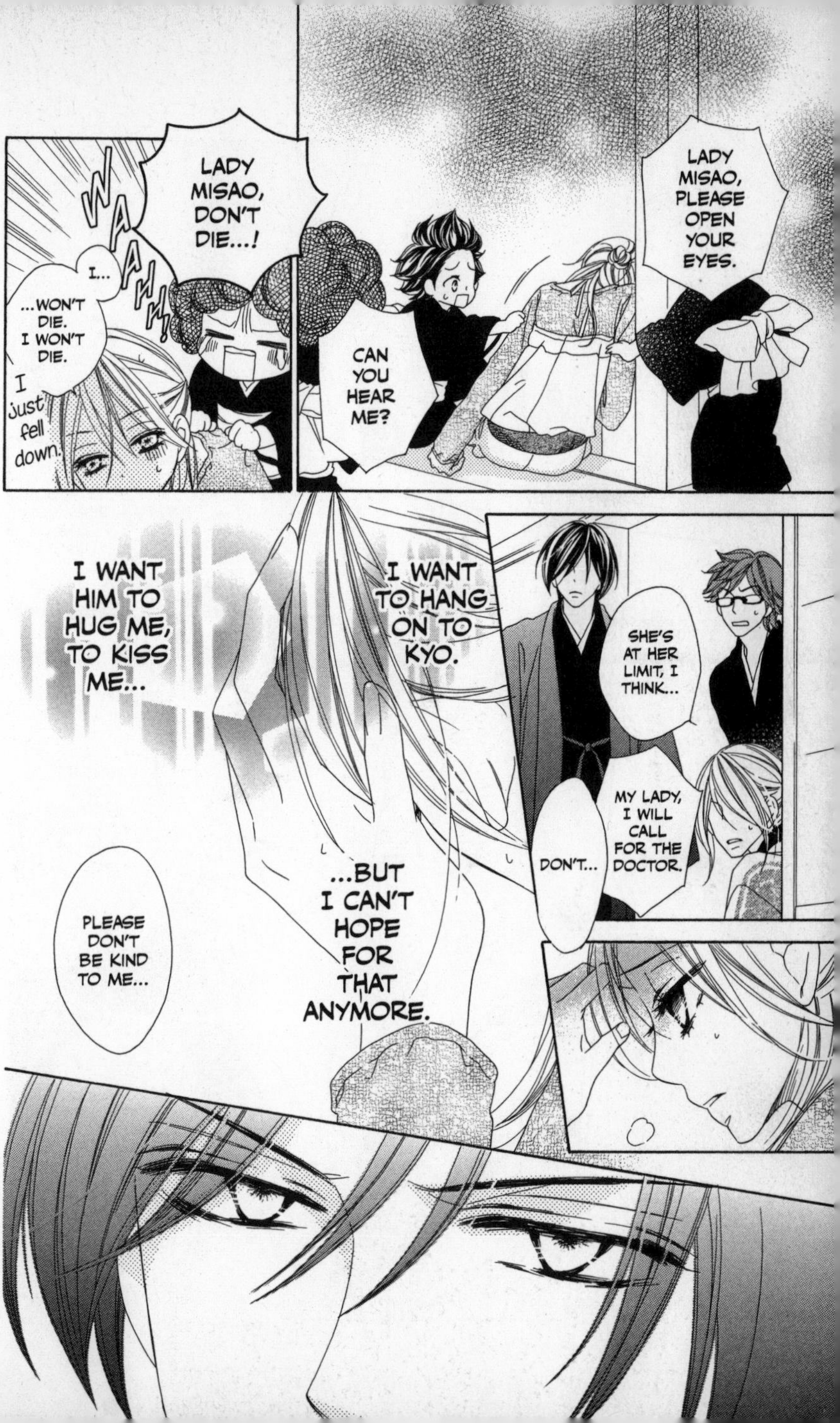

LADY MISAO, PLEASE OPEN YOUR EYES.
CAN YOU HEAR ME?
LADY MISAO, DON'T DIE...!
WAAHH!
I...
...WON'T DIE. I WON'T DIE.
I just fell down.
SHE'S AT HER LIMIT, I THINK...
MY LADY, I WILL CALL FOR THE DOCTOR.
DON'T...
I WANT TO HANG ON TO KYO.
I WANT HIM TO HUG ME, TO KISS ME...
...BUT I CAN'T HOPE FOR THAT ANYMORE.
PLEASE DON'T BE KIND TO ME...

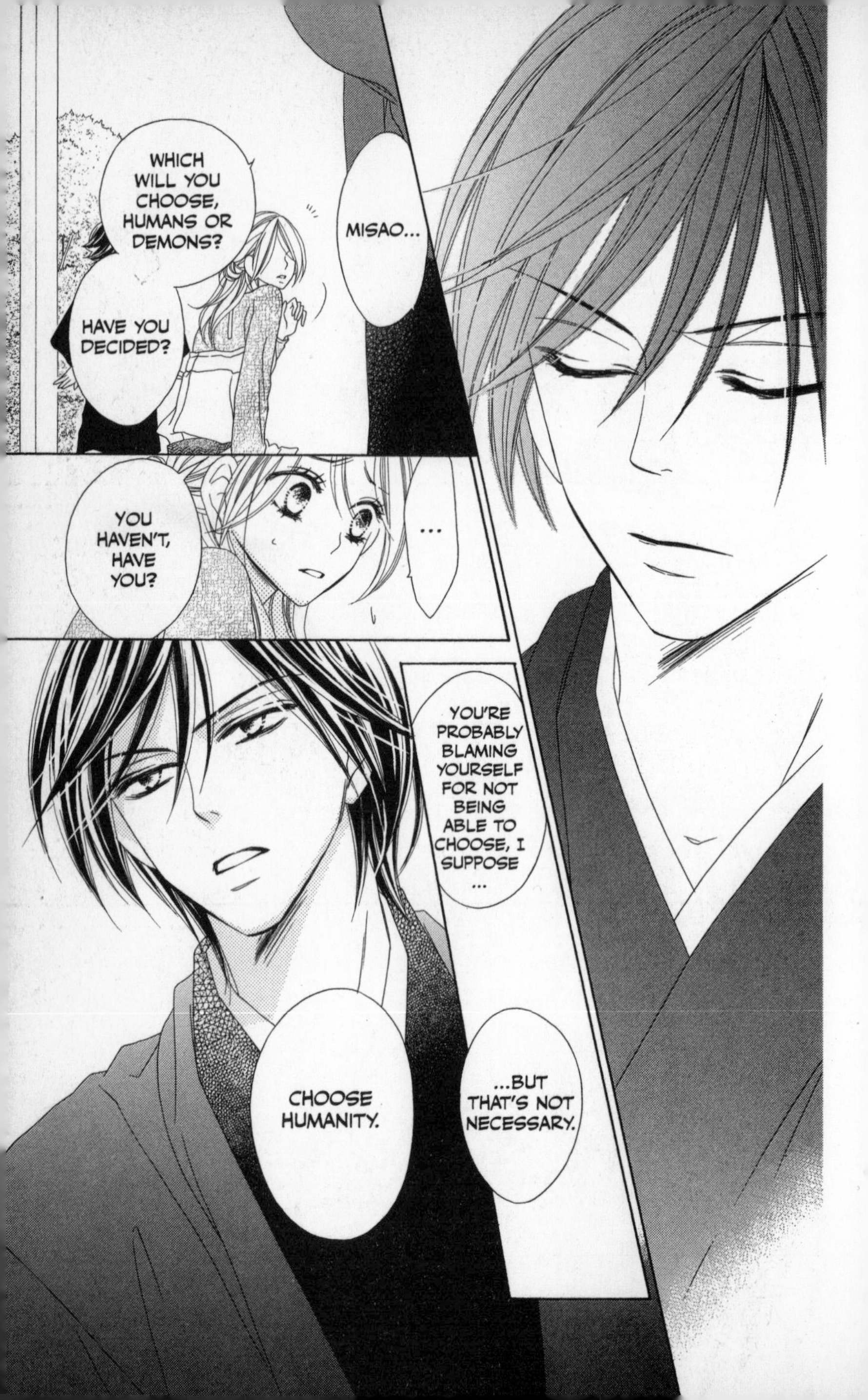
MISAO...
WHICH WILL YOU CHOOSE, HUMANS OR DEMONS?
HAVE YOU DECIDED?
...
YOU HAVEN'T, HAVE YOU?
YOU'RE PROBABLY BLAMING YOURSELF FOR NOT BEING ABLE TO CHOOSE, I SUPPOSE ...
...BUT THAT'S NOT NECESSARY.
CHOOSE HUMANITY.

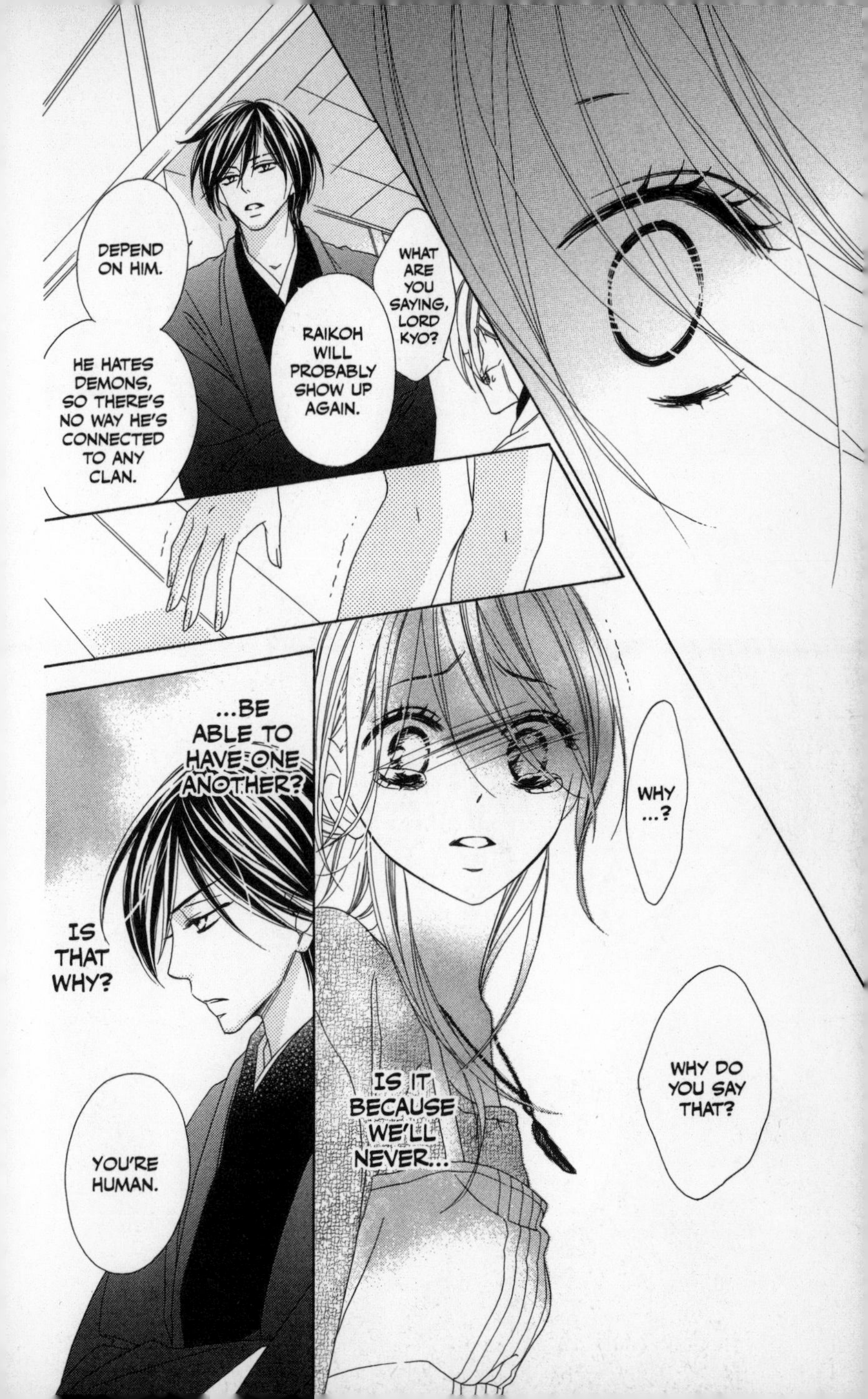
WHAT ARE YOU SAYING, LORD KYO?
RAIKOH WILL PROBABLY SHOW UP AGAIN.
DEPEND ON HIM.
HE HATES DEMONS, SO THERE'S NO WAY HE'S CONNECTED TO ANY CLAN.
WHY ...?
WHY DO YOU SAY THAT?
IS IT BECAUSE WE'LL NEVER...
...BE ABLE TO HAVE ONE ANOTHER?
IS THAT WHY?
YOU'RE HUMAN.

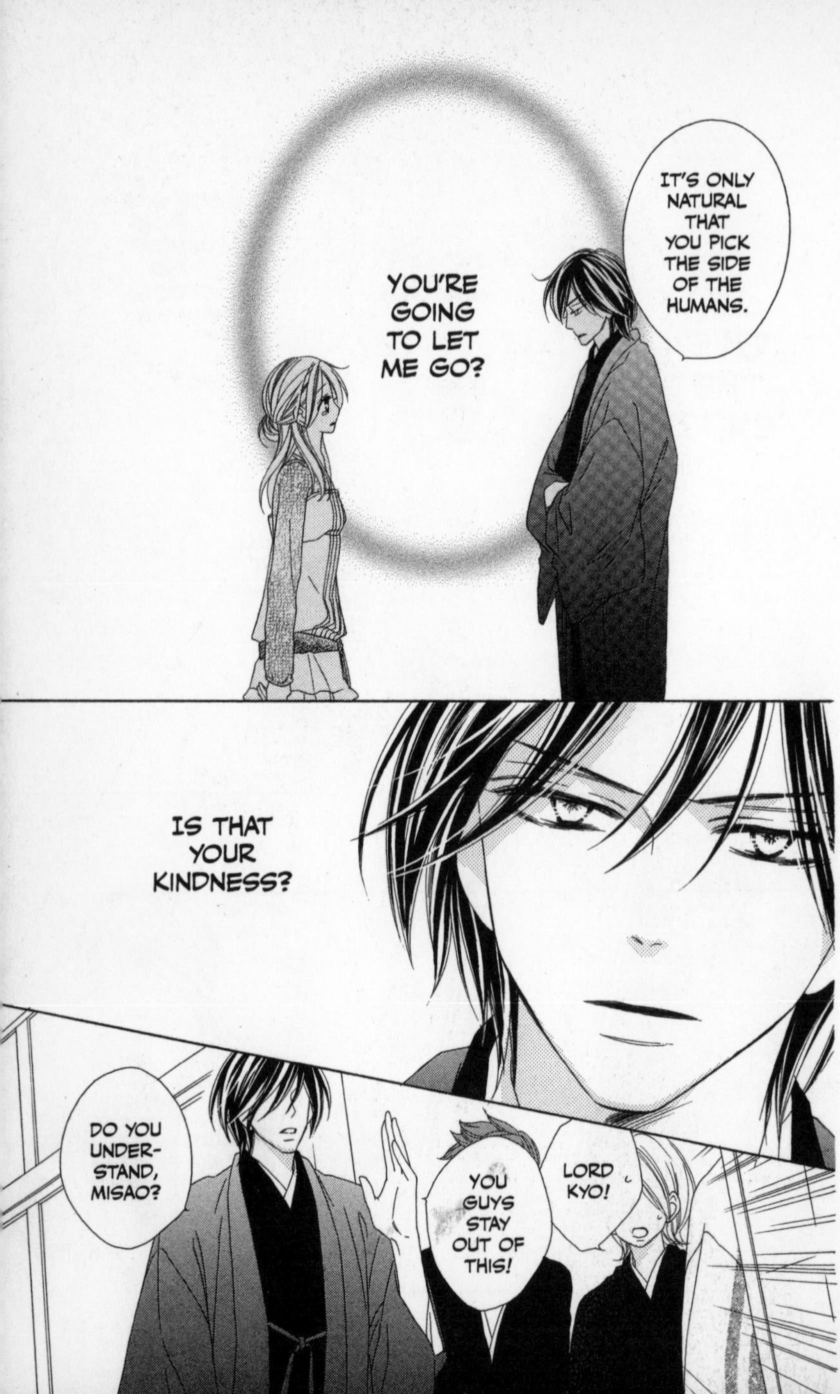
IT'S ONLY NATURAL THAT YOU PICK THE SIDE OF THE HUMANS.
YOU'RE GOING TO LET ME GO?
IS THAT YOUR KINDNESS?
LORD KYO!
YOU GUYS STAY OUT OF THIS!
DO YOU UNDER-STAND, MISAO?

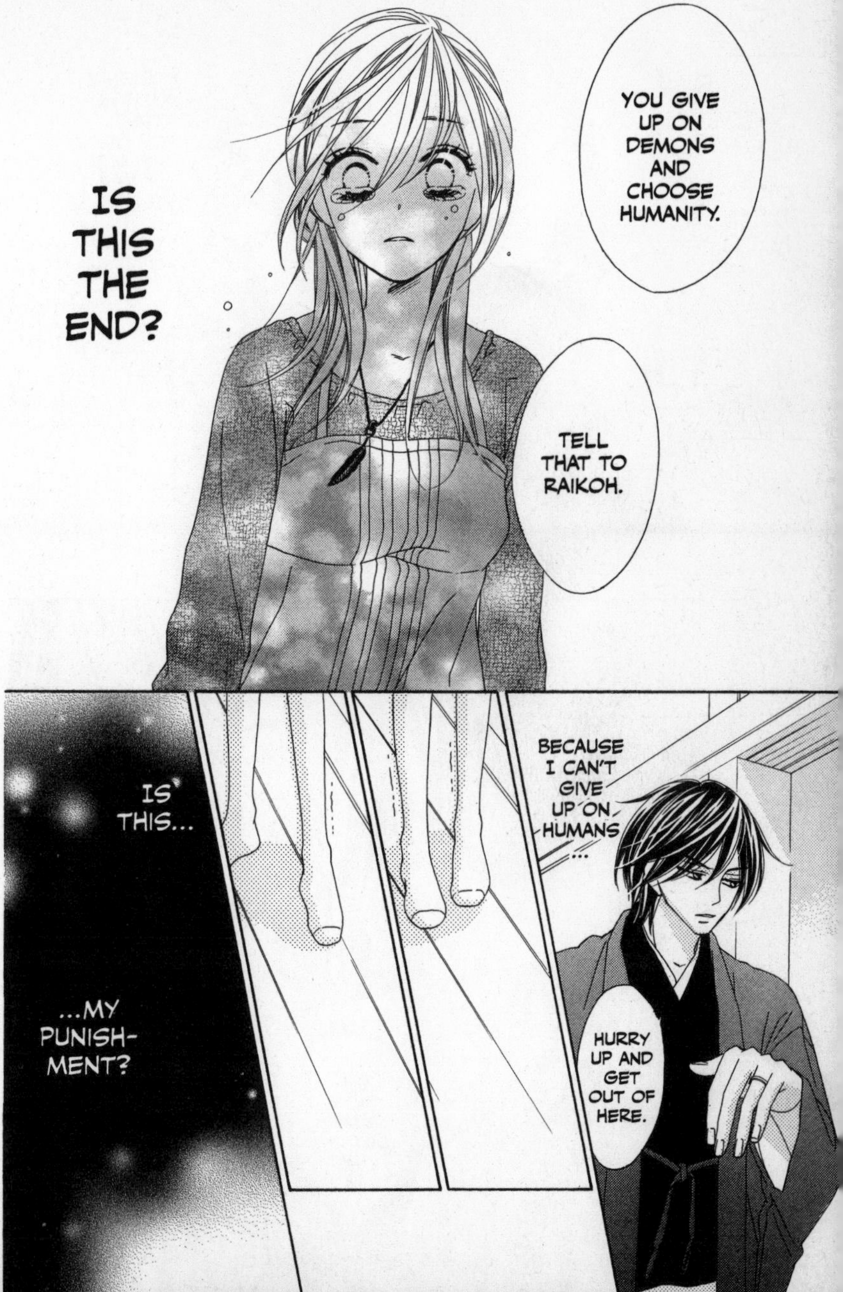
YOU GIVE UP ON DEMONS AND CHOOSE HUMANITY.
TELL THAT TO RAIKOH.
IS THIS THE END?
BECAUSE I CAN'T GIVE UP ON HUMANS...
HURRY UP AND GET OUT OF HERE.
IS THIS...
...MY PUNISH-MENT?

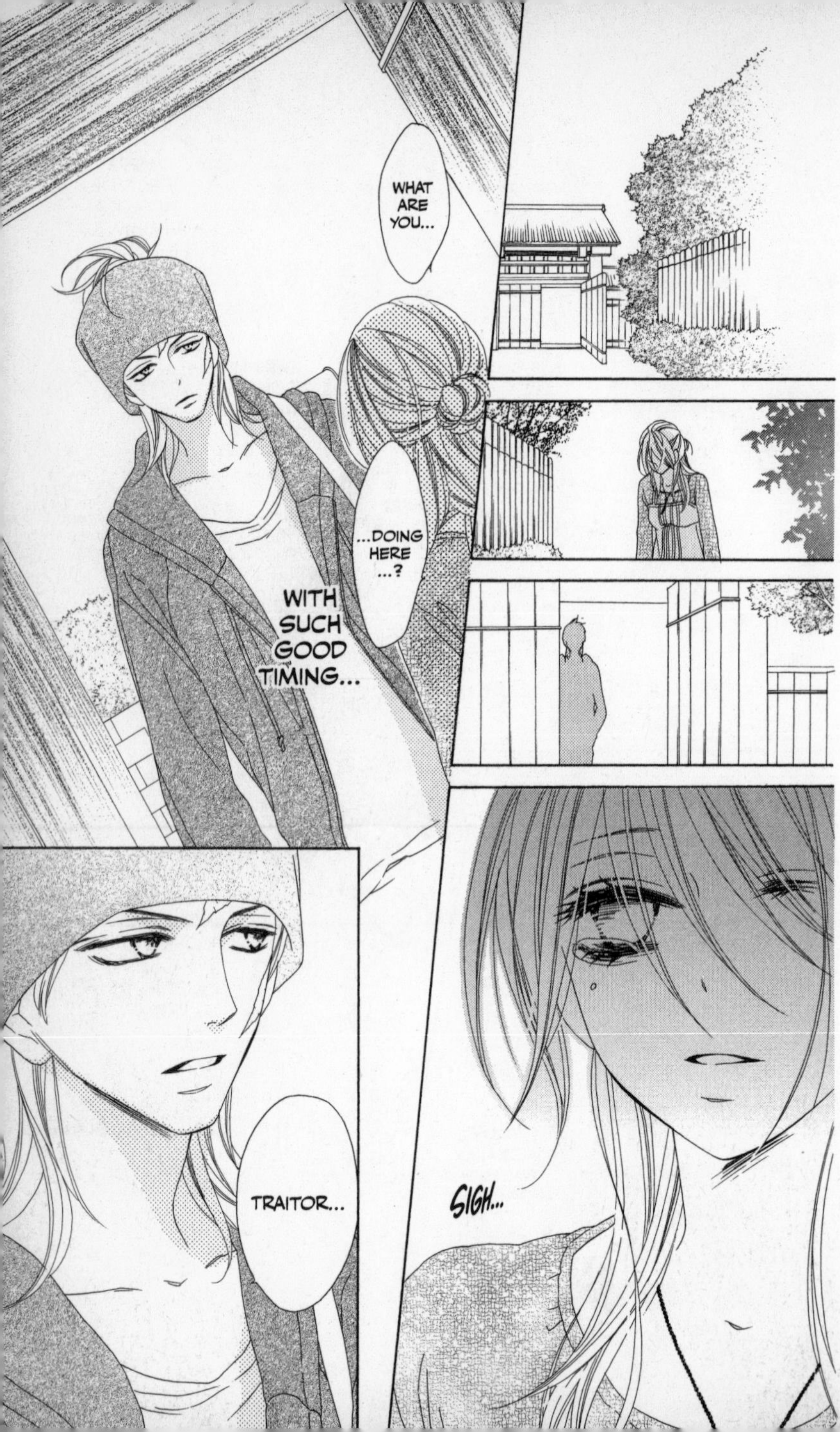
WHAT ARE YOU...
...DOING HERE ...?
WITH SUCH GOOD TIMING...
SIGH...
TRAITOR...

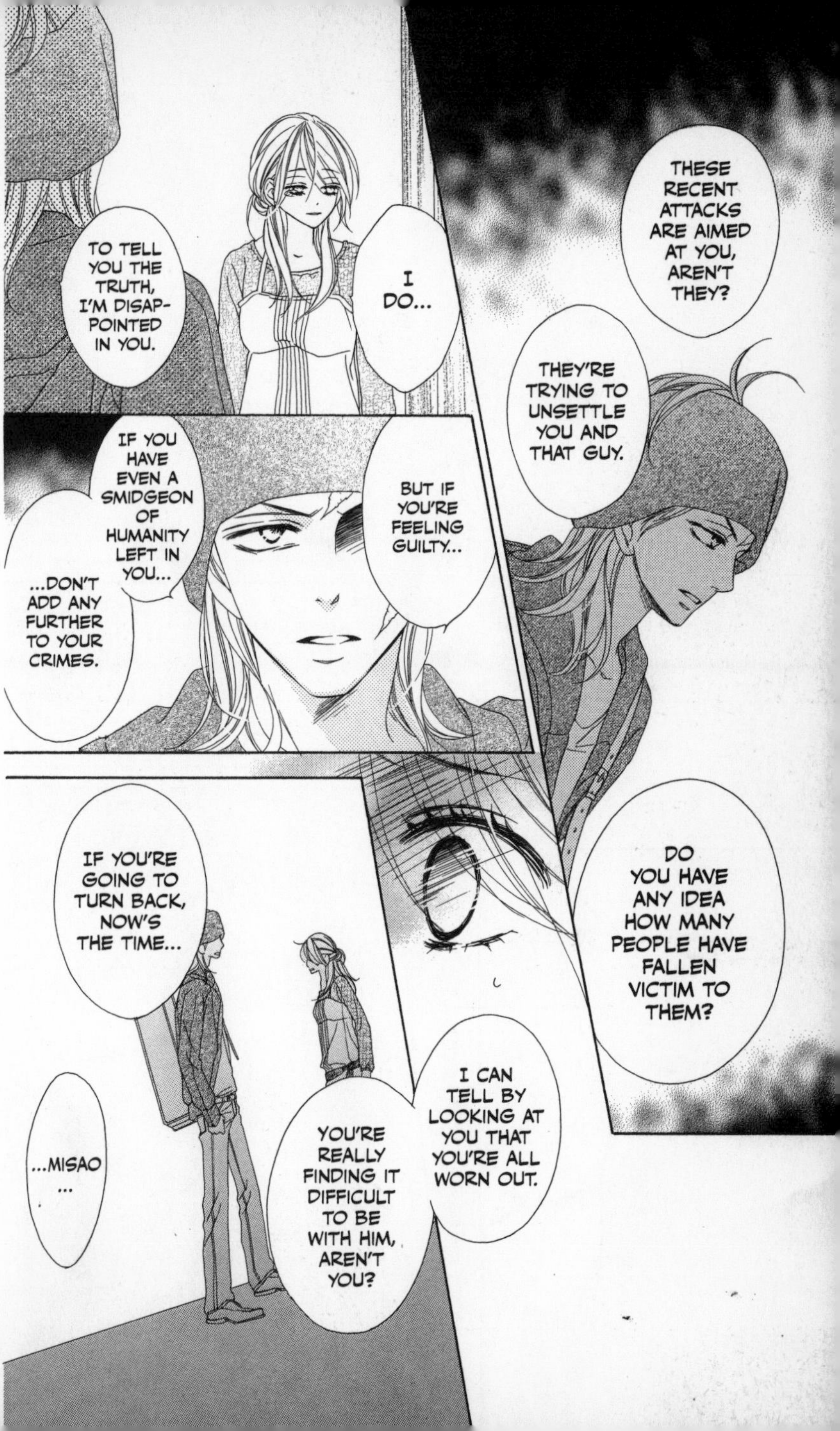
THESE RECENT ATTACKS ARE AIMED AT YOU, AREN'T THEY?
THEY'RE TRYING TO UNSETTLE YOU AND THAT GUY.
DO YOU HAVE ANY IDEA HOW MANY PEOPLE HAVE FALLEN VICTIM TO THEM?
I DO...
TO TELL YOU THE TRUTH, I'M DISAPPOINTED IN YOU.
BUT IF YOU'RE FEELING GUILTY...
IF YOU HAVE EVEN A SMIDGEON OF HUMANITY LEFT IN YOU...
...DON'T ADD ANY FURTHER TO YOUR CRIMES.
I CAN TELL BY LOOKING AT YOU THAT YOU'RE ALL WORN OUT.
YOU'RE REALLY FINDING IT DIFFICULT TO BE WITH HIM, AREN'T YOU?
IF YOU'RE GOING TO TURN BACK, NOW'S THE TIME...
...MISAO...

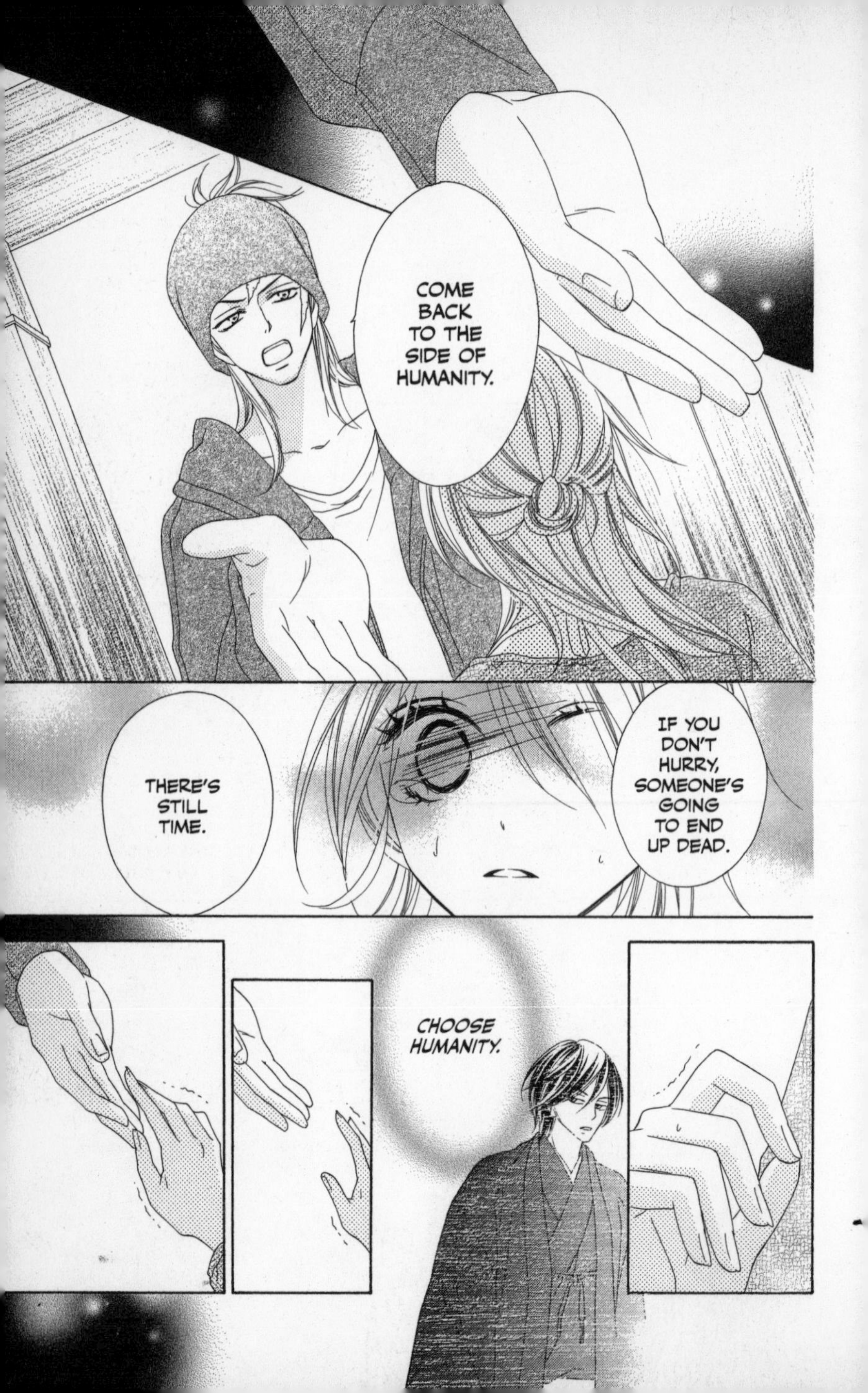
COME BACK TO THE SIDE OF HUMANITY.
IF YOU DON'T HURRY, SOMEONE'S GOING TO END UP DEAD.
THERE'S STILL TIME.
CHOOSE HUMANITY.

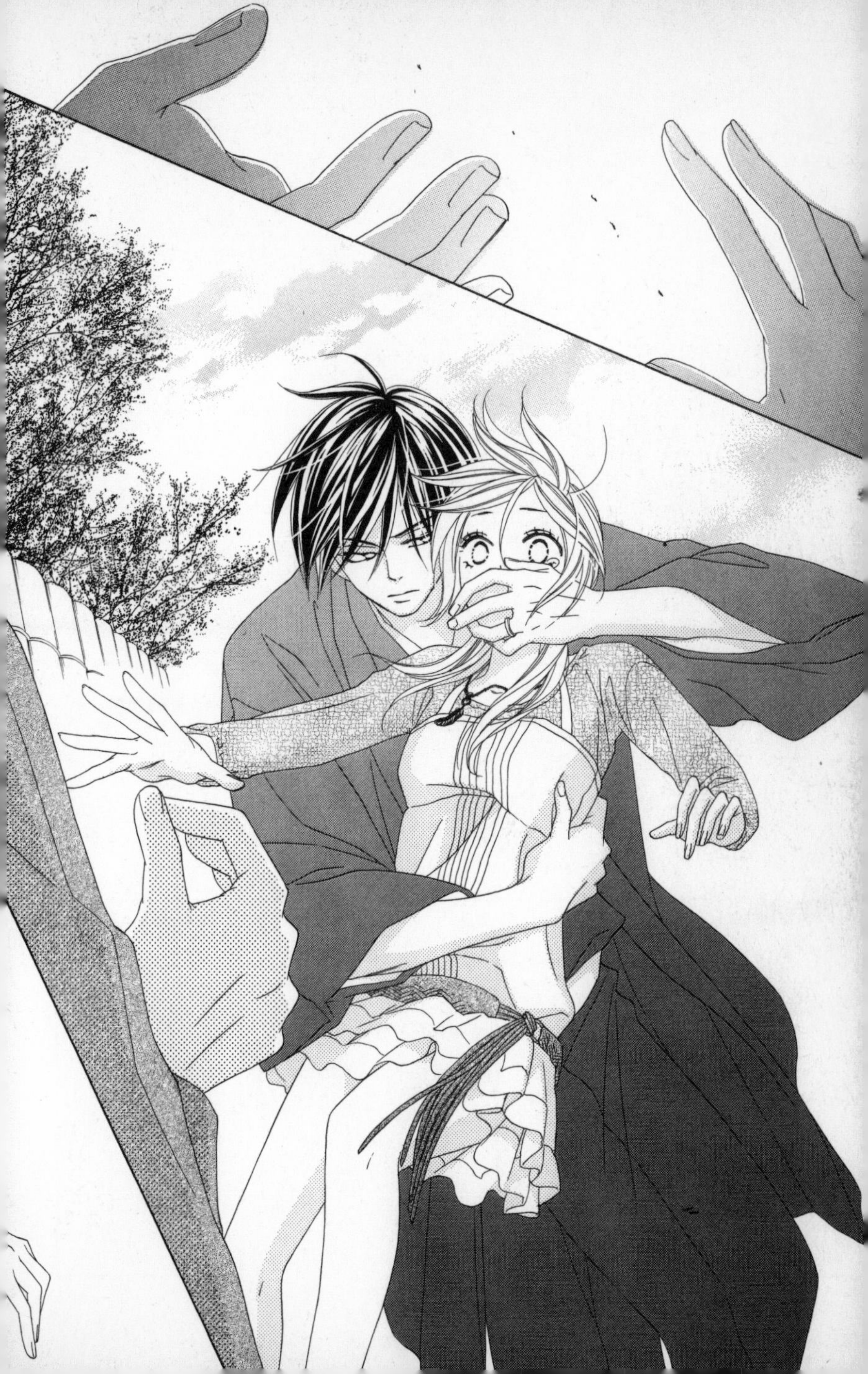

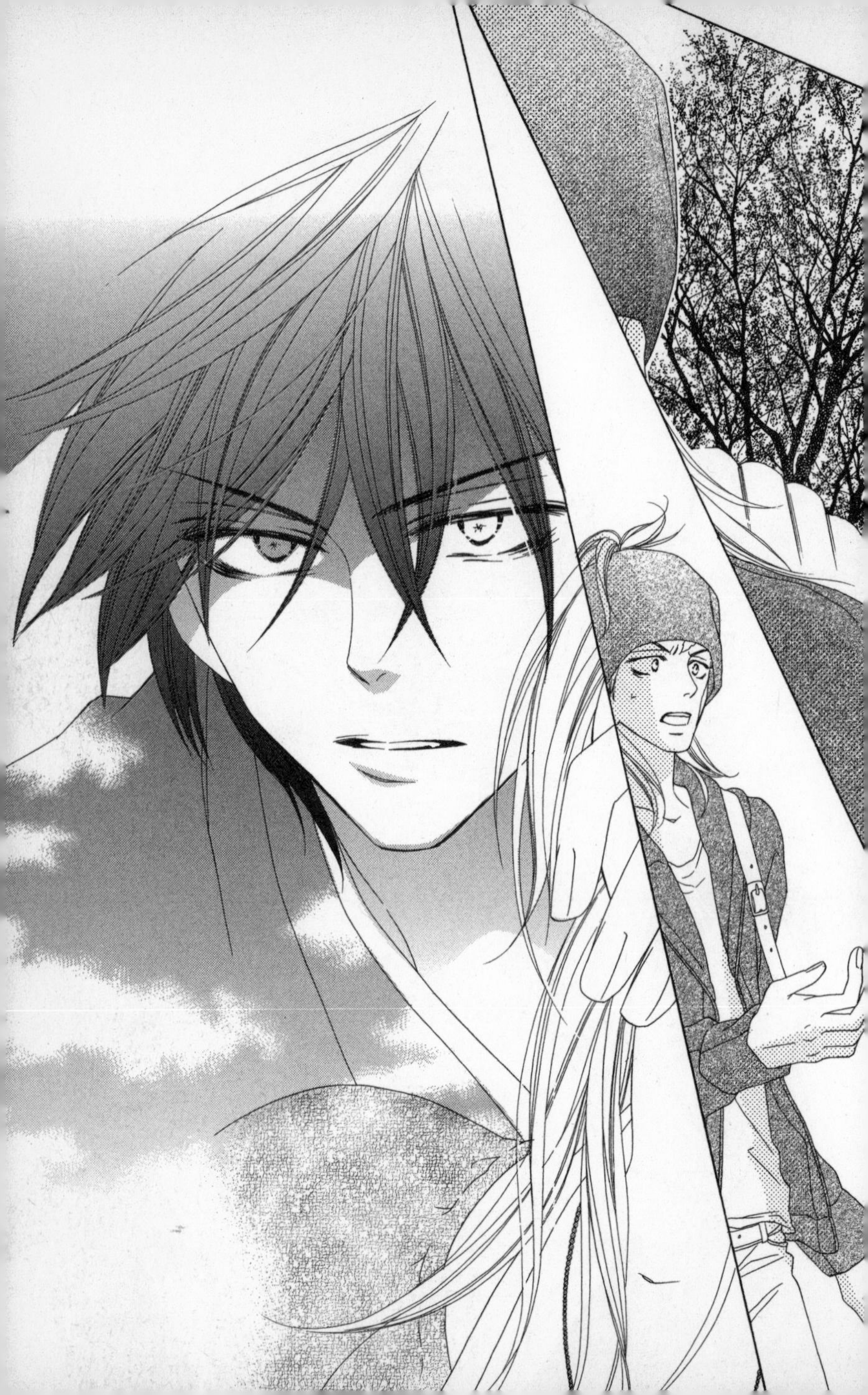

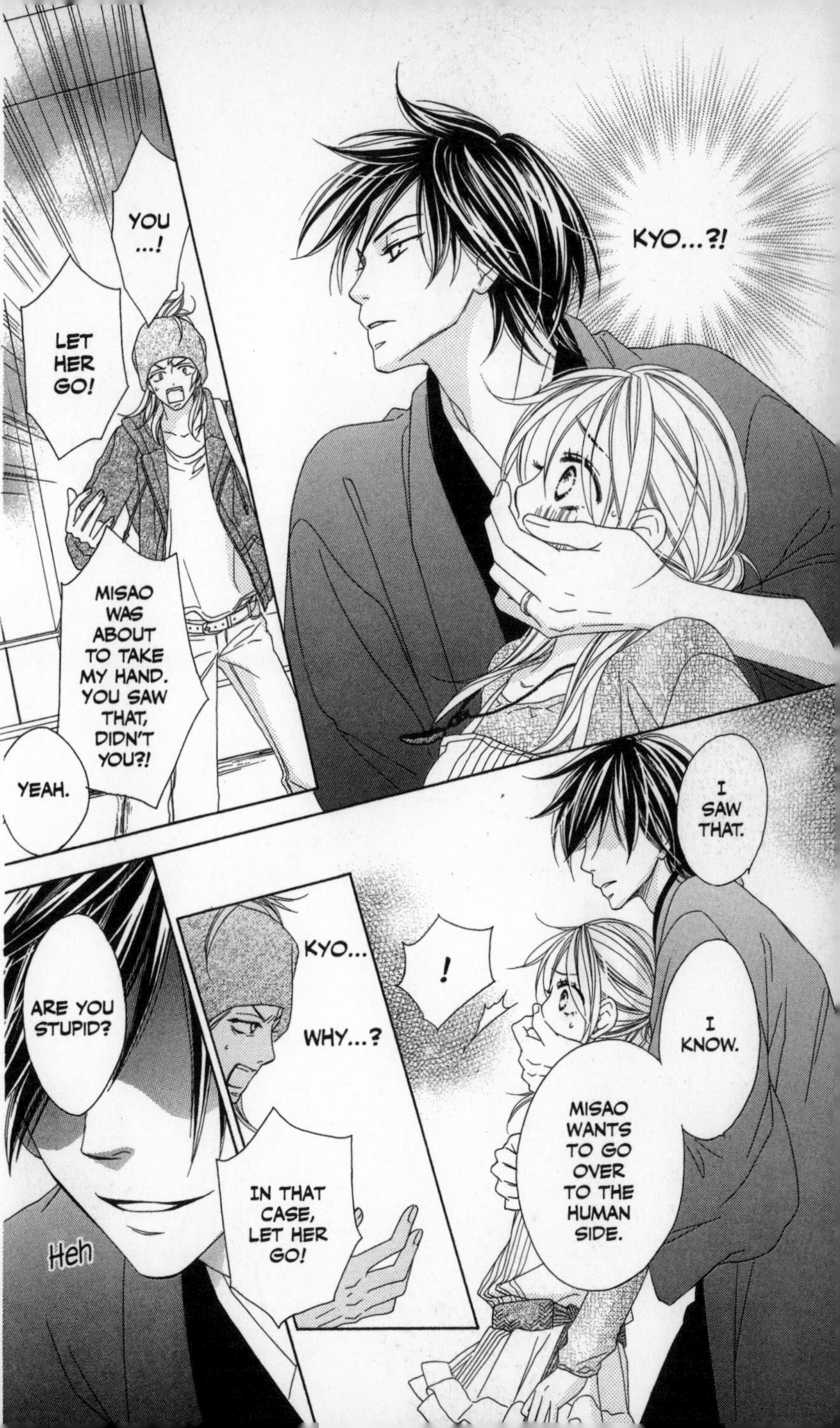
KYO...?!
YOU ...!
LET HER GO!
MISAO WAS ABOUT TO TAKE MY HAND. YOU SAW THAT, DIDN'T YOU?!
YEAH.
I SAW THAT.
!
I KNOW.
MISAO WANTS TO GO OVER TO THE HUMAN SIDE.
KYO...
WHY...?
IN THAT CASE, LET HER GO!
ARE YOU STUPID?
Heh

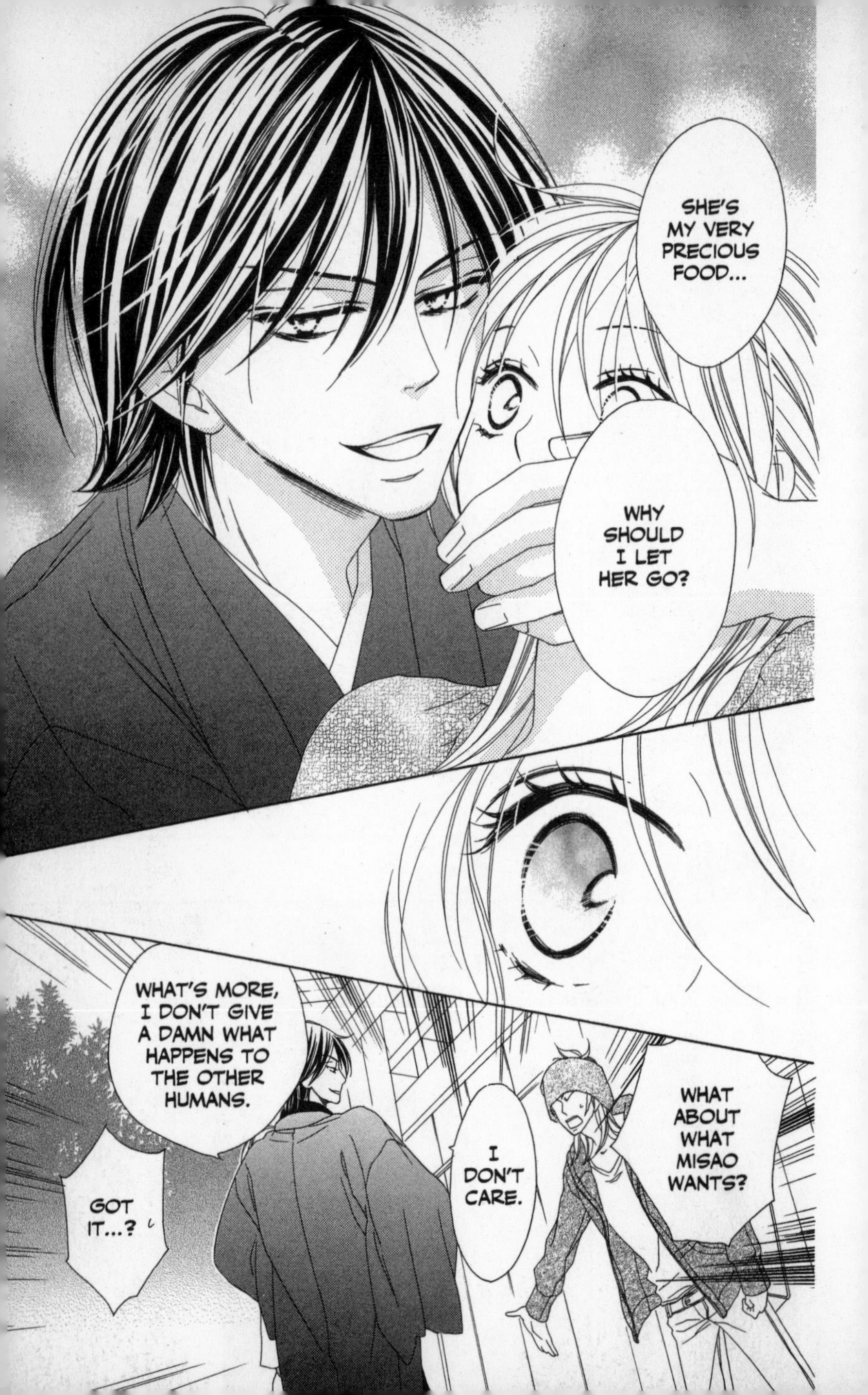
SHE'S MY VERY PRECIOUS FOOD...
WHY SHOULD I LET HER GO?
WHAT ABOUT WHAT MISAO WANTS?
I DON'T CARE.
WHAT'S MORE, I DON'T GIVE A DAMN WHAT HAPPENS TO THE OTHER HUMANS.
GOT IT...?

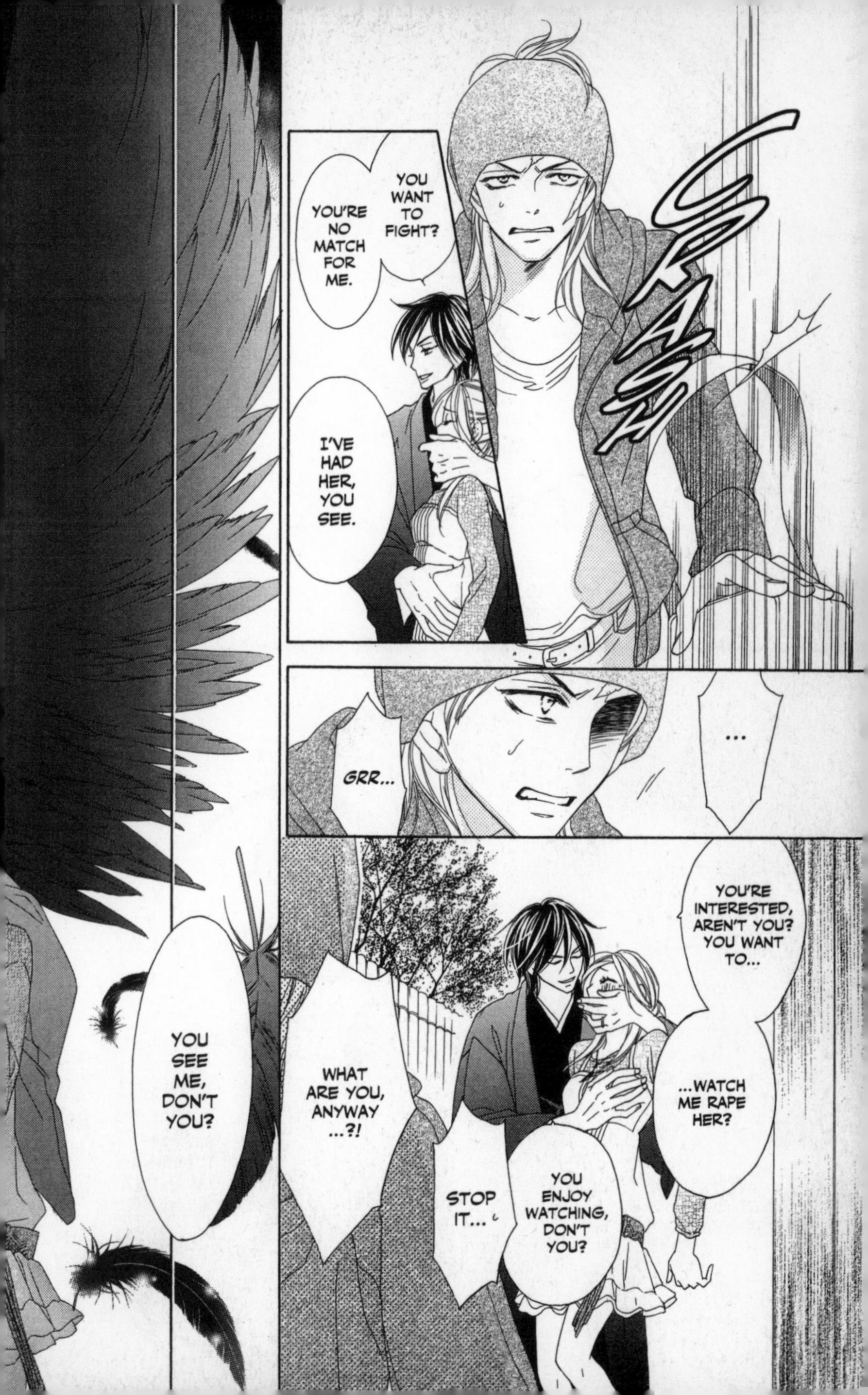
YOU WANT TO FIGHT?
YOU'RE NO MATCH FOR ME.
I'VE HAD HER, YOU SEE.
...
GRR...
YOU'RE INTERESTED, AREN'T YOU? YOU WANT TO...
...WATCH ME RAPE HER?
YOU ENJOY WATCHING, DON'T YOU?
STOP IT...
WHAT ARE YOU, ANYWAY ...?!
YOU SEE ME, DON'T YOU?

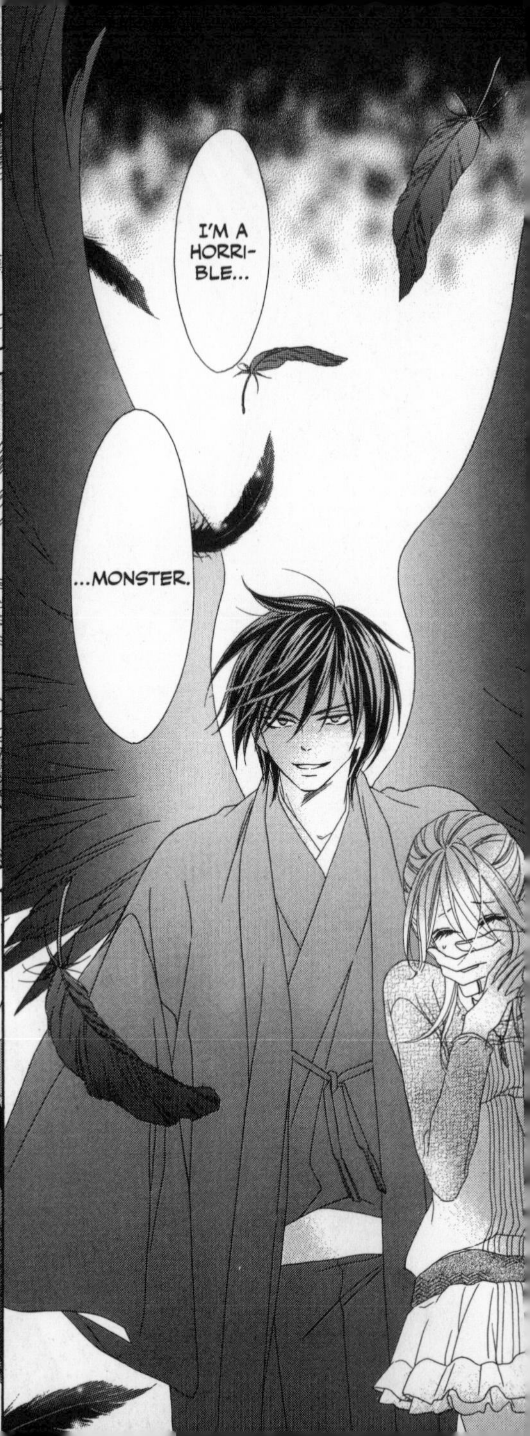
I'M A HORRI-BLE...
...MONSTER.
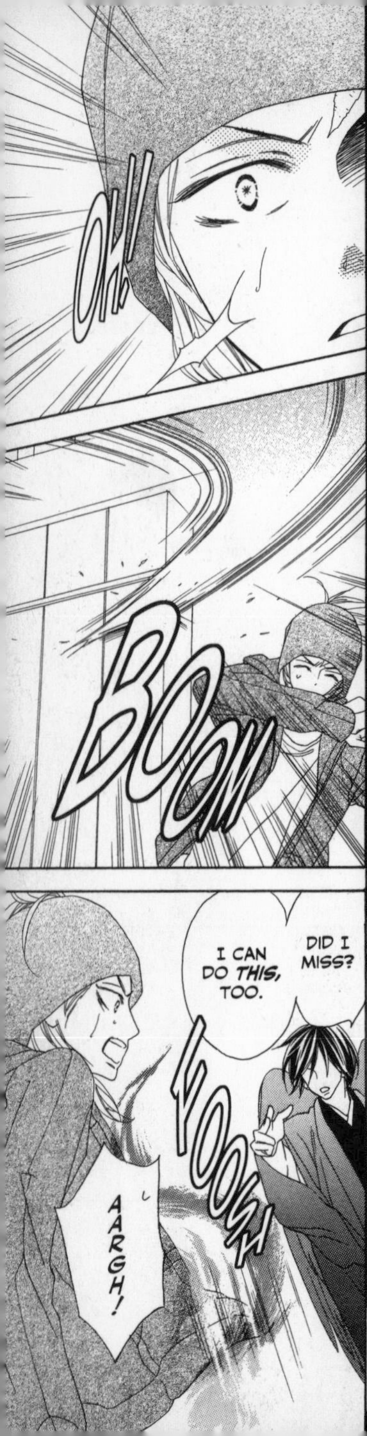
OH!
BOOM
DID I MISS?
I CAN DO THIS, TOO.
VOOM!
AARGH!

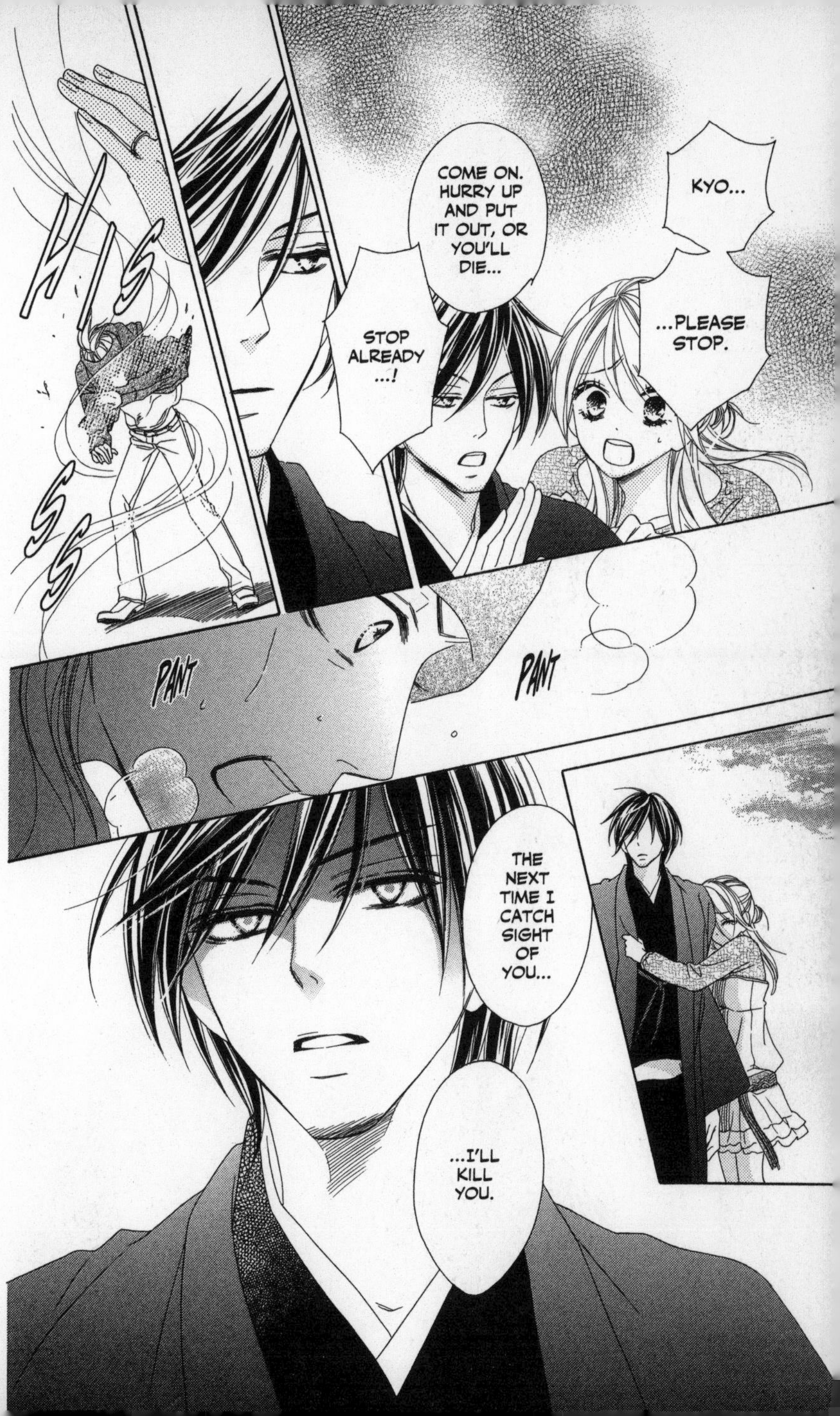
KYO...
...PLEASE STOP.
COME ON. HURRY UP AND PUT IT OUT, OR YOU'LL DIE...
STOP ALREADY ...!
HISS
SSS
PANT
PANT
THE NEXT TIME I CATCH SIGHT OF YOU...
...I'LL KILL YOU.

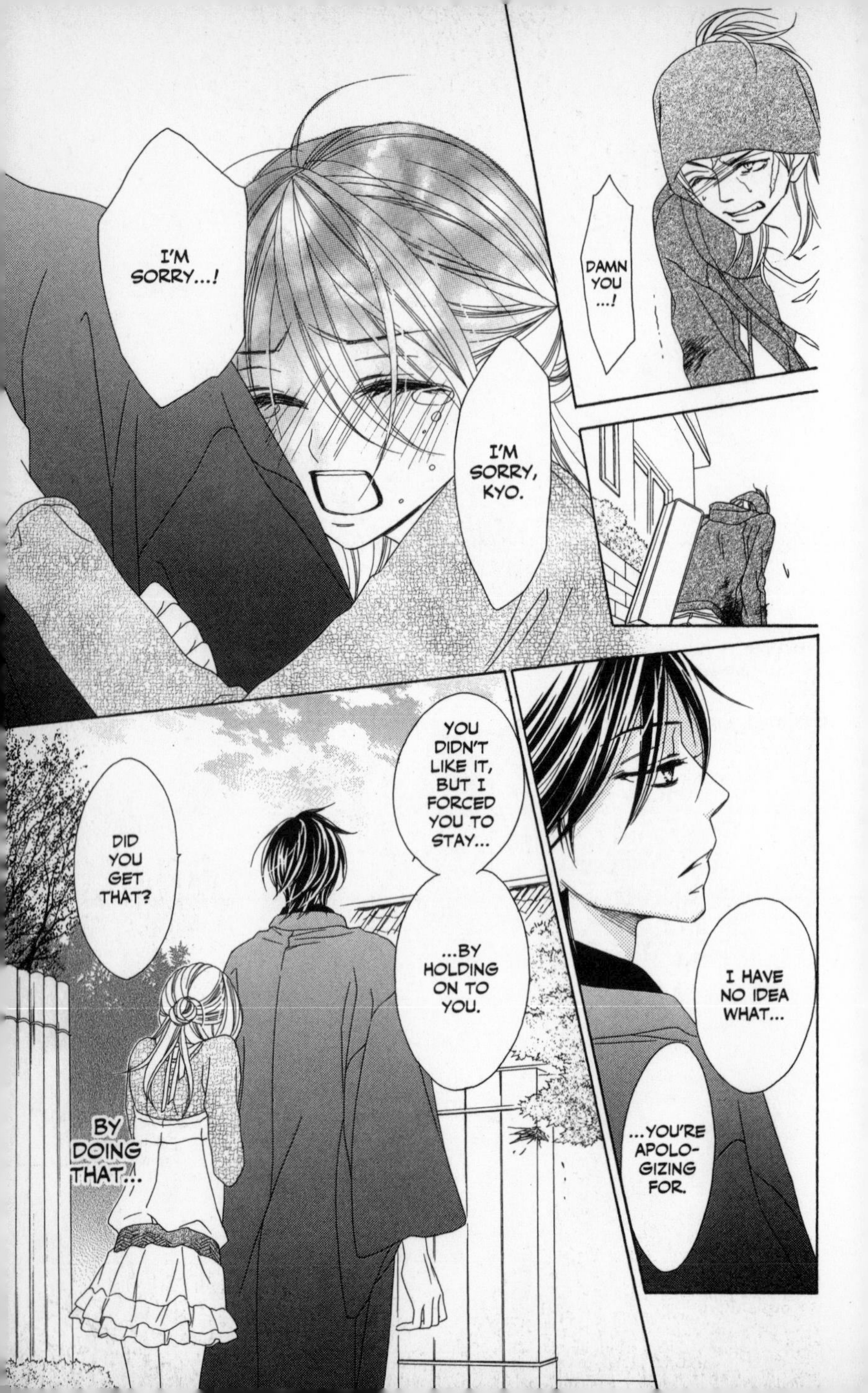
DAMN YOU ...!
I'M SORRY, KYO.
I'M SORRY...!
I HAVE NO IDEA WHAT...
...YOU'RE APOLO- GIZING FOR.
YOU DIDN'T LIKE IT, BUT I FORCED YOU TO STAY...
...BY HOLDING ON TO YOU.
DID YOU GET THAT?
BY DOING THAT...

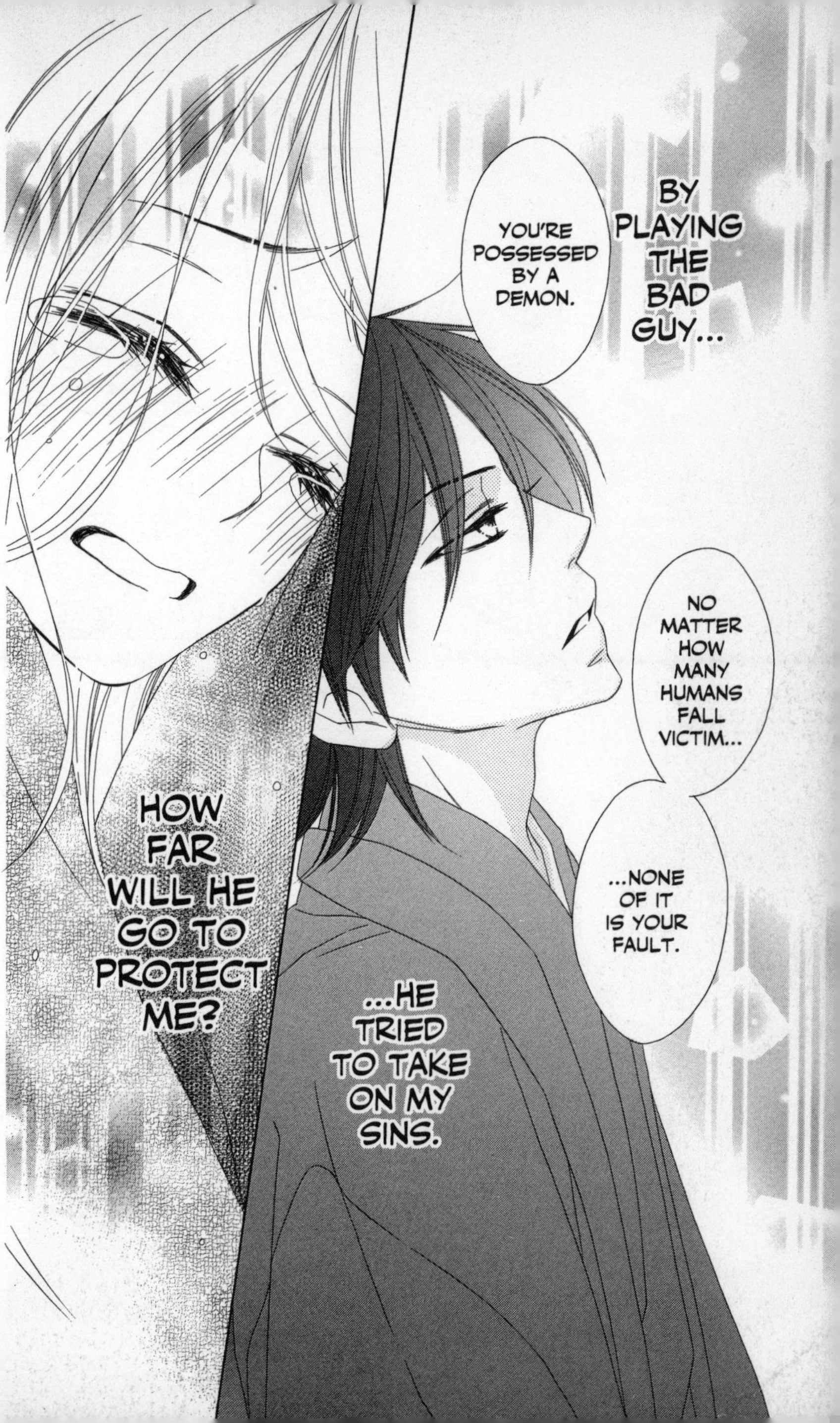
BY PLAYING THE BAD GUY...
YOU'RE POSSESSED BY A DEMON.
NO MATTER HOW MANY HUMANS FALL VICTIM...
...NONE OF IT IS YOUR FAULT.
...HE TRIED TO TAKE ON MY SINS.
HOW FAR WILL HE GO TO PROTECT ME?

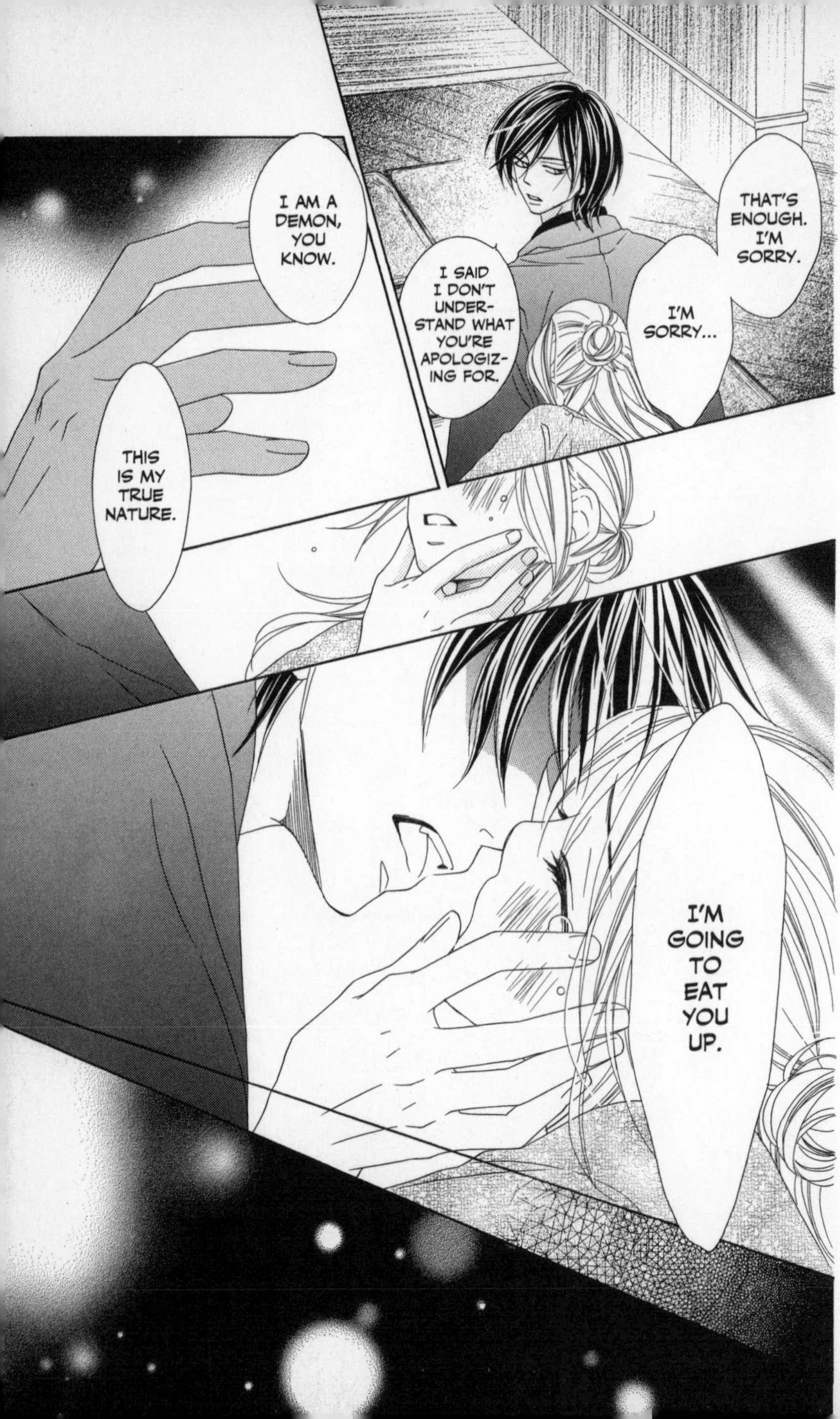
THAT'S ENOUGH. I'M SORRY.
I'M SORRY...
I SAID I DON'T UNDER-STAND WHAT YOU'RE APOLOGIZ-ING FOR.
I AM A DEMON, YOU KNOW.
THIS IS MY TRUE NATURE.
I'M GOING TO EAT YOU UP.

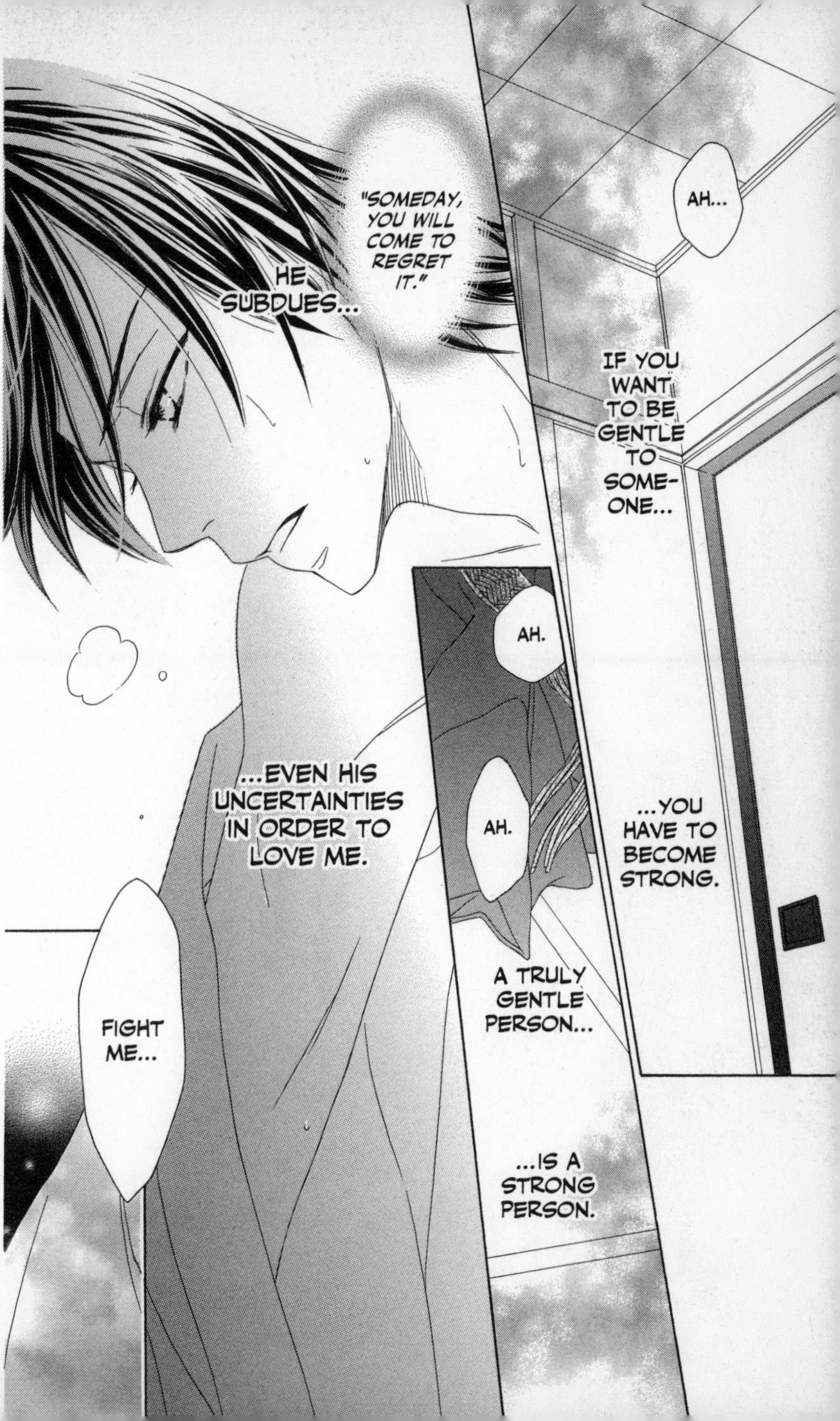
AH...
IF YOU WANT TO BE GENTLE TO SOMEONE...
...YOU HAVE TO BECOME STRONG.
AH.
AH.
A TRULY GENTLE PERSON...
...IS A STRONG PERSON.
"SOMEDAY, YOU WILL COME TO REGRET IT."
HE SUBDUES...
...EVEN HIS UNCERTAINTIES IN ORDER TO LOVE ME.
FIGHT ME...

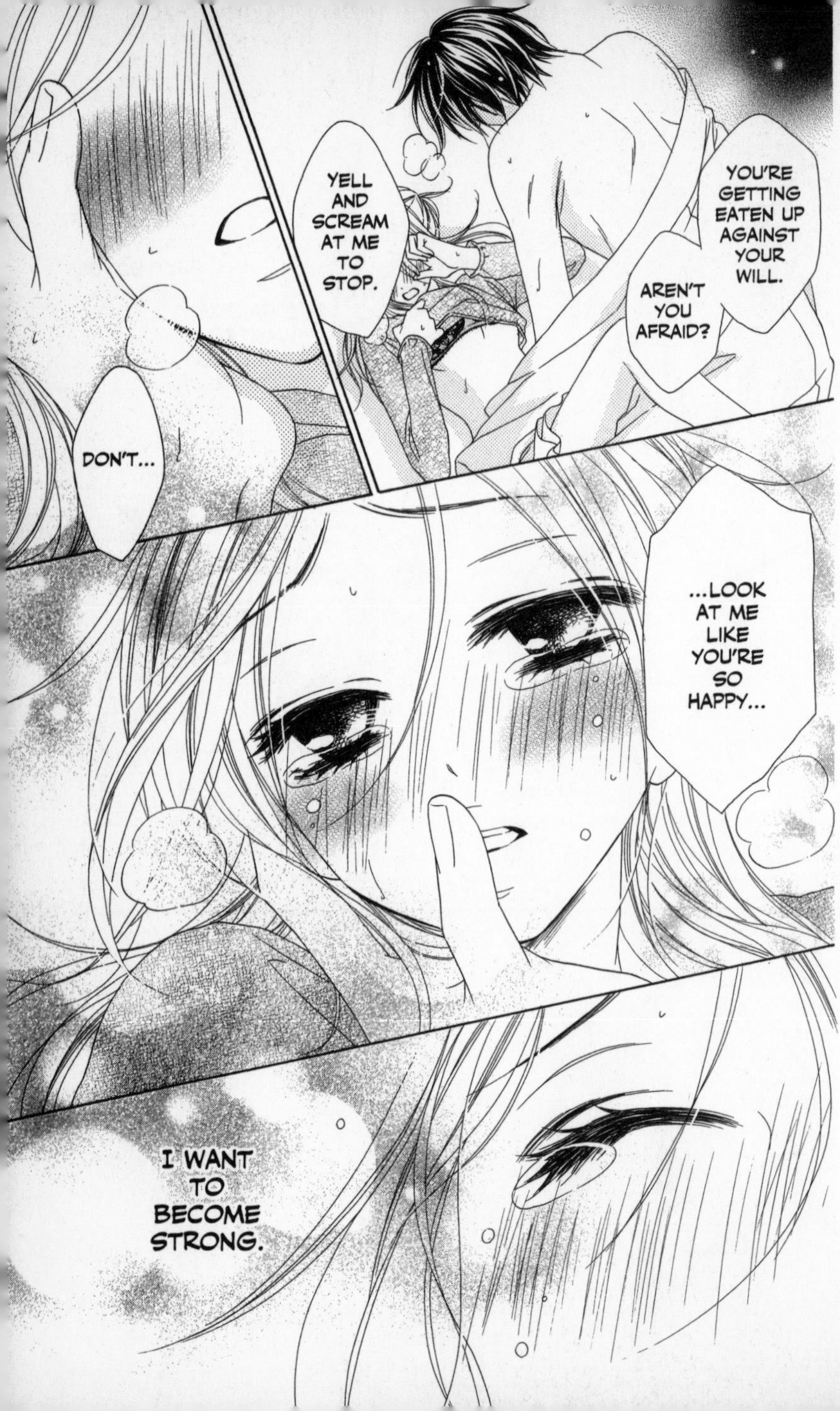
YOU'RE GETTING EATEN UP AGAINST YOUR WILL.
AREN'T YOU AFRAID?
YELL AND SCREAM AT ME TO STOP.
DON'T...
...LOOK AT ME LIKE YOU'RE SO HAPPY...
I WANT TO BECOME STRONG.

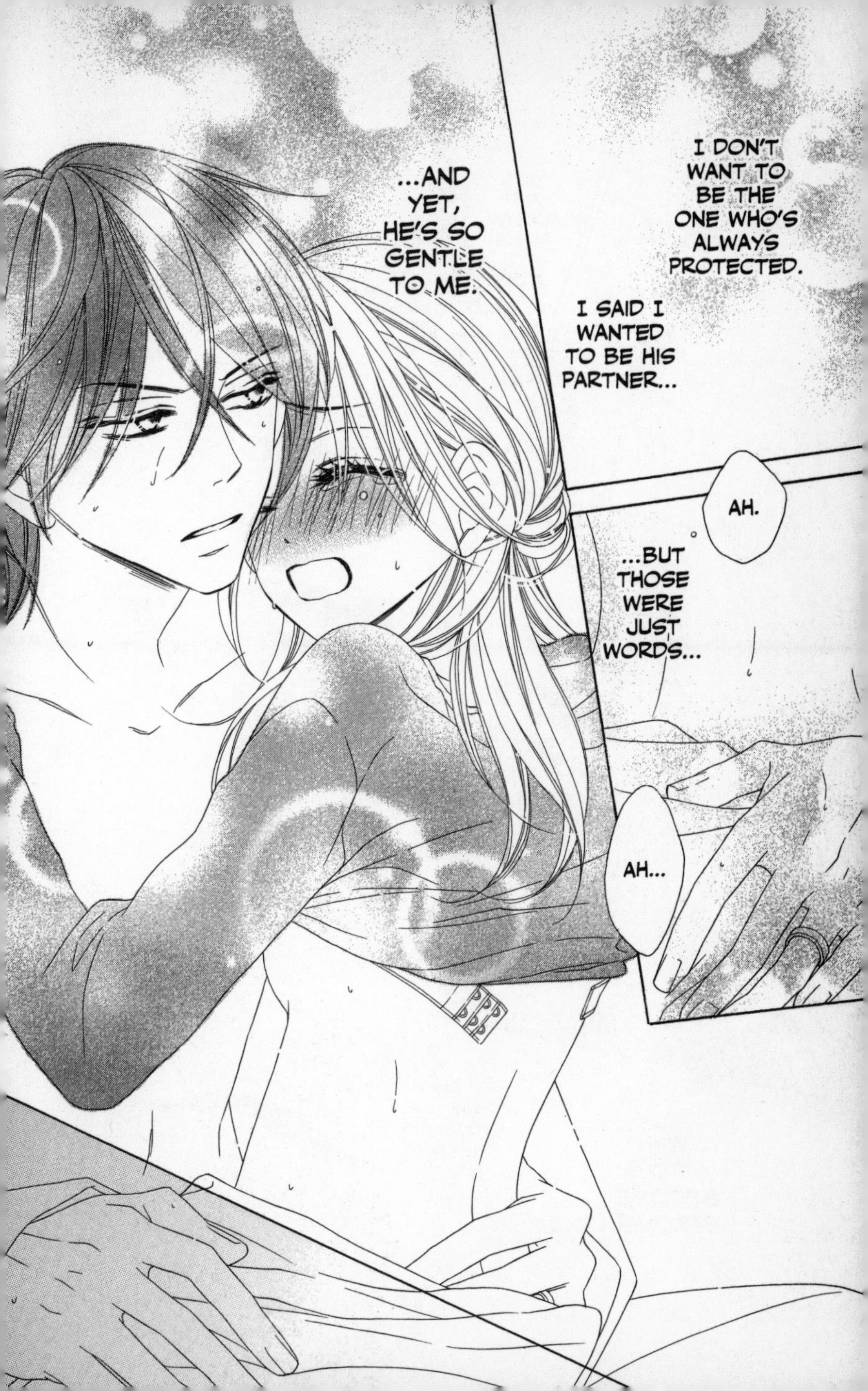
I DON'T WANT TO BE THE ONE WHO'S ALWAYS PROTECTED.
I SAID I WANTED TO BE HIS PARTNER...
AH.
...BUT THOSE WERE JUST WORDS...
AH...
...AND YET, HE'S SO GENTLE TO ME.

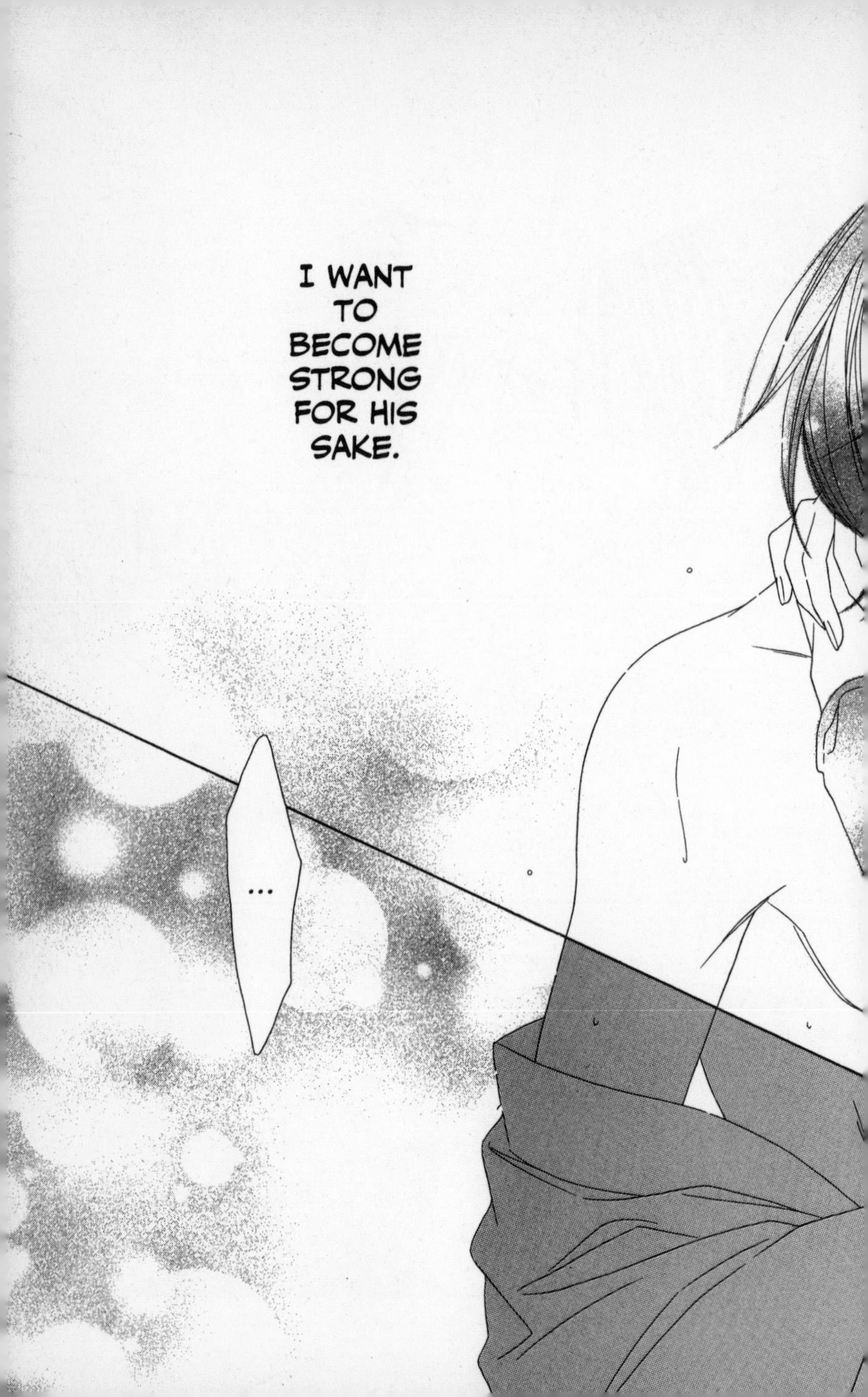
I WANT TO BECOME STRONG FOR HIS SAKE.
...

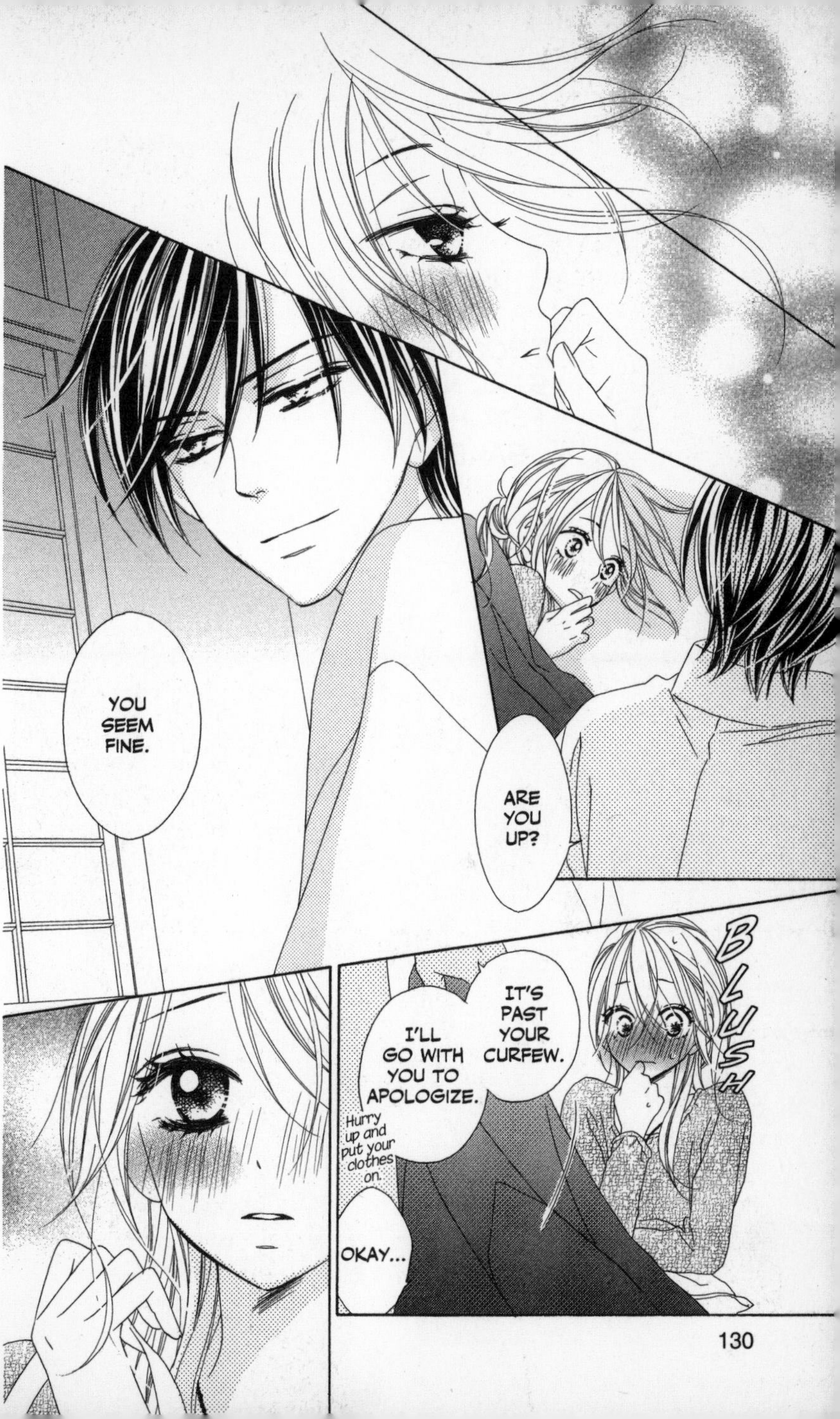
ARE YOU UP?
YOU SEEM FINE.
BLUSH
IT'S PAST YOUR CURFEW.
I'LL GO WITH YOU TO APOLOGIZE.
Hurry up and put your clothes on.
OKAY...

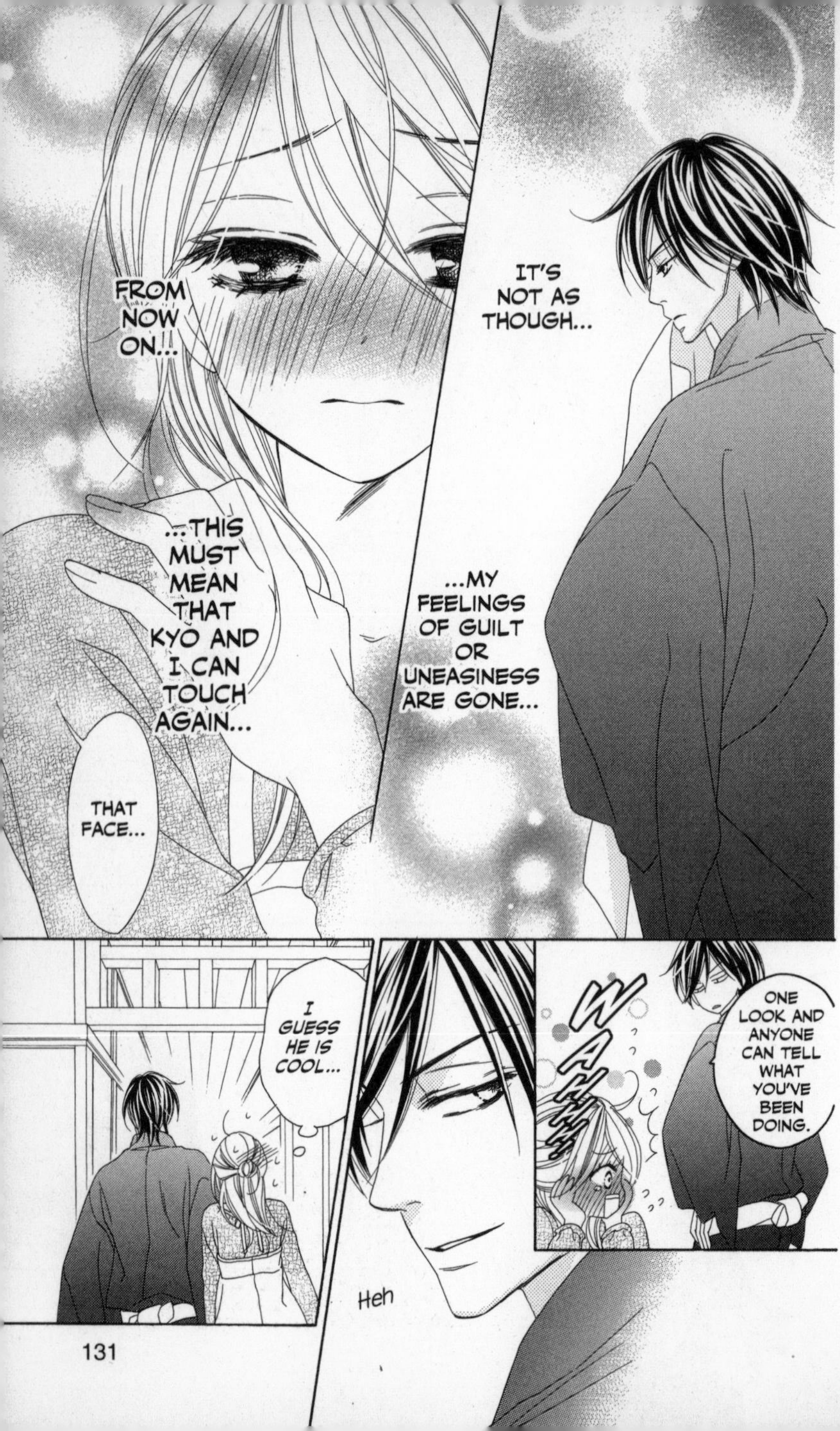
IT'S NOT AS THOUGH...
...MY FEELINGS OF GUILT OR UNEASINESS ARE GONE...
FROM NOW ON...
...THIS MUST MEAN THAT KYO AND I CAN TOUCH AGAIN...
THAT FACE...
WAHHH
ONE LOOK AND ANYONE CAN TELL WHAT YOU'VE BEEN DOING.
Heh
I GUESS HE IS COOL...

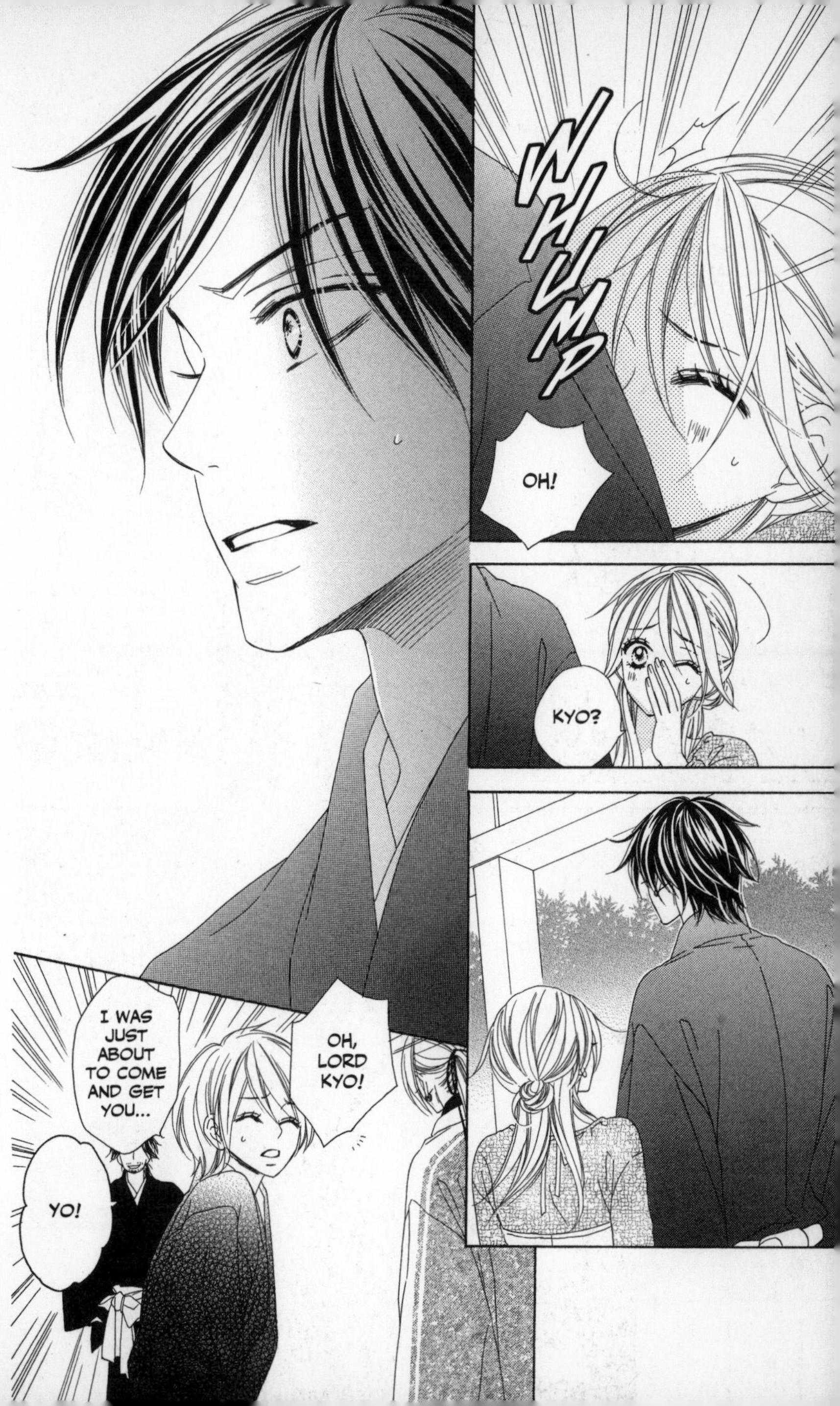
WHUMP
OH!
KYO?
OH, LORD KYO!
I WAS JUST ABOUT TO COME AND GET YOU...
YO!

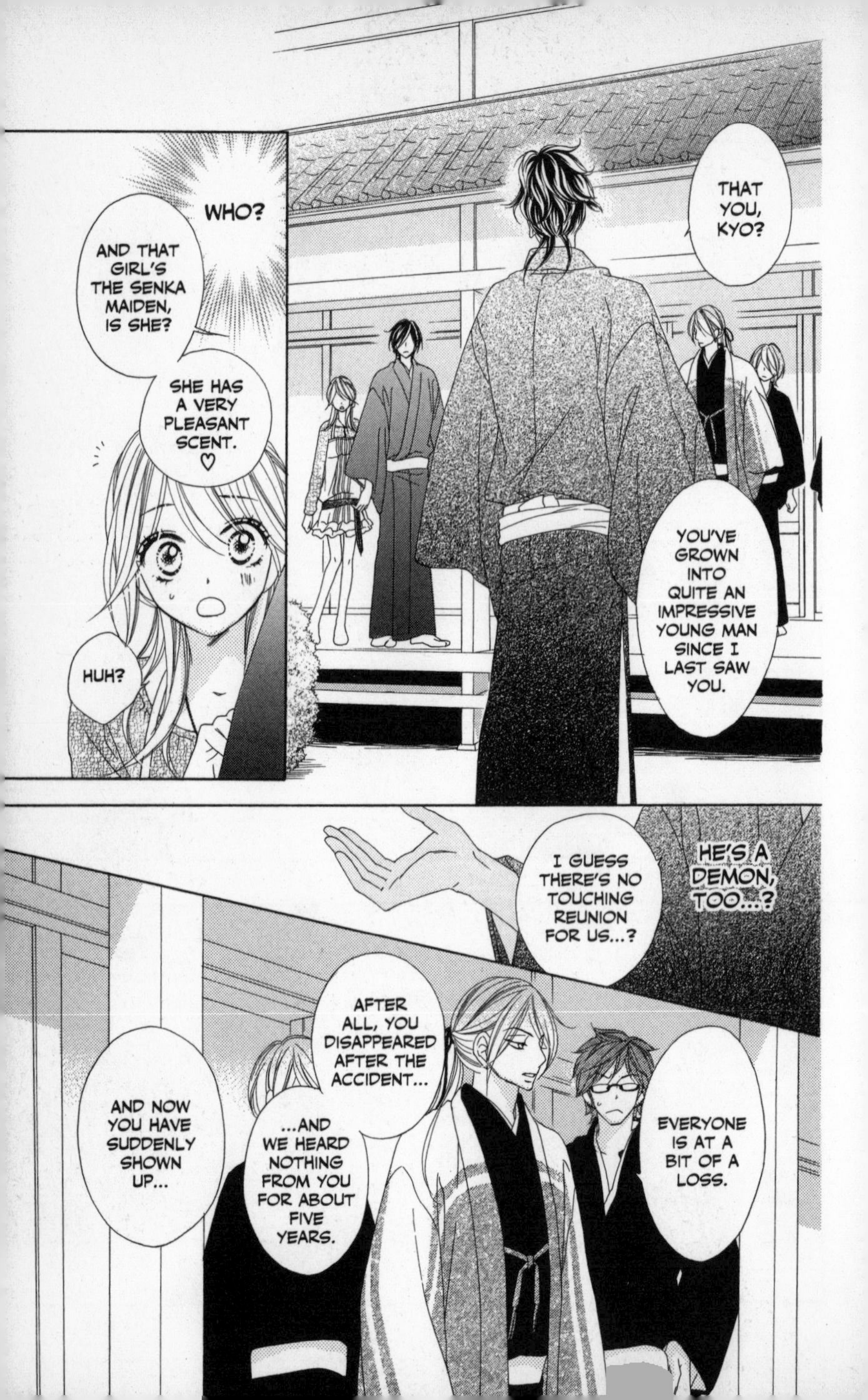
THAT YOU, KYO?
YOU'VE GROWN INTO QUITE AN IMPRESSIVE YOUNG MAN SINCE I LAST SAW YOU.
WHO?
AND THAT GIRL'S THE SENKA MAIDEN, IS SHE?
SHE HAS A VERY PLEASANT SCENT. ♡
HUH?
HE'S A DEMON, TOO...?
I GUESS THERE'S NO TOUCHING REUNION FOR US...?
EVERYONE IS AT A BIT OF A LOSS.
AFTER ALL, YOU DISAPPEARED AFTER THE ACCIDENT...
...AND WE HEARD NOTHING FROM YOU FOR ABOUT FIVE YEARS.
AND NOW YOU HAVE SUDDENLY SHOWN UP...

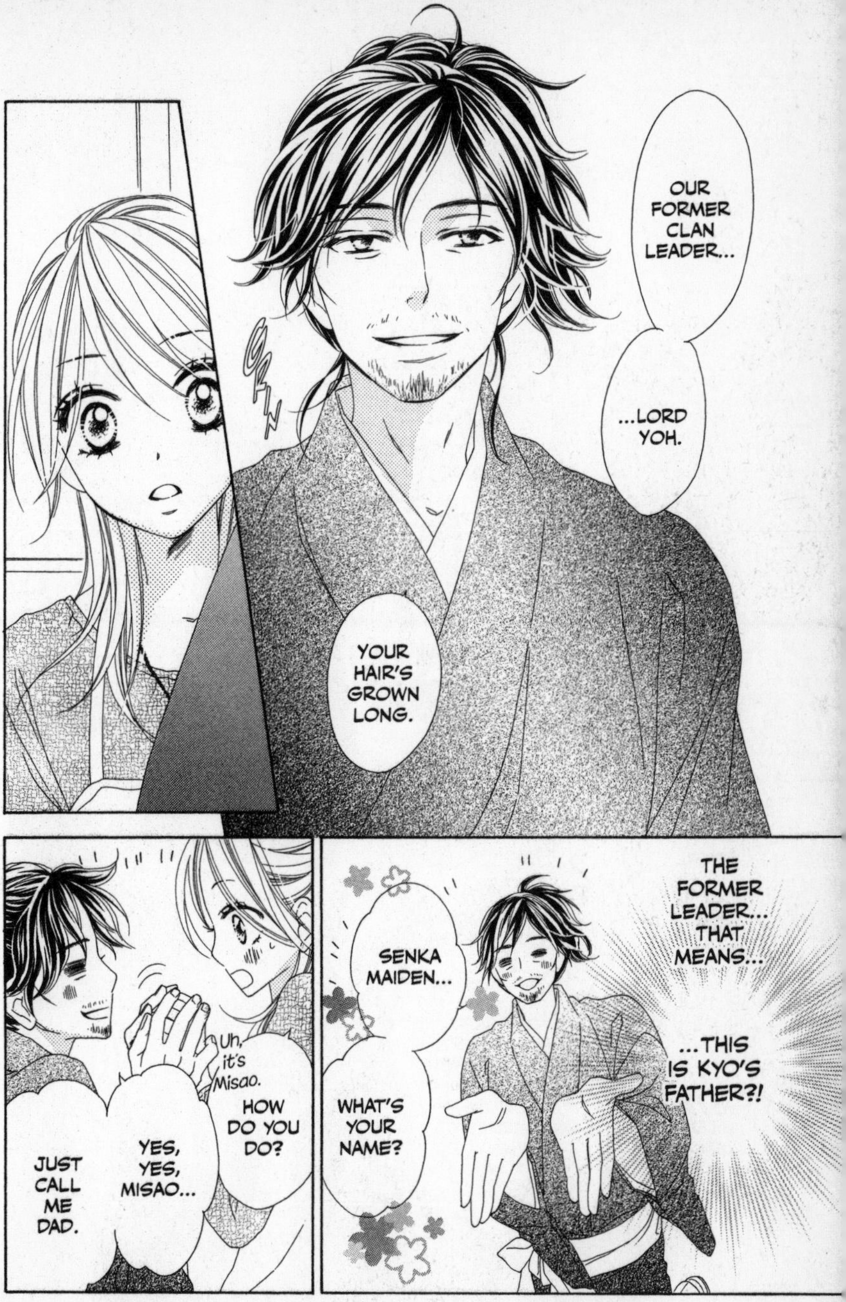
OUR FORMER CLAN LEADER...
...LORD YOH.
YOUR HAIR'S GROWN LONG.
THE FORMER LEADER... THAT MEANS...
...THIS IS KYO'S FATHER?!
SENKA MAIDEN...
WHAT'S YOUR NAME?
Uh, it's Misao.
HOW DO YOU DO?
YES, YES, MISAO...
JUST CALL ME DAD.

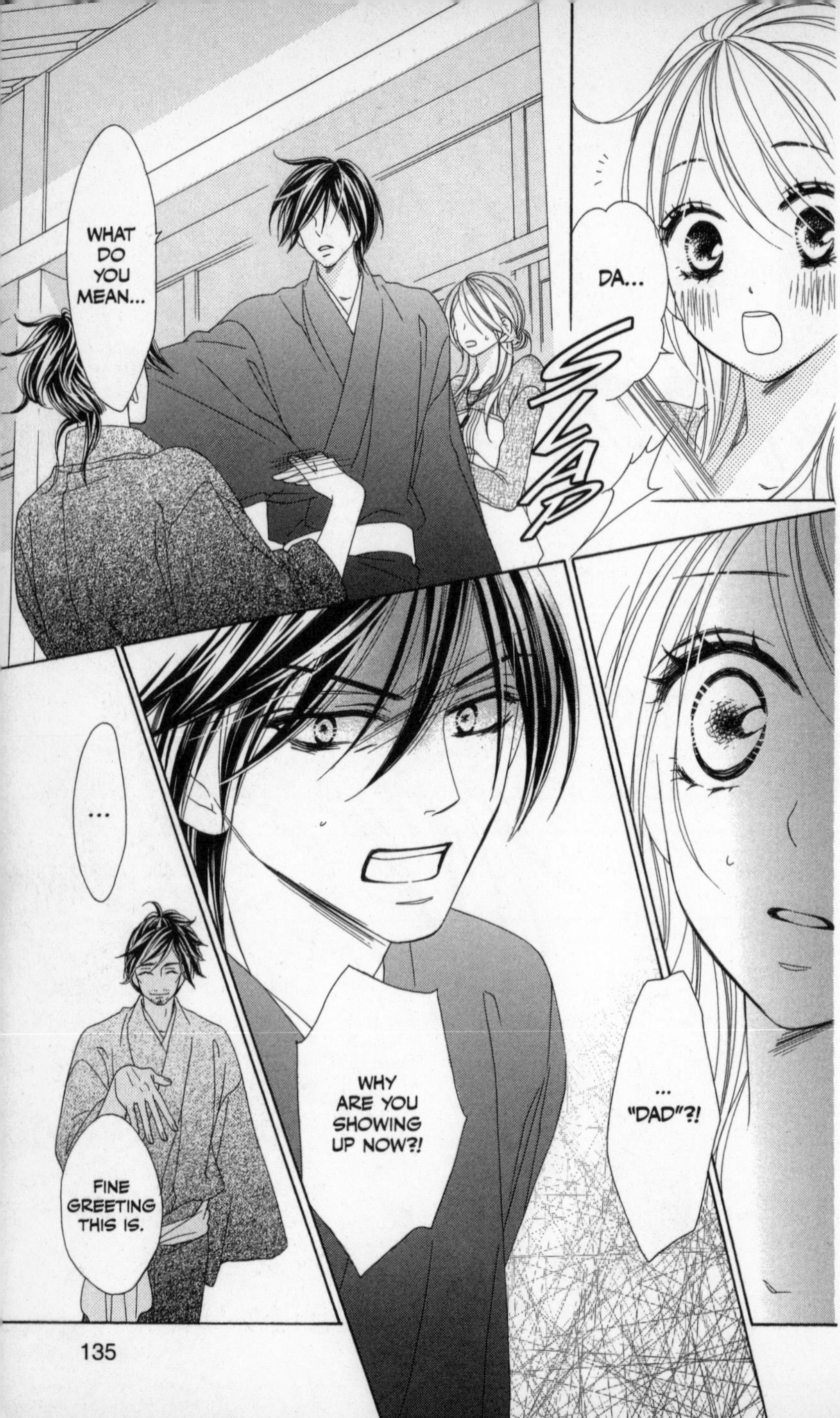
DA...
SLAP
WHAT DO YOU MEAN...
... "DAD"?!
WHY ARE YOU SHOWING UP NOW?!
...
FINE GREETING THIS IS.

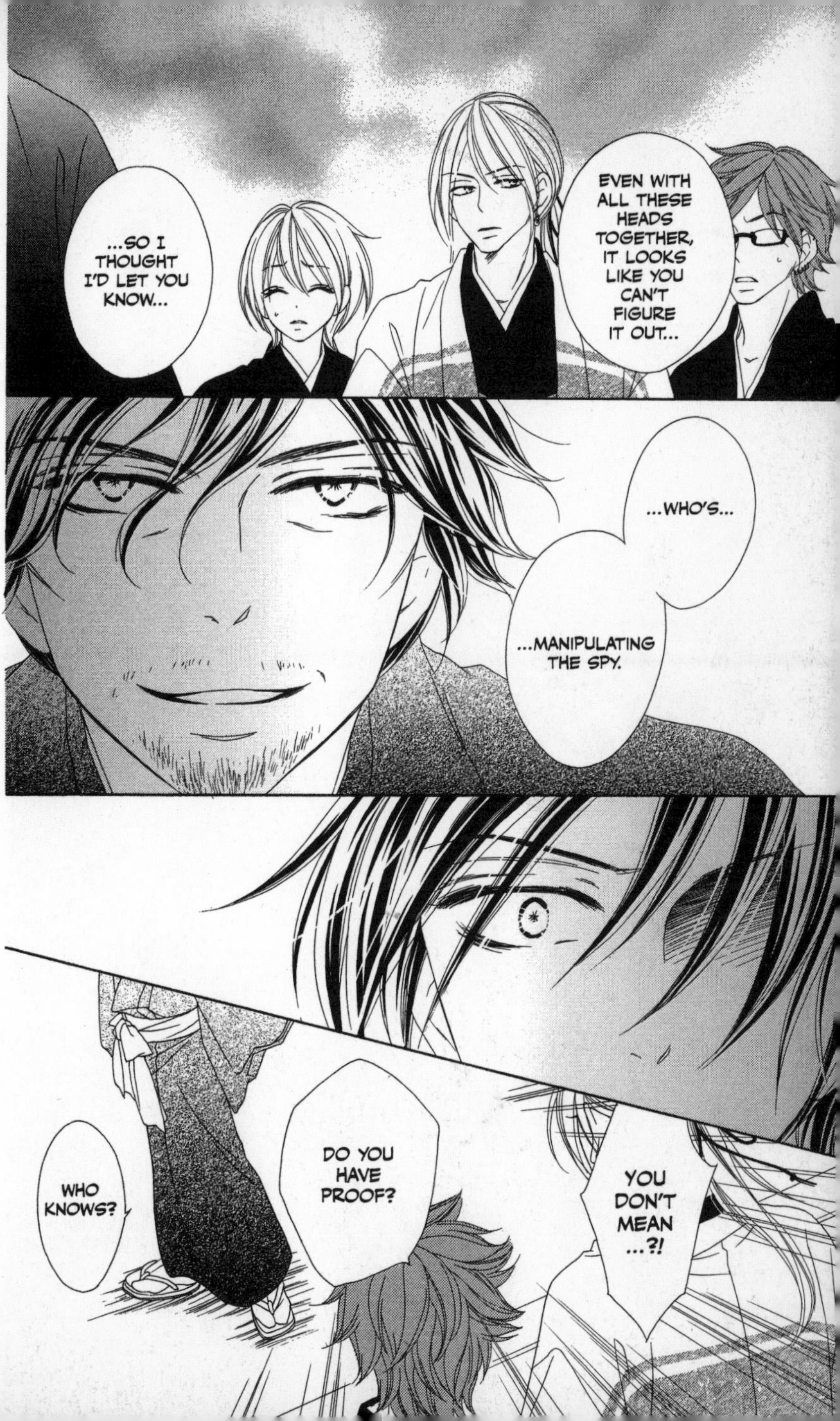
EVEN WITH ALL THESE HEADS TOGETHER, IT LOOKS LIKE YOU CAN'T FIGURE IT OUT...
...SO I THOUGHT I'D LET YOU KNOW...
...WHO'S...
...MANIPULATING THE SPY.
YOU DON'T MEAN ...?!
DO YOU HAVE PROOF?
WHO KNOWS?

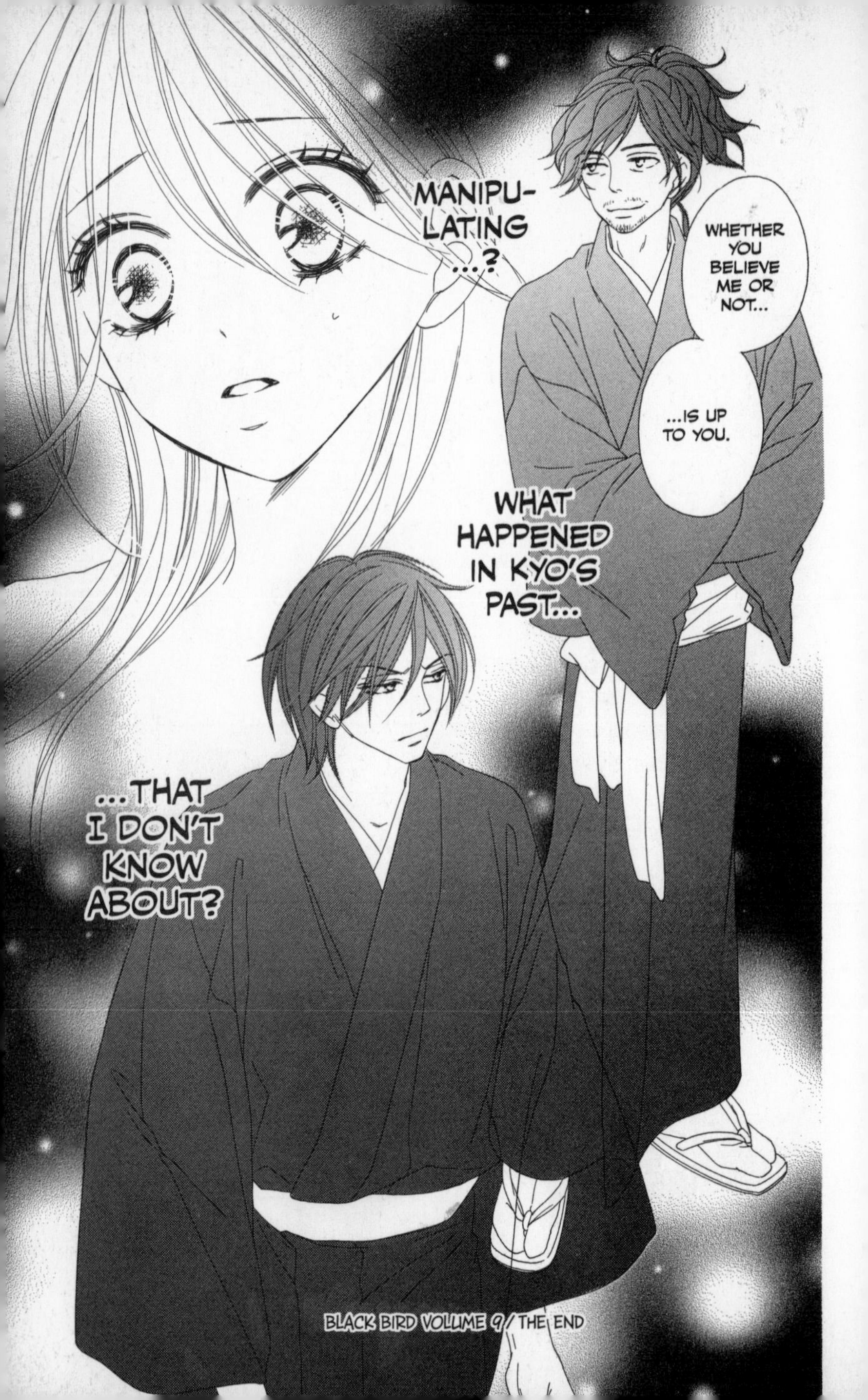
WHETHER YOU BELIEVE ME OR NOT...
...IS UP TO YOU.
MANIPU-LATING ...?
WHAT HAPPENED IN KYO'S PAST...
...THAT I DON'T KNOW ABOUT?
BLACK BIRD VOLUME 9 / THE END

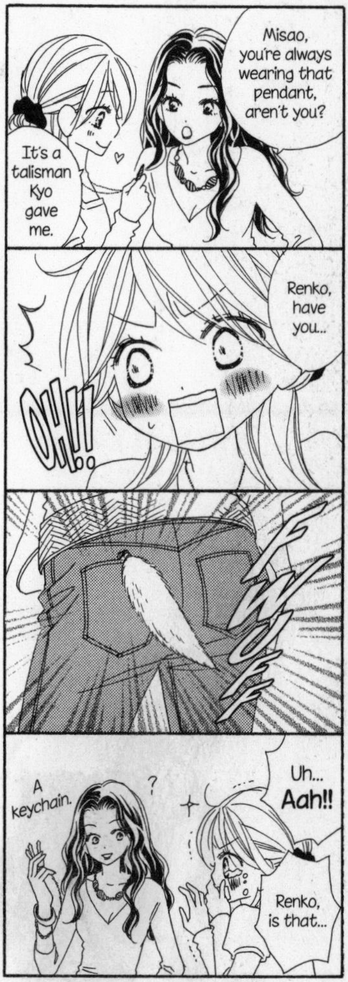
Misao, you're always wearing that pendant, aren't you?
It's a talisman Kyo gave me.
Renko, have you...
OH!!
FWUFF
Uh... Aah!!
Renko, is that...
A keychain.

I don't think anyone has noticed, but the braid that Sagami wears is supposed to be an amulet woven by Ayame using her own flight feathers.

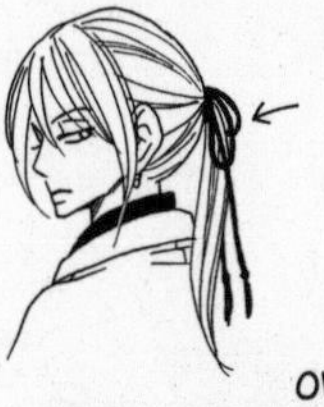

(That's why he wasn't wearing it before their marriage...) There's a reason why it is a braid rather than a pendant, but... I might not write about it until the last episode! But you don't really care, do you...?

Maybe amulets come in many forms, not just pendants.

Could it be like the tale of the grateful crane?

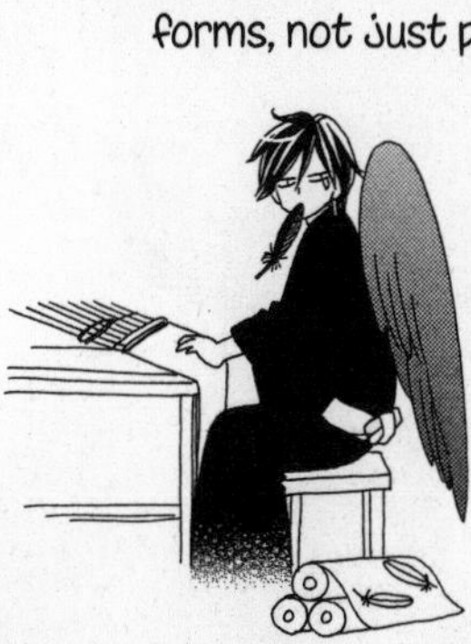

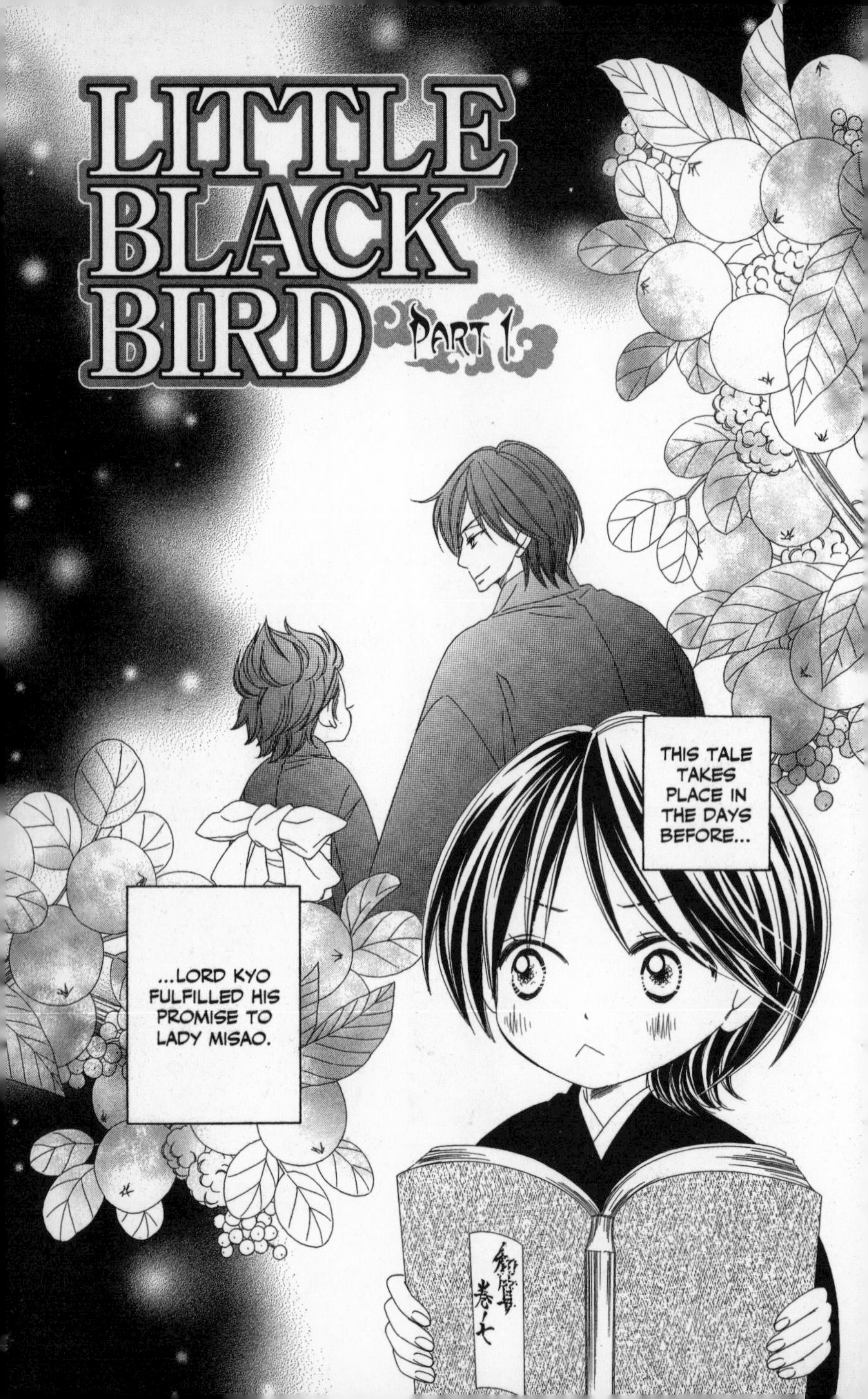
LITTLE BLACK BIRD
PART 1
THIS TALE TAKES PLACE IN THE DAYS BEFORE...
...LORD KYO FULFILLED HIS PROMISE TO LADY MISAO.

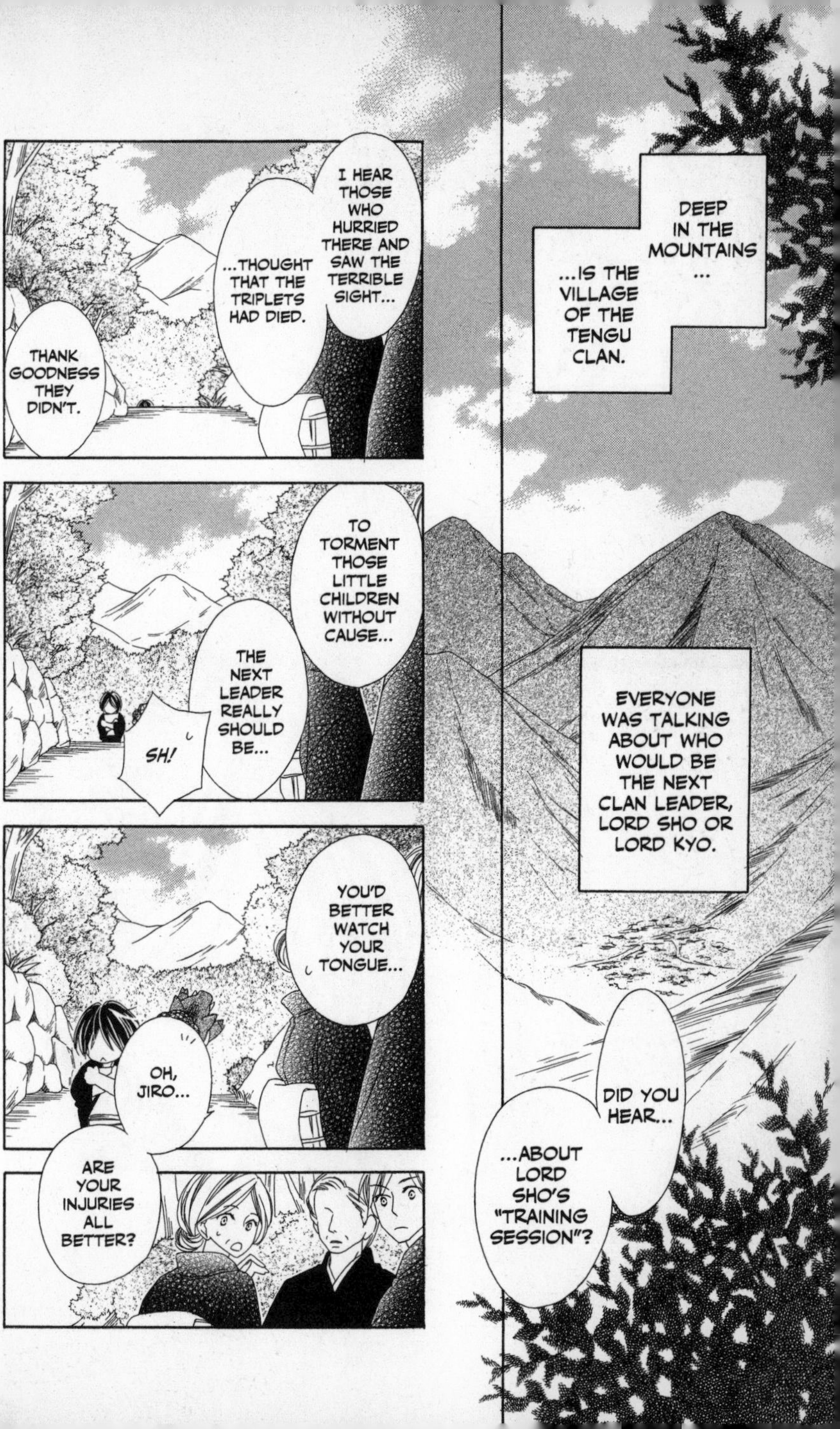
DEEP IN THE MOUNTAINS...
...IS THE VILLAGE OF THE TENGU CLAN.
EVERYONE WAS TALKING ABOUT WHO WOULD BE THE NEXT CLAN LEADER, LORD SHO OR LORD KYO.
DID YOU HEAR...
...ABOUT LORD SHO'S "TRAINING SESSION"?
I HEAR THOSE WHO HURRIED THERE AND SAW THE TERRIBLE SIGHT...
...THOUGHT THAT THE TRIPLETS HAD DIED.
THANK GOODNESS THEY DIDN'T.
TO TORMENT THOSE LITTLE CHILDREN WITHOUT CAUSE...
THE NEXT LEADER REALLY SHOULD BE...
SH!
YOU'D BETTER WATCH YOUR TONGUE...
OH, JIRO...
ARE YOUR INJURIES ALL BETTER?

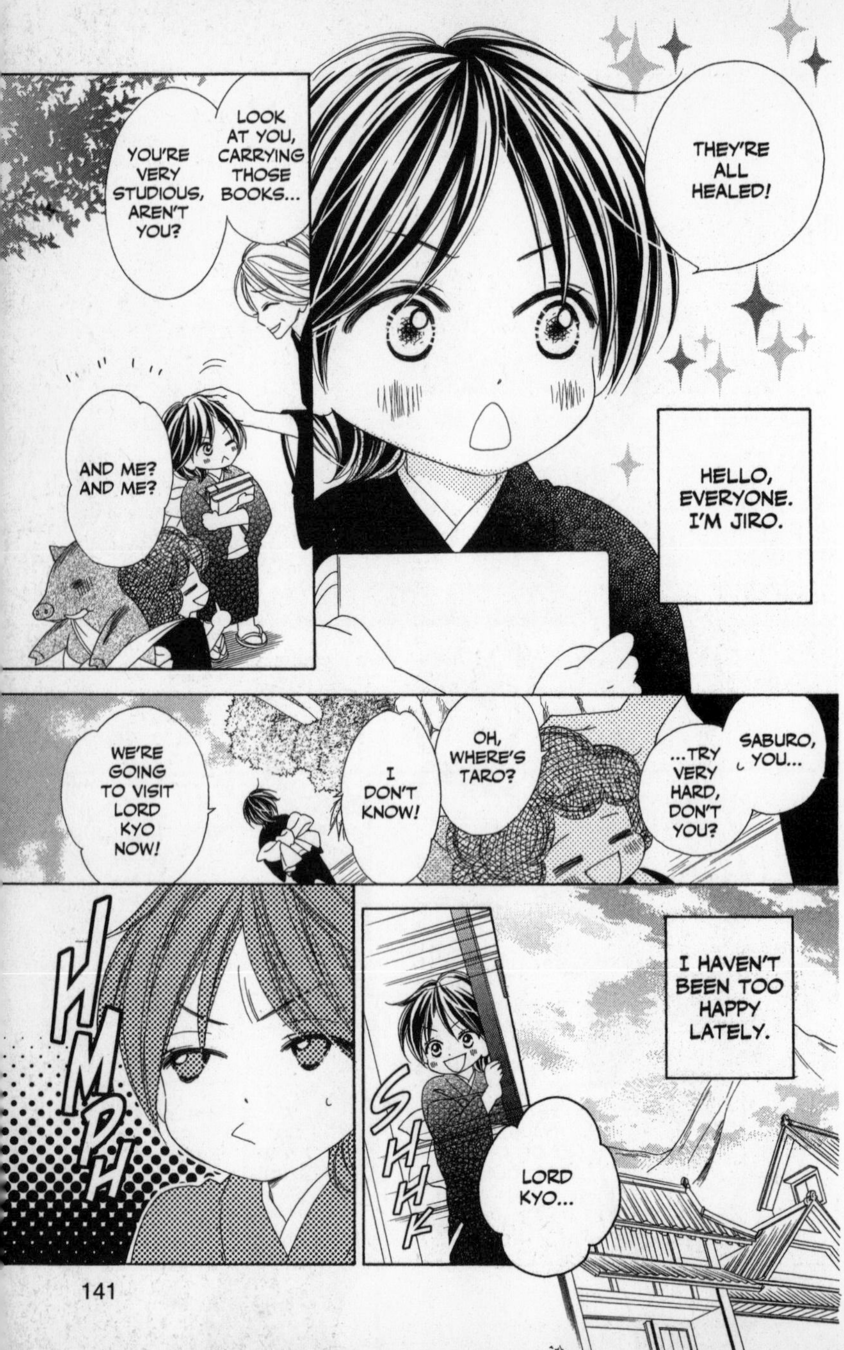
THEY'RE ALL HEALED!
HELLO, EVERYONE. I'M JIRO.
LOOK AT YOU, CARRYING THOSE BOOKS...
YOU'RE VERY STUDIOUS, AREN'T YOU?
AND ME? AND ME?
SABURO, YOU...
...TRY VERY HARD, DON'T YOU?
OH, WHERE'S TARO?
I DON'T KNOW!
WE'RE GOING TO VISIT LORD KYO NOW!
I HAVEN'T BEEN TOO HAPPY LATELY.
SHHK
LORD KYO...
HMMPH

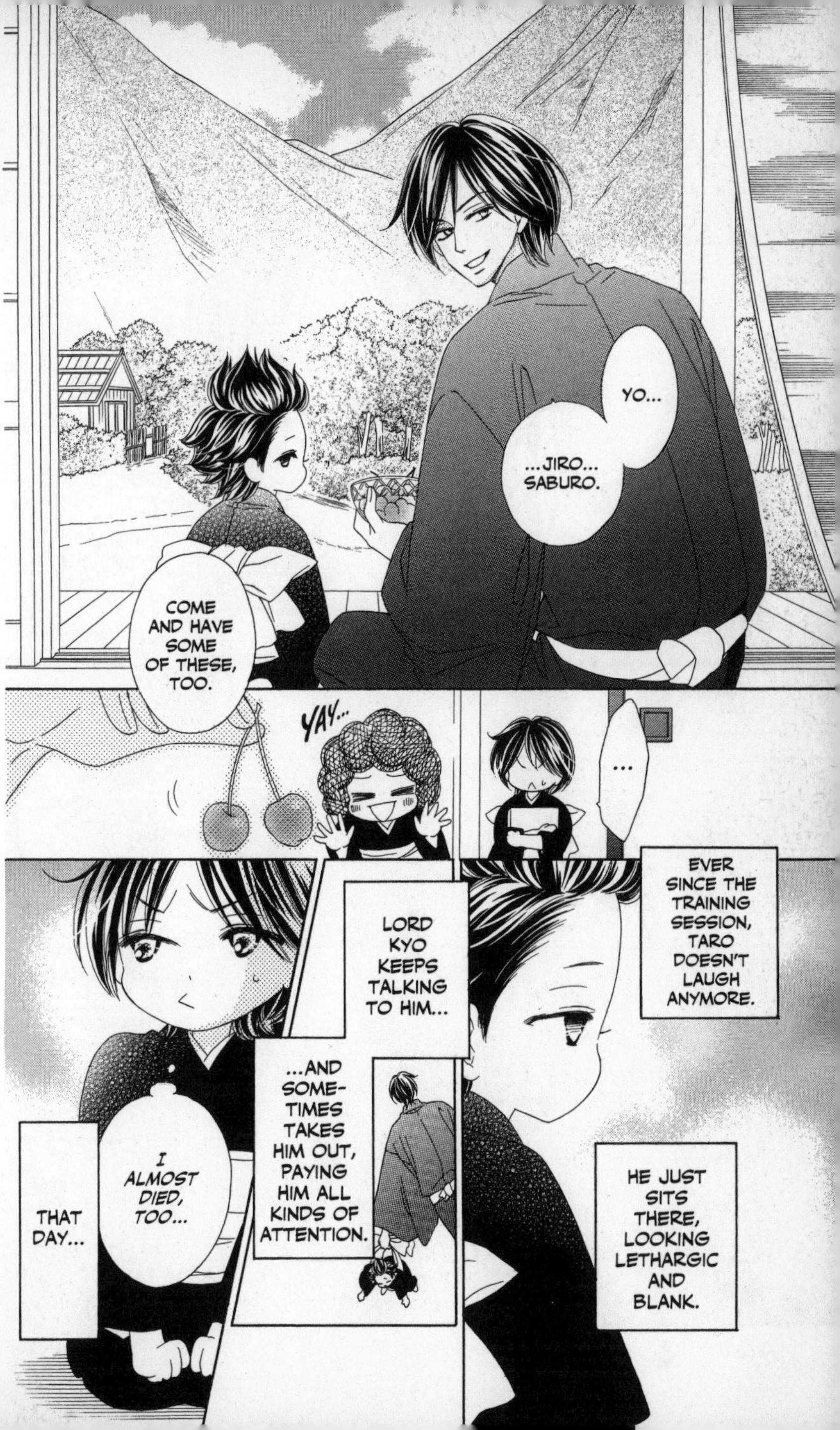
YO...
...JIRO... SABURO.
COME AND HAVE SOME OF THESE, TOO.
...
YAY...
EVER SINCE THE TRAINING SESSION, TARO DOESN'T LAUGH ANYMORE.
HE JUST SITS THERE, LOOKING LETHARGIC AND BLANK.
LORD KYO KEEPS TALKING TO HIM...
...AND SOME-TIMES TAKES HIM OUT, PAYING HIM ALL KINDS OF ATTENTION.
I ALMOST DIED, TOO...
THAT DAY...

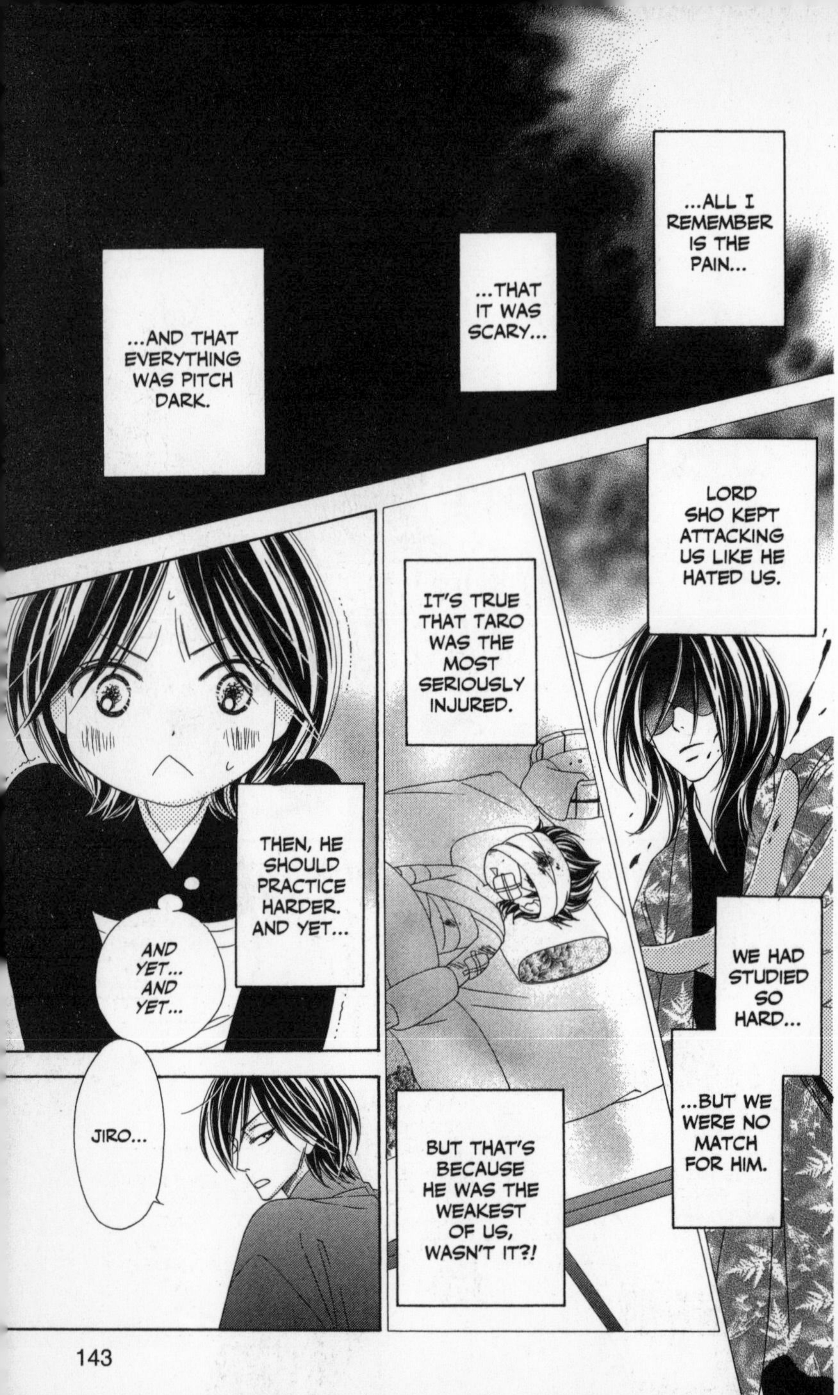
...ALL I REMEMBER IS THE PAIN...
...THAT IT WAS SCARY...
...AND THAT EVERYTHING WAS PITCH DARK.
LORD SHO KEPT ATTACKING US LIKE HE HATED US.
WE HAD STUDIED SO HARD...
...BUT WE WERE NO MATCH FOR HIM.
IT'S TRUE THAT TARO WAS THE MOST SERIOUSLY INJURED.
BUT THAT'S BECAUSE HE WAS THE WEAKEST OF US, WASN'T IT?!
THEN, HE SHOULD PRACTICE HARDER. AND YET...
AND YET... AND YET...
JIRO...

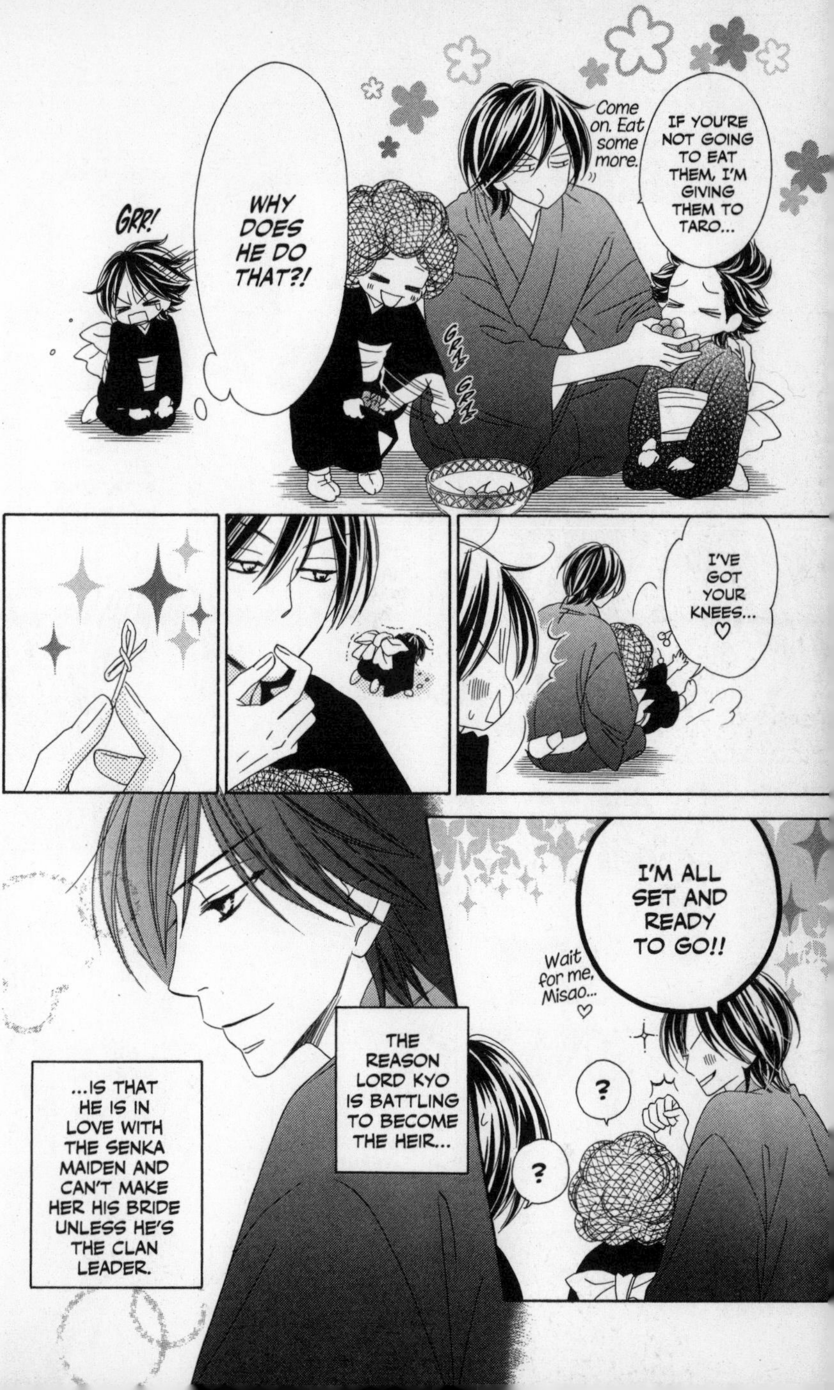
IF YOU'RE NOT GOING TO EAT THEM, I'M GIVING THEM TO TARO...
Come on. Eat some more.
GRM GRM
WHY DOES HE DO THAT?!
GRR!
I'VE GOT YOUR KNEES... ♡
I'M ALL SET AND READY TO GO!!
Wait for me, Misao... ♡
?
?
THE REASON LORD KYO IS BATTLING TO BECOME THE HEIR...
...IS THAT HE IS IN LOVE WITH THE SENKA MAIDEN AND CAN'T MAKE HER HIS BRIDE UNLESS HE'S THE CLAN LEADER.

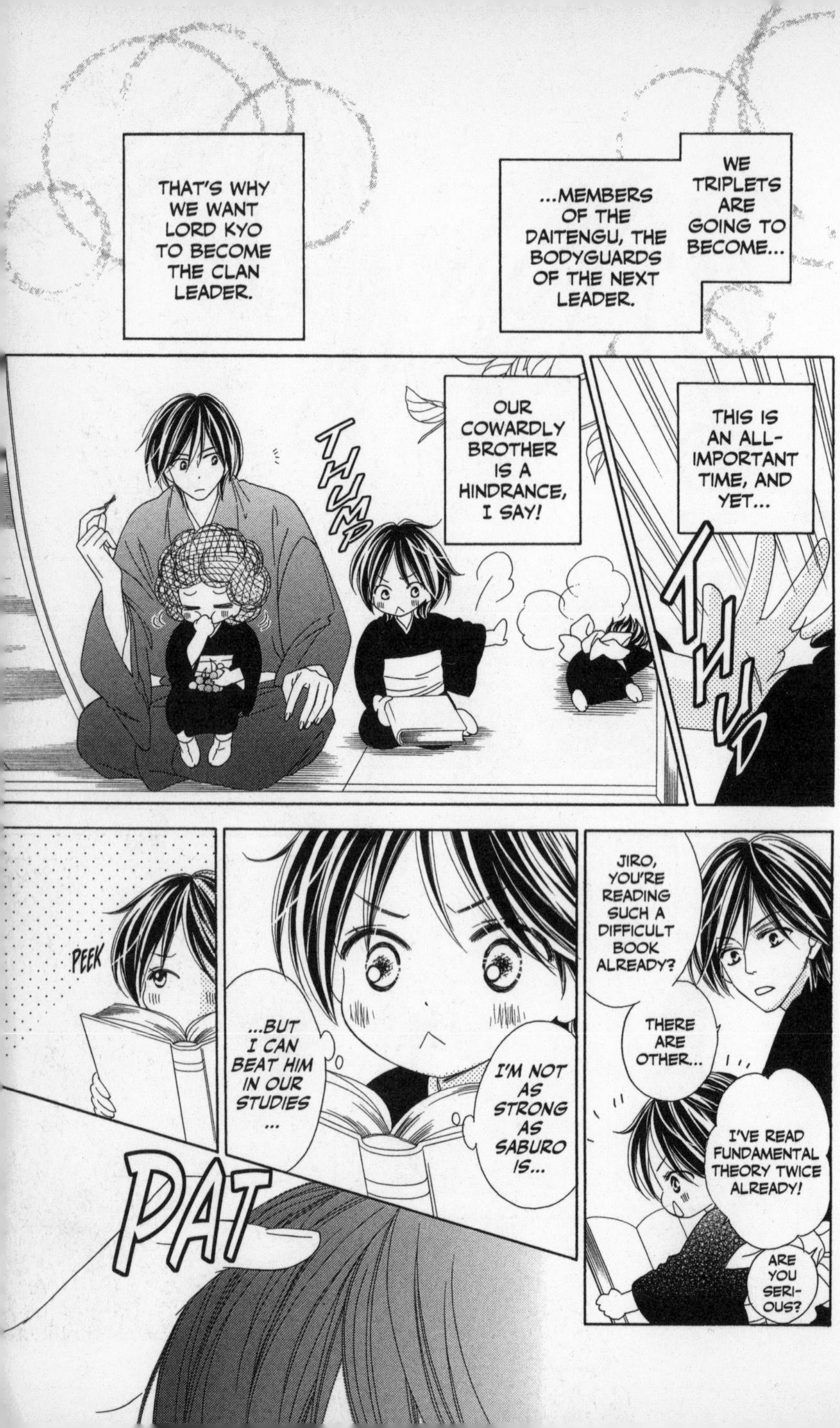
WE TRIPLETS ARE GOING TO BECOME...
...MEMBERS OF THE DAITENGU, THE BODYGUARDS OF THE NEXT LEADER.
THAT'S WHY WE WANT LORD KYO TO BECOME THE CLAN LEADER.
THIS IS AN ALL-IMPORTANT TIME, AND YET...
THUD
OUR COWARDLY BROTHER IS A HINDRANCE, I SAY!
THUMP
JIRO, YOU'RE READING SUCH A DIFFICULT BOOK ALREADY?
THERE ARE OTHER...
I'VE READ FUNDAMENTAL THEORY TWICE ALREADY!
ARE YOU SERI-OUS?
I'M NOT AS STRONG AS SABURO IS...
...BUT I CAN BEAT HIM IN OUR STUDIES...
PEEK
PAT

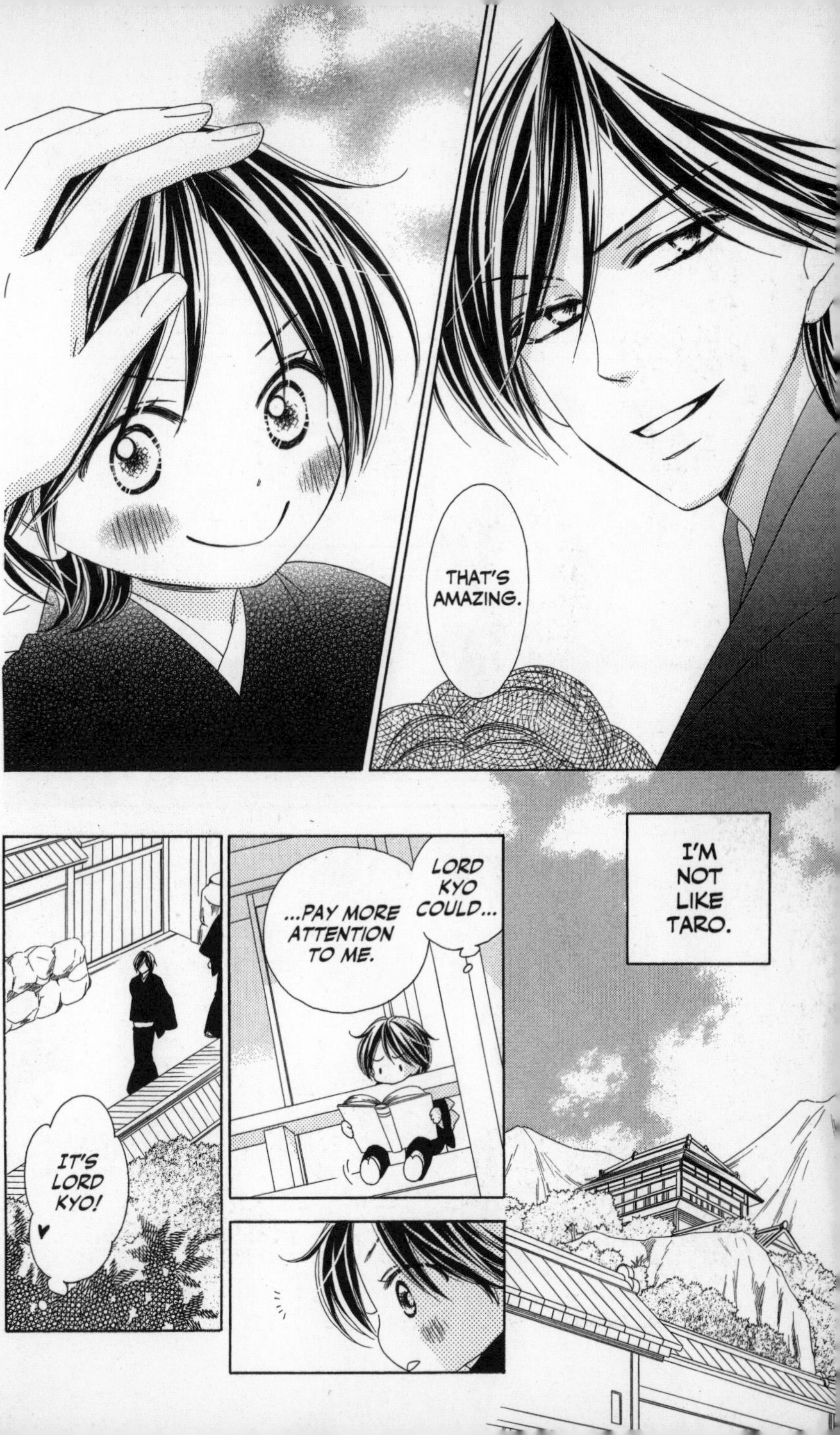
THAT'S AMAZING.
I'M NOT LIKE TARO.
LORD KYO COULD...
...PAY MORE ATTENTION TO ME.
IT'S LORD KYO!

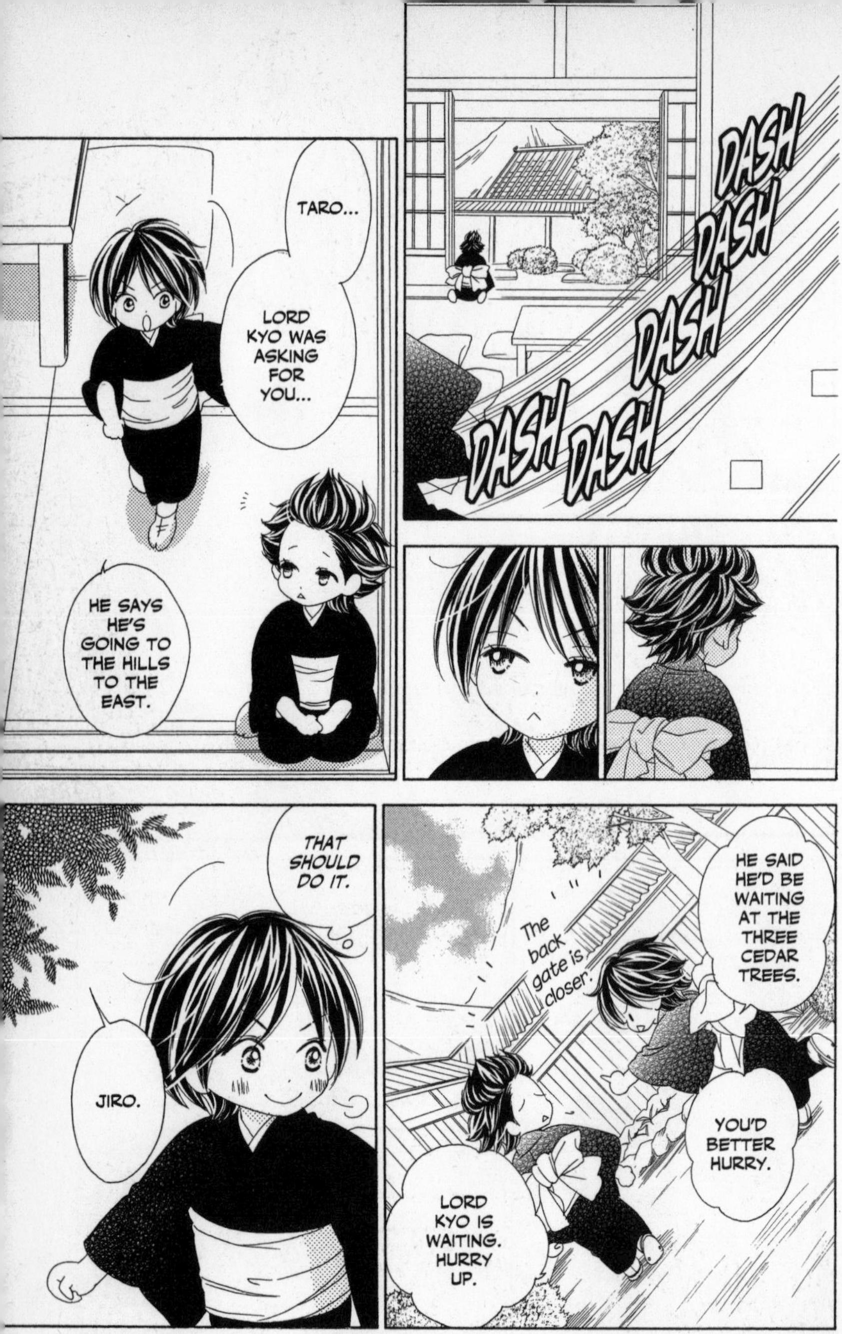
DASH DASH DASH DASH DASH
TARO...
LORD KYO WAS ASKING FOR YOU...
HE SAYS HE'S GOING TO THE HILLS TO THE EAST.
HE SAID HE'D BE WAITING AT THE THREE CEDAR TREES.
The back gate is closer.
YOU'D BETTER HURRY.
LORD KYO IS WAITING. HURRY UP.
THAT SHOULD DO IT.
JIRO.

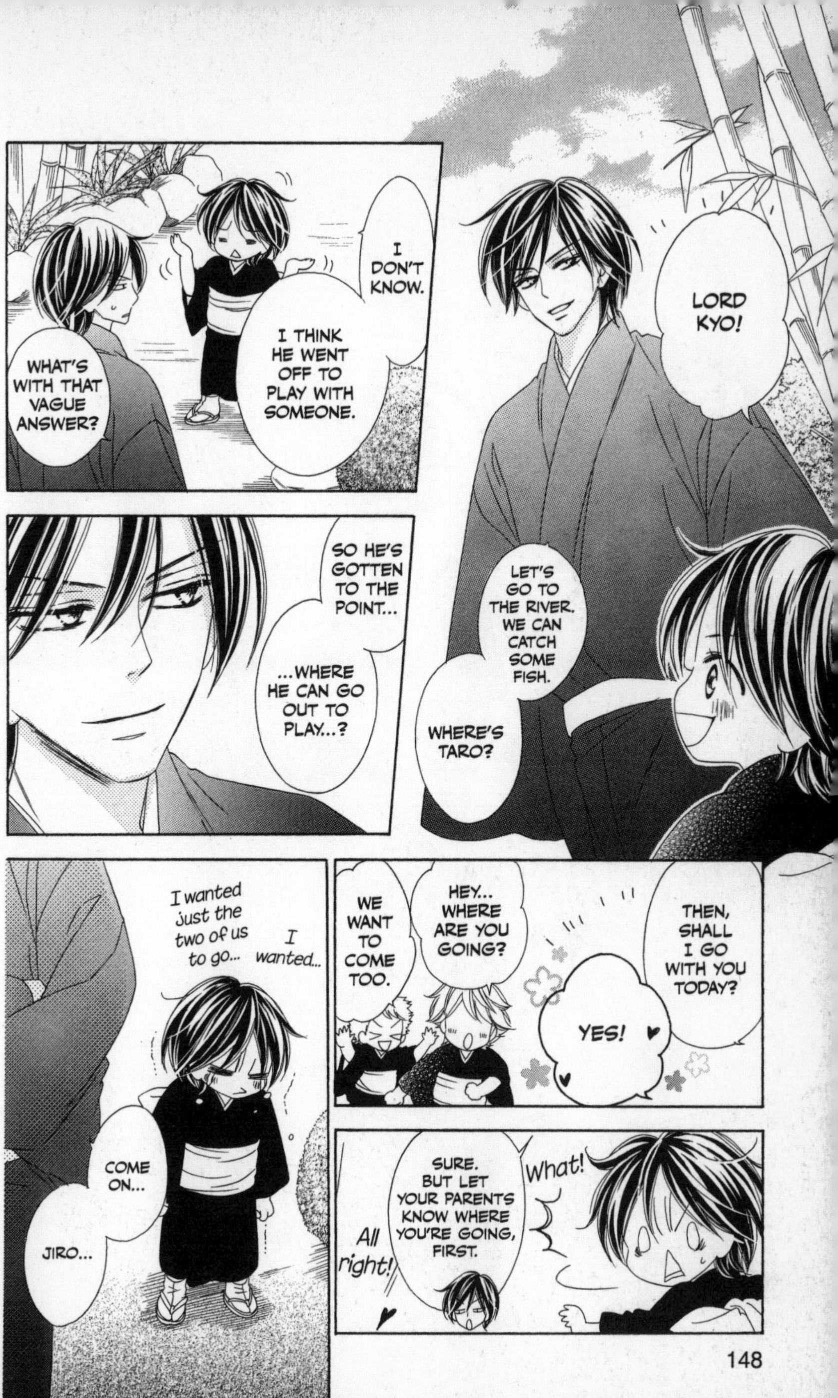
LORD KYO!
LET'S GO TO THE RIVER. WE CAN CATCH SOME FISH.
WHERE'S TARO?
I DON'T KNOW.
I THINK HE WENT OFF TO PLAY WITH SOMEONE.
WHAT'S WITH THAT VAGUE ANSWER?
SO HE'S GOTTEN TO THE POINT...
...WHERE HE CAN GO OUT TO PLAY...?
THEN, SHALL I GO WITH YOU TODAY?
YES!
HEY... WHERE ARE YOU GOING?
WE WANT TO COME TOO.
What!
SURE. BUT LET YOUR PARENTS KNOW WHERE YOU'RE GOING, FIRST.
All right!
I wanted...
I wanted just the two of us to go...
COME ON...
JIRO...

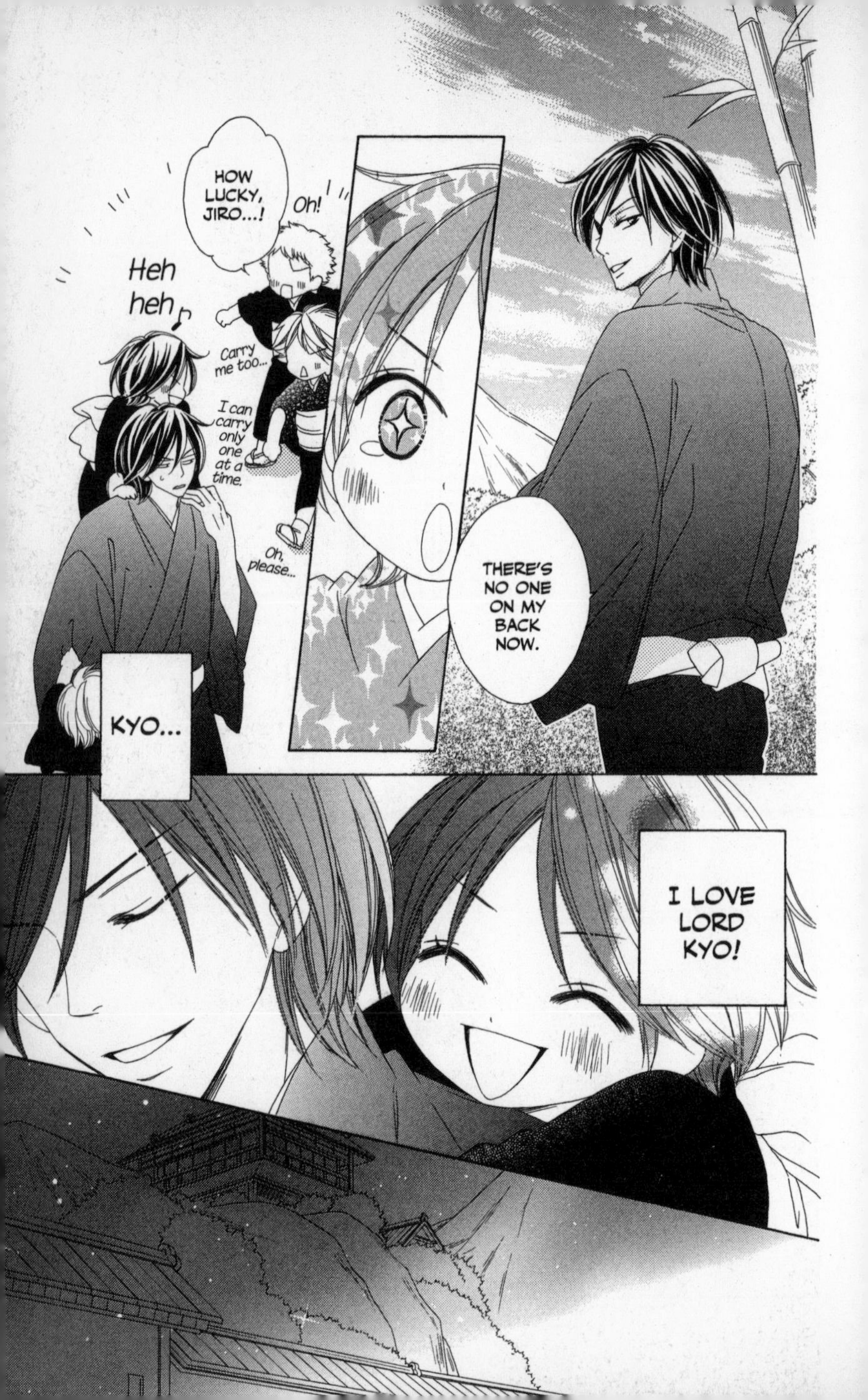
THERE'S NO ONE ON MY BACK NOW.
HOW LUCKY, JIRO...!
Oh!
Heh heh
Carry me too...
I can carry only one at a time.
Oh, please...
KYO...
I LOVE LORD KYO!

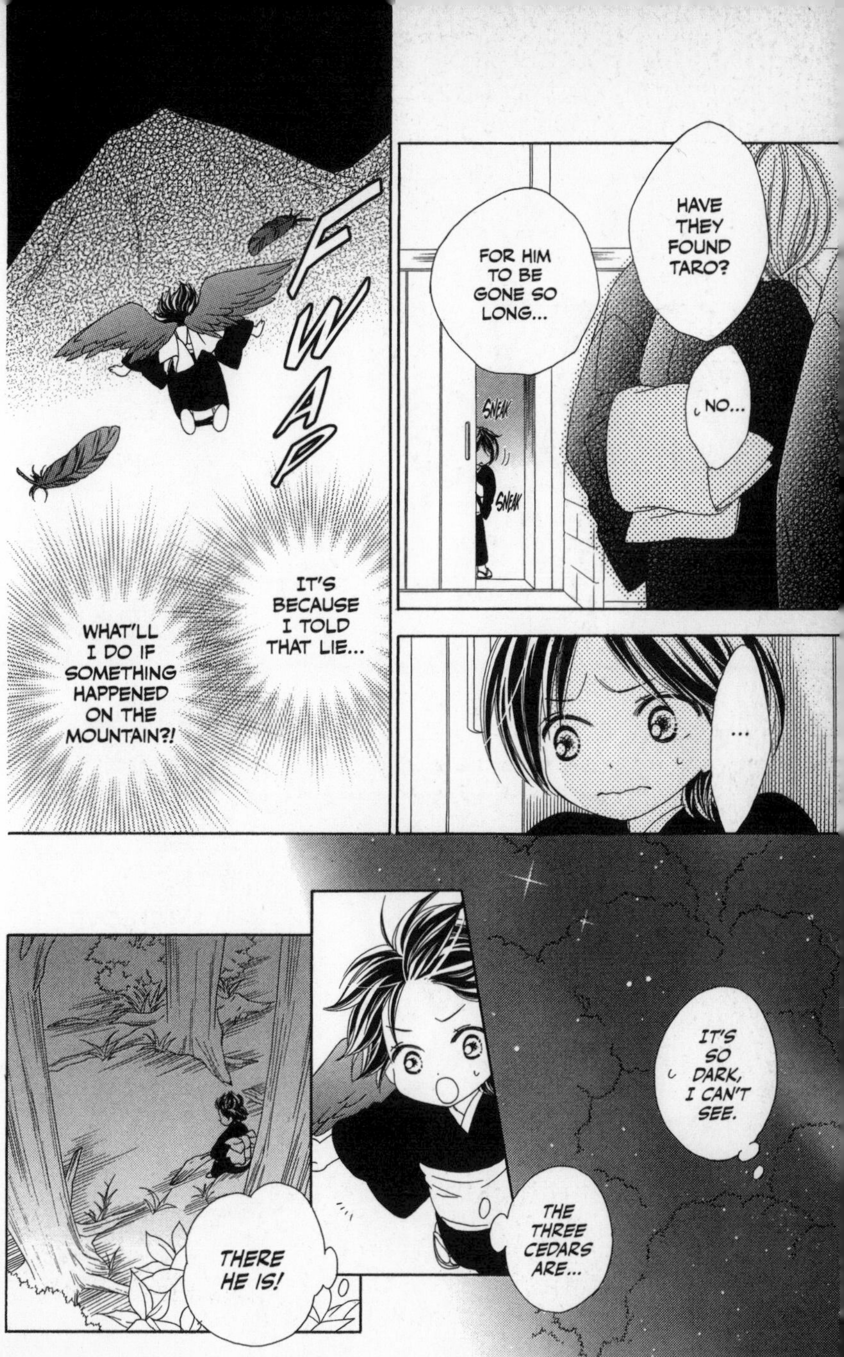
HAVE THEY FOUND TARO?
NO...
FOR HIM TO BE GONE SO LONG...
SNEAK
SNEAK
...
FWAP
IT'S BECAUSE I TOLD THAT LIE...
WHAT'LL I DO IF SOMETHING HAPPENED ON THE MOUNTAIN?!
IT'S SO DARK, I CAN'T SEE.
THE THREE CEDARS ARE...
THERE HE IS!

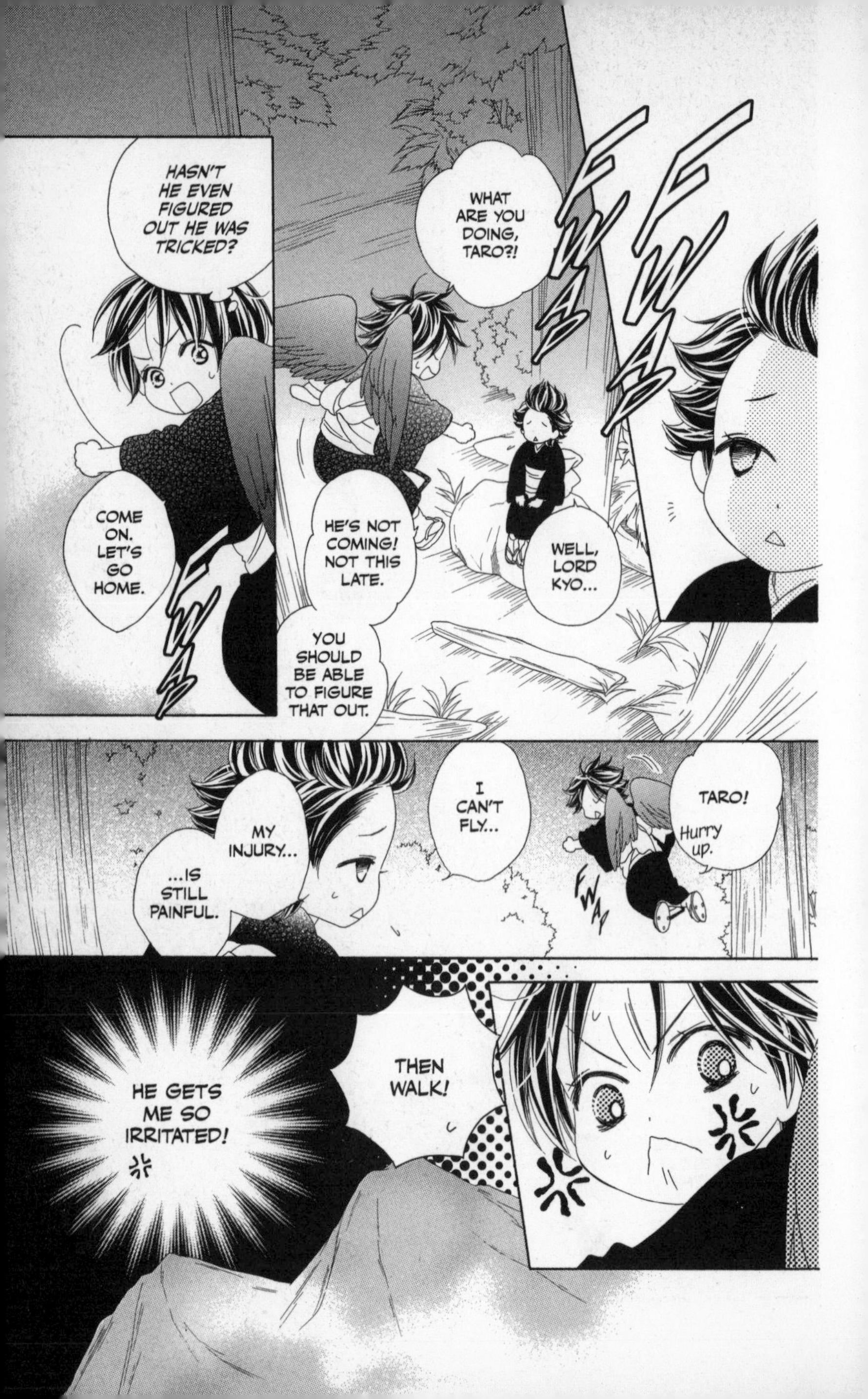
FWAM
FWAM
WHAT ARE YOU DOING, TARO?!
WELL, LORD KYO...
HE'S NOT COMING! NOT THIS LATE.
YOU SHOULD BE ABLE TO FIGURE THAT OUT.
HASN'T HE EVEN FIGURED OUT HE WAS TRICKED?
COME ON. LET'S GO HOME.
FWAM
TARO!
Hurry up.
FWAM
I CAN'T FLY...
MY INJURY...
...IS STILL PAINFUL.
THEN WALK!
HE GETS ME SO IRRITATED!

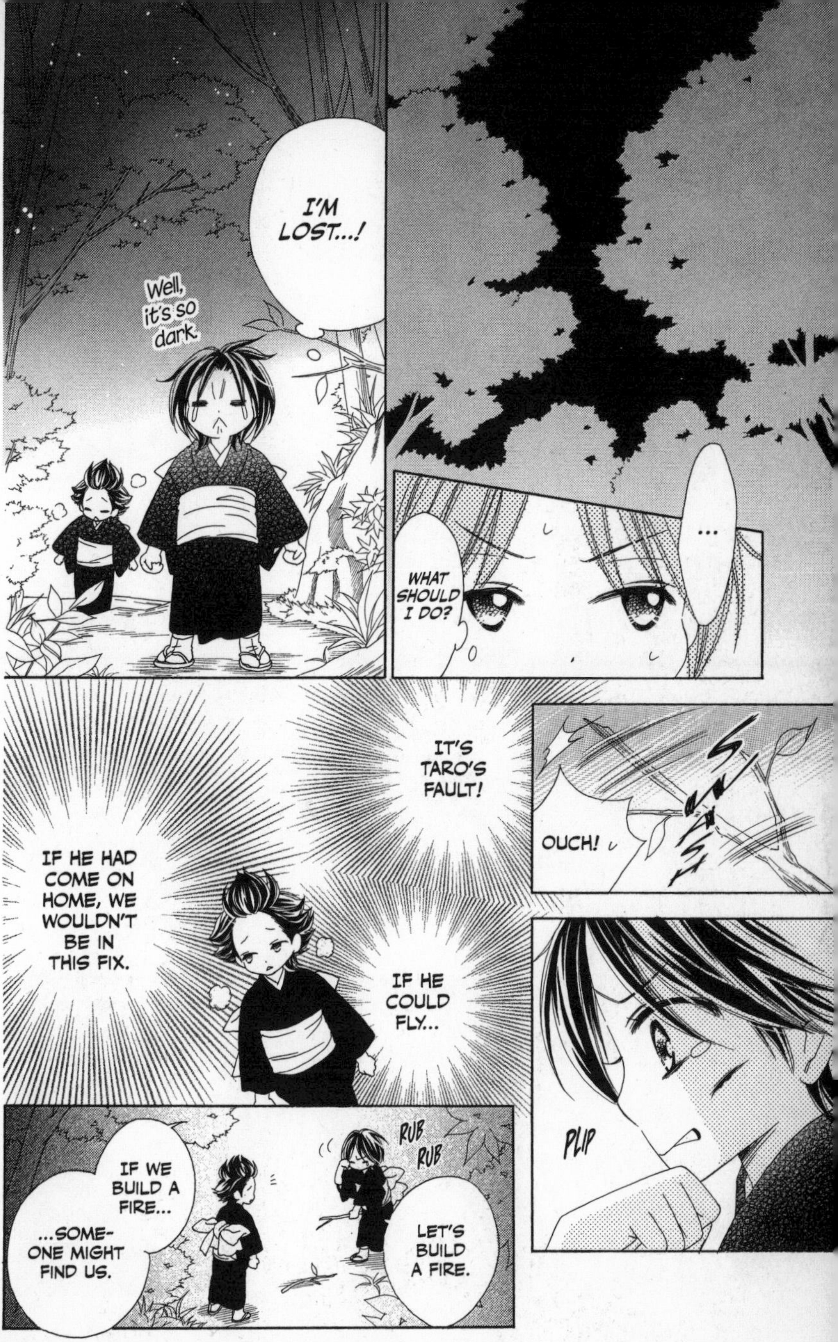
...
WHAT SHOULD I DO?
I'M LOST...!
Well, it's so dark.
OUCH!
PLIP
IT'S TARO'S FAULT!
IF HE HAD COME ON HOME, WE WOULDN'T BE IN THIS FIX.
IF HE COULD FLY...
RUB RUB
LET'S BUILD A FIRE.
IF WE BUILD A FIRE...
...SOME-ONE MIGHT FIND US.

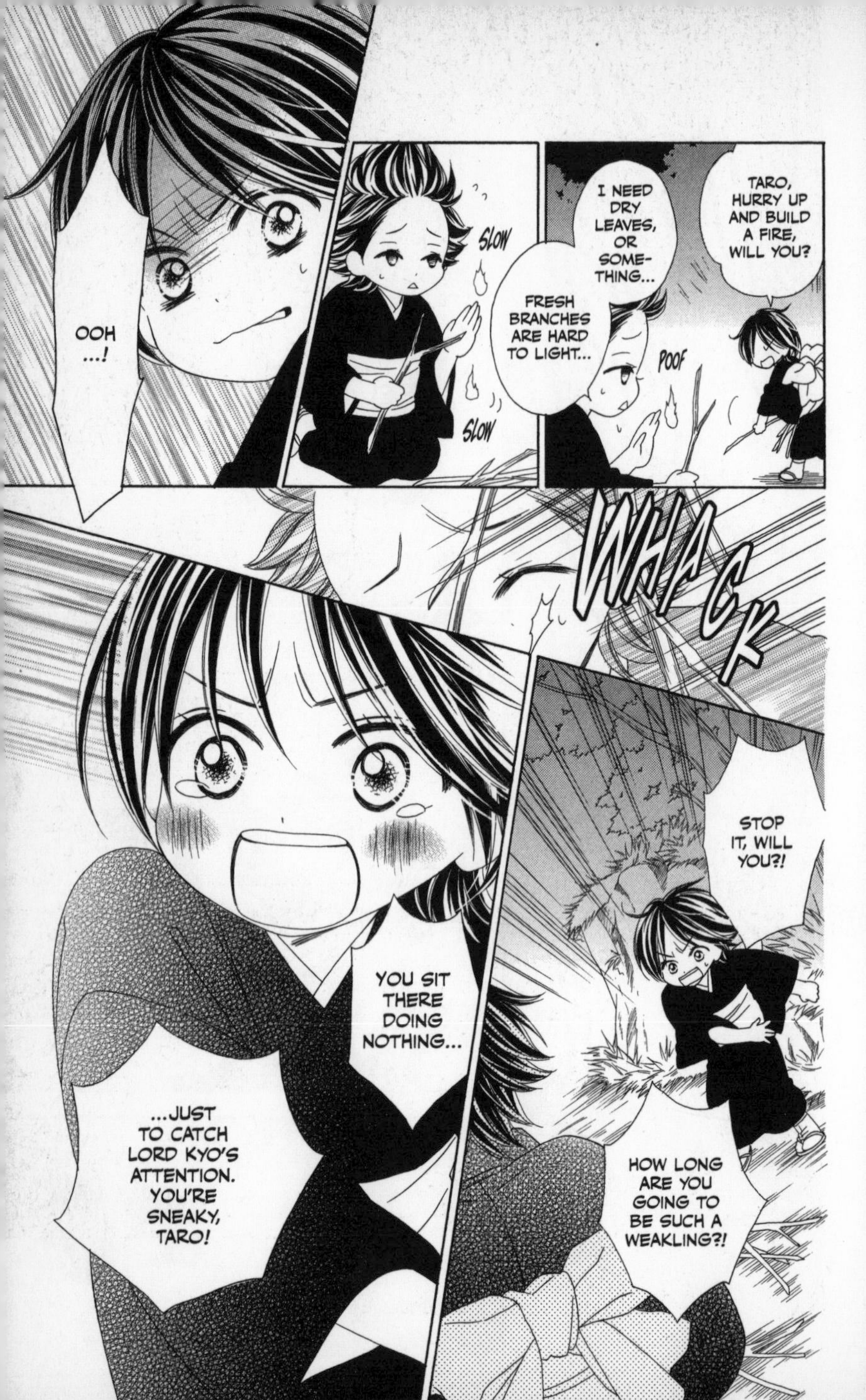
TARO, HURRY UP AND BUILD A FIRE, WILL YOU?
I NEED DRY LEAVES, OR SOME-THING...
FRESH BRANCHES ARE HARD TO LIGHT...
POOF
SLOW
SLOW
OOH ...!
WHACK
STOP IT, WILL YOU?!
HOW LONG ARE YOU GOING TO BE SUCH A WEAKLING?!
YOU SIT THERE DOING NOTHING...
...JUST TO CATCH LORD KYO'S ATTENTION. YOU'RE SNEAKY, TARO!

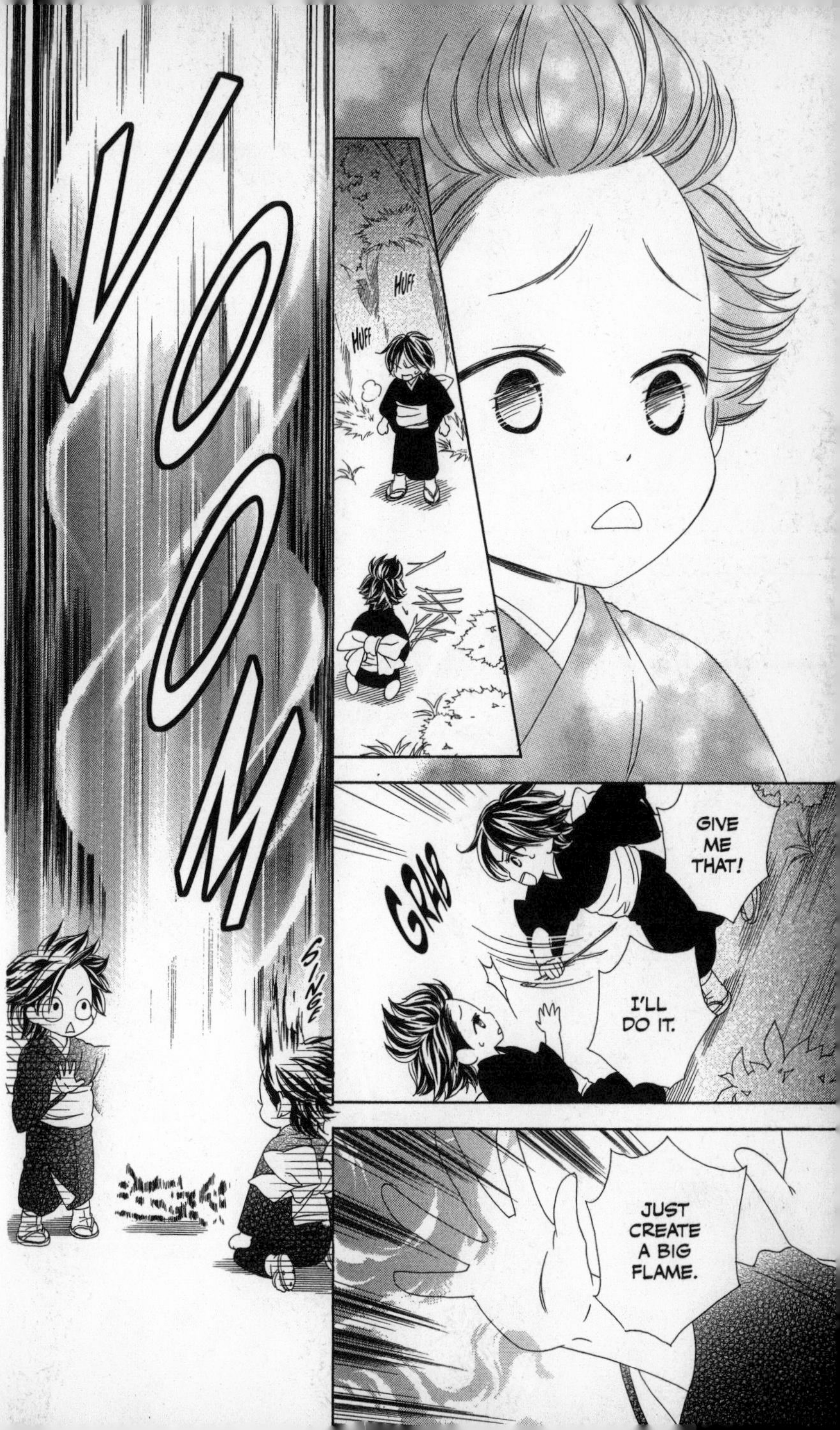
HUFF
HUFF
GIVE ME THAT!
GRAB
I'LL DO IT.
JUST CREATE A BIG FLAME.
VOOM
SINGE

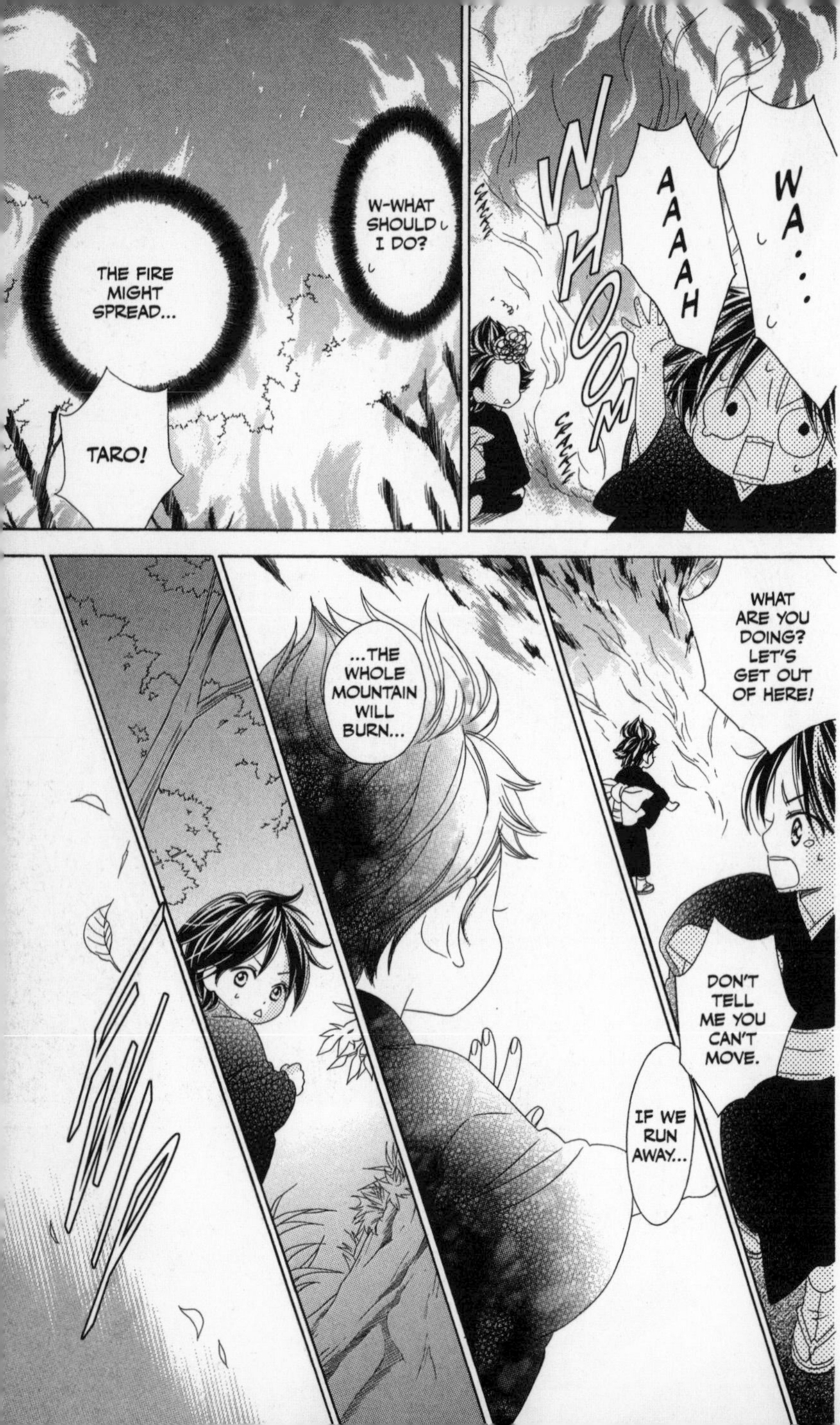
WA...
AAAAH
WHOOM
W-WHAT SHOULD I DO?
THE FIRE MIGHT SPREAD...
TARO!
WHAT ARE YOU DOING? LET'S GET OUT OF HERE!
DON'T TELL ME YOU CAN'T MOVE.
IF WE RUN AWAY...
...THE WHOLE MOUNTAIN WILL BURN...

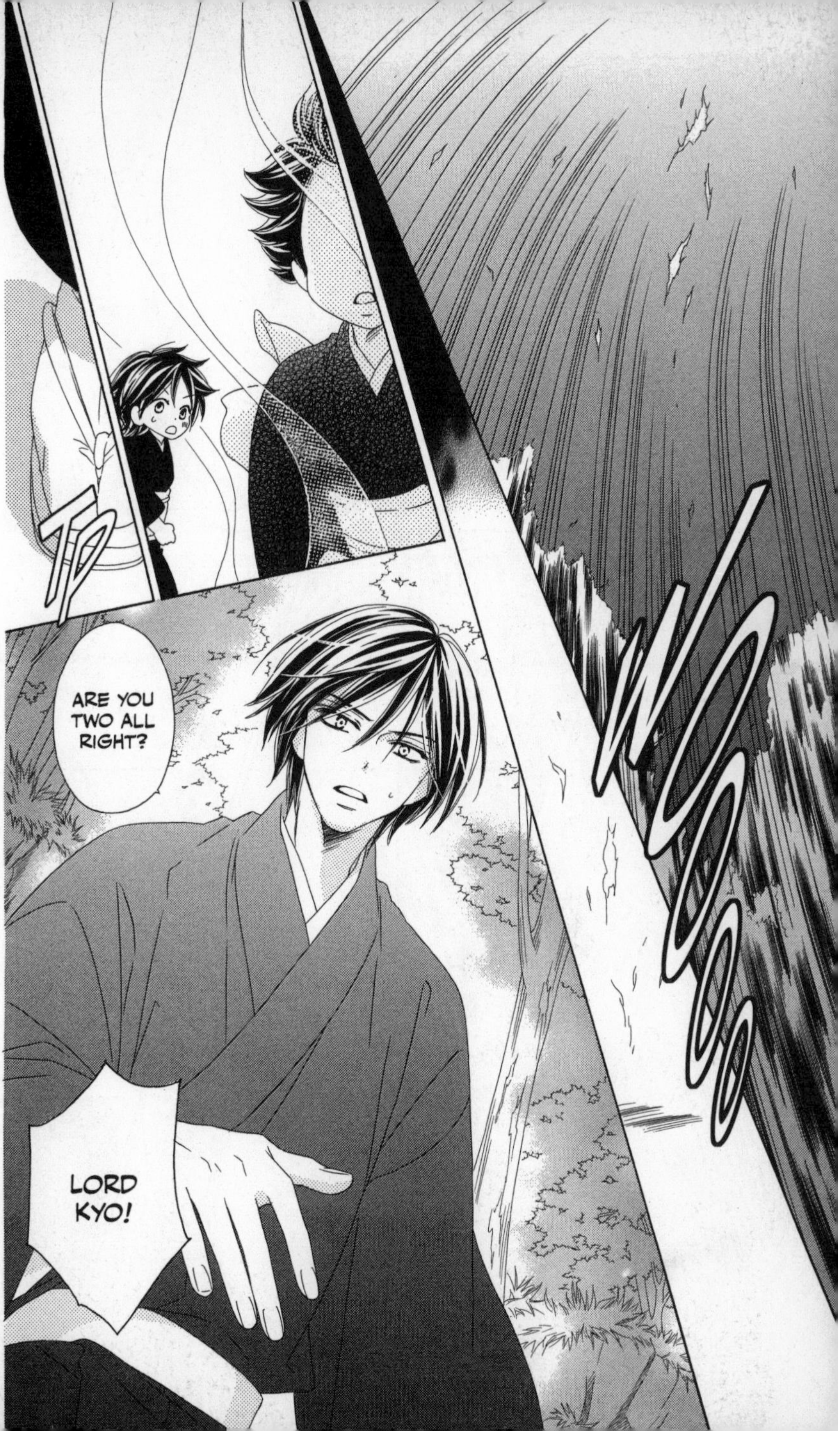
WOOOO
TP
ARE YOU TWO ALL RIGHT?
LORD KYO!

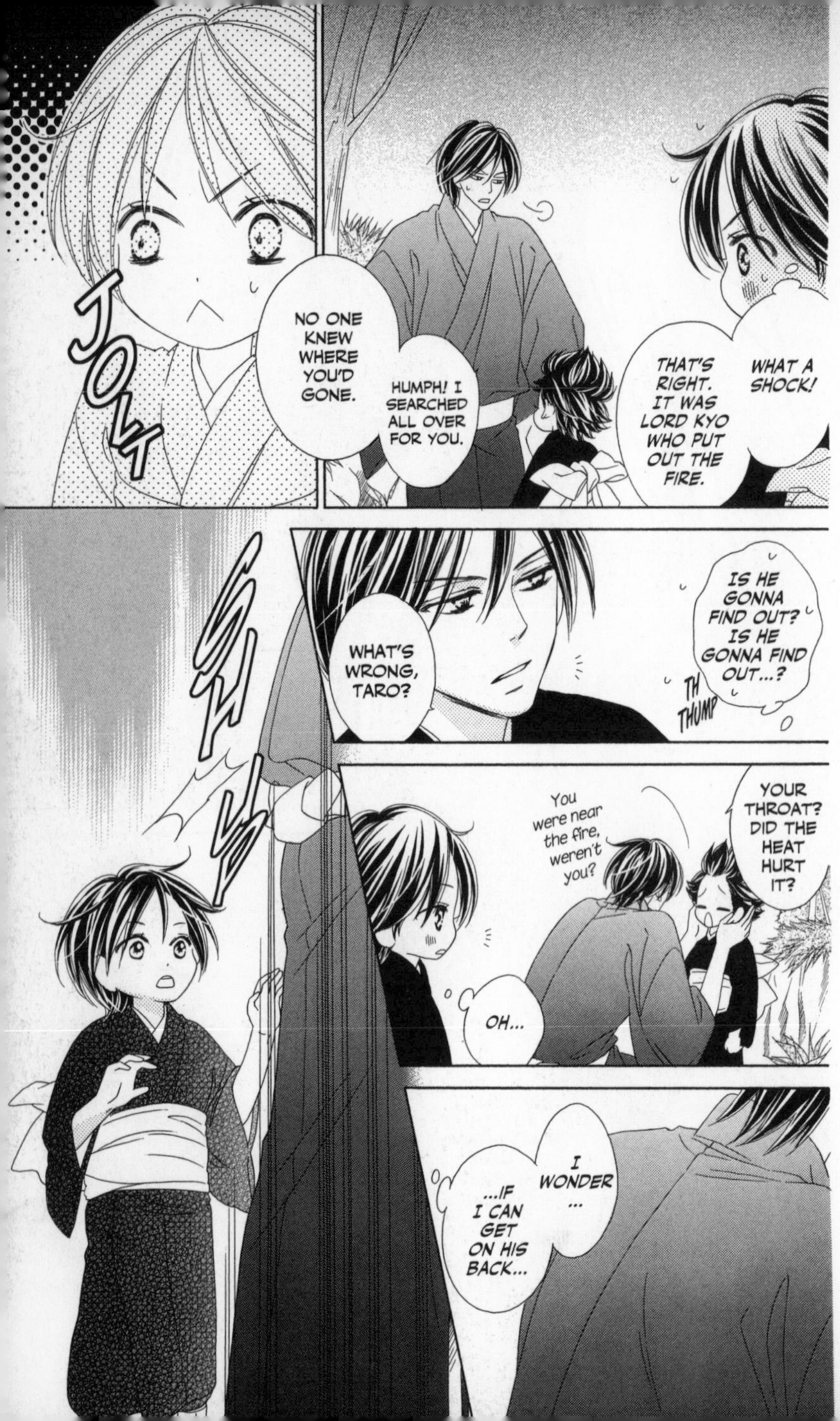
WHAT A SHOCK!
THAT'S RIGHT. IT WAS LORD KYO WHO PUT OUT THE FIRE.
HUMPH! I SEARCHED ALL OVER FOR YOU.
NO ONE KNEW WHERE YOU'D GONE.
JOLT
IS HE GONNA FIND OUT? IS HE GONNA FIND OUT...?
TH THUMP
WHAT'S WRONG, TARO?
YOUR THROAT? DID THE HEAT HURT IT?
You were near the fire, weren't you?
OH...
I WONDER...
...IF I CAN GET ON HIS BACK...

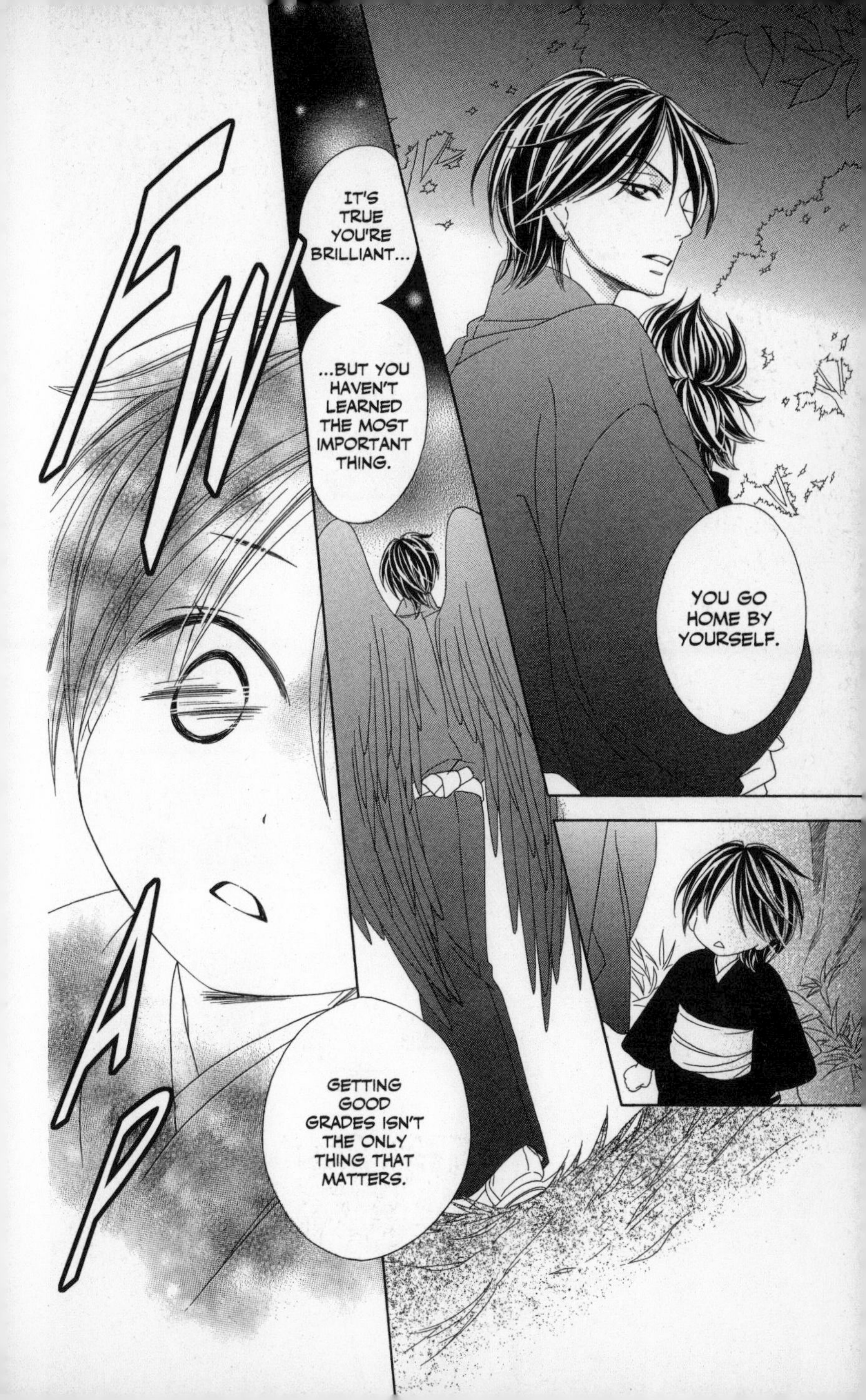
YOU GO HOME BY YOURSELF.
FWAP
IT'S TRUE YOU'RE BRILLIANT...
...BUT YOU HAVEN'T LEARNED THE MOST IMPORTANT THING.
GETTING GOOD GRADES ISN'T THE ONLY THING THAT MATTERS.

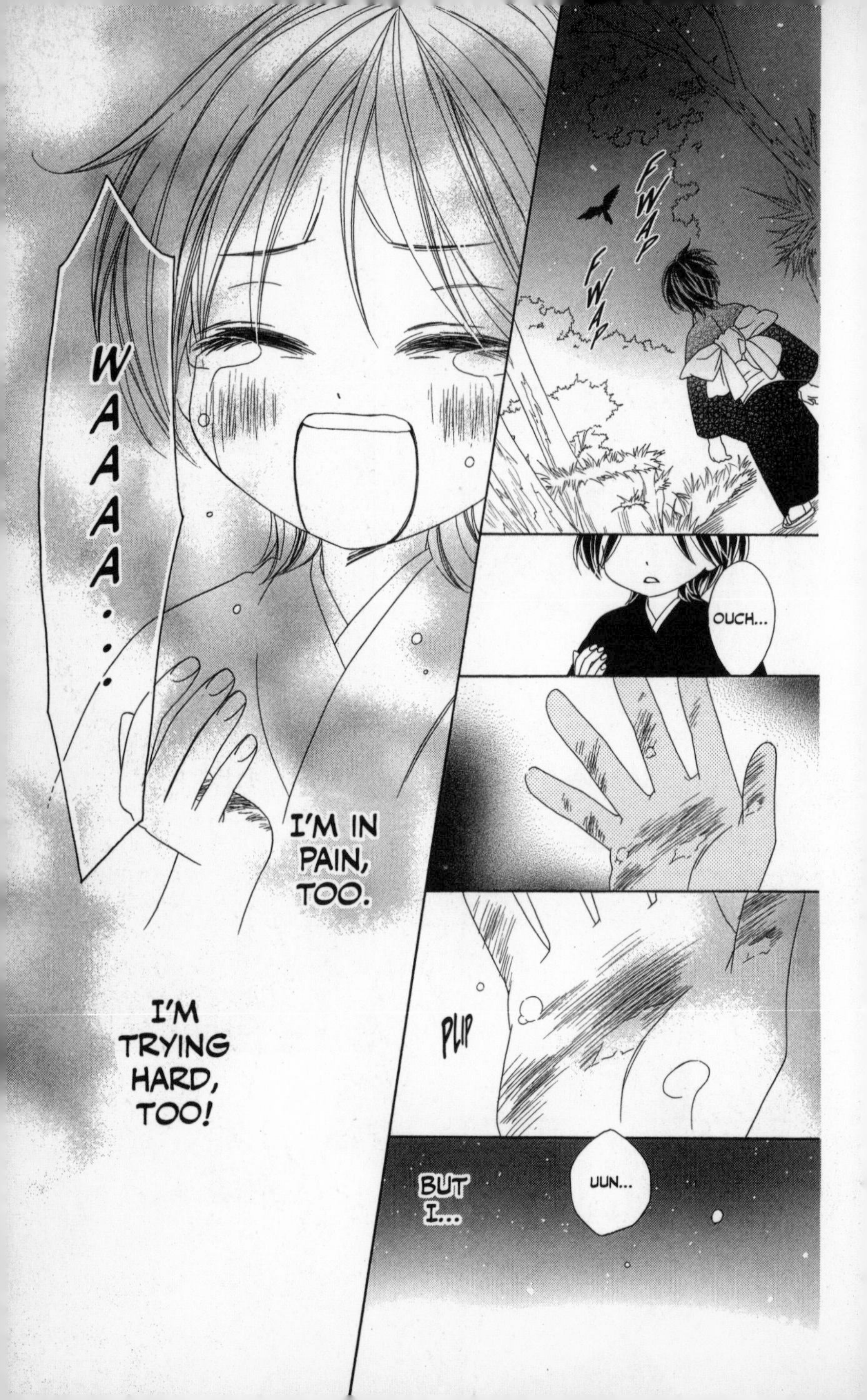
FWAP
FWAP
OUCH...
PLIP
UUN...
BUT I...
WAAAAA...
I'M IN PAIN, TOO.
I'M TRYING HARD, TOO!

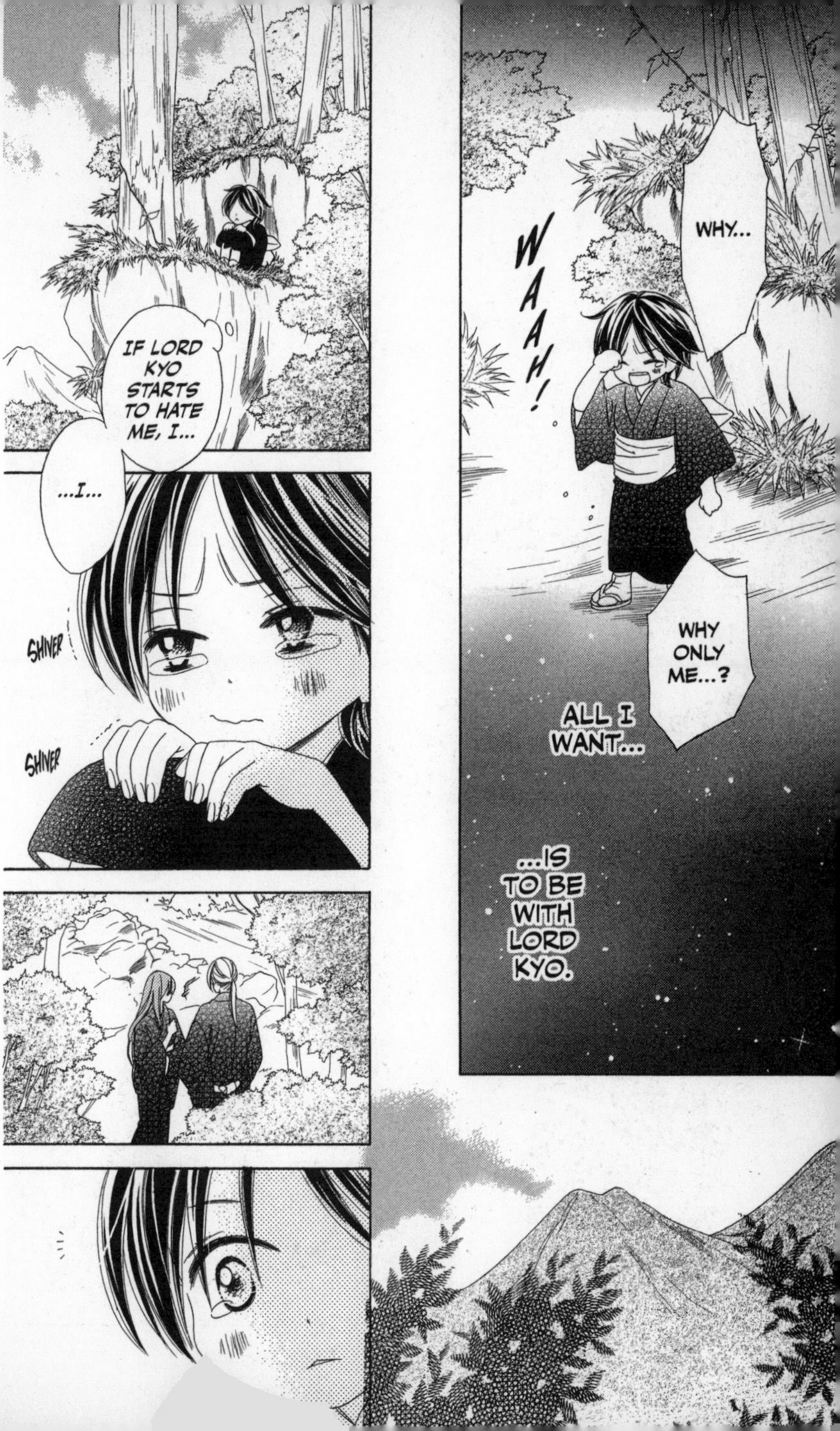WAAAH!
WHY...
WHY ONLY ME...?
ALL I WANT...
...IS TO BE WITH LORD KYO.
IF LORD KYO STARTS TO HATE ME, I...
...I...
SHIVER
SHIVER

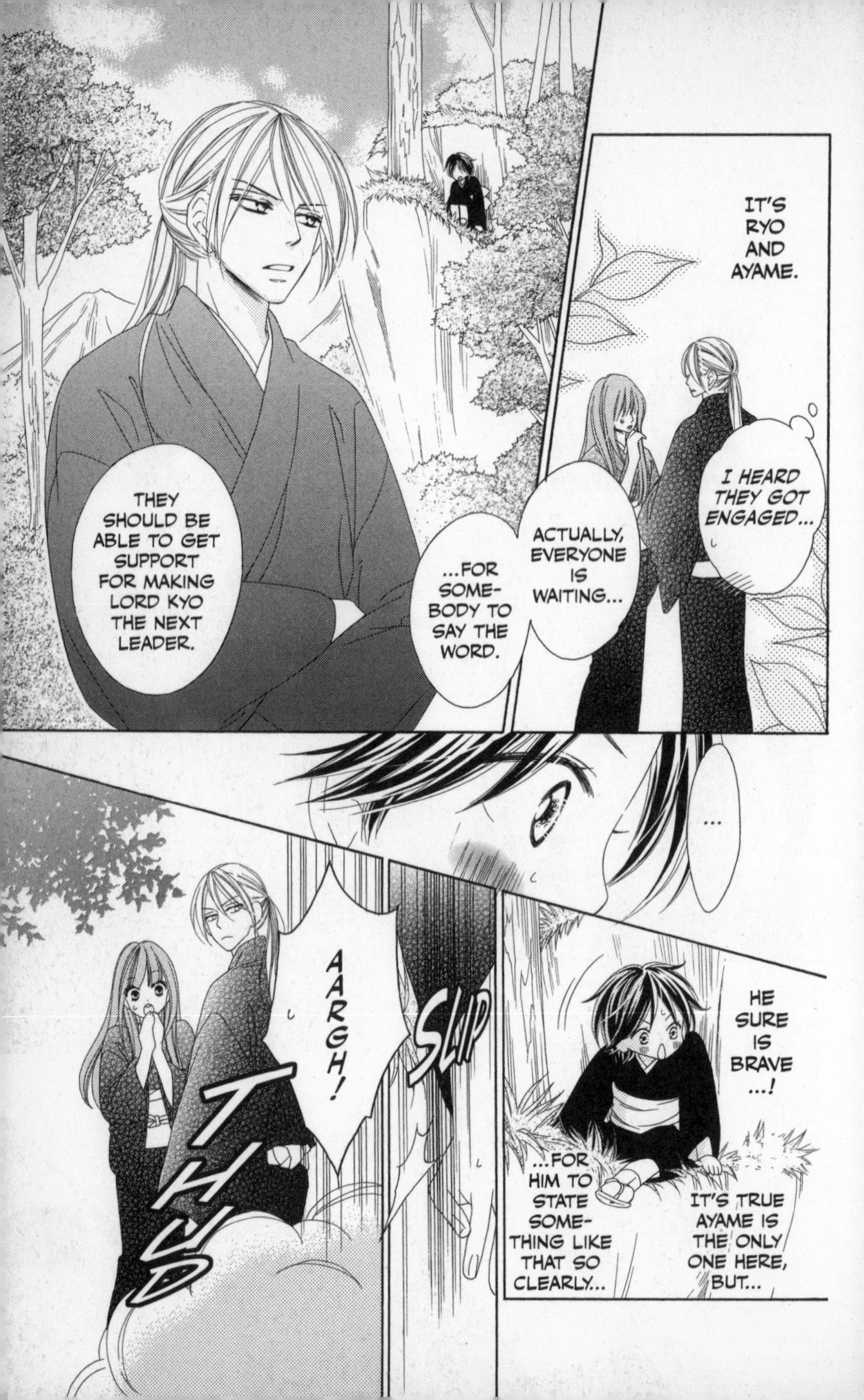
IT'S RYO AND AYAME.
I HEARD THEY GOT ENGAGED...
ACTUALLY, EVERYONE IS WAITING...
...FOR SOME-BODY TO SAY THE WORD.
THEY SHOULD BE ABLE TO GET SUPPORT FOR MAKING LORD KYO THE NEXT LEADER.
...
HE SURE IS BRAVE...!
IT'S TRUE AYAME IS THE ONLY ONE HERE, BUT...
...FOR HIM TO STATE SOME-THING LIKE THAT SO CLEARLY...
SLIP
AARGH!
THUD

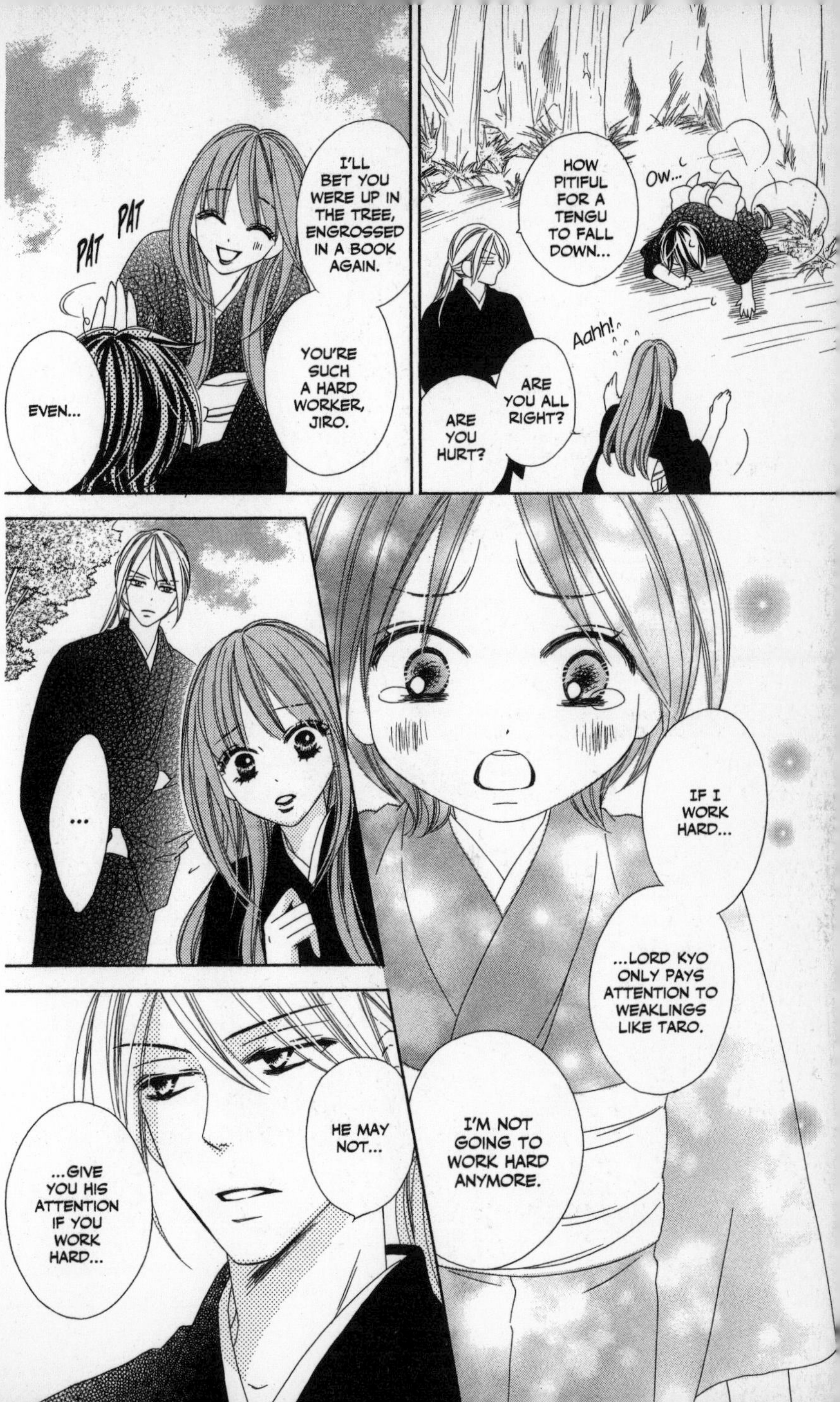
OW...
HOW PITIFUL FOR A TENGU TO FALL DOWN...
Aahh!
ARE YOU ALL RIGHT?
ARE YOU HURT?
I'LL BET YOU WERE UP IN THE TREE, ENGROSSED IN A BOOK AGAIN.
PAT PAT
YOU'RE SUCH A HARD WORKER, JIRO.
EVEN...
IF I WORK HARD...
...LORD KYO ONLY PAYS ATTENTION TO WEAKLINGS LIKE TARO.
I'M NOT GOING TO WORK HARD ANYMORE.
...
HE MAY NOT...
...GIVE YOU HIS ATTENTION IF YOU WORK HARD...

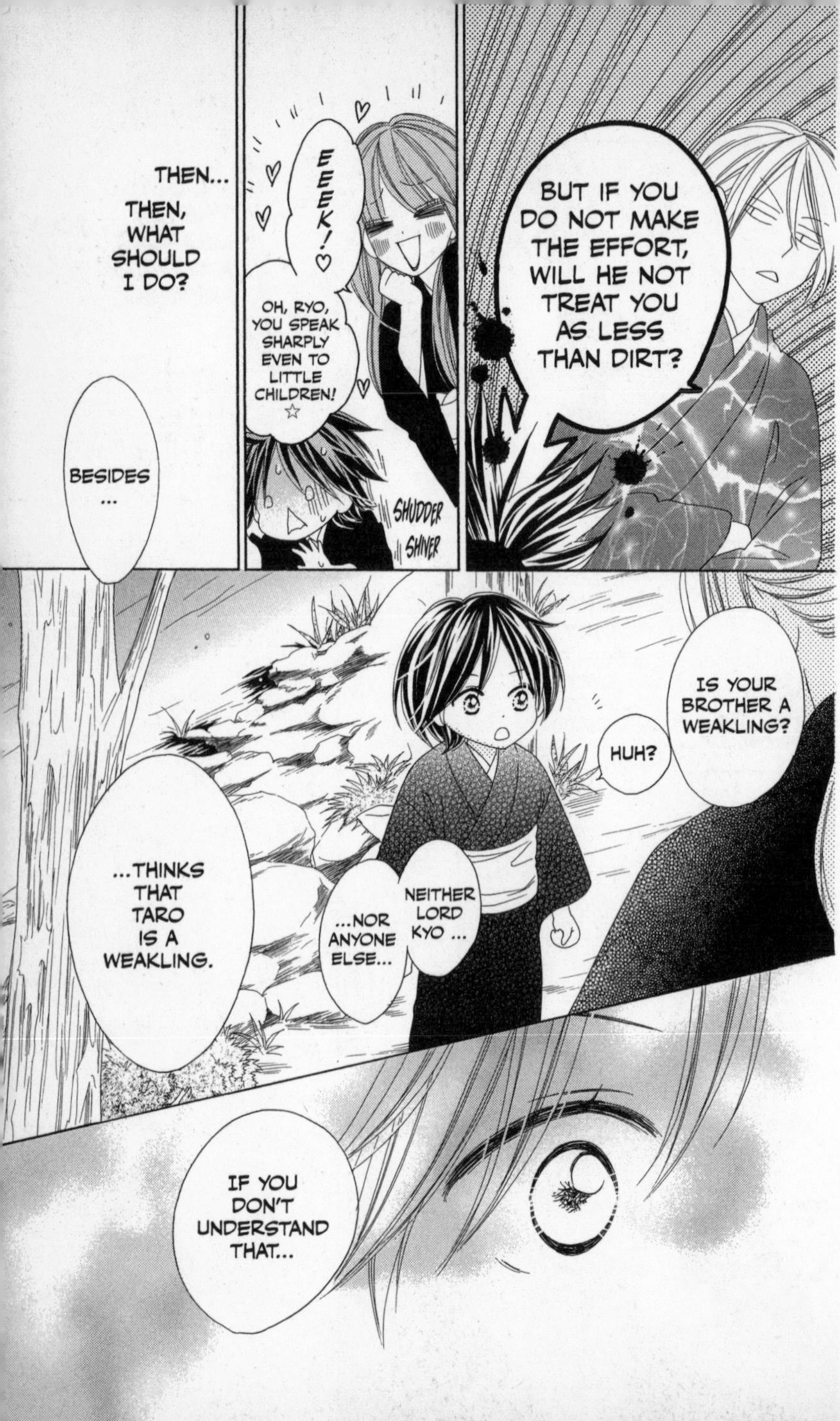
BUT IF YOU DO NOT MAKE THE EFFORT, WILL HE NOT TREAT YOU AS LESS THAN DIRT?
EEEK!♡
OH, RYO, YOU SPEAK SHARPLY EVEN TO LITTLE CHILDREN! ☆
SHUDDER
SHIVER
THEN...
THEN, WHAT SHOULD I DO?
BESIDES...
IS YOUR BROTHER A WEAKLING?
HUH?
NEITHER LORD KYO ...
...NOR ANYONE ELSE...
...THINKS THAT TARO IS A WEAKLING.
IF YOU DON'T UNDERSTAND THAT...

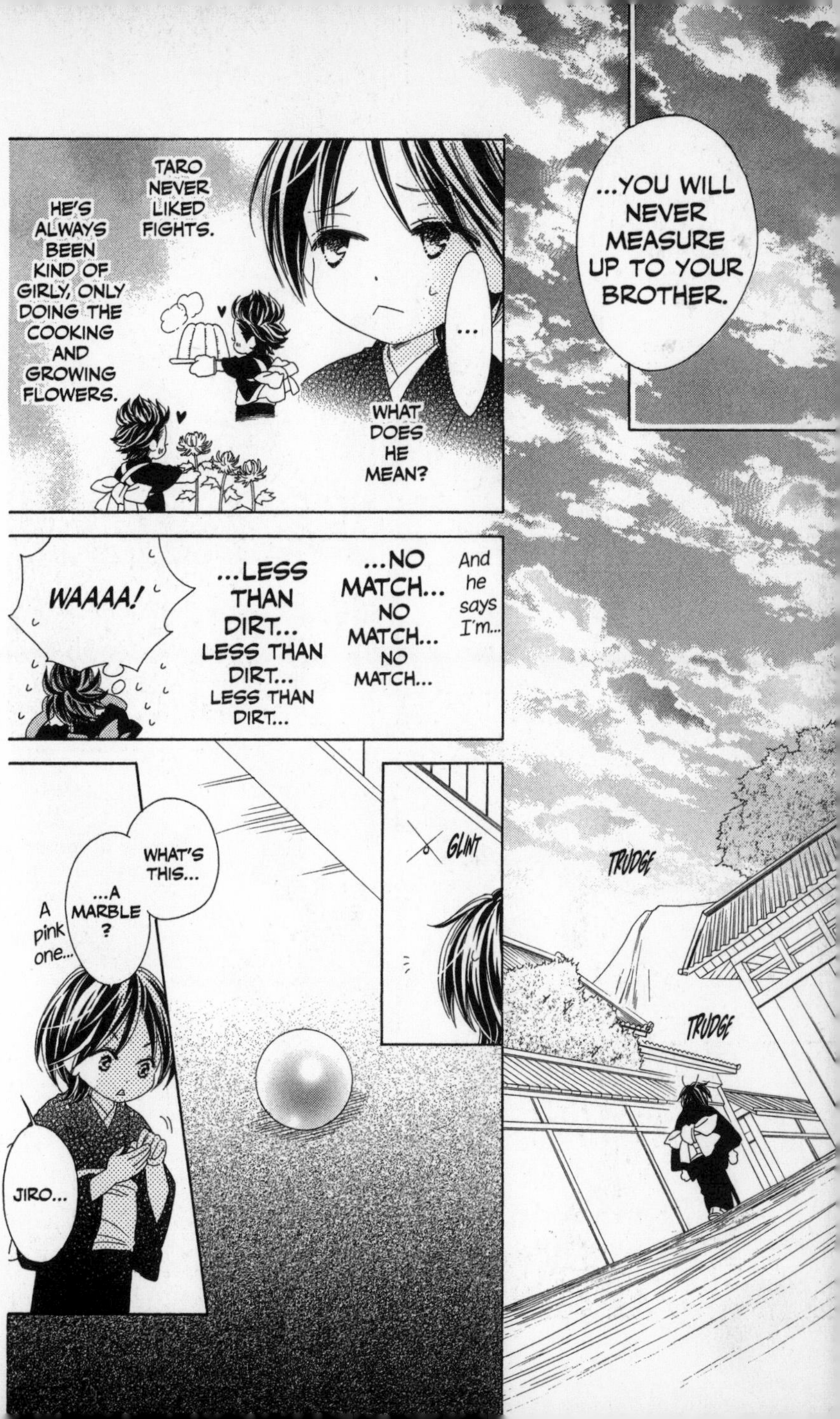
...YOU WILL NEVER MEASURE UP TO YOUR BROTHER.
TRUDGE
TRUDGE
...
WHAT DOES HE MEAN?
TARO NEVER LIKED FIGHTS.
HE'S ALWAYS BEEN KIND OF GIRLY, ONLY DOING THE COOKING AND GROWING FLOWERS.
And he says I'm...
...NO MATCH... NO MATCH... NO MATCH...
...LESS THAN DIRT... LESS THAN DIRT... LESS THAN DIRT...
WAAAA!
GLINT
WHAT'S THIS...
...A MARBLE?
A pink one...
JIRO...

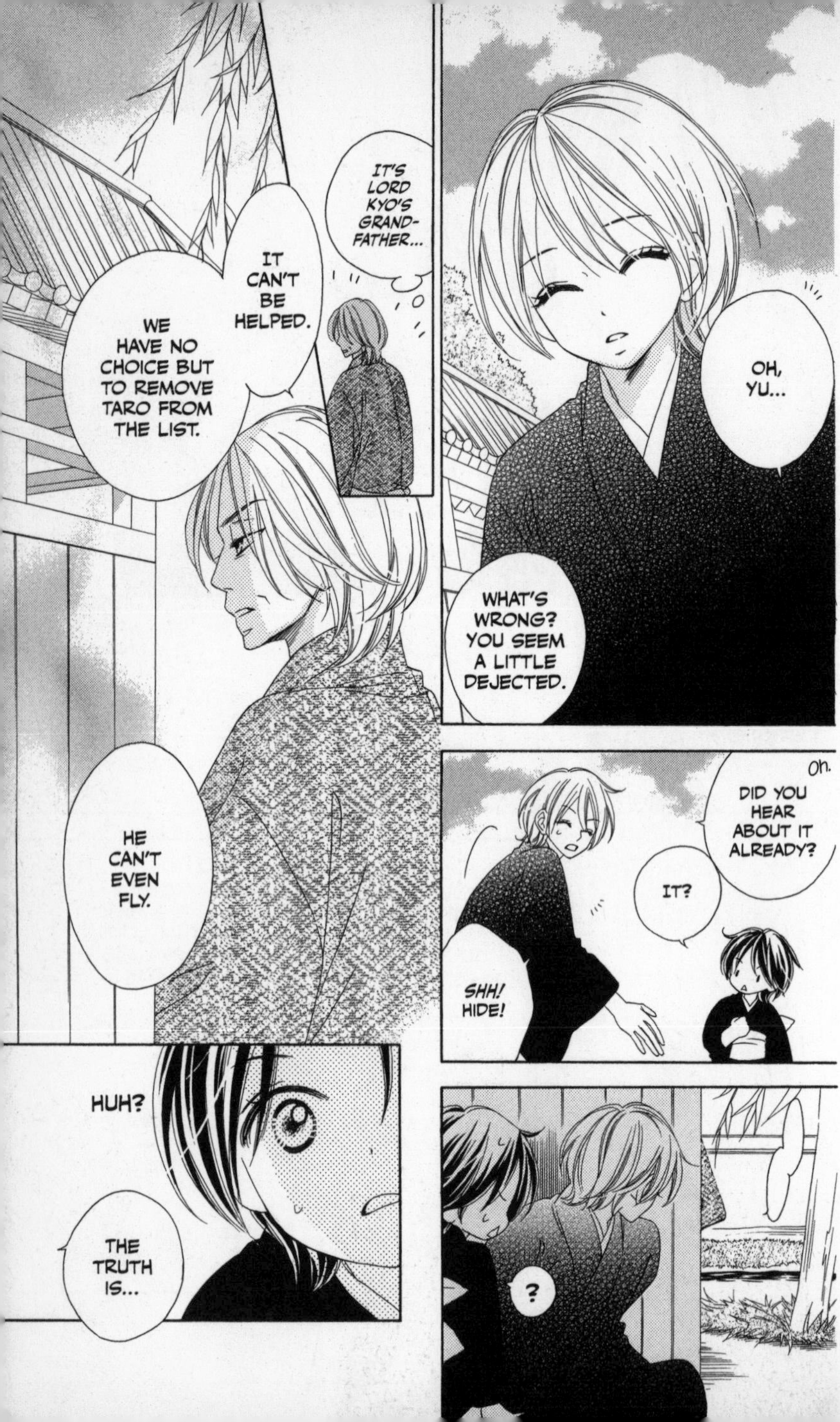
OH, YU...
WHAT'S WRONG? YOU SEEM A LITTLE DEJECTED.
Oh.
DID YOU HEAR ABOUT IT ALREADY?
IT?
SHH! HIDE!
IT'S LORD KYO'S GRANDFATHER...
IT CAN'T BE HELPED.
WE HAVE NO CHOICE BUT TO REMOVE TARO FROM THE LIST.
HE CAN'T EVEN FLY.
?
HUH?
THE TRUTH IS...

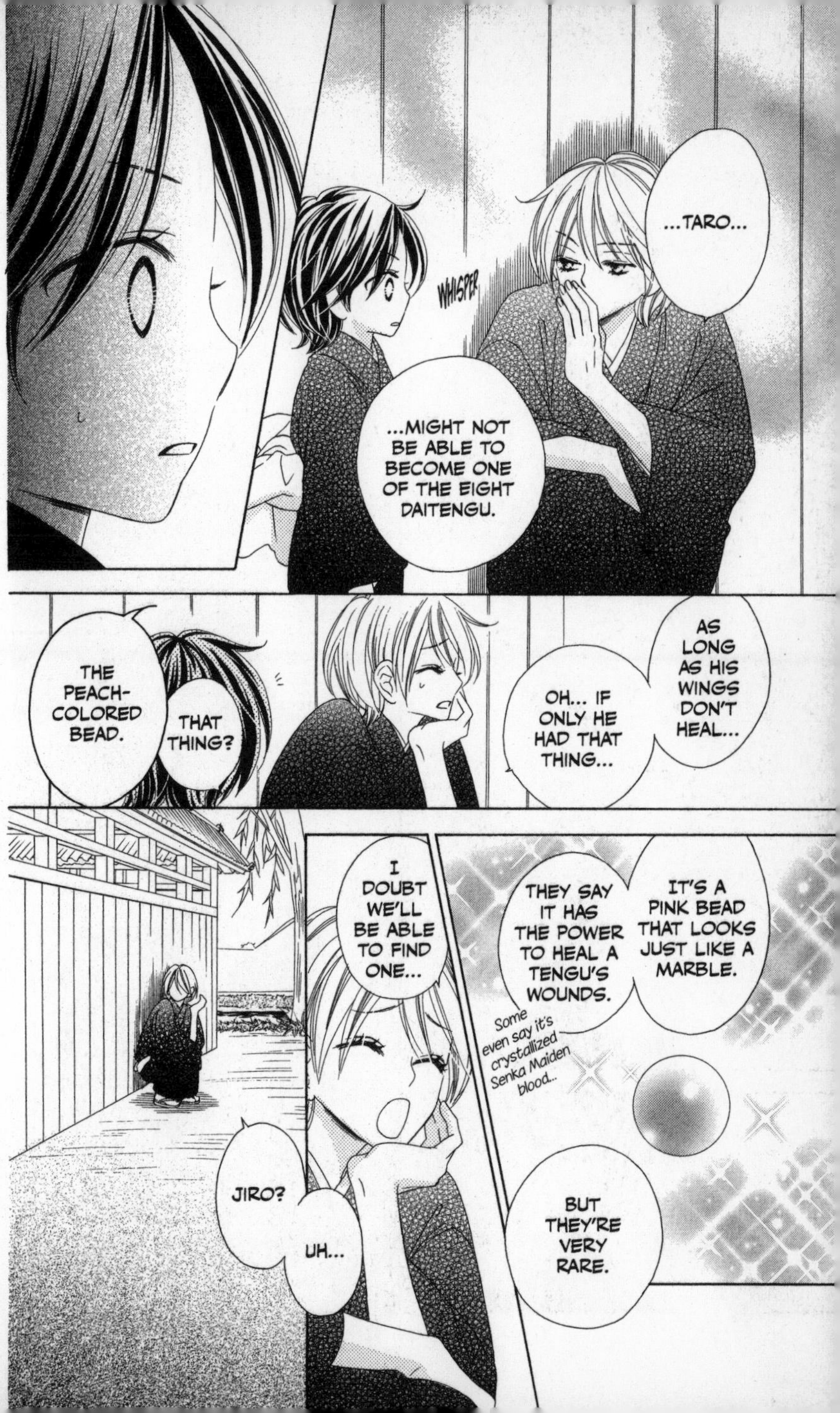
...TARO...
WHISPER
...MIGHT NOT BE ABLE TO BECOME ONE OF THE EIGHT DAITENGU.
AS LONG AS HIS WINGS DON'T HEAL...
OH... IF ONLY HE HAD THAT THING...
THAT THING?
THE PEACH-COLORED BEAD.
IT'S A PINK BEAD THAT LOOKS JUST LIKE A MARBLE.
THEY SAY IT HAS THE POWER TO HEAL A TENGU'S WOUNDS.
Some even say it's crystallized Senka Maiden blood...
BUT THEY'RE VERY RARE.
I DOUBT WE'LL BE ABLE TO FIND ONE...
JIRO?
UH...

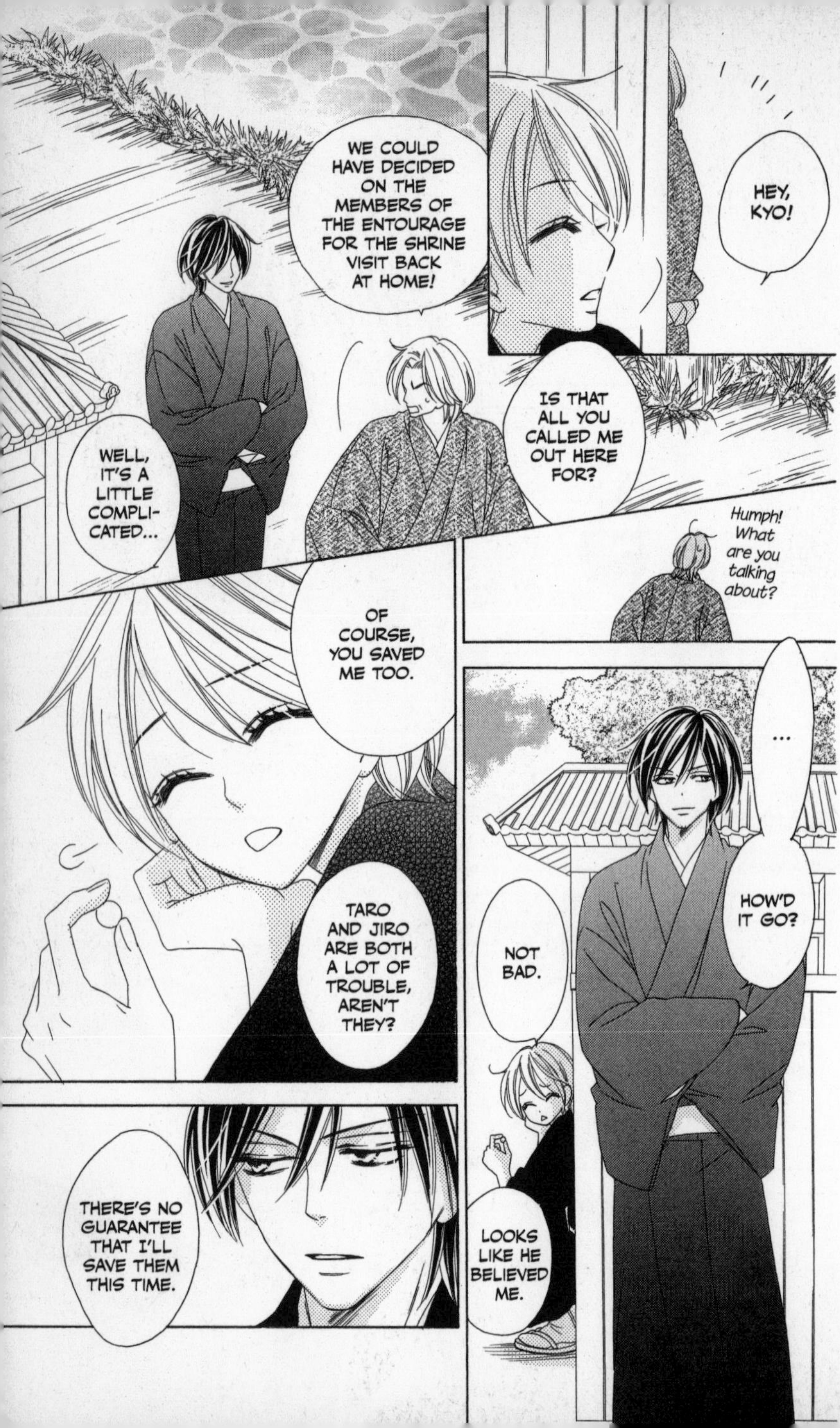
HEY, KYO!
IS THAT ALL YOU CALLED ME OUT HERE FOR?
WE COULD HAVE DECIDED ON THE MEMBERS OF THE ENTOURAGE FOR THE SHRINE VISIT BACK AT HOME!
WELL, IT'S A LITTLE COMPLI-CATED...
Humph! What are you talking about?
...
HOW'D IT GO?
NOT BAD.
LOOKS LIKE HE BELIEVED ME.
OF COURSE, YOU SAVED ME TOO.
TARO AND JIRO ARE BOTH A LOT OF TROUBLE, AREN'T THEY?
THERE'S NO GUARANTEE THAT I'LL SAVE THEM THIS TIME.

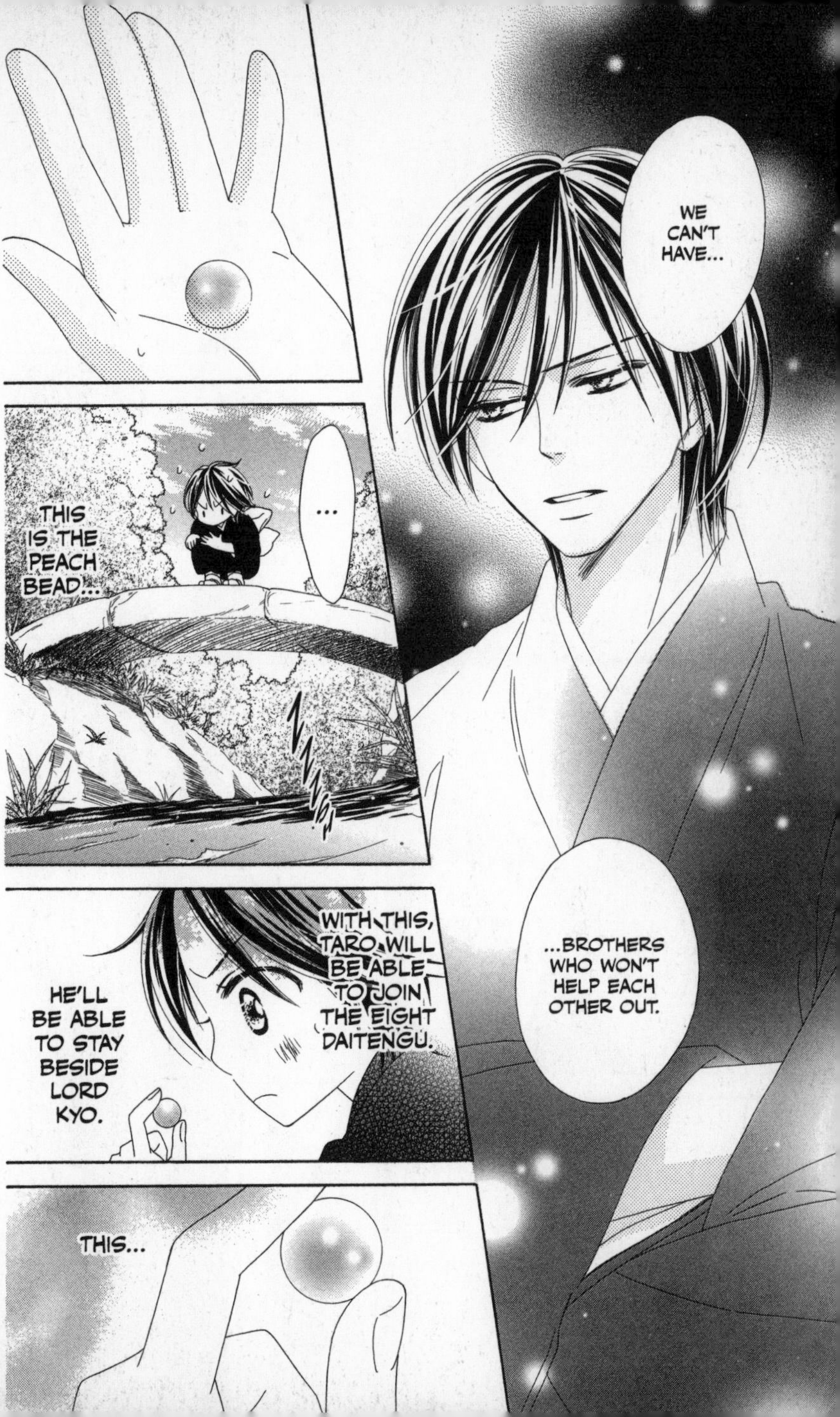
WE CAN'T HAVE...
...BROTHERS WHO WON'T HELP EACH OTHER OUT.
...
THIS IS THE PEACH BEAD...
WITH THIS, TARO WILL BE ABLE TO JOIN THE EIGHT DAITENGU.
HE'LL BE ABLE TO STAY BESIDE LORD KYO.
THIS...

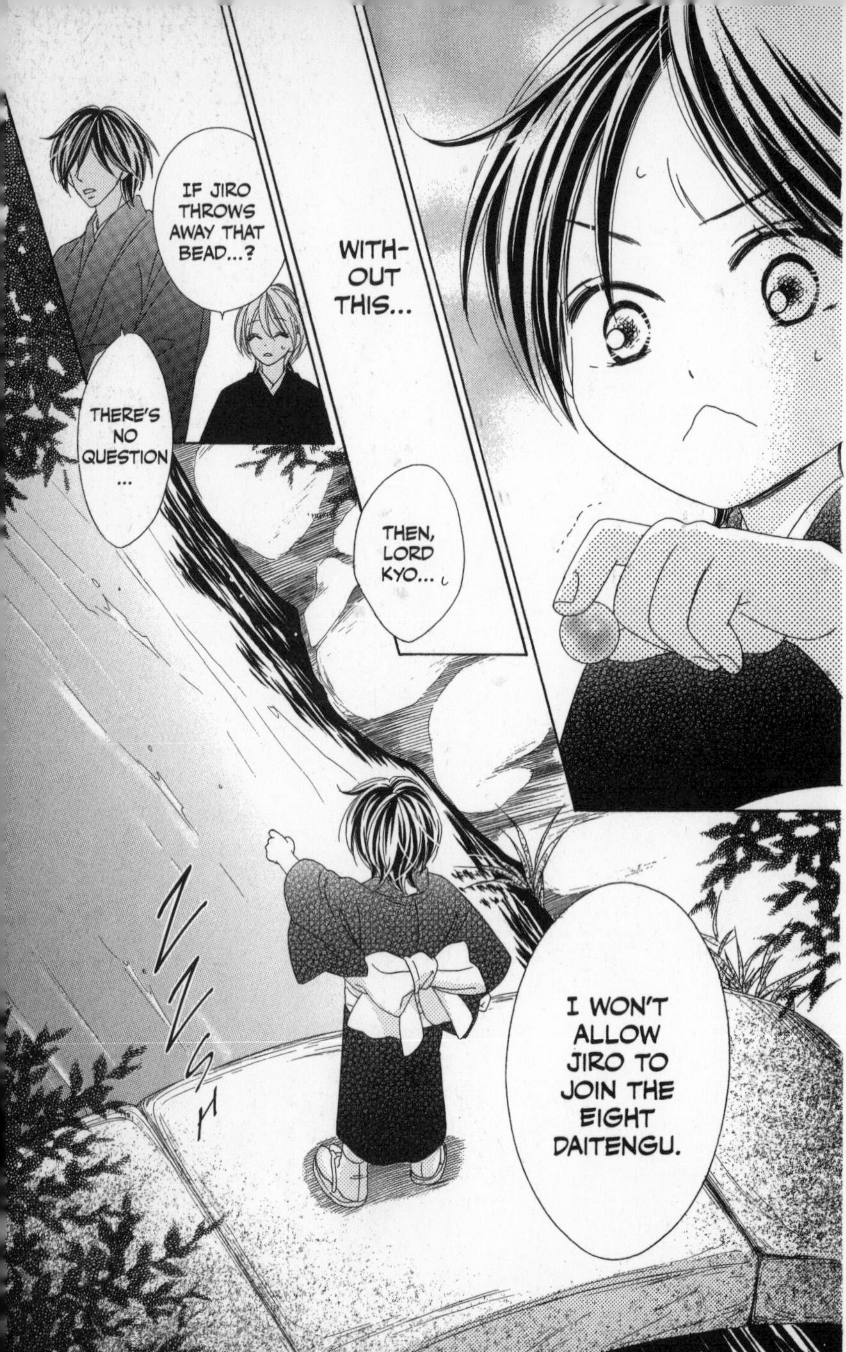
WITH-OUT THIS...
THEN, LORD KYO...
IF JIRO THROWS AWAY THAT BEAD...?
THERE'S NO QUESTION...
I WON'T ALLOW JIRO TO JOIN THE EIGHT DAITENGU.
LITTLE BLACK BIRD PART 1/THE END MAY 2009 BETSUCOMI

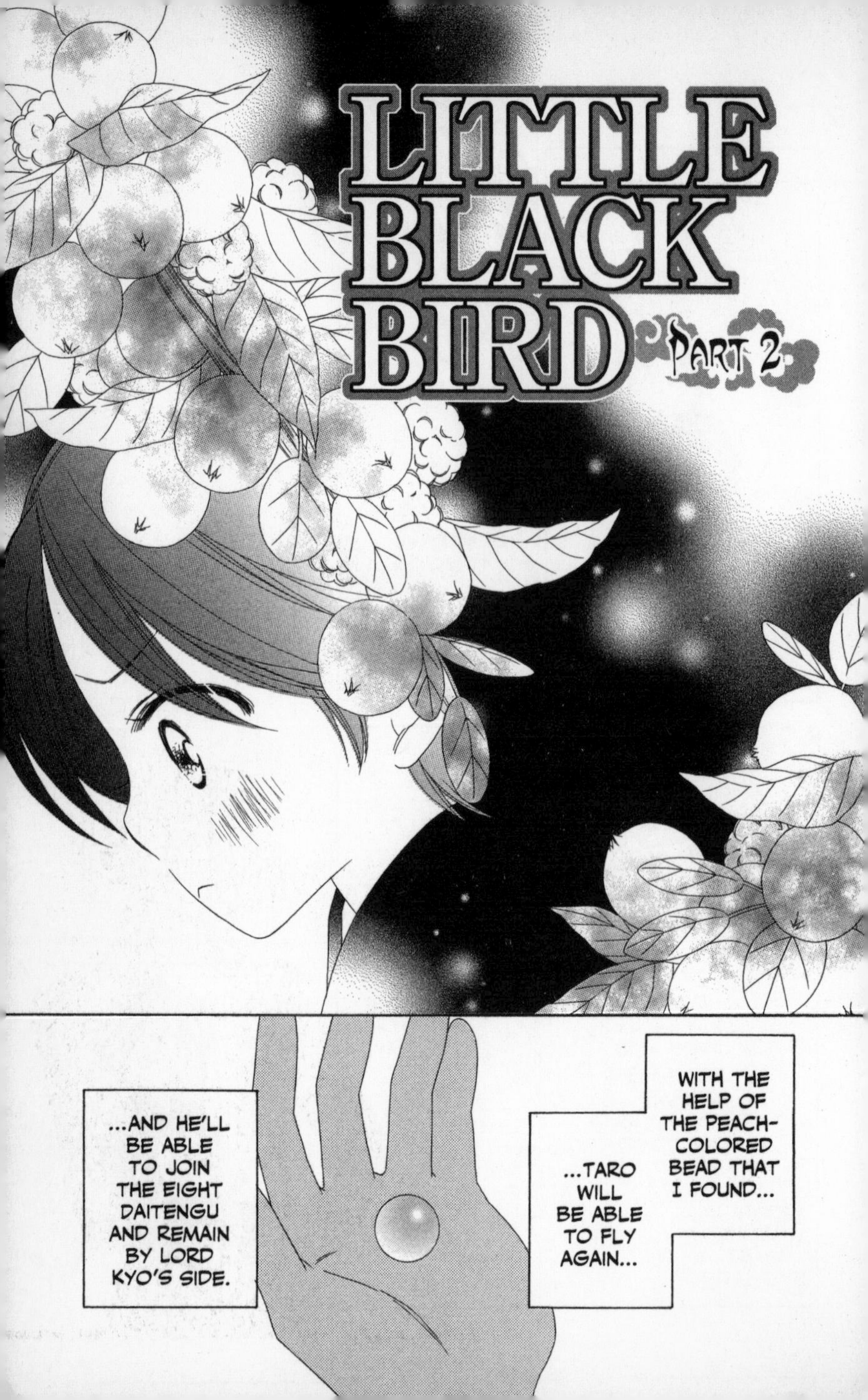
LITTLE BLACK BIRD
PART 2
WITH THE HELP OF THE PEACH-COLORED BEAD THAT I FOUND...
...TARO WILL BE ABLE TO FLY AGAIN...
...AND HE'LL BE ABLE TO JOIN THE EIGHT DAITENGU AND REMAIN BY LORD KYO'S SIDE.

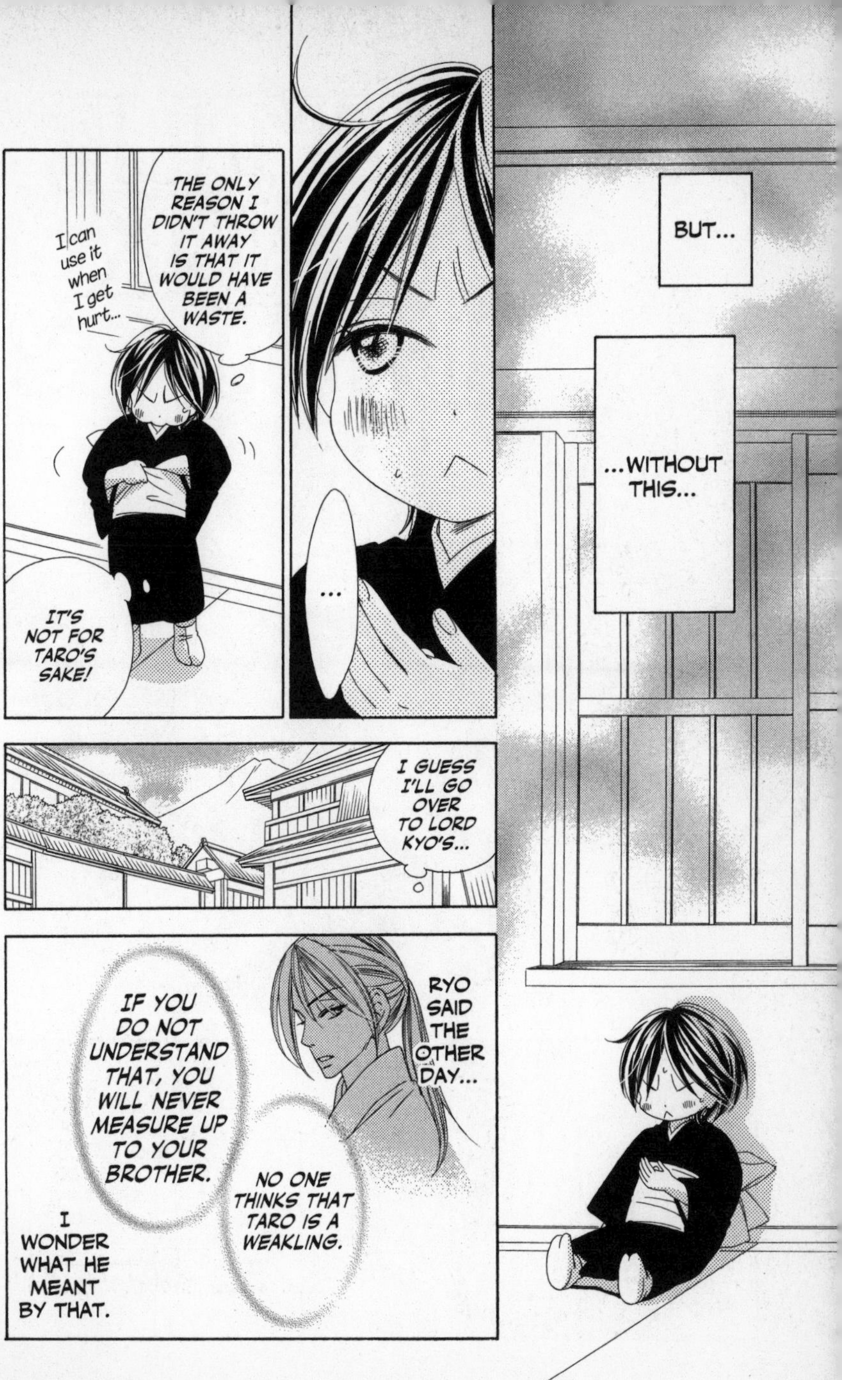
BUT...
...WITHOUT THIS...
...
THE ONLY REASON I DIDN'T THROW IT AWAY IS THAT IT WOULD HAVE BEEN A WASTE.
I can use it when I get hurt...
IT'S NOT FOR TARO'S SAKE!
I GUESS I'LL GO OVER TO LORD KYO'S...
RYO SAID THE OTHER DAY...
IF YOU DO NOT UNDERSTAND THAT, YOU WILL NEVER MEASURE UP TO YOUR BROTHER.
NO ONE THINKS THAT TARO IS A WEAKLING.
I WONDER WHAT HE MEANT BY THAT.

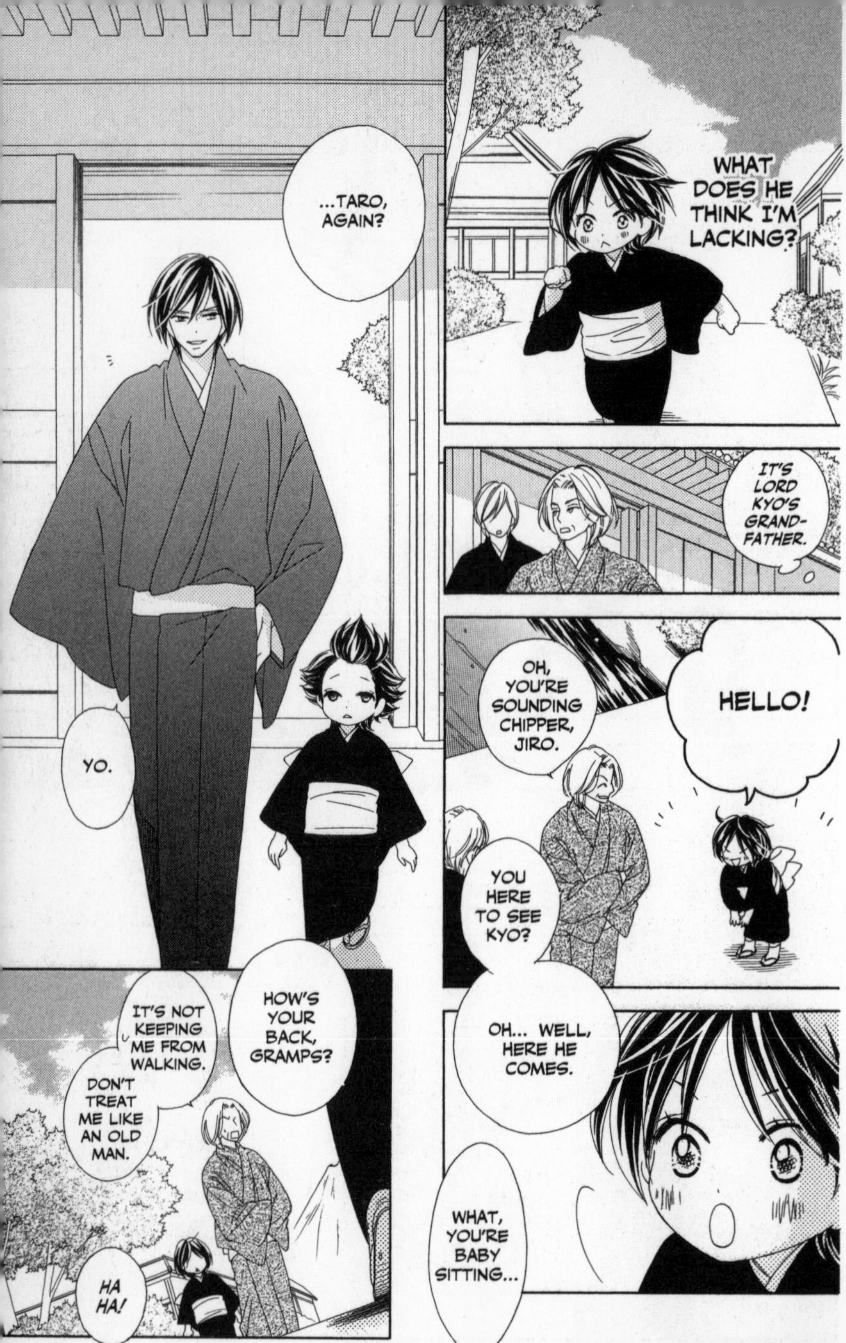
WHAT DOES HE THINK I'M LACKING?
IT'S LORD KYO'S GRAND-FATHER.
HELLO!
OH, YOU'RE SOUNDING CHIPPER, JIRO.
YOU HERE TO SEE KYO?
OH... WELL, HERE HE COMES.
WHAT, YOU'RE BABY SITTING...
...TARO, AGAIN?
YO.
HOW'S YOUR BACK, GRAMPS?
IT'S NOT KEEPING ME FROM WALKING.
DON'T TREAT ME LIKE AN OLD MAN.
HA HA!

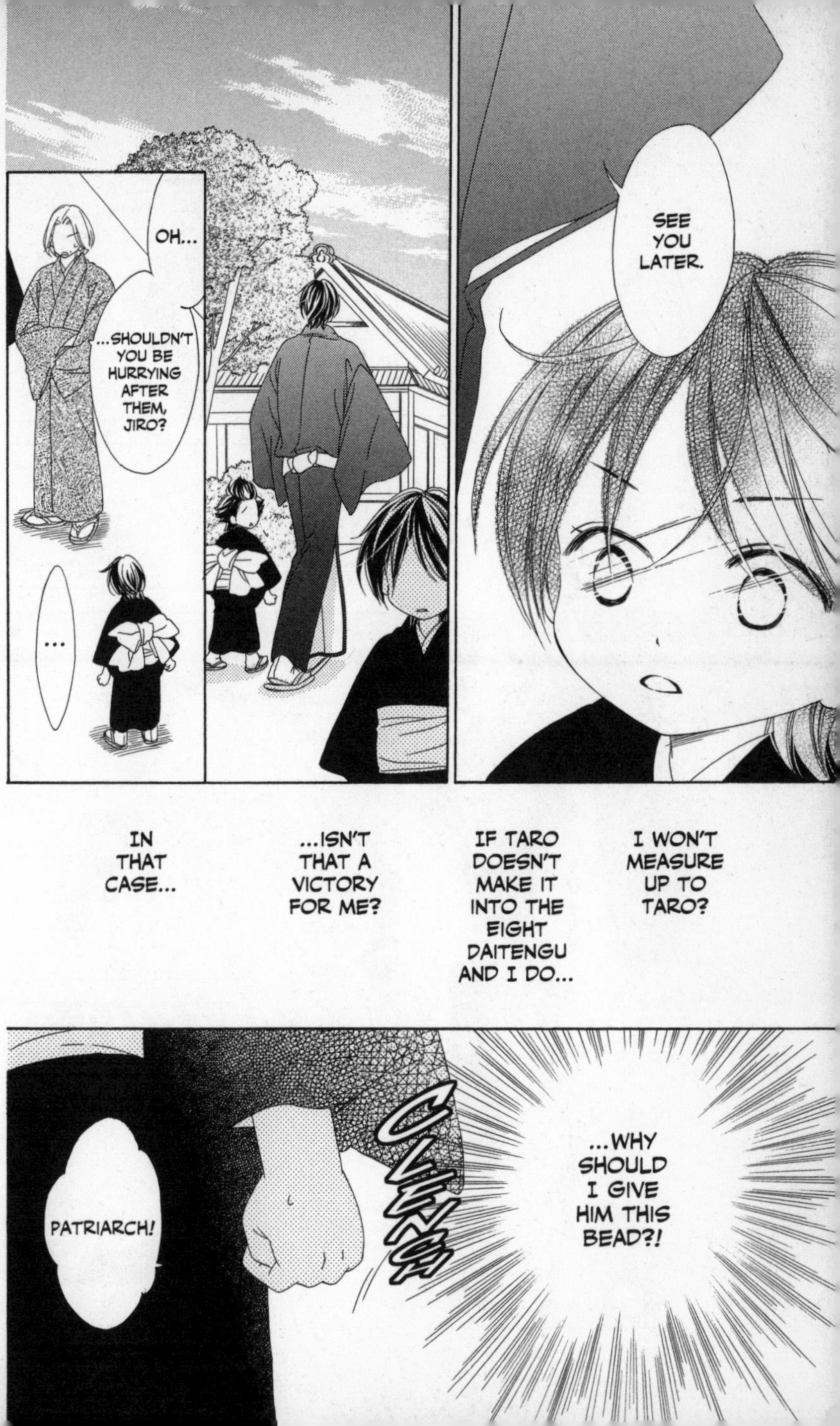
SEE YOU LATER.
OH...
...SHOULDN'T YOU BE HURRYING AFTER THEM, JIRO?
...
I WON'T MEASURE UP TO TARO?
IF TARO DOESN'T MAKE IT INTO THE EIGHT DAITENGU AND I DO...
...ISN'T THAT A VICTORY FOR ME?
IN THAT CASE...
...WHY SHOULD I GIVE HIM THIS BEAD?!
CLENCH
PATRIARCH!

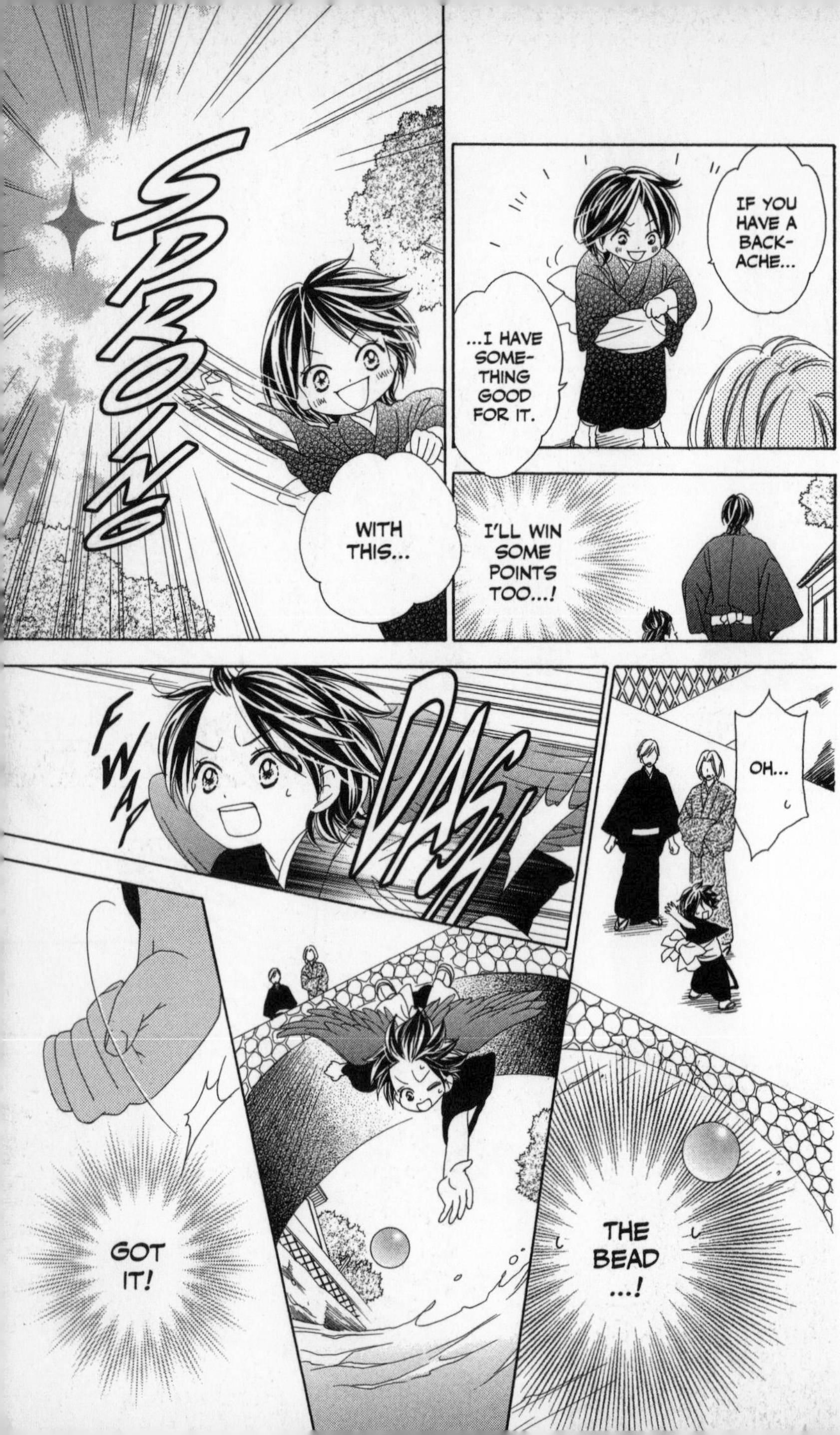
IF YOU HAVE A BACK-ACHE...
...I HAVE SOME-THING GOOD FOR IT.
I'LL WIN SOME POINTS TOO...!
SPROING
WITH THIS...
OH...
FWAP
DASH
THE BEAD ...!
GOT IT!

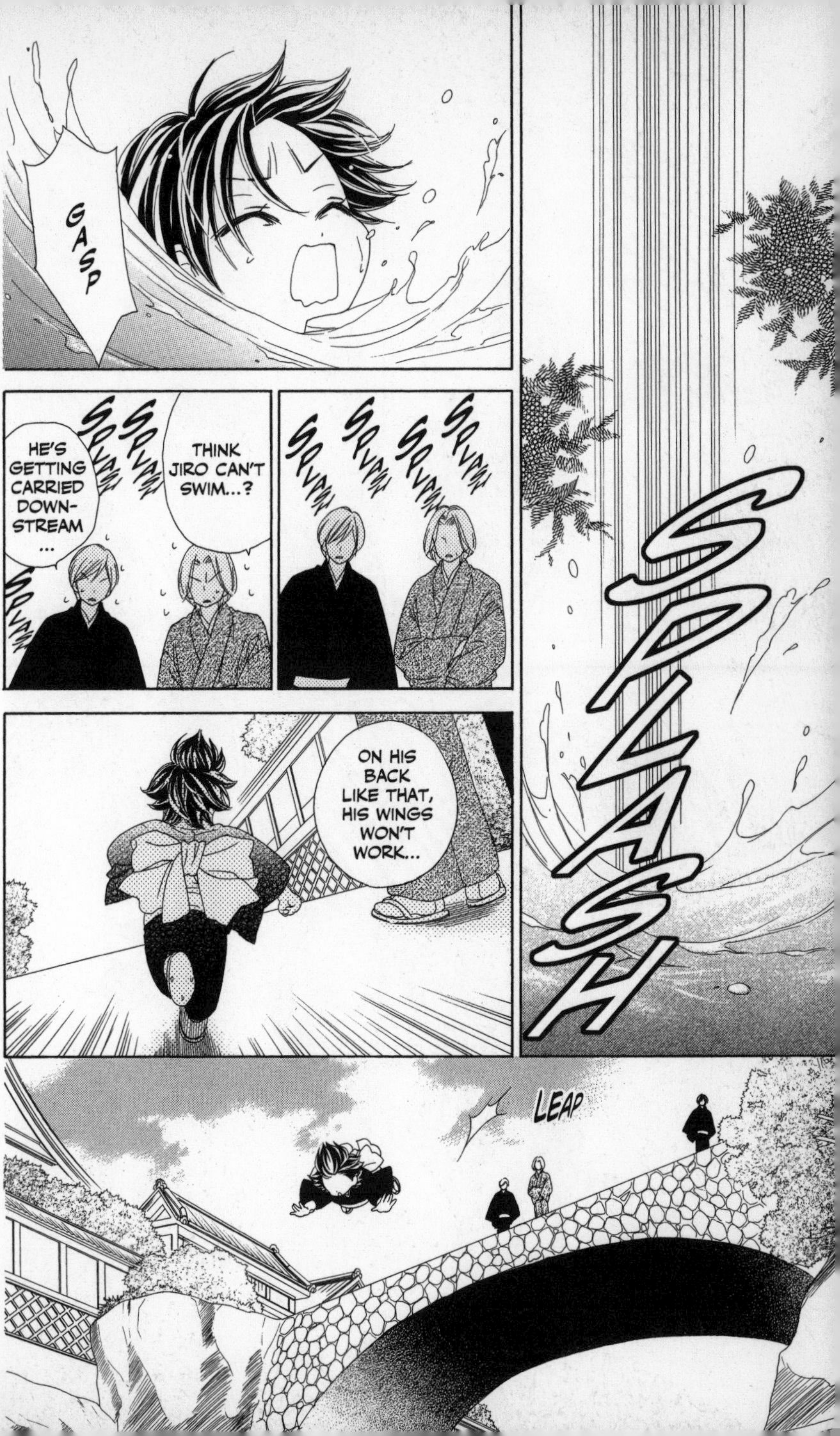
SPLASH
GASP
THINK JIRO CAN'T SWIM...?
HE'S GETTING CARRIED DOWN-STREAM ...
ON HIS BACK LIKE THAT, HIS WINGS WON'T WORK...
LEAP

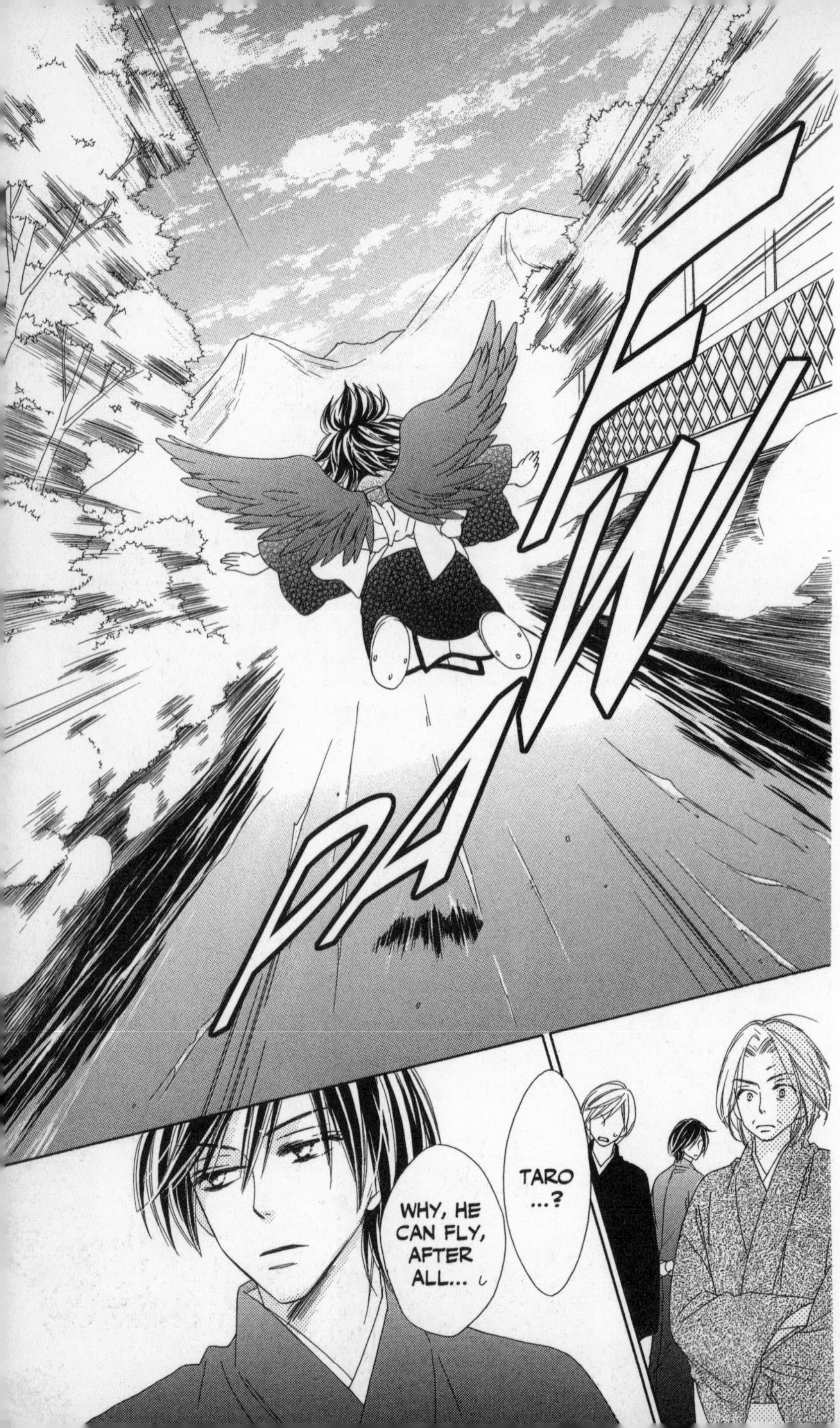
TARO ...?
WHY, HE CAN FLY, AFTER ALL...

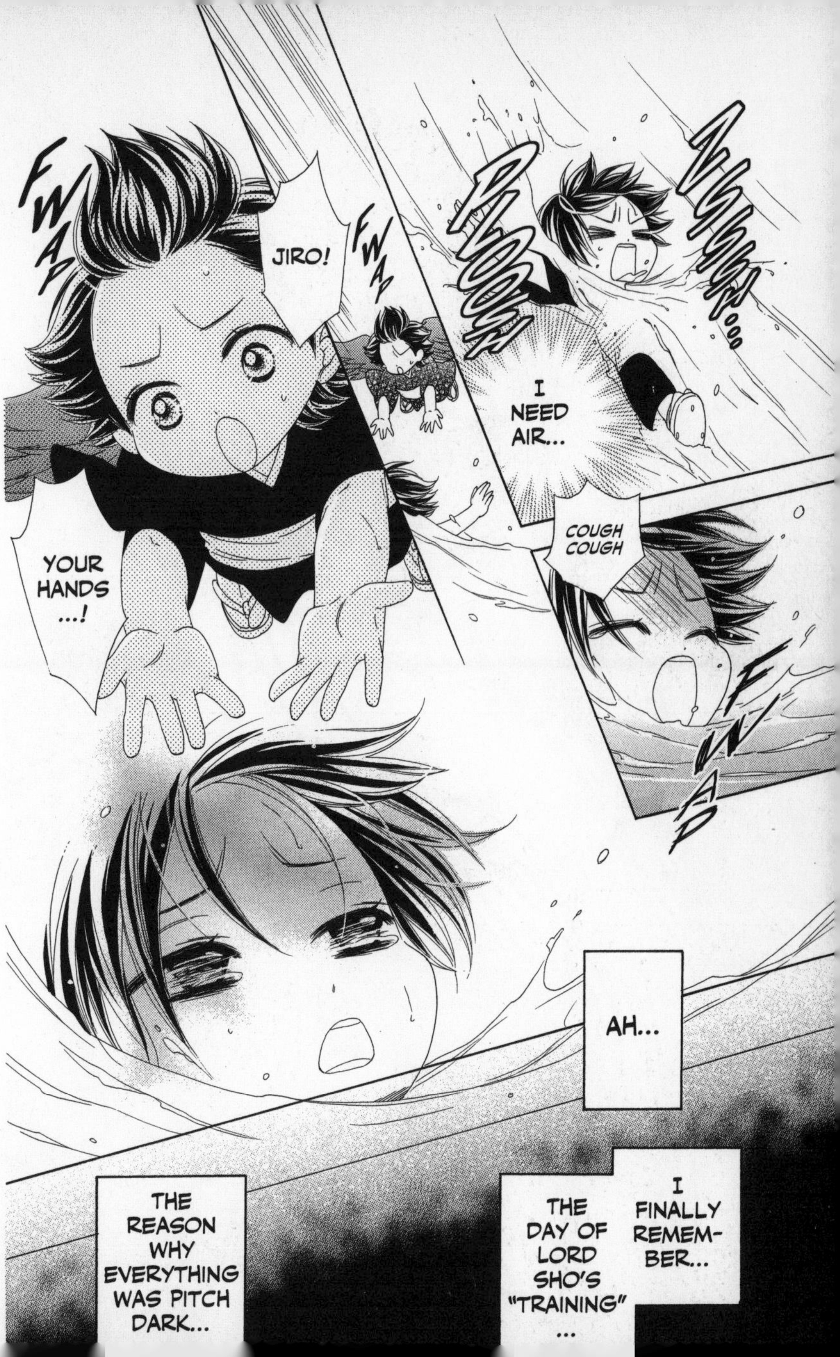
I NEED AIR...
FWAP
JIRO!
FWAP
YOUR HANDS ...!
COUGH COUGH
AH...
I FINALLY REMEMBER...
THE DAY OF LORD SHO'S "TRAINING" ...
THE REASON WHY EVERYTHING WAS PITCH DARK...

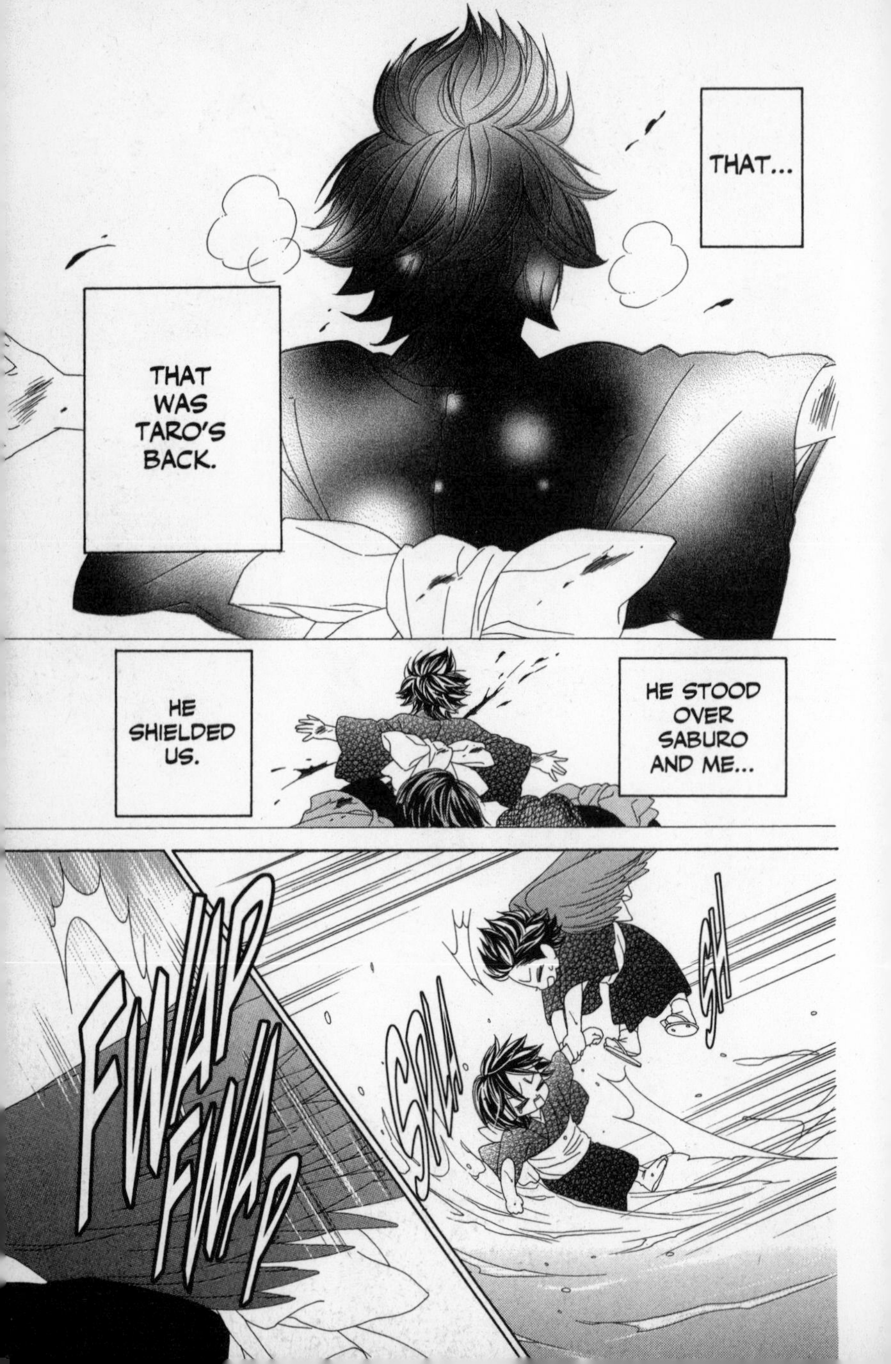
THAT...
THAT WAS TARO'S BACK.
HE STOOD OVER SABURO AND ME...
HE SHIELDED US.
SH
SPLA
FWAP
FWAP

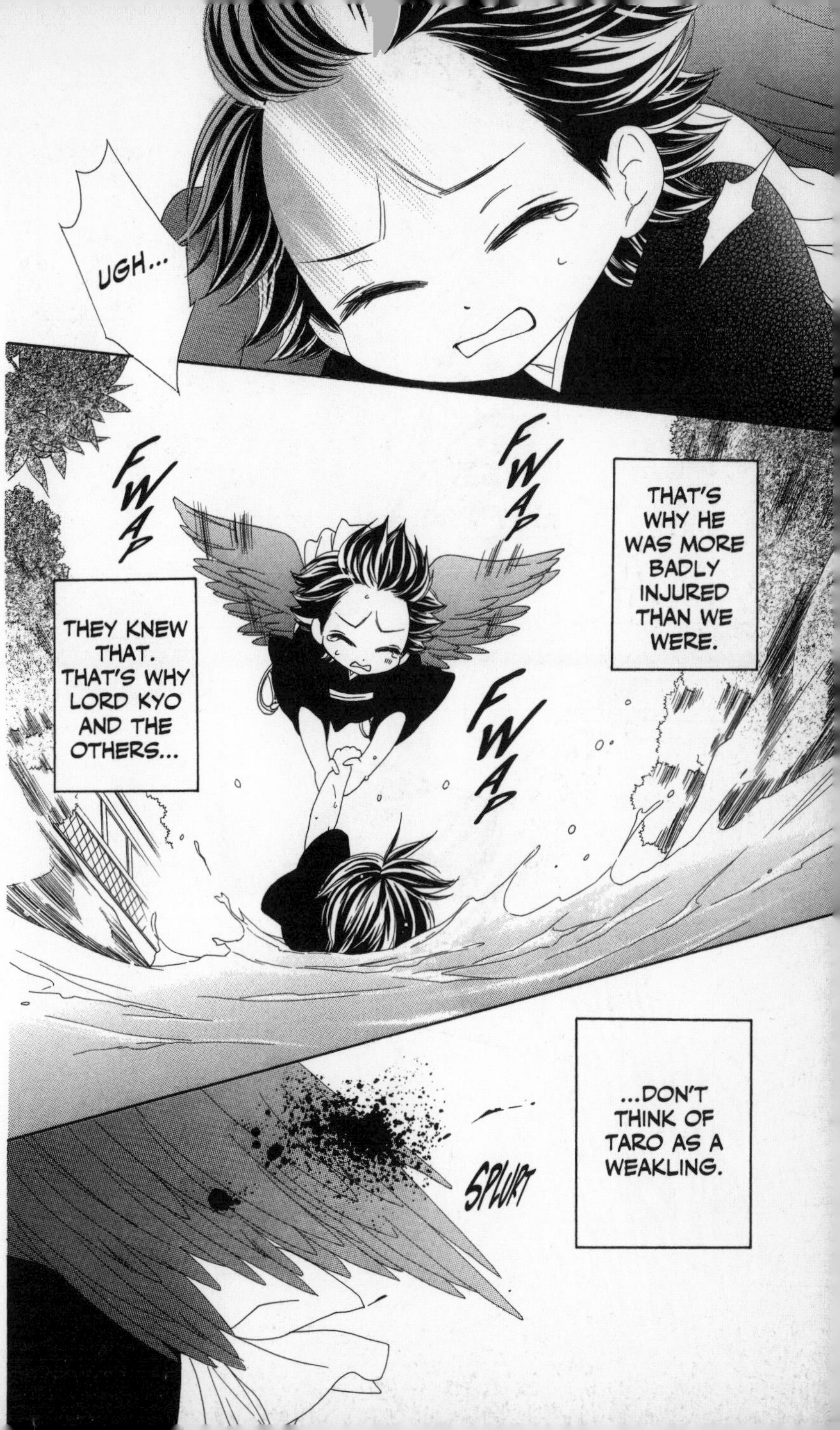
UGH...
THAT'S WHY HE WAS MORE BADLY INJURED THAN WE WERE.
FWAP
FWAP
FWAP
THEY KNEW THAT. THAT'S WHY LORD KYO AND THE OTHERS...
...DON'T THINK OF TARO AS A WEAKLING.
SPLURT

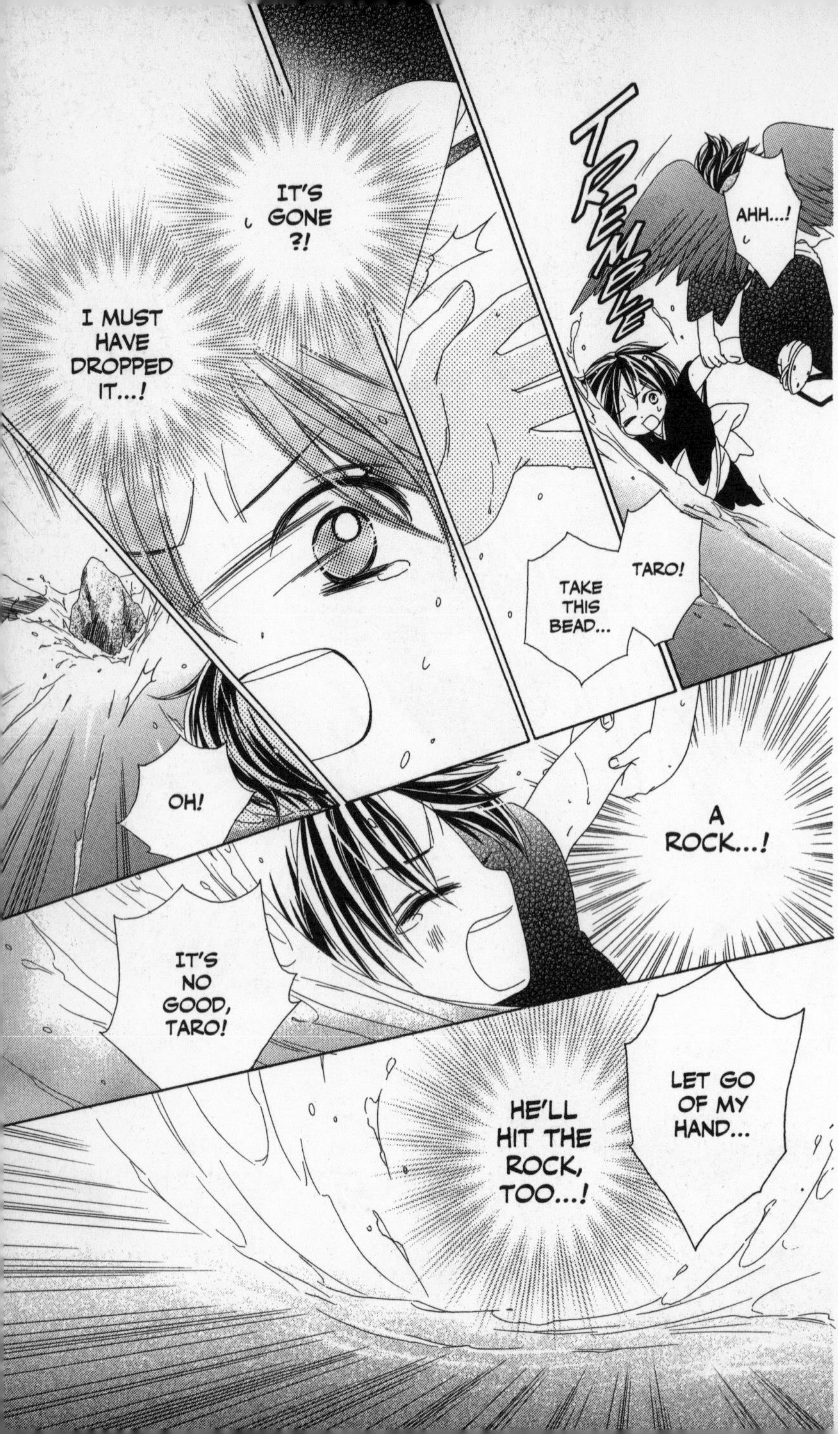
TREMBLE
AHH...!
TARO!
TAKE THIS BEAD...
IT'S GONE?!
I MUST HAVE DROPPED IT...!
OH!
A ROCK...!
IT'S NO GOOD, TARO!
LET GO OF MY HAND...
HE'LL HIT THE ROCK, TOO...!

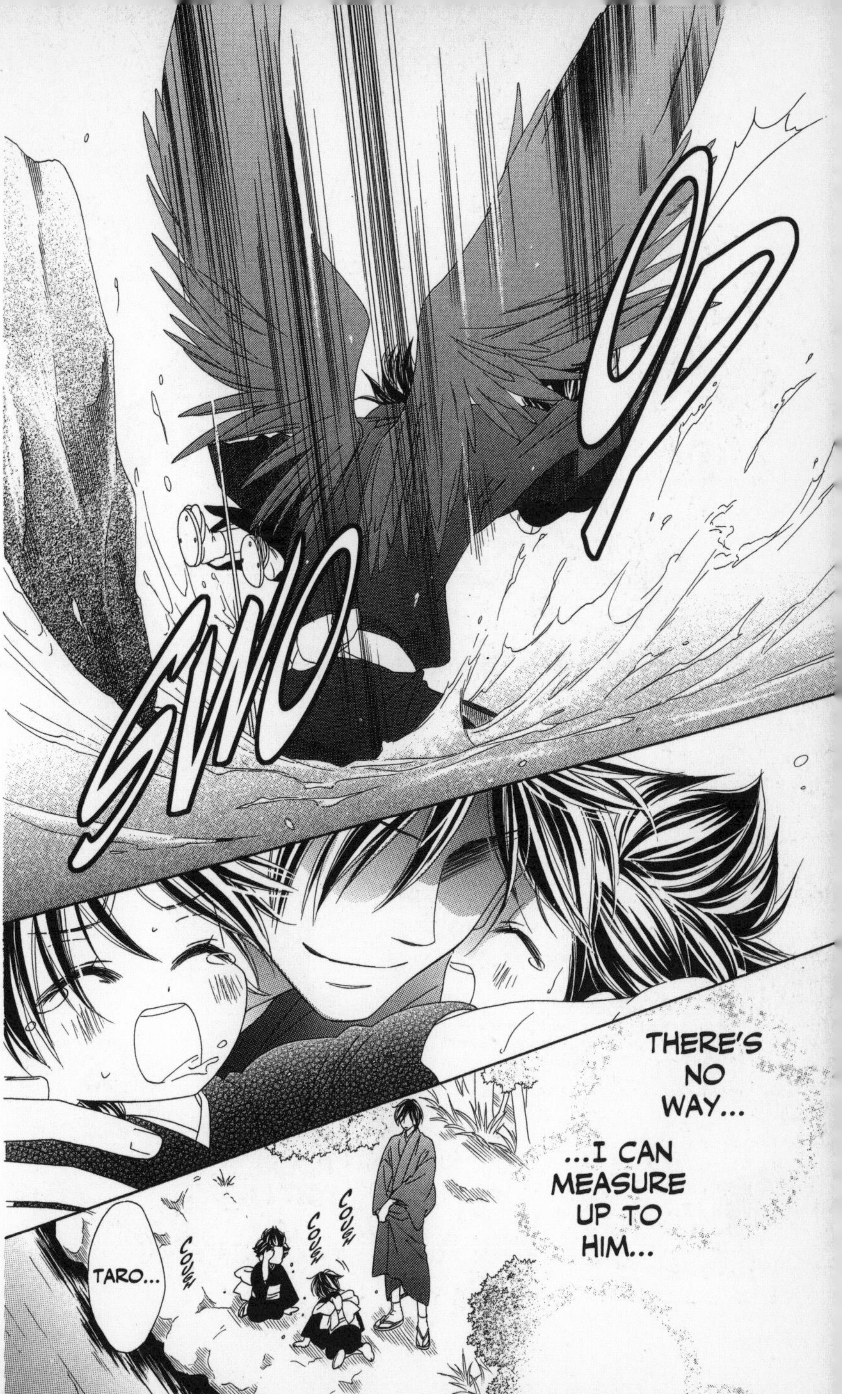
SWOOP
THERE'S NO WAY...
...I CAN MEASURE UP TO HIM...
COUGH COUGH
COUGH
TARO...

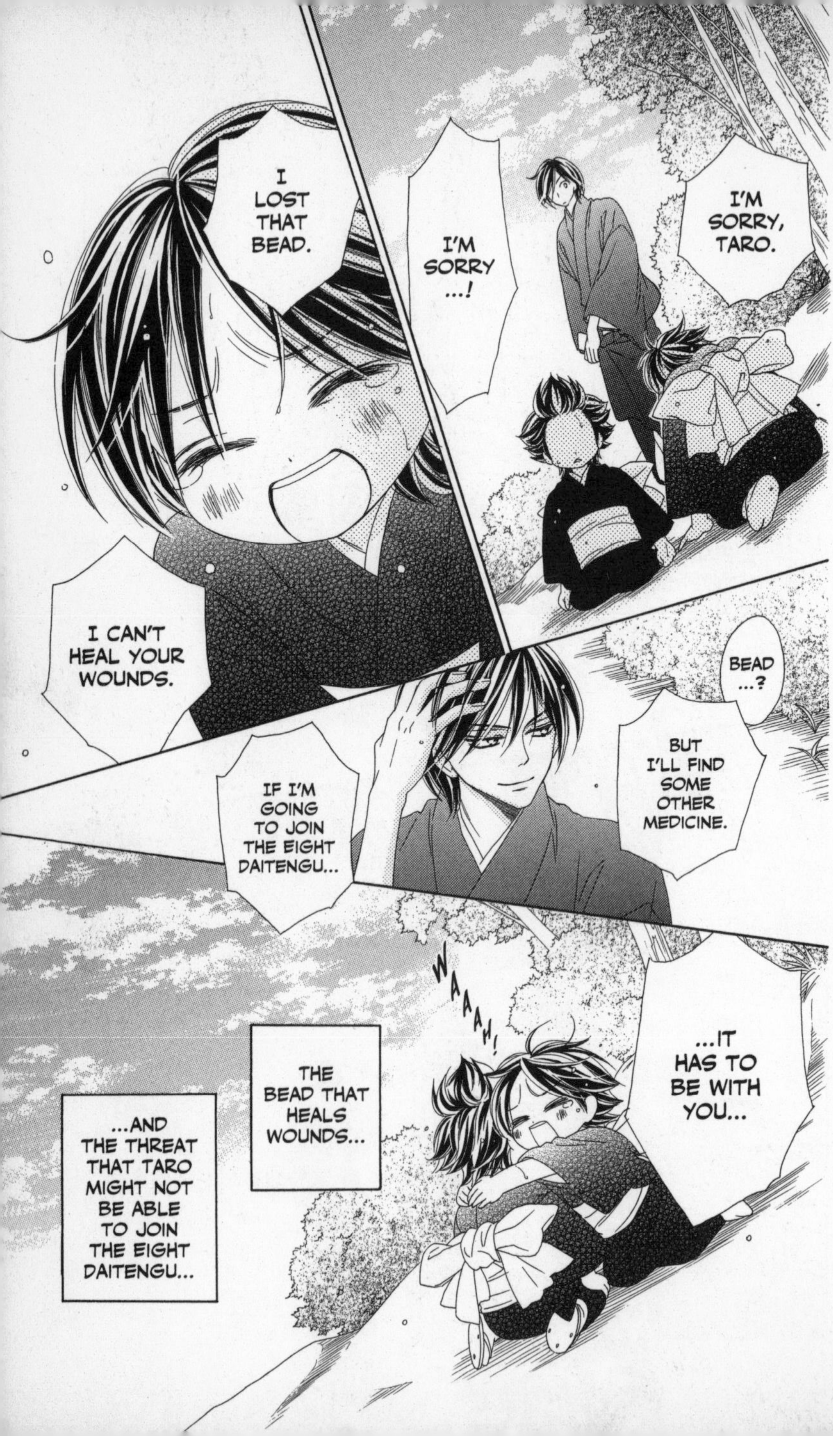
I'M SORRY, TARO.
I'M SORRY ...!
I LOST THAT BEAD.
I CAN'T HEAL YOUR WOUNDS.
BEAD ...?
BUT I'LL FIND SOME OTHER MEDICINE.
IF I'M GOING TO JOIN THE EIGHT DAITENGU...
...IT HAS TO BE WITH YOU...
WAAAAH!
THE BEAD THAT HEALS WOUNDS...
...AND THE THREAT THAT TARO MIGHT NOT BE ABLE TO JOIN THE EIGHT DAITENGU...

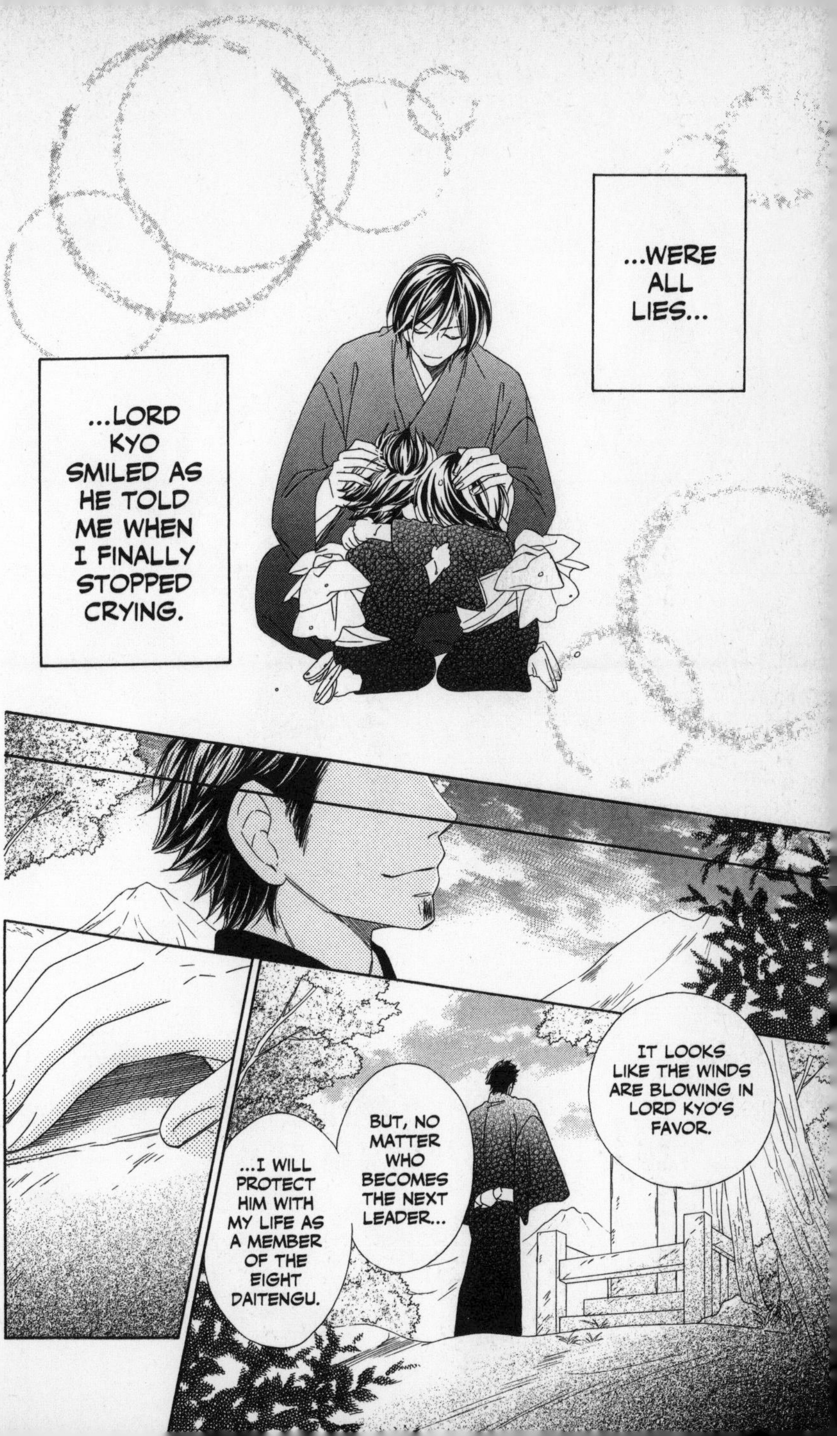
...WERE ALL LIES...
...LORD KYO SMILED AS HE TOLD ME WHEN I FINALLY STOPPED CRYING.
IT LOOKS LIKE THE WINDS ARE BLOWING IN LORD KYO'S FAVOR.
BUT, NO MATTER WHO BECOMES THE NEXT LEADER...
...I WILL PROTECT HIM WITH MY LIFE AS A MEMBER OF THE EIGHT DAITENGU.

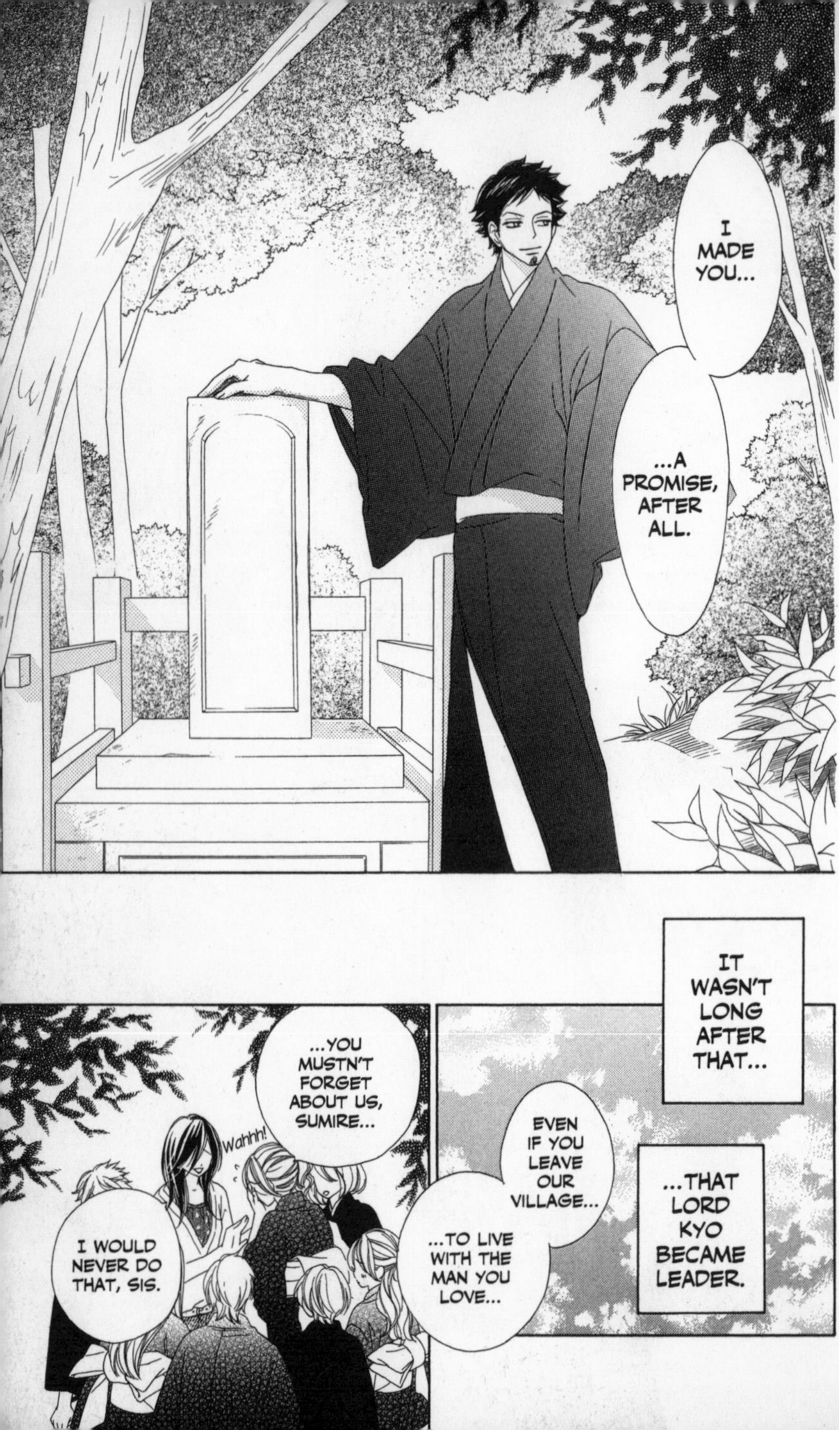
I MADE YOU...
...A PROMISE, AFTER ALL.
IT WASN'T LONG AFTER THAT...
...THAT LORD KYO BECAME LEADER.
EVEN IF YOU LEAVE OUR VILLAGE...
...TO LIVE WITH THE MAN YOU LOVE...
...YOU MUSTN'T FORGET ABOUT US, SUMIRE...
Wahhh!
I WOULD NEVER DO THAT, SIS.

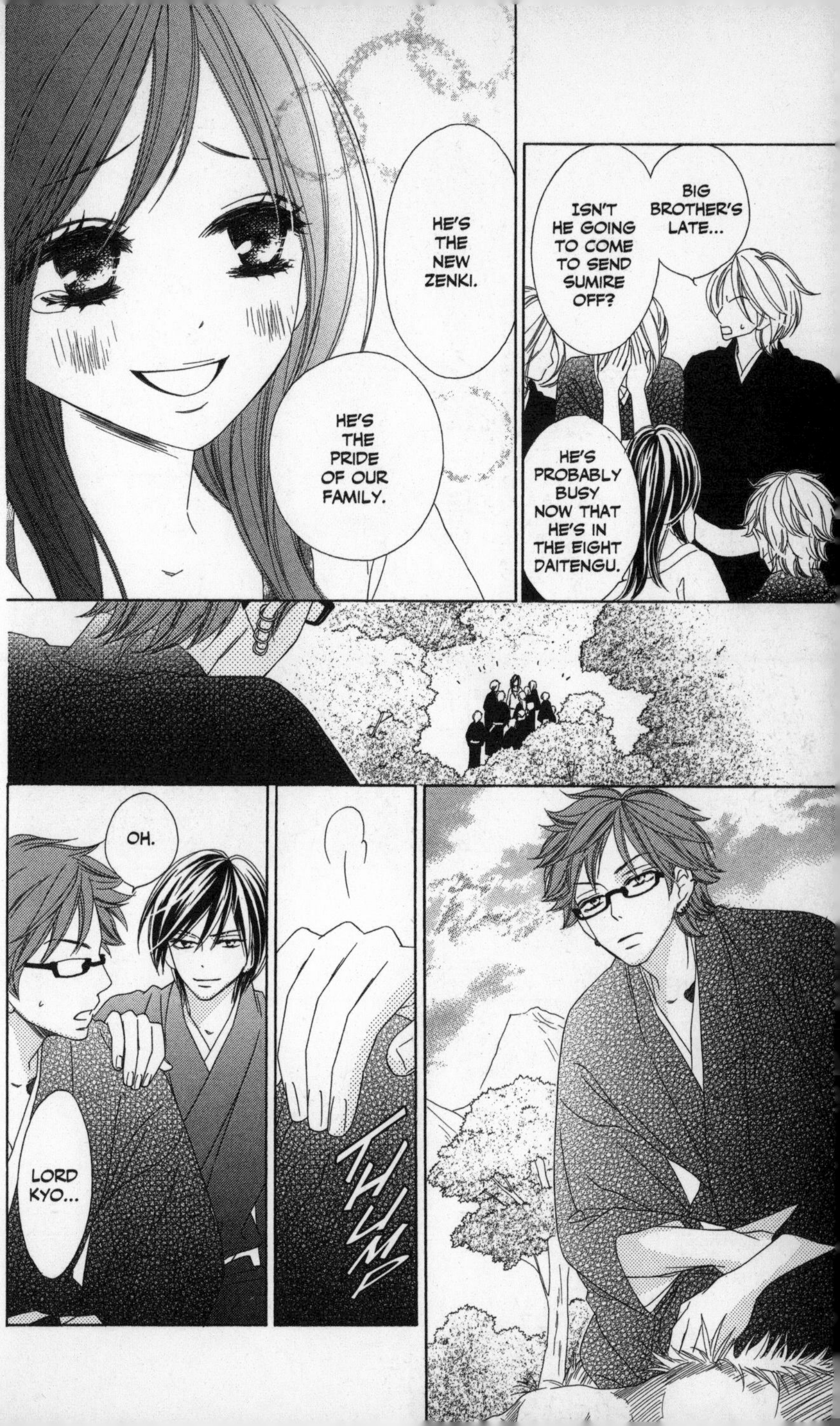
BIG BROTHER'S LATE...
ISN'T HE GOING TO COME TO SEND SUMIRE OFF?
HE'S PROBABLY BUSY NOW THAT HE'S IN THE EIGHT DAITENGU.
HE'S THE NEW ZENKI.
HE'S THE PRIDE OF OUR FAMILY.
THUMP
OH.
LORD KYO...

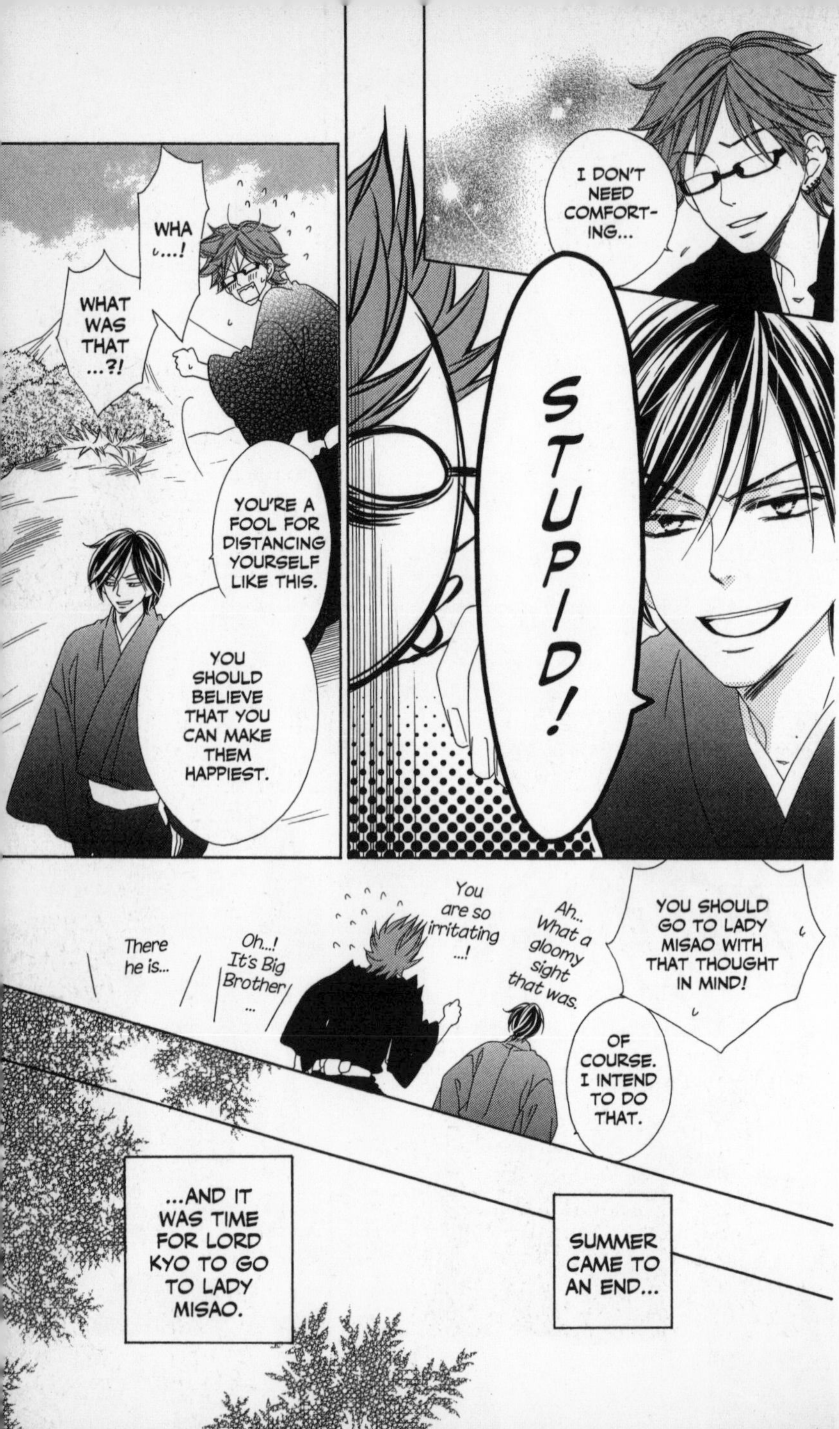
I DON'T NEED COMFORTING...
STUPID!
WHA...!
WHAT WAS THAT...?!
YOU'RE A FOOL FOR DISTANCING YOURSELF LIKE THIS.
YOU SHOULD BELIEVE THAT YOU CAN MAKE THEM HAPPIEST.
YOU SHOULD GO TO LADY MISAO WITH THAT THOUGHT IN MIND!
Ah... What a gloomy sight that was.
You are so irritating...!
OF COURSE. I INTEND TO DO THAT.
Oh...! It's Big Brother...
There he is...
SUMMER CAME TO AN END...
...AND IT WAS TIME FOR LORD KYO TO GO TO LADY MISAO.

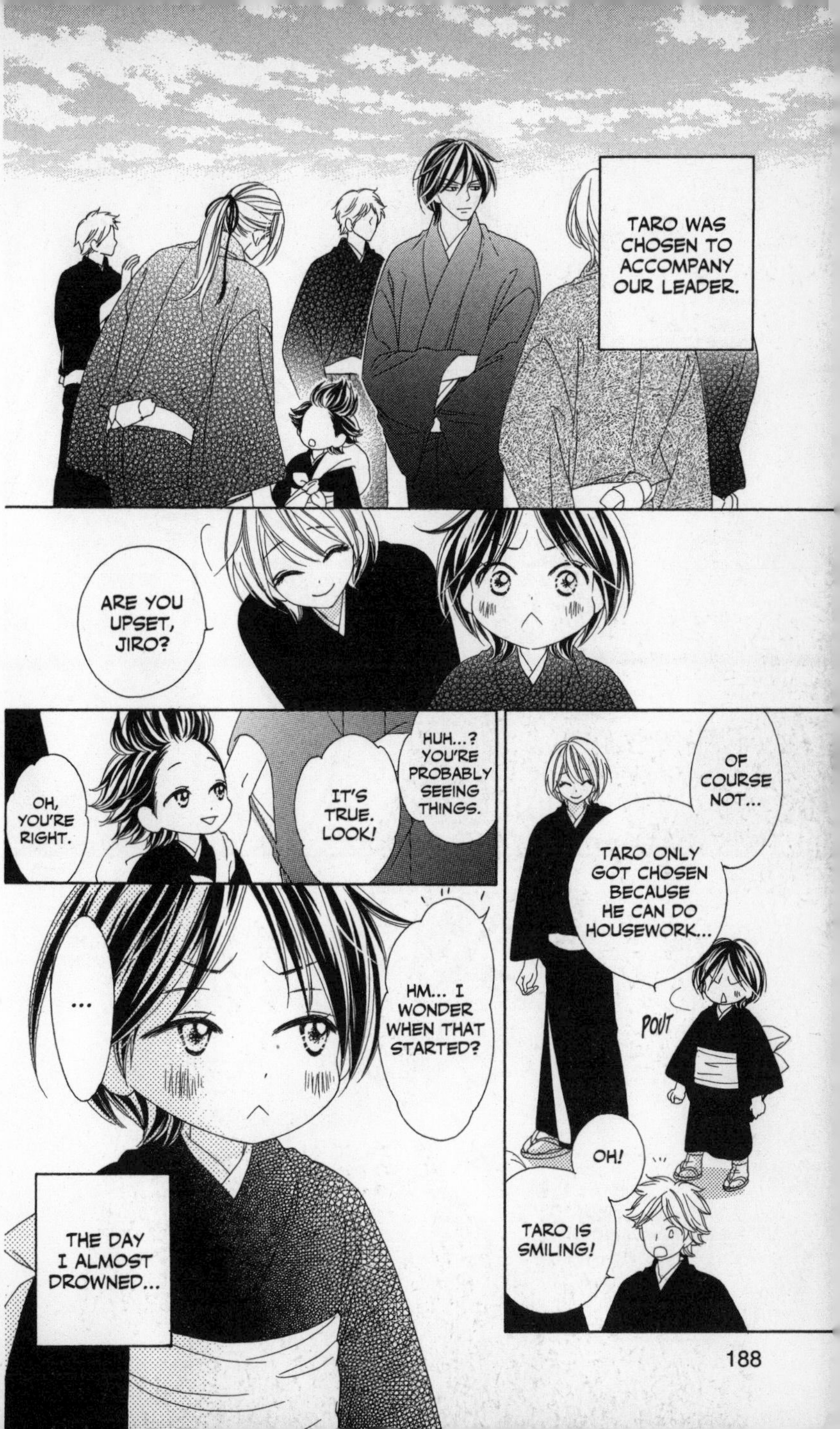

TARO WAS CHOSEN TO ACCOMPANY OUR LEADER.
ARE YOU UPSET, JIRO?
OF COURSE NOT...
TARO ONLY GOT CHOSEN BECAUSE HE CAN DO HOUSEWORK...
POUT
OH!
TARO IS SMILING!
HUH...? YOU'RE PROBABLY SEEING THINGS.
IT'S TRUE. LOOK!
OH, YOU'RE RIGHT.
HM... I WONDER WHEN THAT STARTED?
...
THE DAY I ALMOST DROWNED...

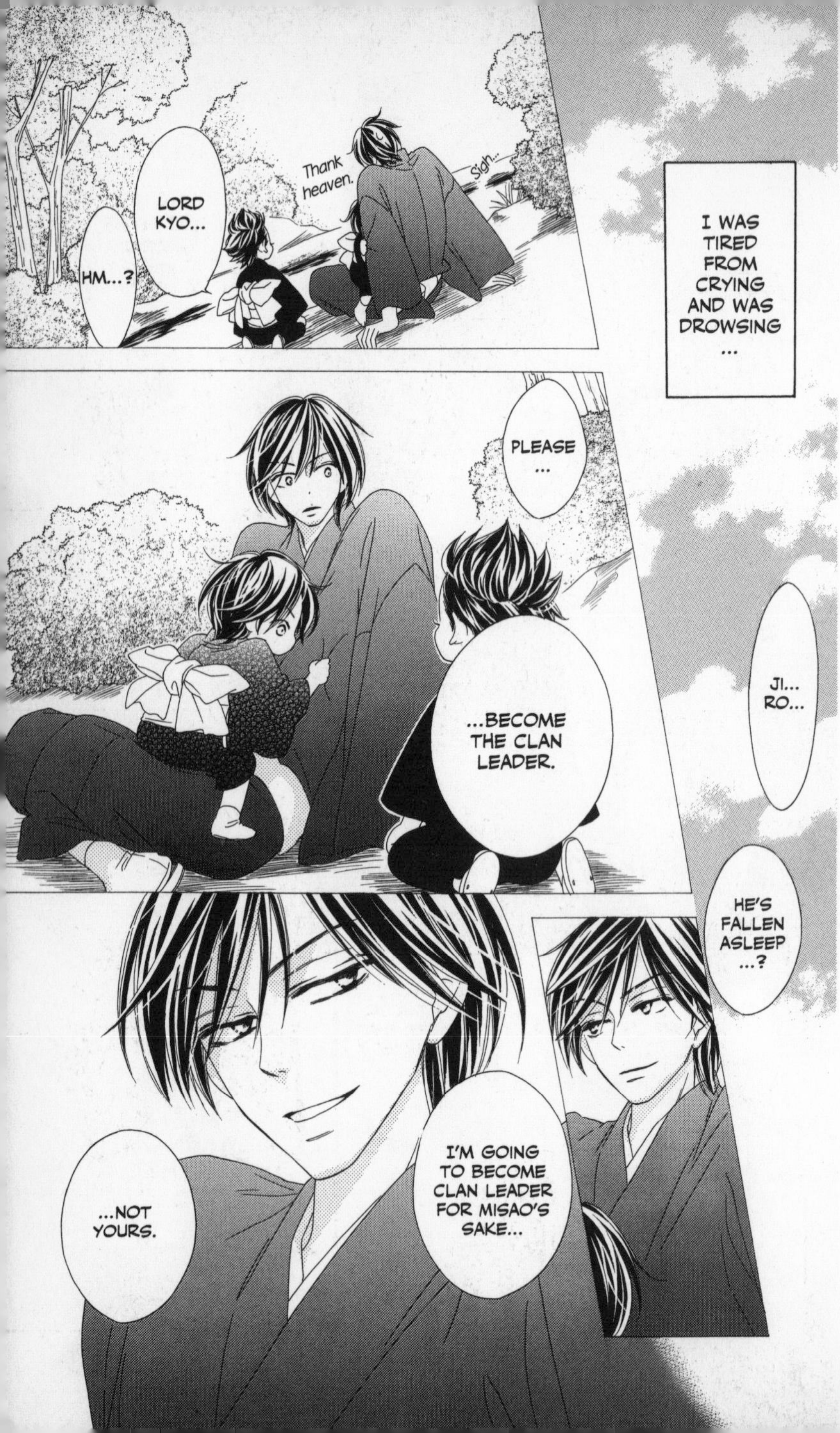
I WAS TIRED FROM CRYING AND WAS DROWSING...
Sigh...
Thank heaven.
LORD KYO...
HM...?
PLEASE...
...BECOME THE CLAN LEADER.
JI... RO...
HE'S FALLEN ASLEEP...?
I'M GOING TO BECOME CLAN LEADER FOR MISAO'S SAKE...
...NOT YOURS.

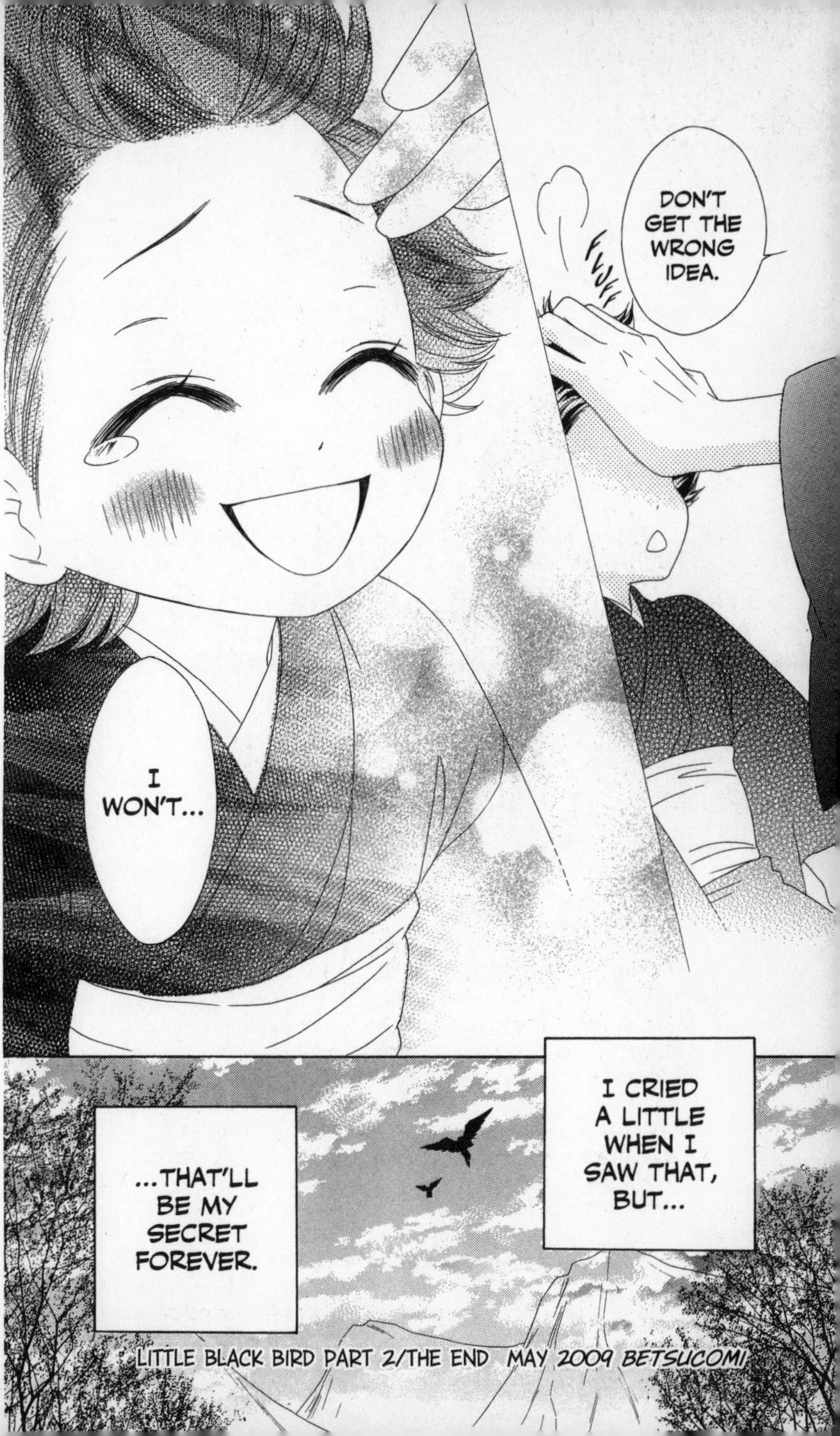
DON'T GET THE WRONG IDEA.
I WON'T...
I CRIED A LITTLE WHEN I SAW THAT, BUT...
...THAT'LL BE MY SECRET FOREVER.
LITTLE BLACK BIRD PART 2/THE END MAY 2009 BETSUCOMI

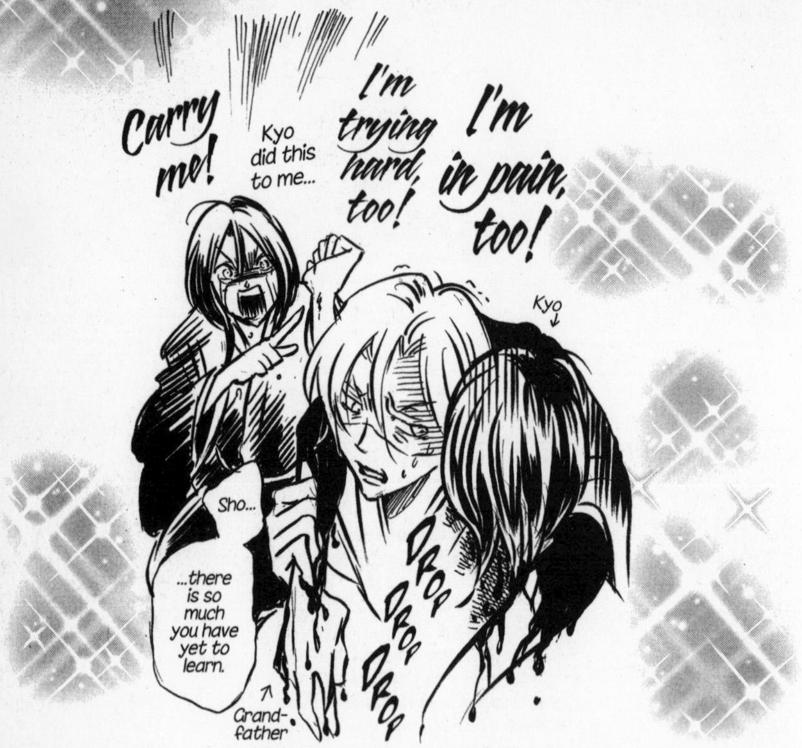
I'm in pain, too!
I'm trying hard, too!
Kyo did this to me...
Carry me!
Kyo
DROP DROP DROP DROP
Sho...
...there is so much you have yet to learn.
Grand-father

And so♡, our wonderful guest, who is appearing in *Black Bird* for the third time, is *Betsucomi's* Yasuko Sensei!!

Sensei, your subject has been Sho all three times... Thank you very much.♡ (She has had my work in her *Cherry na Bokura* volume 1 too.)

The bonus manga in this volume are the ones I think of as the "if I ever get a chance to draw this someday" episodes. I squeezed it all in at once, so it was quite a job getting it all to fit. It turned out to be another weird story...

I pray that I'll see you in the next volume!

An Auspicious Day, September 2009 Kanoko Sakurakoji

桜小路 かのこ

GLOSSARY

PAGE 20, PANEL 5: Red bean rice
Sekihan is a dish eaten at
celebrations, such as those marking
a change in life, like marriage.

PAGE 25, PANEL 2: Opening ceremony
Similar to first day assemblies
at U.S. schools.

PANEL 138, AUTHOR NOTE:
Grateful crane
A Japanese folktale in which an old
couple frees a trapped crane, and in
gratitude the crane returns to them
in the form of a young maiden. She
explains that she is going to weave for
them, and telling the couple not to peek,
locks herself in a room. She weaves
day and night, and finally on the third
night she emerges with a beautiful
cloth that the couple sells for much
money. One night when she has again
locked herself in her weaving room,
the couple is overcome by curiosity
and they peek inside. There they see
the crane in her true form, weaving the
cloth from her own feathers. But because
they peeked, the crane must depart.

Kanoko Sakurakoji was born in downtown Tokyo, and her hobbies include reading, watching plays, traveling and shopping. Her debut title, *Raibu ga Hanetara*, ran in *Bessatsu Shojo Comic* (currently called *Bestucomi*) in 2000, and her 2004 *Bestucomi* title *Backstage Prince* was serialized in VIZ Media's *Shojo Beat* magazine. She won the 54th Shogakukan Manga Award for *Black Bird*.

BLACK BIRD
VOL. 9
Shojo Beat Edition

Story and Art by KANOKO SAKURAKOUJI

© 2007 Kanoko SAKURAKOUJI/Shogakukan
All rights reserved.
Original Japanese edition "BLACK BIRD" published by SHOGAKUKAN Inc.

TRANSLATION JN Productions
TOUCH-UP ART & LETTERING Gia Cam Luc
DESIGN Amy Martin
EDITOR Pancha Diaz

Printed in the U.S.A.

Published by VIZ Media, LLC
P.O. Box 77010
San Francisco, CA 94107

10 9 8 7 6 5 4 3 2 1
First printing, July 2011

www.shojobeat.com   www.viz.com

LAND OF *Fantasy*

MIAKA YÛKI IS AN ORDINARY JUNIOR-HIGH STUDENT WHO IS SUDDENLY WHISKED AWAY INTO THE WORLD OF A BOOK, *THE UNIVERSE OF THE FOUR GODS*. WILL THE BEAUTIFUL CELESTIAL BEINGS SHE ENCOUNTERS AND THE CHANCE TO BECOME A PRIESTESS DIVERT MIAKA FROM EVER RETURNING HOME?

THREE VOLUMES OF THE ORIGINAL *FUSHIGI YÛGI* SERIES COMBINED INTO A LARGER FORMAT WITH AN EXCLUSIVE COVER DESIGN AND BONUS CONTENT

EXPERIENCE THE BEAUTY OF *FUSHIGI YÛGI* WITH THE HARDCOVER ART BOOK

ALSO AVAILABLE: THE *FUSHIGI YÛGI: GENBU KAIDEN* MANGA, THE EIGHT VOLUME PREQUEL TO THIS BEST-SELLING FANTASY SERIES

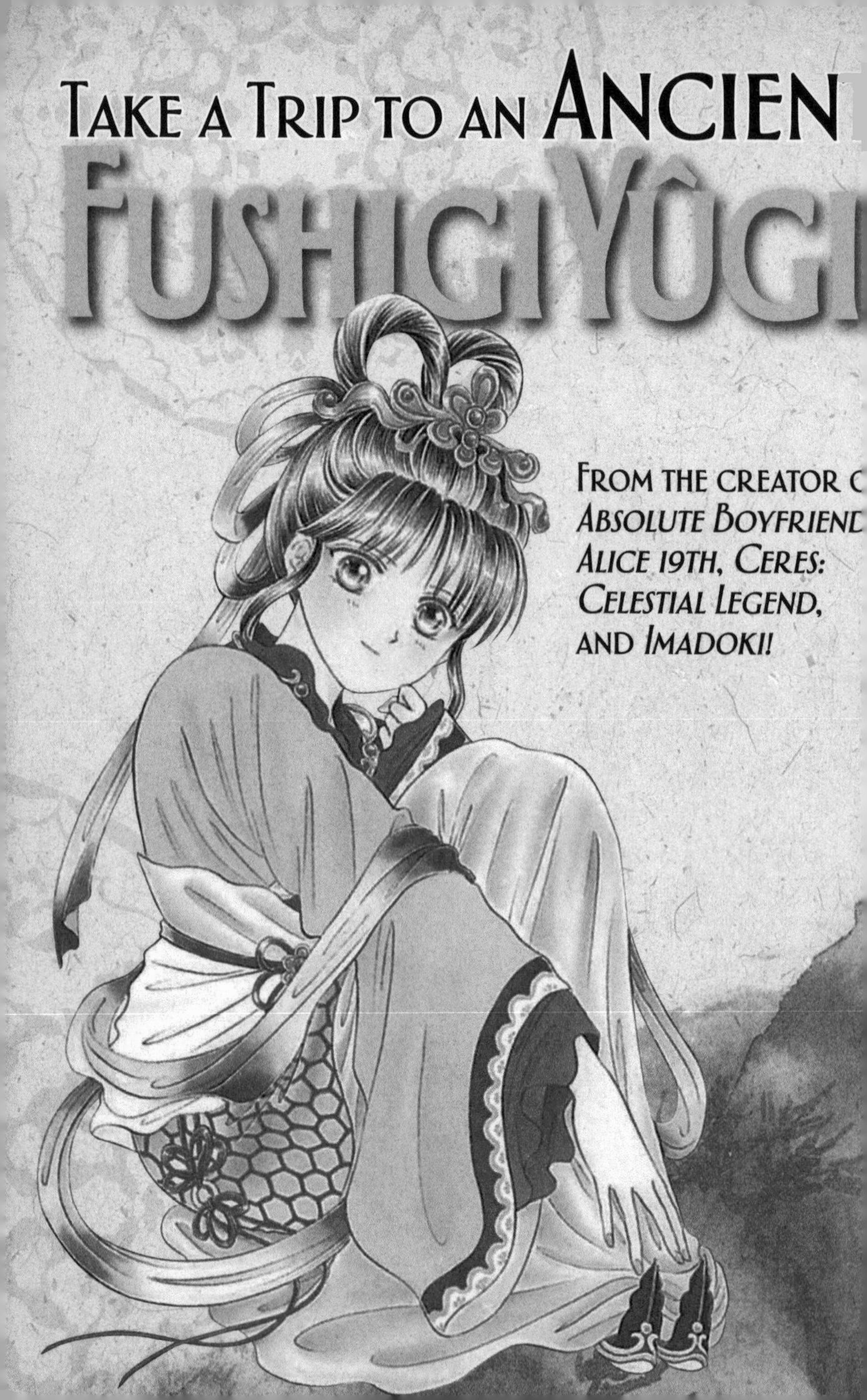
TAKE A TRIP TO AN ANCIEN
FUSHIGI YÛGI
FROM THE CREATOR
ABSOLUTE BOYFRIEN
ALICE 19TH, CERES:
CELESTIAL LEGEND,
AND IMADOKI!

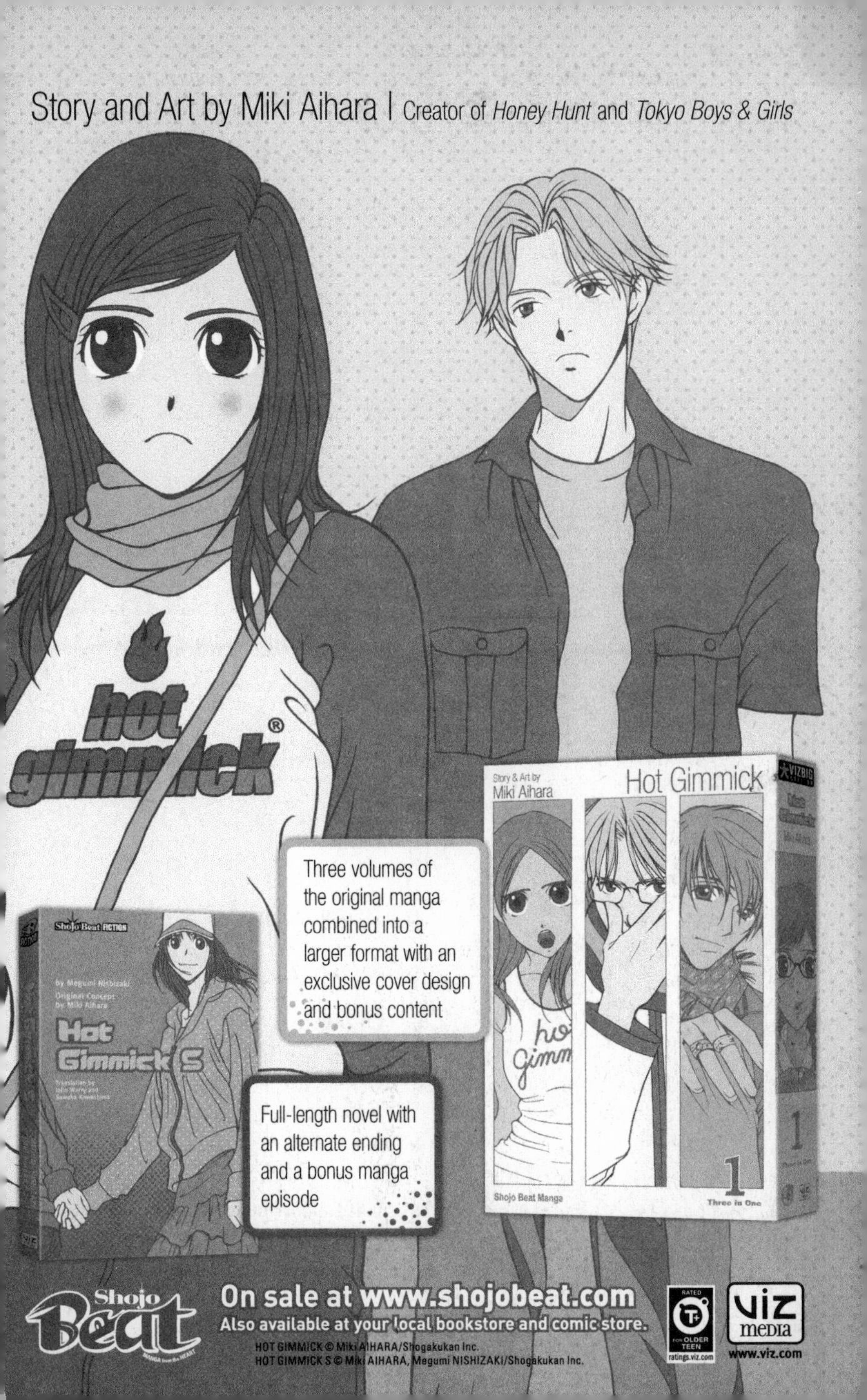
Story and Art by Miki Aihara | Creator of Honey Hunt and Tokyo Boys & Girls
hot gimmick®
Story & Art by
Miki Aihara
Hot Gimmick
Shojo Beat Manga
1
Three in One
Three volumes of the original manga combined into a larger format with an exclusive cover design and bonus content
Shojo Beat FICTION
Hot Gimmick S
Full-length novel with an alternate ending and a bonus manga episode
Shojo Beat
On sale at www.shojobeat.com
Also available at your local bookstore and comic store.
HOT GIMMICK © Miki AIHARA/Shogakukan Inc.
HOT GIMMICK S © Miki AIHARA, Megumi NISHIZAKI/Shogakukan Inc.
RATED T+ FOR OLDER TEEN
ratings.viz.com
VIZ media
www.viz.com

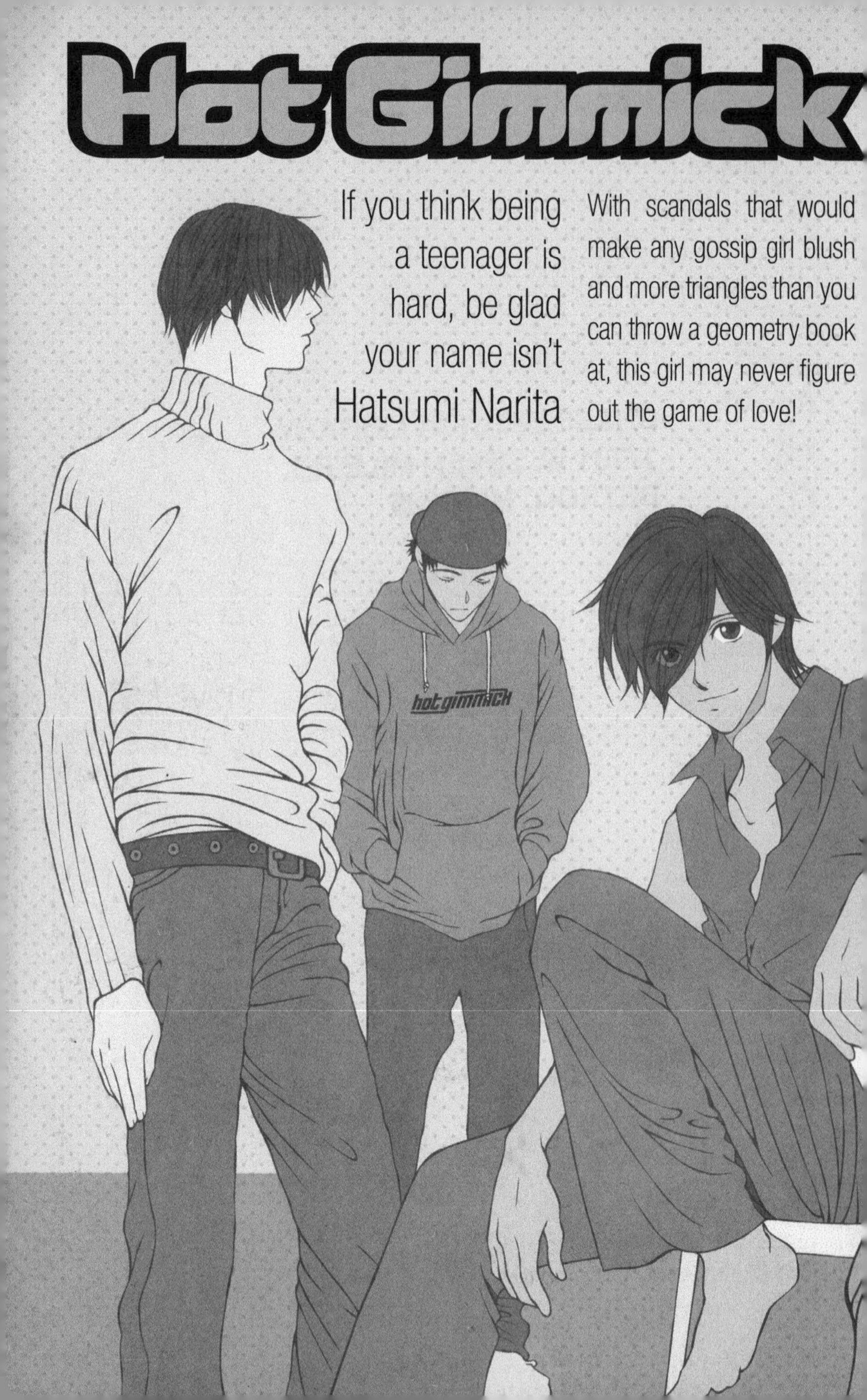

Hot Gimmick
If you think being a teenager is hard, be glad your name isn't Hatsumi Narita
With scandals that would make any gossip girl blush and more triangles than you can throw a geometry book at, this girl may never figure out the game of love!
hotgimmick

We Were There

By Yuki Obata
Also known as the award-winning series *Bokura ga Ita*

Get to the Bottom of a Broken Heart

It's love at first sight when Nanami Takahashi
falls for Motoharu Yano, the most popular boy in
her new class. But he's still grieving his girlfriend
who died the year before. Can Nanami break
through the wall that surrounds Motoharu's heart?

Find out in *We Were There*—
manga series on sale now!